# The Meaning of Educational Change

## Michael Fullan

The Ontario Institute for
Studies in Education

Teachers College, Columbia University
New York and London   1982

Simultaneously published in the U.S.A. by Teachers College Press, 1234 Amsterdam Avenue, New York, N.Y. 10027, and in Canada by OISE Press/ The Ontario Institute for Studies in Education

**Library of Congress Cataloging in Publication Data**

Fullan, Michael.

The meaning of educational change.

Bibliography: p.
Includes index.
1. Curriculum change. I. Title.

LB1570.F86   1982      379.1'54      81-18525
                                     AACR2

ISBN 0-8077-2712-1

Manufactured in the United States of America

87  86  85  84            3  4  5  6

# Contents

To Chris, Maureen, and Josh

# Preface

How to get new educational programs to work in practice has increasingly frustrated and mystified those involved in education over the past two decades. Many educators have attempted to improve programs in reading, mathematics, science, bilingualism, special education, desegregation, using new technologies, involving parents, teaching career and life skills, and the like. Others have been concerned with combating student alienation, teacher stress, stagnation among educational leaders, and disadvantages experienced by the poor, some ethnic groups, and other minorities. In most cases the outcome has been similar. The benefits have not nearly equaled the costs, and all too often the situation has seemed to worsen.

The issue of central interest in this book is not how many new policies have been approved or how many new programs have been developed, but rather what has actually changed in practice—if anything—as a result of our efforts. And how do we know when change is worthwhile? What can teachers, administrators, or policy-makers do when they know something is wrong in our schools? Can rejecting a proposed educational program be more progressive than accepting it? Why are we so often unclear about how to put a new program into practice?

Underlying the above questions is the problem of finding meaning in change. If change attempts are to be successful, individuals and groups must find meaning concerning *what* should change as well as *how* to go about it. Yet it is exceedingly difficult to resolve the problem of meaning when large numbers of people are involved.

Despite these difficulties, through a period of trial and error and persistence during the 1970s it has become more clear why change fails and succeeds. I have attempted to compile the best of theory and practice, including many very recent unpublished sources, in order to explain why change works as it does and what would have to be done to improve our success rate. It is essential to understand both the small picture and the big picture. We have to know what change looks like from the point of view of the individual teacher, student, parent, and administrator if we are to understand the actions and reactions of each; and if we are to comprehend the big picture, we must combine the aggregate knowledge of these individual situations with an understanding of organizational and interorganizational factors which influence the process of change as government departments, intermediate agencies, universities, teacher federations, school systems, and schools interact.

One of the promising features of this new knowledge about change is that successful examples of innovation are based on what might be most accurately labeled "organized common sense." It may not be easy to organize common sense—or rather to prevent other factors from overcoming it when the going gets tough—but explanations of success and of failure as described in this book do make sense. The difficulty in using this knowledge to improve other situations is that it requires contending with several factors at once: leadership, staff development, values and ideas in terms of who benefits, quality materials and programs, and the demands from all quarters for evidence that the new practice is desirable and effective. Managing social change is indeed a multivariate business which requires us to think of and address more than one factor at a time. While the theory and practice of successful educational change do make sense, and do point to clear guidelines for action, it is always the case that particular actions in particular situations require integrating the more general knowledge of change with detailed knowledge of the politics, personalities, and history peculiar to the setting in question.

Emphasizing the integration of the general and the specific is another way of saying that in the final analysis each individual must decide on a course of action for herself or himself. To help in guiding these decisions, I have written this book for individuals at all levels in the educational system. They will find a chapter on their own roles, as well as chapters on other roles and agencies with which they have direct and indirect contact. It is necessary to reflect on and understand both one's own situation and the situations of others around us in order to plan or cope with change. Part I—"Understanding Educational Change"—provides an overview of the sources, processes, and outcomes of change, and the implications for dealing with change. Part II contains chapters on each of the main roles at the local level, examining the day-to-day situations people face and how change is part of these daily realities. In Part III, I return to the larger scene to consider the role of governments, in-service education, and the future of educational change. Each of the fifteen chapters can be read and understood on its own, although the underlying theme and total picture depends on the combined chapters. There is not very much jargon in the book: one cannot claim that meaning is the answer, and then proceed to write an abstruse treatise on the subject. On the other hand, the main findings are amply referenced. For the student of change who wishes to delve into the topic, the bibliography contains some 500 items, many of which are new. For those less interested in the research base, the chapters can be read without attention to the references cited. In short, the book is intended for professionals (policymakers and practitioners) and laypeople interested in education and change at the school, local, regional, and national levels, as well as for university students and professors in faculties of education seeking a textbook on theories and practices of planned educational change.

There is a tension running throughout the book between centralization and decentralization, or between what is referred to as fidelity (attempting to achieve faithful, relatively homogeneous change in large numbers of situations) versus adaptation or variation (permitting and even promoting variety across situations). While I do not resolve this dilemma, the issues are presented at various places in the text.

I should also mention that the focus is on "planned" change attempts regardless of whether we are interested in achieving homogeneity or heterogeneity in practice. I do not dwell on unplanned or naturally occurring changes, although these are no doubt important in any long-term perspective on the evolution of social change. My goal is to highlight the problems involved in bringing about educational change through some deliberate means. While I consider factors involved in implementing $X$ or $Y$ program, the more basic question is how to get good at change—that is, how to increase the *capacity* of individuals and organizations to know when to reject certain change possibilities, to know when and how to pursue and implement others, and to know how to cope with policies and programs which are imposed on them and over which they have little choice.

Dissatisfaction with and interest in improving current efforts at bringing about educational change is a worldwide phenomenon. Although most of the research material I draw upon comes from North American sources, any discussion with those involved in innovative programs in other countries quickly reveals that the nature of problems and many of the principles of success and failure have a great deal in common. It is also encouraging that there is a growing interest within and across countries over the question of implementation or change in practice.

Even well-intentioned change initiatives can create havoc among those who are on the firing line, if support for implementation has been neglected. On the other hand, careful attention to a small number of key details during the implementation process can lead to the experience of success, the satisfaction of mastering some new practice which benefits students, and more fundamentally to the revitalization which is so desperately needed in the lives of educators today. Many of the solutions and the energies needed for widespread school change are already contained in our school systems. Confronting the isolationism and privatism of educational systems and establishing mechanisms for stimulating, adding to, and acting on these solutions and energies represent untapped resources which we can no longer afford to ignore.

I have benefited enormously from a large international "invisible college" of students and doers of educational change with whom I have worked at one time or another and who have freely provided me with information and support. Matt Miles as a coworker, colleague, and friend has given constant help. Matt read the manuscript and made precise and insightful comments to improve its accuracy and clarity. His own work on eduational change with ever-increasing sophistication and comprehensiveness serves as an endless source of ideas for those interested in understanding and doing something about education. David Crandall generously shared information on the mammoth and comprehensive about-to-be-released DESSI study on innovative programs in the U.S., which he is directing. I thank him for his willingness to share unpublished information and for his comments on the manuscript as a whole. Those who have read Seymour Sarason will recognize the imprint of his thinking on this book. His 1971 book *The Culture of the School and the Problem of Change* (2nd ed. 1982) contains insights which have shaped my way of thinking about educational change, as have his other writings during the 1970s.

There is a large number of other educational change workers who have helped and from whom I have learned. In Canada: John Biss, Bev Buchanan, Roger Brulé, George Burns, Des Dixon, Ken Drope, Glenn Eastabrook, Ron Graham, Bart Hildebrand, David Hopkins, David Hunt, Bob Kennedy, Ken Leithwood, Deborah Montgomery, Paul Park, George Podrebarac, Alan Pomfret, Gib Taylor, Walter Werner, and Marv Wideen. In the United States: Paul Berman, Gene Hall, Ron Havelock, Paul Hood, Shirley Hord, Ernest House, Bruce Joyce, Michael Kane, Preston Kronkosky, Rolf Lehming, Ann Lieberman, Susan Loucks, Karen Louis, Milbrey McLaughlin, Fritz Mulhauser, Phil Runkel, Bill Rutherford, Richard Schmuck, Sam Sieber, and Joe Vaughan. In Europe: Ray Bolam, Per Dalin, Harry Gray, Michael Huberman, Rudolf van den Berg, Roland Vandenberghe, Rein van der Vegt, and Wim van Velzen. I thank them all for their contributions.

Closer to home, the Ontario Institute for Studies in Education has been an environment remarkably conducive to sustained work on educational change. With its threefold mandate—graduate studies, research, and field development—OISE has been a natural and fertile ground for confronting the theory–practice question for developing a practical theory of planned change.

Typing the manuscript was in itself an exercise in finding meaning. Lynda Mason not only managed her way through inserts, arrows, and reams of pages to produce with amazing speed and accuracy a coherent copy but also showed continual commitment to the successful completion of the manuscript. Chris Pimblott helped in the final stages of revision and last-minute details. Catherine Cragg in her editorial work displayed a unique combination of the abilities to make precise recommendations and to be flexible and responsive to my own suggestions—even those made late in the editorial process—and cared enough to gain an understanding of the manuscript as a whole. Teachers College Press and OISE were extremely helpful and accommodating publishers at every stage.

My mother and father in different complementary ways supported me in getting started and following through in the study of the sociology of change. My wife, Wendy, was a strong supporter throughout, even though it meant lost weekends, working holidays, and hours spent behind closed doors at the Marshalls' cottage. She must have felt that enough was enough on more than one occasion, but she never wavered in conveying a fundamental feeling that it was a project worth completing.

To all these people, I hope the final product contributes some sense of meaning and value commensurate with at least a fraction of their support.

# Part I

# Understanding Educational Change

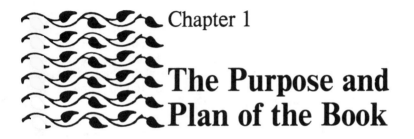 Chapter 1

# The Purpose and Plan of the Book

*Everything must change at one time or another or else a static society will evolve.*

— *Anonymous first-year university student on an English language proficiency test*

One person claims that schools are being bombarded by change; another observes that there is nothing new under the sun. A policy-maker charges that teachers are resistant to change; a teacher complains that administrators introduce change for their own self-aggrandizement and that they neither know what is needed nor understand the classroom. A parent is bewildered by a new practice in reading, open classrooms, and the relevance of education to future jobs. Some argue that the "back to basics" movement is signaling the end of an era of educational experimentation; others say that improving basics does represent a major change; still others say that many more changes are needed regardless of how well basics are taught. One university professor is convinced that schools are only a reflection of society and cannot be expected to bring about change; another professor is equally convinced that schools would be all right if only superintendents and principals had more "vision" as educational leaders and teachers were more motivated to learn new approaches to improving the curriculum. The "innovation establishment" wonder how to get more and more programs institutionalized, while teachers think that it is these same promoters of change who should be institutionalized, not their programs.[1] Students are too distracted by a host of other matters to pay much attention to all the furore.

This book is concerned with educational change affecting elementary and secondary schools. Those involved with schools are constantly embroiled in small- and large-scale change. In Canada this means some 5 million elementary and secondary school students and their parents, 300,000 teachers, and 30,000 school and district administrators, not to mention the thousands of government and university personnel working on educational programs. There are approximately 15,000 schools across Canada and 1,000 local school systems in the ten

---

1 The "innovation establishment" refers to the mass of firmly entrenched sponsors/disseminators of educational change—federal policy-makers, researchers, consultants, developers, project personnel of new programs, publishers, etc., all of whom have a vested interest in promoting educational change. I have never seen an estimate of their numbers, but in the U.S. they must total tens of thousands. Innovation is a big business (although it may be shrinking).

provinces plus the Northwest Territories and the Yukon (Statistics Canada 1980–81; Handbook of Canadian Consumer Markets, 1979). In the United States there are close to 45 million students enrolled in public elementary and secondary schools, over 2 million teachers, 200,000 school and district administrators, and tens of thousands of regional, state, federal, and university-based personnel; the 88,000 schools are organized into over 16,000 school districts (National Center for Education Statistics, 1977–78).

It is impossible to estimate the number of innovative programs. In New York City's board of education, for example, 781 innovative programs were piloted between 1979 and 1981 (Major's Management Report, Supplement, 1980, cited in Mann, 1981). If we broaden the term "innovation" to include all educational changes through legislation, new and revised curricula, and special projects—in short, any practice new to the person attempting to cope with an educational problem—it is clear that change is common fare for school people.

Implicit, but rarely recognized, is the confusion between the terms *change* and *progress*. Resisting certain changes may be more progressive than adopting them, but how do we know? The key to understanding the worth of particular changes, or to achieving desired changes, concerns what I call "the problem of meaning." One of the most fundamental problems in education today is that people do not have a clear, coherent sense of *meaning* about what educational change is for, what it is, and how it proceeds. Thus, there is much faddism, superficiality, confusion, failure of change programs, unwarranted and misdirected resistance, and misunderstood reforms. What we need is a more coherent picture that people who are involved in or affected by educational change can use to *make sense* of what they and others are doing.

The problem of meaning is central to making sense of educational change. In order to achieve greater meaning, we must come to understand both the small and the big pictures. The small picture concerns the subjective meaning or lack of meaning for *individuals* at all levels of the educational system. Neglect of the phenomenology of change—that is, how people actually experience change as distinct from how it might have been intended—is at the heart of the spectacular lack of success of most social reforms. It is also necessary to build and understand the big picture, because educational change after all is a sociopolitical process. This book will have succeeded or failed to the extent that people who are involved in education can read the account and conclude that it makes sense of their individual situations and enables them to understand the broader social forces influencing change.

In the process of examining the individual and collective situations, it is necessary to contend with both the *what* of change and the *how* of change.[2] Meaning must be accomplished in relation to both these aspects. It is possible to be crystal clear about what one wants and be totally inept at achieving it. Or to be skilled at managing change but empty-headed about what changes are most needed. To make matters more difficult, we often do not know what we want, or do not know the actual consequences of a particular direction, until we

2 Put another way (albeit oversimplified), successful educational change involves two components: a theory of education relating to what should change, and a theory of change concerning how to bring about change. The problem of meaning is one of how those involved in change can come to understand what it is that should change and how that can be best accomplished. Of course, the additional problem is that the what and how interact and influence each other.

try to get there. Thus, on the one hand, we need to keep in mind the values and goals and consequences associated with specific educational changes, and on the other hand, we need to comprehend the dynamics of educational change as a sociopolitical process involving all kinds of individual, classroom, school, local, regional, and national factors at work in interactive ways.

Remarkably, it is only in the last twelve years (since about 1970) that we have come to understand how educational change works in practice. In the 1960s educators were busy developing and introducing reforms. In the 1970s they were busy failing at putting them into practice. Out of this rather costly endeavor (psychologically and financially) has come a strong base of evidence about how and why educational reform fails or succeeds. Much of this evidence is very recent and is dispersed in a variety of published and unpublished sources, not yet comprehensively brought together. I draw heavily on this growing body of research in order to show the factual basis for claims made and to provide more specific explanations for why change works as it does. However, this book is not about research in the sense of complicated statistics, jargon, and reams of information without explanation. Most research derives from practice, and I use it to depict and to help explain social reality. Kurt Lewin's well-known saying puts it best: there is nothing as practical as good theory. Or, if you prefer, there is nothing as theoretical as good practice. Conversely, there is nothing as impractical as bad theory, or as atheoretical as bad practice.

In setting the stage for describing the ongoing relationship between theory and practice pertinent to each of the particular roles and agencies involved in educational change, the next section outlines the plan of the remaining chapters. I close the chapter with a brief discussion of "What is school reform for?"—a question which all too frequently gets lost when we are immersed in promoting or resisting given change efforts. Fighting for or against change can easily become an end in itself.

# The plan of the book

I do not attempt to survey the content or substance of all the latest educational innovations. I do, however, use a wide range of specific innovations to explain the practical meaning of educational change. Included in the studies on which I draw are changes in various curriculum areas (e.g., reading, mathematics, science, social studies), microcomputers, career education, open-concept schools, desegregation, special education, Head Start and Follow Through programs, and locally initiated changes as well as those sponsored at the provincial/state and national levels. The materials used derive mainly from attempts at educational reform in Canada and the United States, although several studies referred to from the United Kingdom, as well as any examination of problems of educational innovation in other countries, indicate that the basic problems and principles of educational reform are quite widespread.

The book is divided into three main parts. Part I, "Understanding Educational Change" (chapters 1 through 6), provides a detailed overview of how educational change works. Chapter 2 addresses the issues of what the main sources and purposes of educational change are. It raises questions about who benefits from what types of changes, and about the bases on which decisions to change are made. Evidence is analyzed which leads me to conclude that many decisions about the kinds of educational innovations introduced in school districts are biased, poorly thought out, and unconnected to the stated purposes of education. The sources of innovation and the quality of decisions made indicate that change is not necessarily progress. Change must always be viewed in relation to the particular values, goals, and outcomes it serves: something which is frequently difficult to assess in education, partly because rhetoric differs from reality and consequences cannot easily be determined or measured.

Whether or not the sources of change are suspect, what does it mean to change? Chapter 3 depicts the subjective reality of coping with change, both involuntary and desired change, and makes explicit the objective reality of what we mean when we refer to something as having changed. This chapter defines what change is. Combined with chapter 2, it suggests that not all proposed educational changes either should or could be implemented.

Chapter 4 identifies the main factors which relate to adoption or decisions to change. There are a variety of reasons why individuals or groups decide to embark on a change—personal prestige, bureaucratic self-interest, political responsiveness, concern for solving an unmet need. This chapter raises questions about how and why decisions on particular educational changes are made. How these decisions are made strongly influences what will happen at the follow-up or implementation stage.

Implementation and continuation (or the extent to which change actually occurs and is sustained) is the focus of chapter 5. Since implementation refers to what really happens in practice (as distinct from what was supposed to happen), it is a central theme which runs through all chapters. The short history of implementation research is not pleasant. It shows that planned change attempts rarely succeed as intended. As some old sayings go, "There's many a slip 'twixt the cup and the lip," "The proof is in the pudding," and "The road to hell is paved with good intentions." Honorable motives are even more problematic when we attempt to get others to heaven as well as ourselves—when social rather than individual change is at stake. In fact, I will show that, ironically, in many ways the more committed an individual is to the specific form of change, the less effective he or she will be in getting others to implement it. While the above sayings have been around a long time, it is only in the last twelve years that educators have come to realize that "the proof is in the *putting*": how change is put into practice determines to a large extent how well it fares. As we shall see, some of the most recent evidence indicates that we may be getting better at planning and implementing educational changes. Certainly there is greater clarity about what factors need to be addressed and how to address them.

Chapters 4 and 5 together cover the process of change: from how changes become initiated to how or whether they get put into practice and become institutionalized.[3] What happens at one stage has very powerful consequences for subsequent stages. In the final analysis, chapter 5 provides an overview of

---

3 Most recent authors describe three main stages or phases to educational change—initiation or mobilization, implementation, and continuation or institutionalization (see Berman & McLaughlin, 1977; Berman, 1981; Zaltman, 1973).

the dynamics of how educational changes get implemented/non-implemented and institutionalized/discontinued.

It is one thing to know the events and situations which cause or prevent change from happening; it is an entirely different question to know what to do about it. Chapter 6 delves into the issues of planning and coping with educational change. Many attempts at change fail because no distinction is made between theories of change (what causes change) and theories of chang*ing* (how to influence those causes). And when solutions are attempted, they often create their own problems which are more severe than the original ones (see Sieber, 1979). Understanding the causes of change in societies as complex as ours should lead us to be much more modest in our expectations of change; understanding the difficulties of changing these causes will make us downright discouraged. Nonetheless, in chapter 6 I describe examples of both failure and success at planned change. At a minimum this knowledge offers certain psychological and practical advantages simply through allowing us to become more clear about the process and meaning of change and more realistic about what can be accomplished. By making explicit the problems of planning and coping with change, we gain further understanding of why certain plans fail and others succeed. I also identify some guidelines for how change can be approached or coped with more effectively.

Part I, then, provides the overall framework for thinking about and doing something about educational change. It shows, incidentally, that "rationally planned" strategies are not that rational when it comes to dealing with people and the problem of meaning. Part I does not differentiate in detail what it all means for the everyday teacher, principal, parent, etc. This is the purpose of Part II, "Educational Change at the Local Level," which consists of six chapters (7 through 12) in which I examine what is known about the role of people in different positions at the local-school and school-district levels. In each case, I bring to bear the body of research knowledge (particularly concrete, experiential evidence) on a given role in order to address two sets of questions. The first set of questions concerns the meaning of change for people in the role under discussion—what their experience is and their relationship to the process of educational change. Then, when we have some understanding of the meaning of change for given role incumbents, the second set of questions is directed at generating ideas for what they could or should do about it. These guidelines will range from general suggestions to specific steps to be taken depending on the circumstances.

The six chapters in Part II are organized into these two main themes: "what is" and "what could or should be." In each chapter, I use the framework from Part I to illuminate the meaning of change and the change process in a way which explains why seemingly rational strategies for change do not work. The chapters are designed so that individuals within these roles can gain greater understanding of their place in the context of changes around them. These chapters also enable individuals in one role to gain an understanding of the realities of participants in other roles and thereby a clearer view of the sociology of educational change in the society as a whole.

Chapters 7 to 9 examine change within the school by analyzing the roles of key participants and their organizational relationships. As implementation is the essence of change, it follows that the teacher as implementer is central. Chapter

7 examines the concrete situation of the teacher and shows that change is only one among many problems the teacher faces—in fact, that the conditions for change as well as strategies employed by central policy-makers and administrators provide many more disincentives than benefits. (See Sieber, 1981, for a general analysis of incentives and disincentives in education.) Sociologically speaking, few of us, if placed in the current situation of teachers, would be motivated or able to engage in effective change. Obvious strategies do not seem to work. Teacher participation in curriculum development has not been effective when it comes to other teachers' using the results. In-service training of teachers has been ineffective and wasteful more times than not. Building on earlier chapters, chapter 7 explains why many approaches to change do not work for teachers and suggests some remedies.

More lip service than mind service has been given to the pivotal role of the principal as gatekeeper or facilitator of change. Nothing in the process of change is more agreed on and less understood than the leadership role of the principal. Chapter 8 describes the situation of the principal and his or her current role in facilitating or inhibiting change. As before, to understand what is, we examine specific evidence and situations. It is only through specificity that we can go beyond the generalities of leadership qualities found in much of the literature. In deriving implications for what the role of the principal could or should be, the emphasis will be on the formulation of specific guidelines which deal with the total reality faced by the principal.

People think of students as the potential beneficiaries of change. They think of achievement results, skills, attitudes, and the need for various improvements for the good of the children. They rarely think of students as *participants* in a process of change. Consequently, there is little evidence on what students think about changes and their role regarding them. It is an interesting and worthwhile perspective to attempt to develop the theme of what the role of students is and what it could be. Naturally there will be differences according to the age of students, but chapter 9 will elaborate on the possible meaning of change for children and adolescents.

The remaining three chapters of Part II address the immediate local environment of the school—district administrators, consultants or resource people at the district level, and the parents, community, and school board. A considerable amount of evidence exists that the superintendent and other district administrators are as crucial for determining change within the district as the principal is within the school. Again it will be necessary to examine evidence which will allow us to determine in which ways this is specifically true. What is it that the district administrator does? What is the actual process of events, and what are the results? Chapter 10 analyzes the role of the district administrator as an actual and potential manager of educational change.

There are many different consultants in education variously called curriculum coordinators or consultants, resource teachers, internal change agents, external agents, organization development specialists, disseminators, linking agents, and so on. In chapter 11 I consider the role of consultants broadly divided into two categories—those internal to the district and those external. The intricacies of being a consultant are considerable; the consultant needs to combine subject-matter knowledge, interpersonal skills in working with individuals and small groups, and planned-change or management skills for designing and implementing larger change efforts. Evidence from major studies in recent years, combined with the framework for understanding educational change, enables us to draw some conclusions about how and why some consultants are effective and others are not, and how the roles of internal and external consultants can be better conceptualized and practiced.

In chapter 12 the roles of parents and school boards are examined. The problem of meaning is especially acute for these groups, who are vitally concerned and responsible for educational decisions but who often have limited knowledge. Case-study materials and other research evidence will be used to clarify what communities do vis-à-vis questions of initiating, rejecting, supporting, or blocking particular changes in their schools, and will illustrate the dilemma that schools face about whether or not to involve parents in decisions about change. I will especially take up the question of the role of the individual parent in instruction, decision-making, and otherwise relating to the school and to the education of his or her child.

As Part II analyzes what happens at the local level, the three chapters in Part III return to the regional and national levels. If we are to understand the realities of change at the local level, we must discover how societal agencies, for better or worse, influence change in schools. The role of government agencies represents another dilemma for understanding educational change. On the one hand, important social reforms would probably not be launched without federal or state/provincial impetus. On the other hand, external reforms frequently are not successful and are seen as interfering with local autonomy. We now have enough evidence from governmental change efforts of the 1960s and 1970s to understand why this source of reform is necessary, why it often doesn't work, and what the implications are for altering the approach. Common principles and research findings will be used to analyze how federal and state agencies in the U.S., and how provincial governments in Canada (where education is virtually the sole responsibility of the ten provinces), function in the realm of education. Chapter 13 assesses these issues.

In chapter 14 the training and professional development of school personnel — which itself is a big business — is examined. The mainstream of the analysis concerns the initial preparation of school personnel and especially continuing or in-service efforts, since the latter currently receive a great deal of emphasis in most countries. The ways in which the pre-service education of teachers and administrators does not prepare them at all for the complexities of educational change will be discussed. In-service education or professional development explicitly directed at change also fails in most cases because it is ad hoc, discontinuous, and unconnected to any plan for change which addresses the set of factors identified in chapters 2 through 6, and because it ignores the realities of everyday work of teachers and administrators. Factors affecting change function in interaction and must be treated as such; solutions directed at any one factor in isolation will have minimal impact. The entire question of pre-service and in-service education for teachers and administrators should be thoroughly understood, because it does represent one of the most powerful leverages for improvement.

In the final chapter of the book (chapter 15) I reflect on the problem of change in the context of future trends and expectations for educational change by examining ten themes. The prognosis is discouraging at the level of what has been expected from education since World War II, which has been nothing less than a panacea for societal development. It is optimistic in terms of definite improvements which could be made as a result of knowledge gained about how best to plan and implement educational changes. In several ways we now know what works. Unfortunately this formulation itself is partly a theory of change rather than of changing—to know what works in some situations does not mean we can get it to work in other situations. The basis for hope, however, lies somewhere between the naiveté of the 1960s and the cynicism of the 1970s. In establishing greater hope, we need to figure out what school reform is for, and what it can feasibly accomplish in societies dominated by political and economic forces.

# What is school reform for?

What are schools supposed to do? Does educational change help do it? What are the prospects for improvement? I return to these questions in chapter 15, but it is important to introduce them at this time.

## What are schools for?

What schools are supposed to do is a complicated question. However, the main espoused purposes can be identified. There are at least two major purposes to schooling: to educate students in various academic or cognitive skills and knowledge, and to educate students in the development of individual and social skills and knowledge necessary to function occupationally and sociopolitically in society.[4] Let us label these respectively the cognitive/academic and the personal/social-development purposes of education. Superimposed on these two main purposes in democratic societies is the goal of equality of opportunity and achievement—in John Dewey's phrase, "the opportunity to escape from the limitations of the social group" in which one is born (1916, p. 20).

To assess whether schools are doing their job it would be necessary to have certain *internal* and *external* information. The former refers to how students do in terms of achievement while they are in and as they end their schooling. The latter refers to how students fare occupationally and socially once they leave school. We would want to know how family background relates to performance both internal to schools and in society after schooling has been completed.

I do not intend to answer the question of school performance very thoroughly at this stage. Much has been written about it over the past fifteen years since the Coleman (1966) report. The short answer is that family background correlates strongly with educational performance and occupational achievement. There are some who claim that this is inevitable in capitalist society (Bowles & Gintis, 1976; Jencks et al., 1972, 1979). The claim is that students from more privileged family backgrounds are educationally advantaged by the time they start school, and are favored even more strongly by the middle-class bias of schools while they progress through the grade levels. In any case, stu-

---

4 See Bowles and Gintis (1976, ch. 2) and Sarason and Doris (1979, ch. 18) for very useful discussions of the purposes of schools.

dents from more privileged family backgrounds do perform better academically. The personal/social-development goals may be even more radically affected because they are embedded in the "hidden curriculum." According to these arguments, the hierarchical social order of the school is inimical to many of the espoused personal- and social-development goals related to living and working in a democratic society (e.g., personal and group decision-making abilities).[5] Some authors go so far as to say that even if schools were good at academic and personal development, it might not make a great deal of difference in occupational success (Jencks et al., 1972, 1979).

Countering these gloomy prognoses is a growing body of evidence that schools can and sometimes do make a difference, at least for some educational objectives. The so-called "school effectiveness" research shows that schools in poor areas can and do (depending on their characteristics) help students make significant gains in relation to basic academic achievement (see Brookover, 1981; D'Amico, 1980; Madaus et al., 1980; Lezotte et al., 1980; Edmonds, 1979; in the United Kingdom see Rutter et al., 1979; Halsey et al., 1980). Recent research on successful innovations, which forms some of the evidence in subsequent chapters, also indicates that schools can be moderately successful. Both the school-effects and the school-innovation literatures are relatively silent on personal/social-development goals and achievement, although there seems little doubt that schools emphasize academic achievement over personal/social development.[6]

## What is reform for?

In theory, the purpose of educational change is presumably to help schools accomplish their goals more effectively by replacing some programs or practices with better ones. Throughout the book I will be pursuing this question in terms of whether, how, and under what conditions educational change does improve schools. Change for the sake of change will not help. New programs either make no difference, help improve the situation, or make it worse. The relationship between change and progress,[7] using accomplishments in the cognitive/academic and personal/social-development domains as criteria, can be most forcefully brought home if we ask: What if the majority of educational changes introduced in schools, however unintentionally, actually made matters worse than if nothing had been done? (See chapter 2.) Behind this theme is also the

---

5 Bowles and Gintis (1976) argue that the emphasis on obedience, passivity, and other similar traits is fundamentally determined by the needs of economic institutions in capitalist societies. Others claim that it is related to the fact that schools face similar problems (e.g., to factories) in managing the work of large numbers of people. See the recent special issue of *Interchange* (12, no. 2/3, 1981) on the theme "Rethinking Social Reproduction," especially the articles by Dale and Giroux. No one contends that schools do a good job of addressing personal/social-development goals.

6 Sarason and Doris (1979, p. 399) comment on the preponderance of academic achievement concerns and note that Jencks (1972) could find little information about non-cognitive outcomes: "Jencks finds himself able to devote only one chapter to non-cognitive traits—a chapter of four pages!"

7 For a first-rate and fascinating discussion see Robert Nisbet's *The History of the Idea of Progress* (1980). He concludes that societies are deteriorating rather than progressing. For an antidote read Alvin Toffler's *The Third Wave* (1980).

matter of the relationship between educational and societal change. There are certainly limits to what education can do for the life chances of individuals. While I am most interested in this book in the performance of the educational change system, it should be said that educational reform is no substitute for societal reform. The question is whether it can influence, respond to, or otherwise make a contribution to societal reform. The failure of educational change may be related just as much to the fact that many innovations were never implemented in practice (i.e., real change was never accomplished) as it is to the fact that societal, political, and economic forces inhibit change within the educational system.

What are the prospects for making school reform more effective? I address this issue in the final chapter. To anticipate the answer, the information presented in subsequent chapters suggests that schools can accomplish some changes in practice which improve the conditions and at least short-term outcomes of learning. Whether schools can address the range of cognitive and personal-development goals is another question. Whether what is learned because of schools improves the life chances of individuals is another matter again. Significant improvements within the educational system—modest ones on a societal scale—seem to be possible, although the reader should form her or his own judgment on this issue after examining the evidence.

In the course of experiencing attempts at school reform we have learned that the process of planned educational change is much more complex than had been anticipated. Ironically, as the following chapters indicate, we have also learned that implementing effective reforms is just as much a matter of good common sense as of fancy theories.[8] Alfred North Whitehead referred to the need to go back and forth between complexity and simplicity when he wrote, "The aim of science is to seek the simplest explanations of complex facts [but] seek simplicity and distrust it." While we should be wary of simple explanations, our goal is to render complex phenomena understandable.

I pursue complexity but seek simplicity at both the micro and macro levels of the educational system. In understanding and in coping with educational change it is essential to find out what is happening at the classroom, school, and local levels of education as well as at the regional and national levels.[9] Neither level can be understood in isolation from the other. The process of educational change in modern society is so complex that the greatest initial need is to comprehend its dynamics. Paradoxically, the road to understanding complex social phenomena is through simple and concrete explanations, since the main criterion for *understood complexity* is the extent to which it is meaningful. A minimum of jargon is used in favor of explanations which are understandable to those participating in the educational enterprise. The chapters are written to be useful for any of the participants mentioned in the book, in their quest to make sense not only of their own immediate situations but especially of the totality of educational change and how it can become more meaningful individually and collectively.

---

8 However, it may be the case that good common sense is not very common (or rather that people do not draw enough on their common sense).
9 The Appendix provides brief definitions of the major policies, programs, and research studies referred to in this book. It thus gives the reader a quick and easy guide to the main sources and facilitates reference to them. The Bibliography contains the broader list of the sources used.

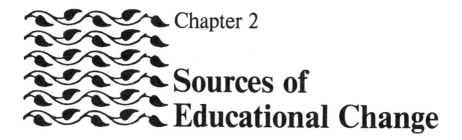

# Chapter 2

# Sources of Educational Change

*When it is not necessary to change, it is necessary not to change.*

— *Joseph de Maistre, 18th-century French philosopher*

The nature of educational and social change must first be understood in terms of its sources and purposes. One does not have to be a historian to accept the fact that a number of major external and internal forces over time create pressures for change. For our purposes we do not even have to understand fully how these pressures specifically come about. At this level, it is sufficient to agree with Levin (1976) that there are three broad ways in which pressures for educational policy change may arise: (1) through natural disasters such as earthquakes, floods, famines, etc.; (2) through external forces such as imported technology and values, and immigration; and (3) through internal contradictions, such as when indigenous changes in technology lead to new social patterns and needs, or when one or more groups in a society perceive a discrepancy between educational values and outcomes affecting themselves or others in whom they have an interest. We can take it as a given that there will always be pressures for educational change in pluralistic and/or externally influenced societies.

What interests us is the more specific manifestations of why people in education decide to push for or promote *particular* changes. It is no denial of the possible good intentions of promoters of educational change to say that a close look at how decisions about change are made, and what decisions are made, will inspire little confidence that the majority of recommended changes are worthwhile or that the most needed changes are being proposed. In examining how and what decisions are made we should keep in mind two critical questions: who benefits from the change (the values question), and how sound or feasible is the idea and approach (the capacity for implementation question)? Both are complex and difficult questions to answer.

To facilitate the discussion, figure 1 presents a very condensed and simplified picture of four possible outcomes. "Actual implementation" refers to whether or not there has been a real change in practice. "Value and technical quality" collapse the two factors related to who benefits and whether or not the program has been technically well developed.[1] The four possible outcomes illustrate why

---

1 These factors, of course, must be separated, for people can value a specific program which is not well developed, or a program can be very well developed which we do not value. For the

**Figure 1     Types of Implementation Outcomes**
**of Adopted Changes**

Actual implementation of the change

|                                        |     | YES | NO  |
| -------------------------------------- | --- | --- | --- |
| Value and technical quality of the change | YES | I   | II  |
|                                        | NO  | III | IV  |

educational changes should be examined closely. Type I, for example, represents what we are presumably striving for: the actual implementation of a quality program which we value. Type II reflects a planning problem in that a valued, technically sound program is not being implemented for whatever reasons (chapter 5 identifies these reasons). We do not, however, often conceive of types III and IV. In type III a change which is not technically well developed or is not valued (by whatever the reference group we use) is being put into practice. In short, a bad change is being introduced.[2] Type IV, interestingly, is a form of success in that a poorly valued or poorly developed change is being rejected in practice. It is a success save for the time, energy, and frustration involved in the course of attempting to implement it (or of combating it). Many of the bandwagon changes of the 1960s may have been of this type; but we really do not know how frequently attempts were made to introduce ill-conceived or inappropriate changes.

Values, quality of innovations, and implementation are infinitely more complex than figure 1 implies. But the point is clear that specific educational changes should be considered on all three counts: Who does it benefit? Is the idea or program technically well developed? Does it result in change in practice?

In the rest of this chapter I describe several examples of problematic sources of educational innovation, and I conclude with a summary of implications for the study and practice of educational change.

# The sources of innovation

The examination of a range of different educational innovations from the 1960s and 1970s should establish without any doubt that it is at least an open question whether the sources of educational change are to be trusted on grounds either of who benefits or of technical soundness.[3] Two major problems stand out: the

---

sake of simplicity I combine them here, but the later discussion in this chapter shows clearly that they are separate.

2 Even if a certain idea is valued because of its goal direction, it may not be sufficiently developed and tested to be practically usable. Far too many innovations, even those with laudable (valued) goals, have been rushed into practice without any clear notion and corresponding resources related to how they could be used in practice (or, more charitably, the technical requirements or means of implementation have been underestimated).

3 Various studies all raise very serious questions about whether educational innovations should be automatically accepted. They cover topics as diverse as open education (Gross et al., 1971;

appropriateness/soundness of innovations which are introduced, and the bias of neglect vis-à-vis needed changes which are never so much as proposed.

## The appropriateness of adopted innovations

Gross et al. (1971) and Smith and Keith (1971) have written the two classic case studies which signaled the problems of implementing educational reform even among people who seemingly desire the change. Both cases illustrate the problems just discussed. The authors concentrate on the failure to develop an adequate design for implementation—technical problems in the management of change and questions about the developmental soundness of the innovations themselves. However, it is more revealing of the assumptions of the time (the late 1960s, when change was assumed to be good) that the authors themselves treat the innovations as givens. Both "innovations" pertained to open education in elementary schools. Gross et al. studied the implementation of a new teacher role to facilitate self-motivation of children; Smith and Keith examined a new open education elementary school. In both cases, the innovations came from broad external forces—generally influenced by the British primary open education model, fueled in the U.S. by university-based supporters of open education, and adopted willingly by school boards at the request of key progressive superintendents. Neither author team questions or even mentions whether the innovations concerned were appropriate for the communities which the two schools served. They simply assumed without any reflection that these "progressive innovations" were good, and that only problems of delivery interfered.

Gross et al. say nothing about the role or rights of the community other than that the school is inner-city (and thereby they assume that a certain open-education role model for teachers is good for this community). Nor do Smith and Keith analyze the innovation in terms of whether it is right for the community. Furthermore, when we consider how the decisions were made and how the main promoters of the change behaved, we have every reason to believe that the changes were adopted by superintendents who were on their way up the career ladder largely as a result of their innovation record. And yet this is not necessarily a description of their conscious motives. They could have been (and probably were) convinced that the innovations in question would solve a great many problems. Intentions do not matter, however, if the quality or appropriateness of the innovation is not fully considered, or if the main sponsors of the program do not remain on the scene for more than a couple of years. I do not know of any systematic studies of the career patterns of "innovative superintendents," but there are too many case-study examples which indicate that one of the main consequences of introducing innovations is career

Smith & Keith, 1971; Sharp & Green, 1975); systems reform (Wolcott, 1977); curriculum reform (Sarason, 1971; Silberman, 1970; Boyd, 1978; Waring, 1978; Krawchenko et al., 1979); education for immigrants and special education (Sarason & Doris, 1979); federal policy-making (Boyd, 1978); computers (House, 1974); career education (Grubb & Lazerson, 1975); innovations in secondary schools (Daft & Becker, 1978); and incentive systems of innovation for public education as a whole (Pincus, 1974). While I criticize the quality of innovations in this chapter, it should be clear that the main point is to be aware of the need to develop sounder programs, and we do seem to be getting better at this (see Crandall et al., forthcoming, and Louis, Rosenblum, & Molitor, 1981).

advancement for the sponsor *and* subsequent failed implementation of the innovation.[4] (See also Carlson, 1972, and the section on career motives in Crandall et al., forthcoming.)

While we consider these examples of open education, I want to reiterate that I am raising two possible types of problems (which become compounded when they interact). One problem relates to whether open education is the most effective reform for particular communities in which it is introduced. The other and equally problematic issue is whether its lack of technical development and failed implementation harmed rather than helped children. It may very well be the case that open education—an innovation "adopted" across North America in the 1960s by nearly all school boards—was harmful (at least as it was implemented) to the educational interests of lower-class children.[5] For example, Sharp and Green (1975) conducted an intensive case study of a progressive primary school in England and demonstrated how the assumptions of open education worked against lower-class children. Some teachers interpreted open education to mean that since all children have potential, they should choose their own learning experiences. When some children (e.g., those from working-class backgrounds) failed to develop, their home background was blamed. The teachers faced with such problem children tended to neglect them, and certainly did not put pressure on them to achieve, "because to do so would be to violate the integrity of the child" (see Whiteside, 1978, p. 28). If failure continued, in the final analysis it would be parental background which would be blamed rather than the possible inappropriateness of the new educational practices being used.

Another type of example which clearly indicates the doubtful origin of some educational innovations comes from Wolcott's (1977) study of a PPBS (Planning-Programming-Budgeting System) innovation adopted by a school district. The "systems"-based innovations of the 1960s arose from a combination of new "theories" and program specifications generated from some university, government, and business quarters. Other analyses (in chapters 3 and 4) will show that this "rationally based" approach to educational reform is not sound. In any case, Wolcott documents the mixture of good motives and shaky reasoning which committed the school district to a multi-year effort. The superintendent became convinced of "the need to better coordinate his schools, to improve the quality of curriculum planning, and to anticipate the growing interest in educational accountability" (p. 34). He became aware of the systems program (eventually called SPECS—School Planning, Evaluation and Communication System) at a summer workshop. In reviewing the decision three years later with some disgruntled teachers, he observed, "... we had to be willing to take a risk. Or, I guess I should say, I took a risk on behalf of the district and

---

4 One might say that since the soundness of the innovations is questionable, it is fortunate that there is little implementation. This is true except for the fact that a great deal of time and frustration is expended to the longer-term detriment of the morale of school people. Their justifiable lack of enthusiasm will make it even more unlikely that *any* kind of changes will be adopted in the future, even worthwhile ones. Negative attitudes accumulate, as do positive ones in cases of success.

5 See Gold and Miles (1981) for a very powerful example of how the community of a middle-class school successfully thwarted an open education school which they did not value; few working-class communities would have attempted or succeeded in similar opposition.

school board" (p. 34). The innovation was beset with problems during the history of its life in the district.

In addition to case studies of individual schools and districts, the nature of decisions at the local level has also been well researched in larger comparative studies. The best known is the study of U.S. federally sponsored educational programs carried out by Berman, McLaughlin, and associates at Rand (see Berman & McLaughlin, vols. I–VIII, 1975–78). They investigated 293 change projects including 29 field studies. They found that school-district decisions to engage in particular reforms were of two types: those reflecting *opportunism*, in which districts were motivated primarily by the desire "to reap federal funds," and those characterized by *problem-solving*, in which the main motivation emerged in response to locally identified needs. As might be expected, projects characterized by the latter orientation tended to be much more successful at achieving desired outcomes and at continuation after federal funds were terminated. The main point, however, is that school districts sometimes adopt innovations which are not intrinsically related to their educational needs:

Local school officials may view the adoption of a change agent project primarily as an opportunity to garner extra, short term resources. In this instance the availability of federal funds rather than the possibility of change in educational practice motivates project adoption. Or, school managers may see change agent projects as a "low cost" way to cope with bureaucratic or political pressures. Innovation *qua* innovation often serves the purely bureaucratic objective of making the district appear up-to-date and progressive in the eyes of the community. Or a change agent project may function to mollify political pressures from groups in the community to "do something" about their special interests. Whatever the particular motivation underlying opportunistic adoption there was an absence of serious educational concerns. (Berman & McLaughlin, 1978, p. 14)

Daft and Becker (1978) carried out a longitudinal study of innovative behavior in 13 high school districts. They examined innovations adopted at two time periods (1959–64 and 1968–72). Related to our contention that innovations are not neutral as to their benefits, the authors found that "college preparatory innovations were clearly in the majority in each period" (p. 42). More specifically, 31 of 35 innovations in the 1959–64 period were clearly directed at college-oriented students, compared with 18 of 29 in the 1968–72 period—with innovations for high school terminating students increasing substantially but still in the minority. Whatever the figures are in other districts or in other eras, innovations must be examined carefully as to their intended beneficiaries (and, as we shall see shortly, the *actual* results for intended beneficiaries may be quite the opposite to stated goals).

Questions about the dependability of decisions and sources of innovation are not only evident at the school and school-district level. They permeate all levels. Thus, the great curriculum reform movement of the 1960s came from a combination of university professors interested in upgrading the quality of discipline-based teaching (usually representing inquiry-oriented teaching) and government sponsorship preoccupied with the importance of producing better scientists and mathematicians. One of the main sources of the impetus (or reinforcement, depending on one's viewpoint) was the launching of Sputnik, which called U.S. technological capacities into question. Sarason analyzes the experience of the new math and concludes:

There are no grounds for assuming that any aspect of the impetus for change came from teachers, parents or children. The teachers were not "hurting" because of the existing curriculum. (Sarason, 1971, p. 36)

A major review of education in 1970 draws a similar conclusion: that the reason the reform movement failed was "the fact that its prime movers were distinguished university scholars"; what was assumed to be its greatest strength turned out to be its greatest weakness (Silberman, 1970, p. 179). The specific reasons cited by Silberman are revealing because they show that well-intentioned, intelligent university authorities and "experts" on education can be dead wrong. The reforms failed because of faulty and overly abstract theories not related or relatable to practice, limited or no contact with and understanding of the school (see also Sarason, 1971), ignorance of the lessons of experiences of the reformers in the 1920s and 1930s, and above all the failure to consider explicitly the relationship between the nature of the proposed innovations and the purposes of schools. Innovations became ends in themselves as the reformers lost sight of the supposed central questions of the purpose of change:

What is education for? What kind of human beings and what kind of society do we want to produce? What methods of instruction and classroom organization as well as what subject matter do we need to produce these results? What knowledge is of most worth? (Silberman, 1970, p. 182)

Curriculum reform in Canada has suffered similar problems. Changes come in the form of curriculum guidelines and programs produced in each of the ten provinces by the respective ministries of education. Although there is provincial autonomy, the guidelines are remarkably similar from province to province in their orientation: inquiry-oriented science and social studies, Canadian studies, "back to basics" via a core curriculum, etc. We can only infer where the ideas contained in the guidelines originated, but they seem to be a strange blend of public, political pressures (emphasizing core curriculum and basic skills) and the pet theories and ideas of progressive university professors and school teachers (emphasizing, e.g., inquiry-oriented learning), the latter groups having been heavily influenced by the "theoretical" developments of the university-based curriculum reform efforts in the 1960s in the United States, reviewed by Silberman. The results are the same—the premature adoption of questionable programs on the grounds of need, feasibility, or technical soundness. Studies of the implementation of language arts curriculum (Simms, 1978) and social studies (Downey et al., 1975; Aoki et al., 1977) in Canada contain ample documentation of the lack of clear need for and/or limitations in the technical development of new curricular policies. Thus, even when there is a need, the development of sound programs frequently lags behind.

Similarly, the role of the governments raises questions about the source of innovation. While at later stages I will argue that pressures for educational reform do need to come from government levels and are legitimate, there is enough evidence to show that the educational basis for decisions is often questionable. Boyd (1978) reviews Moynihan's characterization of "professionalization of reform" (or what I earlier referred to as the innovation establishment). This is an interesting phenomenon to consider, because unlike some of the curriculum changes reviewed above, the federal reforms were directed explicitly at improving conditions for the poor and disadvantaged. Boyd quotes

Moynihan in referring to the professional policy-makers' advisers as people who "tended to measure their success by the number of things they got started"; "the war on poverty was not declared at the behest of the poor; it was declared in their interest by persons confident of their own judgment in such matters" (quoted in Boyd, 1978, pp. 590–91). Boyd himself observes:

A more complete, and charitable interpretation of the professionalization of reform would acknowledge that professionals positioned in national organizations and agencies have an important responsibility to attend to, and anticipate, national needs ... but it nevertheless is hard to deny that the generally liberal-activist ideology of these professionals, in combination with their self-interest in career advancement and the maintenance and enhancement needs of their organizations, must influence their policy recommendations. (p. 590)

House (1974, ch. 8) also seriously questions depending on the federal government as a source of innovations. Referring to the federal "doctrine of transferability" and political turnover, House quotes Gallagher, former Director of the Bureau for Education of the Handicapped, who writes:

The credibility of the Federal government is under serious and justified attack because of its failure to follow through on programs once they have begun. In the second or third year of their efforts—their political glamour worn off—their favored place was taken in the Administration by new, bright, and shiny programs that are polished by hope and unsullied by experience. (p. 207)

The levels of bureaucratic complexity from federal to local districts—each of which adds its own bias and delay to the nature and feasibility of reforms—is also discussed by several authors and is taken up in chapter 5 (see House, 1974, ch. 8; Pressman & Wildavsky, 1973).

The professionalization of reform exists not only among federal policy-makers. I have also indicated that university- and school-based members of professional associations or subject-matter disciplines push for their own versions of reform. Waring (1979) details the historical development of the Nuffield Foundation Science Teaching Project in the United Kingdom, in which a special-interest group (university professors and secondary school teachers of science) lobbied over several years to obtain support for improvement (as they defined it) in the teaching of science. Waring states:

There was too, a belief in the need for every citizen in a technological society to have some knowledge and understanding of science, a need which was so self-evident that the question of what constitutes "relevance" in such an education tended to be ignored. (p. 49)

Similar professional campaigns are evident in sex education. Boyd (1978) refers to a national study by Hottois and Milner (1975), who found:

that the initiative for introducing sex education in most instances came from educators *contrary* to their claims that such instruction was being added to the curriculum in response to public demands for it. In turn, the origin of the whole movement came from a professional sex education "establishment", which was convinced that such instruction was needed, and which actively propagated the idea and showed local educators how to "finesse" the public relations problems involved in introducing it. (Boyd, 1978, p. 591)

Whether or not we are in favor of sex education, it should be clear that ideological convictions are the source of many innovations. Proponents accept the desirability of specific innovations as self-evident. Others who do not share the convictions are equally positive that the innovations are absolutely wrong. The worth of educational change is never self-evident; it is something that goes to the core of the purpose of education in a particular society and must be confronted as such (see Dalin, 1978, p. 16). Conviction is no criterion for determining worth.

Let us consider one final educational example—the computer. House (1974, ch. 7) examines the origins and use of PLATO, an advanced computer-assisted instruction system for junior colleges. He shows that the political economy of obtaining resources for the development and spread of the innovation requires overselling: "The very act of obtaining necessary support often seduces the entrepreneur into making promises impossible to fulfill" (p. 186). In the more optimistic days of the late 1960s PLATO was sold and initially accepted on the promises of major improvements by "experts who should know." Raising the question of the degree of confidence in the quality of the decision, House (p. 192) leaves no doubt as to the answer—"Faith in the future made the PLATO project almost impermeable to data and evaluation."[6] Innovations sponsored by the right combination of resources and organizations come to have a momentum, faith, and life of their own. *Caveat implementer* would be an appropriate rule, except that the majority of participants are helpless victims of this momentum rather than autonomous.

## Bias by neglect

Not only are questionable innovations promoted, but needed changes can also be systematically ignored for decades, as Sarason and Doris (1979) document in their historical analysis of the treatment of immigrants and the mentally handicapped during the past 140 years in the United States. The basis of educational reform originated with the initial purposes of the common school, which was devised "to develop the cognitive skills, and the moral and ethical character that would, according to the leading thought of the time, ensure citizens capable of participating in a complex, ever more industrialized society as productive, law abiding, and socially responsible members" (Sarason & Doris, 1979, p. 7). Immigrants and the handicapped were seen as creating problems for the system in fulfilling its main mandate. In examining the history of attempts to deal with mental retardation, Sarason and Doris note that the "same" speech about the inhumane conditions in institutions for the mentally retarded was given in 1843 and again in 1967 in the same state legislature. They comment:

The fact is that a lot of things have changed in a century, and a lot of well-meaning people have devoted themselves to improving the residential care of the mentally

---

6 The microcomputer will probably fare better, because it is a *better innovation* in terms of usability and individual access (see Evans, 1979; Toffler, 1980). Note that the ability to fulfill some of the promise in the field of computer technology is just beginning to emerge some fifteen years after it was touted—a period during which many school systems and individuals were misled by false promises. Yet serious problems remain in its use.

retarded as well as other dependent or handicapped groups, but the end result was another example of the more things change, the more they remain the same. (p. 18)

The authors make similar points in their investigation of the treatment of immigrants, who were disproportionately selected as mentally retarded in need of special education through segregation. (Segregation was the solution in the 19th century and continues in most situations to the present day: see especially Sarason & Doris, chs. 10, 14, and 16.) Reflecting the subtleties of the change process and the need to distinguish between change and progress, Sarason and Doris write: "No one consciously sought to create conditions that were sadistic or evil, and yet time and again the results were inhumane" (p. 18). Indeed, policy-makers were convinced that they were doing the right and proper thing. Sarason and Doris are perhaps overstating the case, because policies have changed (although it took over a hundred years) with recent legislation in both the United States and Canada. As they themselves amply describe, these policy changes represent the cumulative results of special-interest groups and responsive policy-makers. However, policy change is not practice change—but that is another matter, to be analyzed in chapter 5.

Other examples of innovation bias by neglect can easily be cited. For example, the majority of curriculum innovations are directed at cognitive/academic goals rather than personal/social-development goals. The former are more concrete, easier to implement and measure, and probably more elitist (academic) in their consequences. Individual, interpersonal, and social attitudes and skills appropriate for a democratic society do not receive the equal attention that Dewey (1916) so clearly argued they should and that the rhetoric of formal goal statements of schools and governments implies. Even within certain goal areas which receive emphasis and are desired, there are serious problems pertaining to the bias of relative neglect. For example, the major current emphasis on basic skills (factual content, reading, mathematics, etc.) raises all kinds of questions about relative neglect. The emphasis on basic skills and factual knowledge may be preempting the rest of the curriculum, including higher-order cognitive skills (e.g., problem-solving and other thinking skills); moreover, it may be leading to the almost wholesale neglect of personal- and social-development goals (see Wise, 1979; Galton, Simon, & Croll, 1980). Educational changes are adopted piecemeal without any thought as to whether the sum total of what is expected can feasibly be implemented. If it cannot, as is certainly the case, the more obvious, most easily measured, minimal objectives will be the *de facto* curriculum. Or, with an impossibly large number of priorities, the choice of emphasis may be based on the personal preferences and ideologies of individual teachers and administrators. Relative neglect is central to many issues: whether schools equally address the needs of female students (e.g., in guidance and career education: see Dimond, 1975); whether secondary schools have an academic bias; whether schools provide equal programs for minority groups; etc.

In highlighting the problem of meaning in educational change, the main implication is that innovations should not be taken for granted. What values are involved? Who will the change benefit? How much of a priority is it? How achievable is it? Which areas of potential change are being neglected? All are important questions about the sources and consequences of change.

# Innovations are not ends in themselves

It may seem to the reader that I set out in this chapter to destroy the credibility of educational change. This is not true. There are some excellent innovations available, depending on the specific need and on the approach taken in deciding whether and how to use them. I have attempted to put the sources of change in perspective by suggesting that innovations are not neutral in their benefits, and that there are many reasons other than educational merit which influence decisions to change. A closer examination reveals that innovations can be adopted for symbolic political or personal reasons: to appease community pressure, to appear innovative, to gain more resources. All of these forms represent *symbolic* rather than *real* change. The incentive system of public schools with abstract and unclear goals, lack of performance scrutiny, and a non-competitive market makes it more profitable politically and bureaucratically to "innovate" without risking the costs of real change: "For the schools' purposes, verbal adoption of innovations may be entirely sufficient" (Pincus, 1974, p. 125; see also Miles, 1981, for a discussion of the common properties of schools). Further, the purported neutrality of technical experts obscures "the fact that innovations are still means by which some people organize and control the lives of other people and their children according to their conceptions as to what is preferable. It disguises the reality that some people helped to plan the changes, that some people benefited from them while others did not, and that some consequences were intended while others were not" (Whiteside, 1978, p. 20).

None of this is to deny the fact that there are many educational innovations which are designed to bring about real reform. I will show in subsequent chapters that there are real examples of successful change, and that in the past few years we have come to know what makes for success. Desirable goals and good intentions are not sufficient. The plans and details of implementation are frequently unattended to or their importance underestimated. Reforms which explicitly purport to improve the life chances of the least advantaged groups in society may fail to make a difference, either because on closer examination these groups do not really benefit, or because the plans and resources necessary to accomplish implementation are not adequate to the task.

This chapter has also served to highlight the problem of meaning in educational change, because we cannot be sure about the purposes, possibilities of implementation, or actual outcomes of proposed changes. We should neither accept nor reject all changes uncritically. Nisbet (1969, 1980) has claimed that the "metaphor" of growth and progress in Western thought has seduced us into falsely assuming that change is development. He shows that actual historical events and processes do not sustain the notion of the linearity and inevitability of progress. The corrective to this metaphor is not a counter-metaphor of decay. Rather, the nature of educational changes should be examined according to the specific values, goals, events, and consequences which obtain in concrete situations. Educational innovations are not ends in themselves, but must be subjected to fundamental questions about their relationship to the basic purposes and outcomes of schools—a task made no easier but all the more necessary by the fact that the goals of education in contemporary society and the best means of achieving them are simply not that clear or agreed upon.

The possible approaches to addressing these problems of change must await a further exploration of the meaning of change and its causes. For the time being we may very well take solace in the fact that proposed educational changes which we do not desire will probably not get adequately implemented anyway. But, alas, this also means that educational reforms we value do not stand much of a chance either.

# Chapter 3

# The Meaning of Educational Change

*If there is no meaning in it, that saves a world of trouble, you know, as we needn't try to find any.*

— *King of Hearts in* Alice in Wonderland, *after reading the nonsensical poem of the White Rabbit*

We have become so accustomed to the presence of change that we rarely stop and think what change really means as we are experiencing it at the personal level. More important, we almost never stop to think what it means for those others around us who might be in change situations. The crux of change is how individuals come to grips with this reality. We vastly underestimate both what change is (this chapter) and the factors and processes which account for it (chapters 4 and 5). In answering the former question, let us suspend until the conclusion of this chapter the problem of the reliability of the sources and the purposes of change (chapter 2) and treat change for what it is—a fact of life. The clarification process which I propose to follow is in four parts. The first task is to consider the more general problem of the meaning of individual change in society at large, not as confined to education. Second, I then elaborate on the *subjective* meaning of change among individuals in the field of education. Third, I organize these ideas more comprehensively to arrive at a description of the *objective* meaning of change, which more formally attempts to make sense of the components of educational change. The test of the validity of this objective description will indeed be whether it orders and makes sense of the confusion and complexity of educators' subjective realities. Lastly, I elaborate on the implications of subjective and objective realities for understanding educational change.

## The general problem of the meaning of change

The titles of some of the more general accounts of individual change and reality in modern society provide us with as succinct an introduction to the problem as any—*Loss and Change* (Marris, 1975), *Beyond the Stable State* (Schon, 1971), *The Social Construction of Reality* (Berger & Luckmann, 1967), *The Micro Millen-*

*ium* (Evans, 1979), *Future Shock* (Toffler, 1970), and *The Third Wave* (Toffler, 1980).

At a later point I will distinguish between voluntary and imposed change. Nevertheless, Marris makes the case that *all* real change involves loss, anxiety, and struggle. Failure to recognize this phenomenon as natural and inevitable has meant that we tend to ignore important aspects of change and misinterpret others. As Marris states early in his book, "Once the anxieties of loss were understood, both the tenacity of conservatism and the ambivalence of transitional institutions became clearer" (p. 2).

According to Marris:

Whether the change is sought or resisted, and happens by chance or design; whether we look at it from the standpoint of reformers or those they manipulate, of individuals or institutions, the response is characteristically ambivalent. (p. 7)

New experiences are always initially reacted to in the context of some "familiar, reliable construction of reality" in which people must be able to attach personal meaning to the experiences regardless of how meaningful they might be to others. Marris does not see this "conservative impulse" as incompatible with growth: "It seeks to consolidate skills and attachments, whose secure possession provides the assurance to master something new" (p. 22).

Change may come about either because it is imposed on us (by natural events or deliberate reform) or because we voluntarily participate in or even initiate change when we find dissatisfaction, inconsistency, or intolerability in our current situation. In either case, the meaning of change will rarely be clear at the outset and ambivalence will pervade the transition. Any innovation "cannot be assimilated unless its *meaning* is shared" (Marris, p. 121, my italics).

I quote at some length one of the most revealing and fundamental passages to our theme:

No one can resolve the crisis of reintegration on behalf of another. Every attempt to pre-empt conflict, argument, protest by rational planning, can only be abortive: however reasonable the proposed changes, the process of implementing them must still allow the impulse of rejection to play itself out. When those who have power to manipulate changes act as if they have only to explain, and when their explanations are not at once accepted, shrug off opposition as ignorance or prejudice, they express a profound contempt for the meaning of lives other than their own. For the reformers have already assimilated these changes to their purposes, and worked out a reformulation which makes sense to them, perhaps through months or years of analysis and debate. If they deny others the chance to do the same, they treat them as puppets dangling by the threads of their own conceptions. (Marris, p. 166)

Schon (1971) has developed essentially the same theme. All real change involves "passing through the zones of uncertainty ... the situation of being at sea, of being lost, of confronting more information than you can handle" (p. 12).

"Dynamic conservatism" in both Marris's and Schon's formulation is not simply an individual but a social phenomenon. Individuals (e.g., teachers) are members of social systems (e.g., schools) which have shared senses of meaning:

Dynamic conservatism is by no means always attributable to the stupidity of individuals within social systems, although their stupidity is frequently invoked by those seeking to introduce change .... The power of social systems over individuals becomes understandable, I think, only if we see that social systems provide ... a framework of theory, values and related technology which enables individuals to make sense of their lives.[1] Threats to the social system threaten this framework. (Marris, p. 51)

Toffler (1970, 1980), of course, has popularized some aspects of the phenomenon of information overload, anxiety, and stress as a result of the rapidity and uncertainty of change. The future may not be upon us, or change may not be as ubiquitous as Toffler claims, but there should be no doubt that instances of real change do exist in education and elsewhere, and when they appear they do result in a sense of future shock.

The implications of the principles and ideas described by Marris and others are profound in relation to our understanding of educational change in two senses—one concerning the meaning of change, and the other regarding the process of change. In the rest of this chapter, I will begin to apply these principles to specific examples of the meaning of educational change by introducing concepts pertaining to different dimensions and degrees of change. In chapters 4 through 6 the implications for the management of change will be documented in an examination of a large body of evidence on the causes and processes of change.

The point of this section is that real change, whether desired or not, whether imposed or voluntarily pursued, represents a serious personal and collective experience characterized by ambivalence and uncertainty, and if the change works out it can result in a sense of mastery, accomplishment, and professional growth (see Huberman's 1981 case study for an example). The anxieties of uncertainty and the joys of mastery are central to the subjective meaning of educational change, and to success or failure—facts which have not been recognized or appreciated in most attempts at reform.

# The subjective meaning of educational change

The details of the multiple phenomenologies of the different role incumbents in the educational enterprise will be taken up in each of the relevant chapters in Parts II and III. In this section, my purpose is to establish the importance and meaning of the subjective reality of change.[2] For illustration I will use examples taken from the world of the teacher, but the reader should refer to chapter 7 for a more complete treatment of the teacher's situation, and to other chapters for the various relevant realities of other participants.

The appropriate starting point for considering change, as Nisbet (1969, pp. 270–71) indicates, is the existing reality: "If we look at actual behavior, in place

1 For a comprehensive treatment of the origins and continuance of the social construction of meaning, see Berger and Luckmann (1967).
2 The description of subjective meaning tries to capture the modal individual in a given group. There is no sociologism that all individuals in the same role have the same orientation. I will be discussing variations in response in later chapters.

and in time, we find over and over that persistence in time is the far more common condition of things .... [O]n the empirical record, fixity, not change is the required point of departure for the study of *not merely social order but social change*" (Nisbet's emphasis).

For example, the daily subjective reality of teachers is very well described by Jackson (1968), Smith and Geoffrey (1968), Lortie (1975), House and Lapan (1978), and Huberman (1980). The picture is one of limited development of technical culture: teachers are uncertain about how to influence students, especially about non-cognitive goals, and even whether they are having an influence; they experience students as individuals in specific circumstances who, taken as a classroom of individuals, are being influenced by multiple and differing forces for which generalizations are not possible; teaching decisions are often made on pragmatic trial-and-error grounds with little chance for reflection or thinking through the rationale; teachers must deal with constant daily disruptions, within the classroom in managing discipline and interpersonal conflicts, and from outside the classroom in collecting money for school events, making announcements, dealing with the principal, parents, central office staff, etc.; they must get through the daily grind; the rewards are having a few good days, covering the curriculum, getting a lesson across, having an impact on one or two individual students (success stories); they constantly feel the critical shortage of time. (See Jackson, 1968, Smith & Geoffrey, 1968, Lortie, 1975, and House & Lapan, 1978, for details and further discussion.) Huberman (1978, 1980), based on his own investigations and reviews of other research, summarizes those characteristics using three dimensions:

Multidimensionality: the classroom as a crowded place with several activities and functions to be carried out (discipline, supplies, instruction, relationships, etc.)
Simultaneity: interacting with one pupil and monitoring the others, preparing the next question or exercise, directing simultaneous groups, etc.
Unpredictability: anything can happen; a well planned lesson may fall flat; what works with one child is ineffective for another; one feels one's way through the day; classes have different "personalities" from year to year. (Huberman, 1978, p. 4)

Enter "the hyperrationalization of change" (Wise, 1977, 1979) and we add insult to injury. The rational assumptions, abstraction, and descriptions of a proposed new curriculum do not make sense in the capricious world of the teacher:

Many proposals for change strike them as frivolous—they do not address issues of boundedness, psychic rewards, time scheduling, student disruption, interpersonal support, and so forth. (Lortie, 1975, p. 235)

In short, there is no reason for the teacher to believe in the change, and few incentives (and large costs) to find out whether a given change will turn out to be worthwhile. As House (1974) explains:

The personal costs of trying new innovations are often high ... and seldom is there any indication that innovations are worth the investment. Innovations are acts of faith. They require that one believe that they will ultimately bear fruit and be worth the personal investment, often without the hope of an immediate return. Costs are also high. The amount of energy and time required to learn the new skills or roles associated with the new innovation is a useful index to the magnitude of resistance. (p. 73)[3]

Predictably, "rational" solutions to the above problems have backfired because they ignore the culture of the school (Sarason, 1971). Two of the most popular, but in themselves superficial, solutions consist of the use of general goals (on the assumption that teachers should specify the change according to their own situation) and of voluntary populations (on the assumption that people who choose to participate will implement the change). The result has been two forms of non-change: *false clarity* without change and *painful unclarity* without change. As to the former, Goodlad, Klein, et al. (1970) comment on the presence of specific educational reforms (e.g., team teaching, individualization) in 158 classrooms which they examined across the United States. They found:

A very subjective but nonetheless general impression of those who gathered and those who studied the data was that some of the highly recommended and publicized innovations of the past decade or so were dimly conceived, and, at best, partially implemented in the schools claiming them. The novel features seemed to be blunted in the effort to twist the innovation into familiar conceptual frames or established patterns of schooling. For example, team teaching more often than not was some form of departmentalization .... Similarly, the new content of curriculum projects tended to be conveyed into the baggage of traditional methodology .... [Principals and teachers] claimed individualization of instruction, use of a wide range of instructional materials, a sense of purpose, group processes, and inductive or discovery methods when our records showed little or no evidence of them. (pp. 72–73)

Other studies of attempted change show that not all teachers experience even the comfort of false clarity. Both Gross et al. (1971) and Charters and Pellegrin (1973) in their investigation of four cases of differentiated staffing (to name just two of many studies) found that abstract goals combined with a mandate for teachers to operationalize them resulted in confusion, frustration, anxiety, and abandonment of the effort.

The function of the ambiguity of change goals and the dilemma of explicitness will be analyzed in the following chapter. At this stage, we can register the observation that in the subjective realm of change, false clarity occurs when people *think* that they have changed but have only assimilated the superficial trappings of the new practice. Painful unclarity is experienced when unclear innovations are attempted under conditions which do not support the development of the subjective meaning of the change. Loucks and Hall's (1979) research clearly shows that the assumptions of introducers of change are out of whack with the "stages of concerns" of teachers. At initial stages, teachers are often more concerned about how the change will affect them personally, in terms of their in-classroom and extra-classroom work, than they are about a description of the goals and supposed benefits of the program. In brief, change is usually not introduced in a way which takes into account the subjective reality of teachers.

Essential to the discussion in this section are three themes. First, the typical situation of teachers or anyone else in ongoing organizations is one of fixity and

---

3 See also House and Lapan (1978), ch. 10.

a welter of forces keeping things that way. Second, there is little room, so to speak, for change. When change is imposed from outside, it is bitterly resented. When it is voluntarily engaged in, it is threatening and confusing. In any event, the transformation of subjective realities is the essence of change. Third, there is a strong tendency for people to adjust to the "near occasion" of change, by changing as little as possible—either assimilating or abandoning changes which they have initially been willing to try, or fighting or ignoring imposed change. Marris (1975, p. 16) gives a good description of the fundamental meaning of the threat of change:

Occupational identity represents the accumulated wisdom of how to handle the job, derived from their own experience and the experience of all who have had the job before or share it with them. Change threatens to invalidate this experience robbing them of the skills they have learned and confusing their purposes, upsetting the subtle rationalizations and compensations by which they reconciled the different aspects of their situation.

The extent to which proposals for change are defined according to only one person's or one group's reality (e.g., the policy-maker's or administrator's) is the extent to which they will encounter problems in implementation.[4] This is not to say that subjective realities *should* define what is to change, but only that they are powerful constraints to change or protections against undesirable or thoughtless change (depending on your viewpoint and the particular change).

Defining the objective reality of innovations will move us one step closer to an understanding of the nature of educational change, which in my view is an essential precondition for formulating our own subjective response to the question of when change is progress.

# The objective reality of educational change

People do not understand the nature or ramifications of most educational changes. They become involved in change voluntarily or involuntarily and in either case experience ambivalence about its meaning, form, or consequences. I have implied that there are a number of things at stake—changes in goals, skills, philosophy or beliefs, behavior, etc. Subjectively these different aspects are experienced in a diffuse, incoherent manner. Change is often not conceived of as being *multidimensional*. Objectively, it is possible to clarify the meaning of an educational change by identifying and describing its main separate dimensions. Ignorance of these dimensions explains a number of interesting phenomena in the field of educational change: for example, why some people accept an innovation they do not understand; why some aspects of a change are implemented and others not; and why strategies for change neglect certain essential components.

---

4 See Lighthall's (1973) brilliant critique of Smith and Keith's (1971) failure to recognize "the multiple realities" in their otherwise fine case study. See also McLean (1979) for a similar argument as to why educational research has limited impact on teachers.

The concept of objective reality is tricky (see Berger & Luckmann, 1967, section II: Society as Objective Reality; and Schutz, 1970). Reality is always defined by concrete individuals and groups. But individuals and groups interact to produce social phenomena (constitutions, laws, policies, educational change programs) which exist outside any given individual. There is also the danger that the objective reality is only the reflection of the producers of change and thus simply a glorified version of *their* subjective conceptions. As Berger and Luckmann (1967) put it, we can minimize this problem by following the practice of posing double questions: "What is the existing conception of reality on a given issue?" followed quickly by "Says who?" (p. 116). With this caution in mind, I would now like to turn to the possibility of defining educational change.

## What is change in practice?

The implementation of educational change involves "change in practice." But what exactly does this mean? Although change in practice can occur at many levels—the teacher, the school, the school district, etc.—I will use as an illustration the classroom or teacher level because this level is closest to instruction and learning. When we ask which aspects of current practice would be altered, if given educational changes were to be implemented, the complexity of defining and accomplishing actual change begins to surface. The difficulty is that educational change is not a single entity. It is to a certain extent *multidimensional*. There are at least three components or dimensions at stake in implementing any new program or policy: (1) the possible use of new or revised *materials* (direct instructional resources such as curriculum materials or technologies), (2) the possible use of new *teaching approaches* (i.e., new teaching strategies or activities), and (3) the possible alteration of *beliefs* (e.g., pedagogical assumptions and theories underlying particular new policies or programs).[5]

All three aspects of change are necessary because together they represent the means of achieving a particular educational goal or set of goals.[6] It is clear that any individual may implement none, one, two, or all three dimensions. A teacher could use new curriculum materials or technologies without altering the teaching approach. Or a teacher could use the materials and alter some teaching behaviors without coming to grips with the conceptions or beliefs underlying the change.

Before we turn to some illustrations of the three dimensions of change in practice, three difficulties should be noted. First, in identifying the three aspects of change, there is no assumption about who develops the materials, defines the teaching approaches, and decides on the beliefs. Whether these are done by an external curriculum developer or a group of teachers is an open question

---

5 See Fullan and Park (1981, p. 6), Leithwood (1981), and Hall and Loucks (1981) for more elaborate discussions of the notion of different dimensions of implementation. Werner (1980) discusses the role of beliefs in implementation. It is possible to add a few other dimensions, but the three referred to here are central.

6 Whether or not they do achieve the goal is another question depending on the quality and appropriateness of the change for the task at hand. My point is the logical one that the change has to *occur in practice* along the three dimensions in order for it to have a chance of affecting the outcome.

(see chapters 4 and 5). Second, and partly related, there is a dilemma and tension running through the educational change literature in which two different emphases or perspectives are evident: the fidelity perspective, and the mutual-adaptation or evolutionary perspective. The fidelity approach to change, as the label indicates, is based on the assumption that an already developed innovation exists and the task is to get individuals and groups of individuals to implement it faithfully in practice—that is, to use it as it is "supposed to be used" as intended by the developer. The mutual-adaptation or evolutionary perspective stresses that change often is (and should be) a result of adaptations and decisions taken by users as they work with particular new policies or programs, with the policy or program and the situation of the user mutually determining the outcome.[7] Third, we can see that it is very difficult to define once and for all exactly what the objective dimensions of change are in respect to materials, teaching approach, and beliefs, because they may get transformed, further developed, or otherwise altered during implementation (and this is the essence of the evolutionary perspective). Nonetheless, there is value in conceptualizing change (in order to define it over time) in terms of the three dimensions. Some examples illustrate this point.

In considering examples, it should be recognized that individual innovations or programs vary in terms of whether they entail significant change on the three dimensions in relation to the current practices of particular groups of individuals; but I suggest that the majority of educational innovations extant in the field involve substantial changes in regard to these criteria.[8] Numerous examples could be used to illustrate the objective reality of the dimensions of change. I will draw on three studies—one on a provincewide curriculum on language arts, one on open education, and one on mainstreaming. Portraying these changes again raises the question "Is not the reality described simply the subjective proposals of developers and decision-makers?" This may or may not be the case in terms of content, but my main interest is in demonstrating that there are different *dimensions* of change, and that they do often take on a socially legitimated life of their own. Once we understand the dimensions, we are in a better position to argue the desirability of the content of change because we can argue concretely.

Simms (1978) conducted a detailed study in one of the provinces in Canada on the use of an elementary language arts program. A few of the main objectives of the program are stated as follows:

— developing competencies in receiving information (critically) through listening, reading, viewing, touching, tasting, smelling;

---

7 For a discussion of the two different perspectives on implementation which elaborates on the above issues and contains other ideas on what is a very complex topic, see Berman (1980), Farrar et al. (1979), Hall and Loucks (1981), Majone and Wildavsky (1978), and Fullan and Pomfret (1977). If we were to get into a finer-grained debate, there is some argument for distinguishing between adaptation and evolution (see Fullan, 1981a).

8 I would also propose that innovations which do not include changes on most of these dimensions are really not significant changes at all. For example, the use of a new textbook or materials without any alteration in teaching strategies is a minor change at best—an example of "the more things change the more they remain the same" (Sarason, 1971). Put in terms of the theme of this book, real change involves changes in conceptions and role behavior, which is why it is so difficult to achieve.

— understanding the communication process as well as their role as receivers, processors or expressors in that process. (Quoted in Simms, p. 96)

The three dimensions of potential change can be illustrated by reference to the basic document. For example, implications for pedagogical *beliefs* are contained in the following passage:

The basic focus is on the child as a flexible user of language. If language is to be truly useful (functional) we must begin with the present experience and competence of the child and fit our teaching into the natural language situation, which is an integrated, whole situation. It should be emphasized that the developing philosophy is one of total integration of all aspects of language arts. In this sense, integration refers to the treatment of all the communication skills as closely interrelated. (pp. 90–91)

References to possible alterations in *teaching approaches* are stated throughout the document. Teaching methodologies include providing opportunities for active involvement of the child, using a variety of resources and techniques (viewing, reading, speaking, informal drama, mime, photography, etc.), and using "the inductive method ... frequently in small groups and individual teaching situations" (pp. 366–77). The core of the methodology is the "diagnostic approach," which involves eight steps in cycle—set objectives, design a task, set criteria, collect sample of work, analyze sample, diagnose strengths and weaknesses, plan instruction by charting individual and group needs, and teach the needed skill (pp. 376–77). We need not proceed to describe the content of *curriculum materials and resources*—the third dimension—but the difficulties of clarifying and accomplishing changes in practice involving the interrelationship of beliefs, teaching approaches, and resources should be clear.[9]

By employing the distinction between surface curriculum and deep structure in analyzing open education, Bussis, Chittenden, and Amarel (1976) have played right into our theme. They found that open-education teachers differed fundamentally in their use of open-education dimensions. Some teachers operated at the level of surface curriculum, focusing on materials and seeing that students were "busy." They tried to address open-education goals *literally*, but they did not comprehend the underlying purpose. For example, they wanted to ensure that children were "learning to share materials, to take turns, to respect the properties of others, and so on—with the focus of concern being the manifestation of these behaviors rather than concomitant attitudes and understanding" (Bussis et al., p. 59). It was these teachers who reacted to the problem of ambiguity by requesting further guidance on "what exactly has to be covered." Other teachers had developed a basic understanding of the principles of open education and concrete activities which reflected them. They were "able to move back and forth between classroom activities and organizing priorities, using a specific encounter to illustrate a broader concern and relating broader priorities back to specific instances" (p. 61). Reflexivity, purposefulness, and awareness characterized these teachers, but not in a linear way; for example, they would do something out of intuition and then reflect on its meaning in

---

9 The impact of the language arts program is described in chapter 5. The reader may want to make some predictions based on the twin phenomena of the unreliability of sources and the subjective meaning of order and change.

relation to overall purpose. Assumptions about and orientations to children varied similarly. Teachers ranged from those who felt that children's ability to choose was unreliable and idiosyncratic (some could, others couldn't) to those who assumed and experienced that *all* children have interests and who were able to relate individualized interests to common educational goals across the curriculum (pp. 95–98).

In the pages of quotes from teachers and in their own analysis, Bussis et al. clearly demonstrate (although not using the same words) the nature of the dimensions of change at work. Some examples: teachers who saw open education as literally covering subject content but who had no underlying rationale (p. 57); those "who were reasonably articulate in indicating priorities for children [but] were more vague in describing concrete connections between these priorities and classroom activities" (p. 69); still others who "may provide the classroom with rich materials *on the faith* that they will promote certain learning priorities" (p. 74, their emphasis).

In the words of our dimensions, it is possible to change "on the surface" by endorsing certain goals, using specific materials, and even imitating the behavior *without specifically understanding* the principles and rationale of the change. Moreover, in reference to beliefs it is possible to value and even be articulate about the goals of the change without understanding their implications for practice:[10]

... action based on valuing and faith is not very likely to lead to an enlargement or strengthening of the teacher's own understanding. The potential informational support available in feedback to the teacher is not received because it is not recognized. (Bussis et al., p. 74)

In summary, for our purposes there are three critical lessons to be learned from the Bussis et al. investigation. First, change is multidimensional and can vary accordingly within the same person as well as within groups. Second, there are some deep changes at stake, once we realize that people's basic conceptions of education and skills are involved—that is, their occupational identity, their sense of competence, and their self-concept. The need and difficulty for individuals to develop a sense of meaning about change is manifest. Third, compounding the second lesson is the fact that change consists of a sophisticated and none-too-clear *dynamic interrelationship* of the three dimensions of change.[11] Beliefs guide and are informed by teaching strategies and activities; the effective use of materials depends on their articulation with beliefs and teaching approaches; and so on. Many innovations entail changes in some aspects of educational beliefs, teaching behavior, use of new materials, and more. Whether or not people develop meaning in relation to these aspects is fundamentally the problem.

Recent special education legislation and policies in Canada and the United States emphasize every child's right to a full education. The practice known as

---

10 The opposite is also possible: "being conceptually equipped to implement without [having] a commitment to the program philosophy" (Bussis et al., p. 168).

11 Giacquinta's (1979) findings from a national U.S. study of open education shows just how fatal the complexities of open education have turned out to be. He found limited and inconsistent meaning and understanding of the concept, high proportions of "never tried it," and high rates of discontinuance (Giacquinta & Kazlow, 1979).

mainstreaming provides another example of the misunderstood complexities and multiple components of change (see Sarason & Doris, 1979, for a detailed account). Sarason and Doris realize the problem in the first lines of their chapter on mainstreaming:

The speed with which mainstreaming as a concept, value and public policy has emerged in our society is little short of amazing. Indeed, the change has come about so fast and with such apparent general approbation as to raise a question about what people understand about mainstreaming and its implications for schools .... Because we may think mainstreaming is desirable is no excuse for assuming that institutional realities will accommodate our hopes. (p. 355)

It is not necessary to give a complete litany of the dimensional implications of mainstreaming for schools, but some of the philosophical, role-change, and materials consequences both inside and outside the classroom are evident in the following excerpts from Sarason and Doris:

For effective mainstreaming, regular classroom teachers must have the strong and coordinated backing of special education teachers and support personnel. (Ryor, quoted in Sarason and Doris, p. 372)

The law mandates the involvement of parents and lay groups in "overseeing, evaluating, and operating special education programs" through regional and state advisory committees, a majority of whose members are parents of handicapped children. (p. 376)

Success requires "integrated diagnosis, prescription, and follow through" with "an individual education prescription for each handicapped child", and "to be done well this not only requires time but harmonious relationships among school personnel." (p. 389)

Mainstreaming is one of the more complex changes on the current educational scene, and as such it highlights the dimensions of change and the magnitude of the task in bringing about major educational reform—valuing new beliefs; cognitively understanding the interrelationship between the philosophical principles and concrete diagnosis and treatment; changing the roles and role relationships between regular classroom teachers and special education teachers, and between school personnel and community members and professionals outside the school.

We could take other educational changes to illustrate the significance of the different dimensions of change. Virtually every program change states or implies all three aspects, whether we refer to language arts, social studies, career education, use of microcomputers, Head Start or Follow Through programs, special education, and so on. The point is that educational change programs do have an objective reality which may be more or less definable in terms of what beliefs, teaching practices, and resources they encompass.

Why worry about all three aspects of change? Why not be content to develop quality innovations and provide access to them? The answer is simply that such an approach does not adequately recognize how individuals come to confront or avoid behavioral and conceptual implications of change. The innovation as a set of materials and resources is the most visible aspect of change, and the easiest to employ, but only literally. Change in teaching approach or style in using new materials presents greater difficulty if new skills must be acquired and new ways of conducting instructional activities established. Changes in beliefs are yet more difficult: they challenge the core values held by individuals regarding the purposes of education; moreover, beliefs are often not explicit, discussed, or understood, but rather are buried at the level of unstated assumptions. And the development of a clear belief system is essential, because it provides a set of criteria for overall planning and a screen for sifting valuable from not-so-valuable learning opportunities that inevitably arise during instruction (recall Bussis et al., 1976). The ultimate question, of course, is how essential are all three dimensions of change. The use of new materials by themselves may accomplish certain educational objectives, but it seems obvious that developing new teaching skills and approaches and understanding conceptually what and why something should be done, and to what end, represents much more fundamental change, and as such takes longer.[12]

Specific educational programs and policies differ in how great a change is at stake. The extent of change must always be defined in reference to concrete situations and individuals, because the degree of potential change consists in the discrepancy between the state of existing practice on the part of particular individuals and the future state where a change might take them. The very recent large-scale Study of Dissemination Efforts Supporting School Improvement (the DESSI study—see Appendix) demonstrates the critical importance of defining the extent of change in terms of individuals' starting points (Crandall et al., forthcoming). This study, to which I will refer at various places in subsequent chapters, found that teachers, under the right supportive conditions, used new materials and altered teaching practices consistent with innovations adopted by their schools or districts.[13]

In summary, the purpose of acknowledging the objective reality of change lies in the recognition that there are new policies and programs "out there" and that they may be more or less specific in terms of what they imply for changes in materials, teaching practices, and beliefs. The real crunch comes in the *relationships* between these new programs or policies and the thousands of subjective realities embedded in people's individual and organizational contexts and their personal histories. How these subjective realities are addressed or ignored is crucial for whether potential changes become meaningful at the level of individual use and effectiveness. It is perhaps worth repeating that changes in actual practice along the three dimensions—in materials, teaching approaches, beliefs—what *people do and think*—determine the outcome of change.[14]

---

12 The whole matter of strategies of change is left until later chapters. How best to deal with conceptions (e.g., beliefs) and behavior (e.g., teaching approaches) is complicated, but some of the implications include the need for addressing them on a *continuous* basis during implementation, and the possibility that beliefs can be most effectively discussed *after* people have had at least some behavioral experience in attempting new practices.

13 The DESSI study also contains a clear discussion and corresponding evidence on the fidelity perspective: i.e., the question of faithfully implementing innovations which have been developed external to a group of users.

14 It is also appropriate here to compare "change in practice" with the recent "time on task" research. The latter, based in the so-called "school effects" literature, documents that the amount of time spent by teachers and students engaged in instructional tasks is related to student achievement (see Fisher et al., 1978; Karweit, 1981; and chapter 7). The argument regarding implementation is similar: the more time teachers spend thinking about and using a new practice, the more it will affect student learning.

# Implications of the subjective and objective realities

As we integrate the ideas of chapters 2 and 3, there are seven major observations to be made concerning: (1) the soundness of proposed changes; (2) understanding the failure of well-intentioned change; (3) guidelines for understanding the nature and feasibility of particular changes; (4) implications for planning; (5) the realities of the status quo; (6) the deepness of change; and (7) the question of valuing.

First, as we have seen in the previous chapter, not all change proposals are "authentic." There may be a variety of reasons why change decisions are made, not all of which represent sustained commitments. Moreover, if the subjective and objective implications of implementing real change are as profound as I have suggested, there is no way that even a fraction of the changes coming down the pike could be implemented. All new programs could not possibly be fully implemented, and could not be developed to the point that they become meaningful. And if they were, it might be discovered that some are unsound, meaningless ideas in the first place. As the King of Hearts says at the beginning of this chapter, we needn't try to find any meaning if there is no meaning in it—good advice for maintaining sanity when change seems senseless. Change strategies or strange chatteries? Sometimes it is difficult to discern the difference.

A second version of the inauthenticity of change relates to new programs or policies which are very sincerely hoped for, and adopted naively, with their adopters not realizing and perhaps never realizing the implications. This phenomenon accounts for the false clarity in Goodlad and Klein's (1970) findings that teachers *thought* they were using a new approach but actually were not;[15] it also accounts for Sarason's observation about mainstreaming, where a large number of people endorse an innovation because of value agreement without realizing what specific changes might be involved. Knowing the subjective and objective dimensions of change helps us to understand these occurrences.

Third, the objective dimensions can be and have been used to analyze given changes in order to understand what they are and how feasible and desirable they might be (see Leithwood, 1981). For example, we might examine a particular curriculum change or direction and discover that (a) the goals are specific and clear, but the means of implementation are vague, or (b) beliefs and goals are abstract, vague, and unconnected with other dimensions (e.g., teaching strategies), or (c) the number of changes implied (e.g., the number of different teaching activities) is overwhelming or incoherent when taken together. Such an analysis could lead to any one of a number of conclusions— the proposed change is hopelessly incoherent; the proposed change is *too* coherent (i.e., prescriptive); the change has possibilities but needs further

---

15 As Watzlawick et al. (1974, p. 79) quotes Laing: "If I don't know I don't know, I think I know."

development and/or resources during implementation, and if they are not available further work is unfeasible.

Fourth, and related to the third point, the analysis of the subjective and objective aspects can be useful for more specific and effective planning of changes that we do want. Whether the change is external or self-chosen, if we know where we currently are in relation to a particular policy or program change, we can develop plans to address the different dimensions in attempting to bring about specific changes in practice.[16]

Fifth, the status quo is full of fixity which leaves little room for change. We must understand the *existing* realities of the major participants in relation to the feasibility of any change. In Parts II and III we will see that understanding the *different* realities of the main groups of participants goes a long way in explaining the total picture; that is, the sum total of subjective meanings provides a more comprehensive picture of educational change as a whole.

Sixth, change can be very deep, striking at the core of learned skills and beliefs and conceptions of education, creating doubts about purposes, sense of competence, and self-concept. If these problems are ignored or glossed over, superficial change will occur at best; at worst, people will retreat into a self-protective cocoon, unreflectively rejecting all proposed changes. Even changes which do not seem to be complex to the promoter of change may raise numerous doubts and uncertainties on the part of those not familiar with it.

But now the question: How do we know if a particular change is valuable, and who decides? Sarason and Doris (1979, p. 361) give some indication of the difficulty and indeed impossibility of coming up with a definitive answer:

Institutional custom and practice are effective bulwarks to forces for change and this, we too easily forget, has both good and bad features. On the one hand, we do not want our institutions to change in response to every new fad or idea and, on the other hand, we do not want them blindly to preserve the status quo. In regard to mainstreaming, how one regards the oppositional stance of our schools and university training centers will depend on how one feels about mainstreaming. If one is for mainstreaming, then one will tend to view opposition as another instance of stone-age attitudes. If one is against mainstreaming, one will tend to view it as another misguided effort that will further dilute the quality of education of everyone.

The short answer is that a change is good depending on one's values, whether or not it gets implemented, and with what consequences. Some people blindly support certain changes which they value, oblivious to questions of implementation and consequences. Others are unsure of the value of change because they are only too well aware of the lack of clarity and uncertainty that permeates the transition from values to goals, to adoption, through implementation, to outcomes.[17]

What I have been saying has nothing to do with the *intentions* of promoters of change. It mainly says that no matter how honorable the motives, each and every individual who is necessary for effective implementation will experience some concerns of meaning about new practices, goals, beliefs, and means of

---

16 This is a simplified version of a complex and difficult process, which is more fully taken up in the next two chapters.

17 This uncertainty is compounded by the difficulties of *ever* knowing the true impact of change, because of the myriad forces affecting schooling and its outcomes.

implementation. Clear statements at the outset may help, but do not eliminate the problem; the psychological process of learning and understanding something new does not happen in a flash (or for most educational changes in several flashes). The presence or absence of mechanisms to address the ongoing problem of meaning—at the beginning and as people try out ideas—is crucial for success, because it is at the individual level that change does or does not occur.[18]

So far I have dwelt on the problem of meaning in relation to the content of innovations. I have suggested that individuals have to become clear about new educational practices which they wish (and/or someone else wishes them) to implement. This is meaning, if you will, about the content and theory of educational practice. Affecting the likelihood of obtaining meaning about the desirability and workability of specific educational practices is the question of *how* new practices are introduced. The latter concerns the theory of change—a complex social process in which people have just as many problems understanding what is happening and why.[19] I start in chapter 4 near the beginning of the process with how educational changes get decided on or adopted in the first place.

---

18 This principle is true whether change is imposed on individuals or whether they voluntarily decide to do something new. Basic to this process is the reality that learning a new skill and entertaining new conceptions create doubts and feelings of awkwardness or incompetence especially when we first try something (see, for example, Joyce & Showers, 1981). Of course, in saying that change occurs at the individual level, it should be recognized that organizational changes are often necessary to provide supportive or stimulating conditions to foster change in practice.
19 I mentioned in chapter 1 that educational change involves two main aspects: what changes to implement (theories of education) and how to implement them (theories of change). There are dangers in separating these two aspects, because they do interact. But it is helpful to realize this distinction in planning or analyzing specific change efforts.

# Chapter 4

# The Causes
# and Processes
# of Adoption

*The pressures [for change] seem to subside with the act of adoption followed by the appearance of implementation.*

— *Berman and McLaughlin (1979), p. 1*

There is no shortage of recommendations about how the ills of education *should* be rectified. But the remedies remain pie in the sky as long as competing "shoulds" fight it out without an understanding of what *is*. The next two chapters contain a description of the educational change process and an explanation of why it works as it does.

The number and dynamics of factors which interact and affect the process of educational change are too overwhelming to compute in anything resembling a fully determined way. Moreover, there is little agreement or clarity on the outcomes or on how to get there except perhaps in the area of basic skills at the elementary school level, and even here there is nothing close to a consensus.[1] And whatever conviction there is usually turns out to be based on belief and advocacy of certain values rather than on knowledge of the change process.

Most researchers now see three broad phases to the change process. Phase I—variously labeled initiation, mobilization, or adoption—consists of the process which leads up to and includes a decision to adopt or proceed with a change. Phase II—implementation or initial use (usually the first two or three years of use)—involves the first experiences of attempting to put an idea or program into practice. Phase III—called continuation, incorporation, routinization, or institutionalization—refers to whether the change gets built in as an ongoing part of the system or disappears by way of a decision to discard or through attrition (see Berman & McLaughlin, 1978; Rosenblum & Louis, 1979; Yin et al., 1977; Zaltman et al., 1973). Figure 2 depicts the three phases and adds the concept of outcome to provide a more complete overview of the change process.

In simple terms, someone or some group for whatever reasons initiates or promotes a certain program or direction of change. The direction of change, which may be more or less defined at the early stages, moves to a phase of attempted use (implementation), which is more or less effective in that use

---

1 See March (1972) for a description of the problem that one often cannot clarify educational goals and decide whether they are desirable *a priori*. Many goals and especially their means of implementation only become clear as one attempts to achieve them.

**Figure 2    A Simplified Overview of the Change Process**

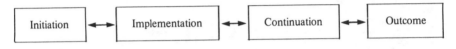

may or may not be accomplished. Continuation is an extension of the implementation phase in that the new program is sustained beyond the first year or two (or whatever time frame we choose). Outcome, depending on the objectives, can refer to several different types of results, and can be thought of generally as the degree of school improvement in relation to given criteria. Results could include, for example, improved student learning and attitudes; new skills, attitudes, or satisfaction on the part of teachers and other school personnel; or improved problem-solving capacity of the school as an organization.

Figure 2 presents only the general image of a much more detailed and snarled process. First, there are numerous factors operating at each phase. Second, as the two-way arrows imply, it is not a linear process but rather one in which events at one phase can feed back to alter decisions taken at previous stages, which then proceed to work their way through in a continuous interactive way. For example, a decision at the initiation phase to use a specific program may be substantially modified during implementation, and so on. A useful distinction to keep in mind is whether the process is characterized more by a programmatic or fidelity emphasis or more by a mutually adaptive or evolutionary mode.[2]

The third set of variables which are unspecified in figure 2 concern the scope of change and the question of who develops and initiates the change. The scope can range from large-scale externally developed innovations to locally produced ones. In either of these cases the teacher as user may or may not be centrally involved in development and/or decisions to proceed. Thus, the concept "initiation" leaves open the question of who develops or initiates the change. The question is taken up at various places in the rest of this chapter and in relevant chapters on particular roles.

The fourth complication in figure 2 is that the total time perspective as well as subphases cannot be precisely demarcated. The initiation phase may be in the works for years, but even later specific decision-making and pre-implementation planning activities can be lengthy. Implementation for most changes takes two or more years; only then can we consider that the change has really had a chance to become implemented.[3] The line between implementation and continuation is somewhat hazy or arbitrary unless a specific implementation period has been agreed upon (for example, a two-year period tied to external funds). Outcomes can be assessed in the relatively short run, but we would not expect many results until the change had had a chance to become implemented. In this

2 I have already introduced this distinction (see Berman, 1981; Fullan, 1981a).

3 The DESSI study found that this time-line can be shorter if the innovation has been previously developed and validated (Crandall et al., forthcoming). Routine uses of new materials and practices may be accomplished in one year, but alterations in beliefs or conceptual understanding take longer (see Huberman's 1981 case study).

sense implementation is the *means* to achieving certain outcomes; evaluations have limited value and can be misleading if they only provide information on outcomes (see Fullan, 1980; Fullan & Park, 1981).

In any case, the total time frame from initiation to institutionalization is lengthy; even moderately complex changes take from three to five years.[4] Of course, information can and should be gathered and assessments made throughout the process. The single most important idea arising from figure 2 is that *change is a process, not an event* (Hall & Loucks, 1977; Fullan & Park, 1981)—a lesson learned the hard way by those who put all their energies into developing an innovation or passing a piece of legislation without thinking through what would have to happen beyond that point.

What happens at one stage strongly affects subsequent stages, but new determinants also appear. Because the processes are so entangled, I will endeavor to identify a list of the main factors and to describe their influence at each stage. The ideas in chapters 4 and 5 will be used to help explain why the processes of adoption, implementation, and continuation function as they do. This discussion will set the stage for chapter 6, in which the difficult questions of the relationships among broad strategies of change, the processes, and intended and unintended outcomes will be explored: What is the difference between and differential impact of sweeping approaches to reform (the alternative of grandeur) and gradualistic strategies (the alternative of incrementalism)?[5] What can we say about the impact of educational change (both intended and unintended) on attitudes, achievement, and capacities for further change? What are some guidelines and alternatives for approaching and coping with educational change more effectively?

The most immediate question, however, is which factors influence whether or not changes get adopted in the first place. Answering this question will provide an important basis for understanding the subsequent course of the changes.[6]

# Factors affecting adoption

At a general level, we might assume that specific educational changes are introduced because they are desirable according to certain educational values and meet a given need better than existing practices. This is not the way it always or even usually operates. The import of the process of initiation or adoption must be considered in the context of three larger questions:[7] How broad is the uni-

---

4 The time involved clearly can be more or less, depending on the number of people involved and the scope and complexity of the change (see Crandall et al., forthcoming).

5 See Smith and Keith (1971); Yin et al. (1977).

6 In each of the three phases I describe the main factors at work. Several of these relate to the roles of specific groups (e.g., teachers, community, federal government). The in-depth exploration of these groups is contained in the relevant chapters in Parts II and III. In this chapter their place and impact on the change process is examined for the purpose of gaining an overview of how and why the change process functions as it does.

7 I define adoption as the decision to proceed (or the process leading up to and including the decision) with a change which affects more than one person. This, of course, can be done in an authoritarian or a participatory manner.

| Chart 1 | Factors Associated with Adoption |
|---|---|
| 1. | Existence and quality of innovations |
| 2. | Access to information |
| 3. | Advocacy from central administrators |
| 4. | Teacher pressure/support |
| 5. | Consultants and change agents |
| 6. | Community pressure/support/apathy/opposition |
| 7. | Availability of federal or other funds |
| 8. | New central legislation or policy (federal/state/provincial) |
| 9. | Problem-solving incentives for adoption |
| 10. | Bureaucratic incentives for adoption |

verse for potential adoptions? What is the access, selectivity, and process of selection from this universe? What is the impact of the process of adoption on subsequent stages? (The last question will be examined in chapter 5.)

A summary list of specific factors affecting adoption derived from recent literature is contained in chart 1. We would get hopelessly bogged down if we attempted to identify all possible variables in every situation, but the list shows the main ones on which I could locate evidence across several studies. The ten factors, depending on their presence or absence, influence or result in decisions to reject or adopt specific change programs, policies, or directions.[8] This list is not presented in any elegant theoretical form. My first priority is to describe in understandable language what is happening in actual situations.

## 1. Existence and quality of innovations

Educational innovations do exist in plentiful numbers. The question is what innovations are out there. It is well beyond the scope of my study to investigate the world of invention and development. Therefore, it will be impossible to draw systematic data-based conclusions about the content of available changes. The answer probably is that there are all kinds of innovations in existence which could address a wide range of values, as we would expect in any pluralistic or heterogeneous society.

Innovations are usually developed in response to the incentive system of the society. Market conditions (federal tenders, government-sponsored development, saleability in terms of values, cost, etc.) serve to delimit the educational changes likely to be generated. Boyd (1978, pp. 370–71) states that conflict avoidance is a major market determiner in the school textbook industry in the United States. Consequently, publishers try to please the *national* market, being careful to exclude material that might offend given communities or subgroups in the country. In this way, material appropriate for many other communities or subgroups with different values is less likely to be produced, and controversial material which might form the very basis of addressing some of the social goals of education (e.g., in social studies curriculum) is less likely to

---

8 Different combinations *among* factors is also important. For example, community pressure or support combined with a problem-solving orientation will have quite different consequences from when it is combined with a bureaucratic orientation.

be developed. Boyd also points out that many teachers and local districts do not have the resources to produce their own curriculum and therefore are dependent on available materials. A counter-tendency, as Boyd indicates, occurs when government agencies and foundations sponsor the development of new materials; for example, a variety of policies and programs for disadvantaged groups are sponsored directly or indirectly by government agencies.

Along with the question of what innovations are available is the issue of the quality of new programs. I have stated that program clarity and quality have been a major problem since the innovation boom of the 1960s. The situation has improved immensely in some program areas (e.g., the teaching of basic skills at the elementary school level). In the United States, the National Diffusion Network (NDN) contains 140 validated innovations judged to be of proven quality (see Appendix; Neill, 1981). The R&D Utilization evaluation found that quality was rated high by teachers and other school personnel who adopted a number of R&D products in seven program areas (see RDU in Appendix; also Louis & Rosenblum, 1981). Regarding the existence or availability of needed innovations, the RDU researchers discovered that there was a scarcity of programs in the areas of career education, basic skills at the secondary level, in-service training, and district-wide planning. The recent large-scale Study of Dissemination Efforts Supporting School Improvement (DESSI: see Appendix; Crandall et al., forthcoming), which included NDN innovations, found many examples of the adoption of educational programs perceived by adopters to be of high quality.[9]

Quality, of course, is difficult to assess and agree on. I can only skim the surface of the problem here. It does seem, however, that quality is improving in some areas, as we would expect it to after years of trial and error. Because of the importance of the problem of meaning, it is interesting to consider the relationship between clarity and adoption. Given what I have said up to this point, it should not be surprising that perceived clarity of an innovation bears no necessary relationship to adoption (although it does to implementation); in other words, many educational changes have been "adopted" without any clear notion as to their specific meaning. It is quite likely that this practice is changing as a result of experience and tighter resources. People in education have been burned often enough in the past to be much more careful in making decisions about taking on unproven new change programs; and limited resources force them to be more choosy.

None of this discussion assumes that innovations are simply "out there." For some people interested in particular solutions, there are programs externally available, but even those undergo significant modifications (e.g., in materials, in specific instructional activities) as people adapt them to their own situations. Others may develop their own new programs.

Leaving aside for the moment the question of who develops or initiates change, and reflecting on the question of existence of innovations, we may

---

9 A panel of experts evaluate the quality of innovations proposed for inclusion in the NDN. Only those which pass the test are included. The specific criteria used to "validate" NDN innovations are described in Lebby (1981). The main criteria are: Has the program caused a positive change to occur? Where has it been tried? Is the change large enough and observed often enough? Is the evidence sound? Is the program transferable to other locations?

conclude that the universe of innovations is rather plentiful as a result of pluralistic sponsors, but not as unrestricted and as equitable as might be necessary to address the educational needs of various groups in society. And many people (e.g., teachers, parents) who have particular needs currently unmet do not have the time, skills, or resources to develop solutions.

## 2. Access to information

More specifically operative for adoption is the selectivity which occurs as a result of differential access to information. The primacy of personal contact in the diffusion of innovations has been known for years (Katz et al., 1963), and its importance in education is concisely summarized by House (1974, ch. 1). District administrators and other central office personnel such as coordinators and consultants spend large amounts of time at conferences and workshops within ongoing professional networks of communication among their peers (Carlson, 1972; House, 1974, ch. 3 on the "educational entrepreneur"). Teachers are much less likely to come into contact with new ideas, for they are restricted to the classroom and have a limited network of professionally based interaction within their schools or with their professional peers outside (see chapter 7).[10] Teachers do receive informational literature, and most attend workshops here and there, but they do not have the opportunity for *continuous personal contact* which would be necessary for becoming aware of and following up innovative ideas (House & Lapan, 1978, p. 177).

All communities, and especially those whose members have limited formal education, are at a double disadvantage: they are unfamiliar with and not confident about technical matters, and they have almost no personal contact (or the time and energy to develop contact) with even a small part of the educational universe. School boards have more direct responsibility in this realm, but also are dependent on central administrators. (This does not mean that boards are unable to put pressure on administrators.) Finally, access to innovations, as is obvious but rarely emphasized, depends on an infrastructure of communication—ease of transportation, resources, and density of population and ideas in the geographical area. Urban school districts and large-size school districts enjoy favorable conditions; rural and small-size school districts do not. House (1974, ch. 2) uses a mathematical model and data on the spread of the Illinois Program for Gifted Children, which shows exactly this pattern over a number of years. Research on the U.S. federally funded Experimental Schools (ES) program involving ten rural school districts corroborates the problem of lack of access and difficulties of communication about new ideas faced by such districts (Rosenblum & Louis, 1979, pp. 305–59; Herriott & Gross, 1979; see also ES in Appendix). Daft and Becker (1978) found also that district size was related to adoption of innovation in thirteen high school districts. On reflection, all of this is common sense, but it is seldom recognized as biasing the adoption process from the beginning.

---

10 It bears repeating that I am not implying that all members of a group function the same way. There are many individuals who are exceptions, but the sociological pressure is otherwise and eventually exerts its influence on the majority of people in the role.

# 3. Advocacy from
# central administrators

Educational adoption never occurs without an advocate, and one of the most powerful is the chief district administrator, with his or her staff, especially in combination with school board support or mandate. The district administration may not be interested in innovation and little may happen. But when there is an interest for whatever reason—mandate from a board, or a reform-minded or career-oriented administrator—it is the superintendent and central staff who combine access, internal authority, and resources necessary to seek out external funds for a particular change program and/or to obtain board support. Numerous studies have found this to be the case: the Experimental Schools (ES) rural district program (Rosenblum & Louis, 1979); the Rand Change Agent study (Berman & McLaughlin, 1977); Berman and McLaughlin et al.'s (1979) more intensive study of five school districts; Miles's (1978) research on new schools; Carlson's (1972) and Havelock and Havelock's (1973) investigations of the school superintendent; and McKinney and Westbury's (1975) review of curriculum change in Indiana from 1940 to 1970. All of these studies show that the chief district administrator and central district staff are an extremely important source of advocacy, support, and adoption of new programs.

Daft and Becker (1978) also examined the role of administrators in the adoption of high school innovations. They found that the advocacy and initiation of change by administrators was central to the adoption of many of the innovative programs for high school terminating students (as distinguished from changes in programs for college-bound students, which were more likely to be initiated by teachers). In other words, district administrators may be an important source for district-wide changes which favor groups which might otherwise be neglected. (Rosenblum & Louis, 1979, found the same thing.) By the same token administrators can be equally powerful at blocking changes they do not like. Sarason (1971, pp. 221–22) reminds us that we do not have much knowledge about change proposals which *never get to the adoption stage*—a fairly high proportion, according to principals and teachers with whom Sarason talked. Whatever the case, central administrators are often powerful advocates and can sponsor or block adoption of change programs.[11] Their impact on implementation will be examined in chapter 5, but a more detailed analysis must be deferred until chapter 10.

# 4. Teacher advocacy

While teachers as a group have less opportunity to come into contact with new ideas and less time and energy to follow through on those that they do become aware of, most teachers do innovate. It is difficult to piece together the subtleties of this process, but we do have some evidence and some inferences which can be made. Daft and Becker (1978) discovered that teacher professionalism (aggregate level of education as indicated by a master's degree) in a high school

---

11 In speaking of district administrators, I include the chief executive officer and other senior administrators (e.g., superintendents, program directors in line positions)—see chapter 10.

district was positively correlated with initiation by teachers and adoption of innovations for college-bound students (and negatively correlated with adoptions of innovations for high school terminating students). They also found that a higher ratio of district support staff to teachers facilitated the adoption process, as staff helped teachers to push for and obtain resources for new programs which teachers wanted but didn't have the time or contacts to pursue.

Research on the Pilot State Dissemination Program (see Appendix), in which field agents were used on an ongoing basis to stimulate knowledge utilization in school districts in seven areas in the United States, confirms the need that teachers have for outside facilitation (Sieber, 1974; Louis & Sieber, 1979). The more recent DESSI and RDU studies corroborate this finding and extend our knowledge of how the process works (Crandall et al., forthcoming; Louis & Rosenblum, 1981). As long as the needs of teachers were the point of departure for information search, the teachers used the services much more than did teachers in adjacent areas without field agent help (Sieber, 1974).

In addition to the importance of outside facilitation, there is a strong body of evidence which indicates that fellow teachers are often the preferred and most influential source of ideas. Typical of this research is Aoki et al.'s (1977) study of social science teachers in their use of provincewide curriculum guidelines in British Columbia. Ideas from colleagues, however, may be more essential for implementation or effective use than for initial adoption decisions. Also recall that teachers do not have much collective access to innovations; nor do they have much opportunity to interact about those with which they do come into contact. In short, they do not have this opportunity very frequently, but when they do (as when they or someone else organizes the opportunity), their interaction can be a very powerful source of influence on adoption and especially on use (see chapters 5 and 7 and the 1982 AFT project).

These findings taken together indicate that many teachers are willing to adopt change at the individual classroom level, and will do so under the right conditions (e.g., an innovation which is clear and practical, a supportive district administration and principal, opportunity to interact with other teachers, and outside resource help). There are several qualifiers: most teachers do not have adequate information access, time, or energy; the innovations they do adopt will be individualistic (and unlikely to spread to other teachers); and understandably they will be less likely to advocate district-wide reforms (their main concern being their own classroom), for which legislation, administrators, and/ or community pressure are needed. Rosenblum & Louis (1979), among others, found that advocacy from district administrators was necessary for district-wide reform efforts.[12]

## 5. Linking agents

I have already indicated how linking agents or consultants (district support staff, state/provincial or federal field agents, etc.) may help teachers to adopt innovations which teachers want. We need only add that they may also be instrumental in school district adoptions. Thus, external agents interested in as many

---

12 For a useful review of the role of teachers and other practitioners in decision-making about innovation, see Hood and Blackwell (1980). Their conclusions are similar to those stated here.

adoptions as they can get may find it more efficient to convince central district staff to make a favorable decision. Inside the district, central support staff are more likely to respond to the expectation of central administrators than to individual teachers, and in any case frequently have the job of writing proposals to obtain external funds for district programs. How closely the selected programs are likely to be related to the needs of teachers and others in the district will depend on whether the seekers of funds are oriented to bureaucratic grants-personship or to problem-solving processes. See Berman, McLaughlin, et al. (1979) for a description of five different district patterns. On the role of external linking agents, the most recent and elaborate analyses are contained in the research studies on RDU (Louis & Rosenblum, 1981; Louis, 1981) and DESSI (Crandall et al., forthcoming).[13]

## 6. Community pressure/support/opposition/apathy

Since communities vary and characteristics of school districts differ greatly, different combinations of factors will result in various adoption patterns—a perennial problem in understanding change processes. But when some of the main combinations are examined, we can make sense of the paradox that some communities support innovation, others block it, most are apathetic, and even more are all of those things at one time or another.

In general terms, and depending on the circumstances, communities can either (1) put pressure on district administrators (directly or through school boards) to "do something" about a problem, (2) oppose certain potential adoptions about which they become aware, or (3) do nothing (passive support or apathy). The meaning of these patterns is clarified by considering some evidence.

The most predictable initial pressure for change from the community is likely to come as a result of population shifts.[14] Berman, McLaughlin, et al.'s (1979) study of five school districts demonstrates that major demographic changes (rapid growth in population, or a change in composition which results in different social-class and cultural mixes) lead to the development of community efforts and demands for change. McKinney and Westbury's (1975) longitudinal study showed the same phenomenon. How the demands are handled depends very much on the problem-solving vs. bureaucratic orientations to be discussed below. In other words, demands may or may not result in adoption depending on a combination of factors—but the point is that communities can instigate educational change. (In one of the Berman and McLaughlin cases, for example, population growth led to community activism in a previously stagnant school system, election of new board members, hiring of an innovative superintendent, facilitation of change by other central staff, principals, teachers, etc., etc.)

---

13 These studies build on some of the earlier conceptual contributions on the role of linking agents (Havelock, 1969; Crandall, 1977) and have the additional advantage of being empirically based. See also Cox and Havelock (1982) and chapter 11.

14 Yin et al. (1977, p. 1) indicate similar origins of change for innovations in urban technology. Changes come from many other sources as well, but we are concerned here with community pressure. Also, more stable communities can "passively support" or be indifferent to adoptions proposed by administrative and professional staff.

Schaffarzick's study of 34 San Francisco Bay area districts is also very revealing. He found that 62% of the curriculum decision cases in his sample did not involve lay participation (cited in Boyd, 1978, p. 613). Community apathy and indifference characterized these decisions. However, in the 19 cases which involved conflict and bargaining, the community groups nearly always prevailed. Boyd (1978) also indicates that conflict avoidance is a major orientation of school boards and administrators. Innovations which involve major value differences (e.g., the teaching of evolution, sex education) can easily be blocked by a local minority at the adoption stage or shortly thereafter if the minority play up the controversiality of the change (regardless of whether their claims are accurate). Further to the selective role of communities, Daft and Becker (1978) found that highly educated communities correlated substantially with the adoption of innovations for college-bound students, but less well educated communities did *not* correlate with the greater likelihood of programs of benefit to high school terminating students. Bridge (1976, p. 370) makes a similar point: "It is easier to organize parents, particularly lower class parents, to resist perceived threats than it is to organize them to achieve long term positive goals."

In putting these findings together, we can conclude that the role of the community in the adoption process is not straightforward, but it is understandable when we break it down into the following components.

1 Major demographic changes create turbulence in the environment which may lead to adoptions or irreconcilable conflict depending on the presence of other factors listed in chart 1.
2 Most communities do not actively participate in change decisions about educational programs.
3 More highly educated communities do seem to put general pressure on their schools to adopt high-quality academic-oriented changes. They also can react strongly and effectively against proposed changes which they do not like.
4 Less educated communities are less likely to initiate change or put effective pressure on educators to initiate changes on their behalf. They are also less likely to become activated against changes because of lack of knowledge, but once activated they too can become effective.

There is a very powerful message implicit in the above statements: namely, *in relatively stable or continuous communities there is a tendency for innovations favoring the least advantaged not to be proposed (the bias of neglect) and there is greater likelihood that educators can introduce new innovations (which they believe in) unbeknownst to the community* (recall the Gross et al. 1971 study). Secondly, demographic shifts do create strong demands for adoption, but what the demands result in is anyone's ball game, for they must interact with other factors in the situation. Chapter 12 examines the role of parents and the community in educational change in more detail.

# 7. Availability of government or other funds

The impact of resources will be traced at all stages of the process. The large-scale Rand Change Agent research (Appendix, FPSEC; Berman & McLaughlin, 1977, 1978) and House et al. (1974) show beyond much doubt that the availability of resources external to the district is a powerful stimulant for adoption.[15] The Rand researchers found that this factor interacts with the problem-solving and bureaucratic factors (factors 9 and 10 below) to produce two quite different patterns, which they label "problem-solving" and "opportunistic." Districts do not have slack resources to undertake major change efforts. Thus, they welcome external funds either as a chance to solve a particular local problem or as an opportunity to obtain extra resources (which they use for other purposes and/or which represent a symbolic act of responding to the need for change). The lack of defined need is not a barrier to adopting a change as long as the change can be presented as a good idea.[16]

In Canada, provincial governments, through the production of curriculum guidelines and government-sponsored task force curriculum development efforts, and foundations such as the Canada Studies Foundation (Anderson & Benoit, 1978) provide adoption materials. The federal government plays virtually no role constitutionally and practically in Canadian school systems (see OECD, 1976, for an overview of education in Canada, and chapter 14).[17] In sum, school districts do not have sufficient resources to adopt many innovations on their own and have been known to accept external funds.

## 8. New central legislation or policy

Most federal projects in the United States are voluntary, but we need to distinguish these projects from new legislation or policy which *mandates* adoption at the local district level. Since we are just talking about "causes of adoption," we need make only two points. First, without the existence of state and federal lobby groups and reform-minded policy-makers, many new social change programs would never get even formally adopted.[18] It is too much of a diversion to explore "the politics of policy-making" at this point, but it is clear that many major educational adoptions are generated through government policy-making and legislation in areas in greatest need of reform, such as special education, desegregation, and vocational education. The second point is that central policies are often left ambiguous and general; it is thus easier for local districts to adopt the policy in principle, but problems emerge at later stages (see Bardach, 1977; Elmore, 1980; Sarason & Doris, 1979; Boyd, 1978, p. 598; Williams & Elmore, 1976).

---

15 We must remember that we are talking about *adoption*—whether a decision is taken to proceed—not whether it leads to effective or any implementation.

16 See House and Lapan's (1978, pp. 169–72) satire on how new programs get started, as they describe a hypothetical adoption of a new program for redheaded children.

17 In effect, in Canada *each* provincial government is the central government for education for school systems within its province. There are not nearly the resources and project/program push for innovation in Canada as in the United States, even allowing for differences in size. In practice, Canada is influenced heavily by innovations developed in the U.S., which are adapted for use in Canada or taken on holus-bolus. This has far-reaching implications, which we cannot take up here. Provincial governments and the Canada Studies Foundation (Anderson & Benoit, 1978) have been attempting to address some aspects of this problem during the past few years.

18 This is not to say that teachers and administrators do not want reform, but that most of them are occupied by the daily demands of coping with their jobs or innovating in their own schools (see chapters 7 and 8).

## 9. Problem-solving orientations

Factors 9 and 10 in many ways guide and sometimes drive the other factors. Berman and McLaughlin (1977) discovered that adoption decisions of school districts were characterized by either a problem-solving or an opportunistic (bureaucratic) orientation. Some districts (for a combination of reasons we return to later) are problem-oriented. They have identified important local needs, are dissatisfied with existing performance, and seek out resources (or respond enthusiastically to opportunities) to address their needs. Berman, McLaughlin, et al.'s (1979) case studies of Lakeville and Sandwood school districts contain concise descriptions and analyses of how problem-solving school districts operate. Daft and Becker (1978) also found that problem-solving orientation correlated highly with the total number of adoptions. So, lest we think that all school districts are stalwarts of stability or masters of the "sleight of change," it is encouraging to know that some districts do make changes in order to address specific local needs and that change can work in the real world (see chapter 10).

## 10. Bureaucratic orientations

We do not know the proportions of problem-solvers and bureaucrats in the school districts of North America. Pincus (1974) would have us believe that the properties of public school systems qua systems make them more bureaucratic than problem-oriented. (Miles, 1981, contains a more elaborate analysis of the properties of school systems.) Pincus claims that compared to the competitive firm, (1) public schools are less motivated to adopt cost-reducing innovations unless the funds so saved become available for other purposes in the district; (2) they are less likely to adopt innovations that change the resource mix or the accustomed authority roles (e.g., that involve behavioral changes in role); and (3) they are more likely to adopt new instructional processes that do not significantly change structure, or adopt new wrinkles in administrative management, because such innovations help to satisfy the demands of the public without exacting heavy costs (Pincus, 1974, pp. 117–18).[19]

Three factors favorable to adoption are identified by Pincus (p. 120): *bureaucratic safety*, as when innovations add resources without requiring behavioral change; *response to external pressure* (in which "adoption" may ease the pressure); and *approval of peer elites* (in the absence of clearly defined output criteria whatever is popular among leading professional peers is sometimes the determining criterion).[20] In other words, "schools tend voluntarily to adopt innovations which promote the schools' self-image" as "up-to-date ... efficient ... professional ... responsive" (p. 122). Stated differently again, it is relatively easy for schools to *adopt* complex, vague, inefficient, costly (especially if someone else is paying) innovations as long as they do not have to *implement* them.

---

19 That is, in terms of the multidimensionality of implementation (chapter 3) schools are more likely to implement superficial changes in content, objectives, and structure than changes in role behavior, conceptions of teaching, etc.

20 Lack of clarity of educational goals and measures of output is a frequently cited problem in education. As I have stated before, to a certain extent this is less of a problem with basic skills, but it remains for higher-order thinking skills and for personal/social-development goals. Moreover, the total balance of the curriculum is unclear, as is the means of best achieving goals.

Pincus's review is analytically rather than empirically based (although he does use illustrations); so we do not know how pervasive these bureaucratic practices are empirically. Certainly both bureaucratic and problem-solving orientations exist depending on the school district. Berman and McLaughlin (1977, 1978) found that opportunistic (as distinct from problem-solving) adoption decisions was the more frequent theme in school districts in their large sample. These authors also give detailed case examples which describe both processes at work: the "illusion of change" approach, in which "the pressures [for change] seem to subside with the act of adoption," and the developmental pattern in which particular pressures were responded to by analysis and adoption of needed changes (Berman & McLaughlin, 1979).

Nelson and Sieber (1976) found interesting adoption patterns in their survey of 32 innovations in urban secondary schools. Using a sample of 679 principals (with an 82% response rate) in all cities of the U.S. with a population of 300,000 or over, Nelson and Sieber discovered (1) that the publicity value of innovations and faddism were major reasons for adoption; (2) that one-fourth of the schools adopted many innovations, but few were of relatively high quality (quality was assessed by a panel of experts); (3) that cost was not a barrier to adoption (the two were *positively* correlated); and (4) that cost was inversely related to quality (i.e., the more costly the innovation, the lower the quality—as judged by a panel of experts). Bureaucratically speaking, then, the political and symbolic value of adoption for schools is often of greater significance than the educational merit and the time and cost necessary for implementation follow-through. But note that the symbolic value is not unimportant. Such adoptions may be necessary for political survival, may be necessary first steps which set the preconditions for real change in practice, or may represent the only change possible in certain situations.

In assessing the nature of adoption decisions, we should remember that all research studies are *timebound*. Much of the above research was conducted in the early 1970s, when failure and confusion were widespread. In more recent research there is a glimmer of hope in that educators seem to be getting better at adopting sounder changes tied more closely to real need (Crandall et al., forthcoming; Louis & Rosenblum, 1981). But it is only a glimmer, because this research is based on samples which are not necessarily representative of the total population. Whatever the situation, we need to understand that there are different ways of making initial decisions about educational change; some of these ways are effective, and others result in the illusion and disillusion of reform.

# Adoption and beyond

Despite the information discussed in this chapter, we do not know very much about the *adoption process*—that is, what happens by way of initiation, mobilization, and planning to prepare for change.[21] Only a few studies have examined this phase closely.

---

21 Furthermore, some of the existing research is misleading. For example, when it is reported that teachers participated in the decision to adopt a new program, it is very difficult to tell what this really means. It may be that there was not much discussion, that teachers did not understand what they were getting into, that the superintendent or principal already had indicated that he or she wanted the change (or indeed that certain decisions had already been taken).

One of the most detailed descriptions of the adoption process is contained in the cross-site analysis of the 12 case studies in the DESSI study (see Appendix and Crandall et al., forthcoming). There were two types of innovations examined: those related to the adoption of NDN innovations, and those related to the development of local innovations through Title IV-C grants (see chapter 14).

The DESSI analysis covers three important aspects of the adoption process: reasons for adoption, the role of career incentives, and the time-line from awareness to adoption and from adoption to start-up of implementation. On the first point, the DESSI researchers found that in 11 of the 12 cases the central office administration was the primary initiator—that is, made the decision to adopt the particular changes.[22] It is interesting to compare the reasons given for adoption by the 41 administrators and 56 teachers involved in the changes. The largest category of response for administrators was "improves classroom instruction" (21 of the 41 cited this as a main reason for adoption), while the largest category for teacher users of the innovation was "administrative pressure" (35 of 56 teachers).[23] In other words, at the initial adoption stage teachers in these cases were responding to administrative initiative. We may also be struck by the multiple reasons given by both administrators and teachers. Adopting an innovation or program direction is a very complicated process, and its impact on implementation can be considerable, although not straightforward to trace, as we shall see in the following chapter.

The role of career incentives is another significant, but understudied, aspect of the adoption and implementation of educational changes. In the case-study component (12 sites) of the DESSI study it was found that there was no apparent career motive for a little fewer than one-half of the teachers (23 of 56) and about one-half of the administrators (21 of 41). The remaining participants revealed a variety of career-related motives involving upward mobility (in the district or outside), enhancing one's status, moving into a more secure position, and so on. The researchers caution that the career incentive was usually only one of several motives and that it was not always obvious at the time of adoption but materialized later. The impact of career incentives on implementation is not clear-cut. When job mobility is high (as it was in the 1960s and early 1970s), career-related innovativeness can be negatively related to implementation, for key supporters move on shortly after an innovation has been initiated and before it can be effectively implemented. However, as the DESSI researchers found, the role of "administrative careerism" is mixed. It appeared in 7 of the 12 sites. For 5 of 7 sites in which it was present, it appeared to inject enthusiasm and energy into the adoption process and mobilized extra resources for implementation. In the other 2 sites strong careerism amplified tensions and conflict already present. Of the 5 sites where careerism was low, the results were also mixed. In 3 of the 5, the implementation was smoother, more task

22 In 4 of the 12 cases some teachers participated in discussions about adoption, and this seemed to have positive effects in 3 of the 4 cases. The dominance of central office staff is to a certain extent a function of central staff having more access to what is available and being in a position to write proposals for external grants.
23 And yet 16 teachers cited "improves classroom instruction" and 4 administrators gave "administrative pressure" as the reason. Respondents could give more than one reason (Crandall et al., forthcoming).

focused and collaborative; but in the other 2 implementation seemed "to suffer" from the lack of central office investment which might have been stronger if a career motive were present (Crandall et al., forthcoming). In other words, the existence of career-related motives along with other reasons for adopting innovations is neither a good nor a bad thing in itself. It is an important aspect of the adoption and follow-through of innovations which should be examined in each case.

The third important contribution of the DESSI analysis concerns the time-line of decisions. The study found that the median length of time from awareness to adoption was 9.5 months, while the median time from the adoption decision to start-up was only 3.5 months. Thus, once the decision is made, things happen quickly—too quickly in the sense that the short time-line provides little opportunity for *planning for implementation*. Or, more precisely, planning for implementation is not recognized as an important component requiring more advance attention. The DESSI study, in general, found that in several sites in which implementation began shortly after the adoption decision, serious problems arose related to the lack of needed training and materials. The transition for those with longer time frames tended to be more successful.[24]

The nature of the adoption process and of its interface with implementation warrants more attention by researchers and planners of change, because of its impact on the outcomes of attempted educational change.[25] It is during the adoption phase that the direction or content of change is set in motion. Decisions are made about *what* is to change, at least in terms of goals and sometimes substance. The process of adoption can generate meaning or confusion, commitment or alienation, or simply ignorance on the part of participants and others to be affected by the change.

What happens beyond adoption is the next critical phase, which I turn to in chapter 5. The two key questions are: *What is the relationship between the adoption process and subsequent implementation? What other factors emerge during implementation which determine whether change in practice occurs?* At this point, we know that adoption decisions occur all the time and come through a variety of sources. We have some inkling that—depending on the source, the process followed, and the combination of contextual conditions in the situation—what happens after adoption will be all over the map. We need more cartographers of implementation—provided that they are prepared to chart continuous earthquakes.

---

24 As with all statements based on single factors, this should be treated with caution. Adoption and implementation depend on several factors which interact in different combinations in different situations.

25 A small number of studies have made important contributions. In addition to the DESSI study, Miles et al. (1978) and Miles (1980) conducted a thorough investigation of the issues and dilemmas in the planning phase in the design of new schools and programs; Rosenblum and Louis (1979) describe the planning activities and their relationship to implementation in the Experimental Schools (ES, see Appendix) project; Molitor (1981) examines the problem-identification and solution-selection process in the RDU study; and Berman (1981) provides a valuable conceptualization and description of the initiation, implementation, and continuation phases of the educational change process.

# Chapter 5

# Causes/Processes of Implementation and Continuation

*Well, the hard work is done. We have the policy passed;
now all you have to do is implement it.*

— *Outgoing deputy minister of education to colleague*

Educational change is technically simple and socially complex, in the words of
Bruce Joyce. While the simplicity of the technical aspect is no doubt overstated,
anyone who has been involved in a major change effort will intuitively grasp the
meaning of and concur with the complexity of the social dimension. A large
part of the problem of educational change may be less a question of dogmatic
resistance and bad intentions (although there is certainly some of both) and
more a question of the difficulties related to planning and coordinating a multi-
level social process involving thousands of people.

There is no need to dwell on the fact that the vast majority of curriculum
development and other educational change "adoptions" in the 1960s and
1970s did not get implemented in practice, even where implementation was
desired (for reviews see Silberman, 1970; Fullan, 1972; Fullan & Pomfret,
1977). Implementation consists of the process of putting into practice an idea,
program, or set of activities new to the people attempting or expected to
change. The change may be externally imposed or voluntarily sought; explicitly
defined in detail in advance or developed and adapted incrementally through
use; designed to be used uniformly or deliberately planned so that users can
make modifications according to their perceptions of the needs of the situation.

In this chapter I identify those factors which affect whether or not an adopted
or decided-upon change happens in practice. The processes beyond adoption
are more intricate, because they involve more people, and real change (as distinct from verbal or "on-paper" decisions) is at stake. I might anticipate the
theme by saying that many attempts at policy and program change have concentrated on product development, legislation, and other "on-paper" changes in a
way which ignored the fact that what people did and did not do was the crucial
variable. This neglect is understandable, for people are much more unpredictable and difficult to deal with than things.[1] Unfortunately, they are also much
more essential for success.

---

1 A statement analogous in thinking style to the saying that schools would be all right if it
weren't for the kids. Implementation would work fine, if people weren't involved.

The positive side is that the persistence of people-related problems in educational change has forged greater knowledge about what makes for success. If we constantly remind ourselves that educational change is *a learning experience for the adults involved* (teachers, administrators, parents, etc.) as well as for children, we will be going a long way in understanding the dynamics of the factors of change described in this chapter.

I must return to the perspective of where implementation fits. To recall figure 2, implementation refers to change in practice after some change has been initiated (adopted). The change process can be thought of in the following phases: (1) factors leading up to and affecting adoption (chapter 4); (2) factors affecting implementation (the adoption process, as we will see, being one of them), which in turn affect the extent of implementation (and continuation) defined as change in practice on the part of teachers and students, which affects (3) outcomes. It is the second category of factors which is isolated and explored in this chapter. The chapter is somewhat long because the implementation process is central to understanding the difficulties and potential of educational change.[2]

# Factors affecting implementation

The idea of implementation and of the factors affecting actual use seems simple enough, but the concept has proven to be exceedingly elusive.[3] However, twelve years of intensive research has produced enough evidence for us to be fairly confident about what factors have the most influence. Although the process is complex in any given situation, the major factors affecting the extent of use can be organized into four main categories (see chart 2).[4] Category A refers to the attributes of the change itself. Categories B and C respectively consist of characteristics of the district and of the school as a unit. Category D concerns factors external to the local school system.

Four general comments should be made about chart 2. First, I have attempted to be comprehensive by identifying the major categories of factors which influence implementation. Within these I have selected all those factors on which there is sufficient evidence to warrant generalizing about how and why the particular factor influences implementation. Over the past two or three years there has been a noteworthy convergence of findings from two relatively distinct bodies of research—that on school innovation and that on school effects.

---

2 For a good recent account of the implementation process see Berman (1981).

3 See Berman (1980, 1981), Berman and McLaughlin (1977), Crandall et al. (forthcoming), Farrar et al. (1979), Fullan (1981a), Fullan and Park (1981), Hargrove (1975), Leithwood (1981), Loucks (1978), Majone and Wildavsky (1978), and Williams (1980) for discussions of the concept of implementation. The two different perspectives on implementation—fidelity/programmatic and mutual-adaptation/evolution—are evident in these writings and reflect the complexity of pinning down the concept.

4 These factors will be discussed in enough detail to make it clear how and why they are important. They are taken up with more specific applications in the appropriate chapters in Parts II and III.

Chart 2      **Factors Affecting Implementation**

**A.**    **Characteristics of the Change**
1.    Need and relevance of the change
2.    Clarity
3.    Complexity
4.    Quality and practicality of program (materials etc.)

**B.**    **Characteristics at the School District Level**
5.    The history of innovative attempts
6.    The adoption process
7.    Central administrative support and involvement
8.    Staff development (in-service) and participation
9.    Time-line and information system (evaluation)
10.    Board and community characteristics

**C.**    **Characteristics at the School Level**
11.    The principal
12.    Teacher–teacher relations
13.    Teacher characteristics and orientations

**D.**    **Characteristics External to the Local System**
14.    Role of government
15.    External assistance

Second, although the list is quite inclusive, it is necessarily oversimplified; each so-called "factor" could be "unpacked" into several subvariables. For example, "staff development and participation" encompasses several variables which characterize effective staff development and participatory involvement in the implementation process (see chapter 14). Or in order to say that the principal can have a significant impact on implementation, it is necessary to describe what he or she actually does which influences change. It would be too cumbersome to attempt to spell out all the specific variables in chart 2 within each category. Their explanations must be left to the discussion of each factor.

Third, describing educational change as one general phenomenon hides variations in large-scale change as compared to small-scale change, differences in units of analysis (e.g., individual classrooms vs. schools, districts, or whole countries), and so on. Again, in order to understand the basic flow of change we need not be concerned with these specifications. But if we were interested in a particular change, we would have to make the necessary adjustments, depending on the unit of our interest. If we were examining small-scale change within an individual school, for example, we would treat the information system, staff development, and such as school-level variables. As it stands, chart 2 places these variables at the district level in order to describe what districts do and how this impacts on the school.

Fourth, we should keep in mind why we are interested in chart 2. I am suggesting that the fifteen factors in the chart causally influence implementation (or more specifically the extent to which teachers and students change their beliefs, behavior, use of new resources, etc.) in the direction of some sought-after change. If any one or more factors are working against implementation, the process will be less effective. Put positively, the more factors supporting implementation, the more change in practice will be accomplished. Finally, we should avoid thinking of the fifteen factors in isolation from each other. They form *a system of variables which interact*. It is difficult to imagine all the details of such a system, but educational change is indeed a dynamic process of interacting variables over time.

## A. Characteristics of the change

Four major aspects pertaining to the nature of the change itself have been found to relate to subsequent implementation: need, clarity, complexity, and quality and practicality of materials (product quality).

### 1. Need

As noted earlier many innovations are attempted without a careful examination of whether or not they address what are perceived to be priority needs. Teachers, for example, frequently do not see the need for an advocated change. Several large-scale studies in the United States confirm the importance of relating need to decisions about innovations or change directions. In the Experimental Schools (ES) project, Rosenblum and Louis (1979, p. 12) found that "the degree to which there was a formal recognition within the school system of unmet needs" was one of the four "readiness factors" which was associated with subsequent implementation. The Rand Change Agent study (FPSEC), it will be remembered, identified problem-solving/decision-making (i.e., identification of a need linked to selection of a program) as strongly related to successful implementation. The RDU project reports that perceived relevance of products is correlated significantly with extent of implementation. Other studies have discovered that implementation is more effective when relatively focused or specific needs are identified (e.g., Emrick & Peterson, 1978; Louis & Sieber, 1979).[5]

### 2. Clarity

Clarity (about goals and means) is a perennial problem in the change process. Even when there is agreement that some kind of change is needed, as when teachers want to improve some area of the curriculum, the adopted change may be not at all clear about what teachers should do differently.[6] Gross et al. (1971) found that the majority of teachers were unable to identify the essential features of the innovation they were using. Problems related to clarity have been found in virtually every study of significant change (e.g., Aoki et al., 1977; Charters & Pellegrin, 1973; Miles, 1978; Simms, 1978; Weatherley, 1979). In short, lack of clarity—diffuse goals and unspecified means of implementation—represents a major problem at the implementation stage; teachers and others find that the change is simply not very clear as to what it means in practice.

Legislation and many other new policies and programs are sometimes deliberately stated at a general level in order to avoid conflict and promote accept-

---

5 However, if specific needs are identified and those who are supposed to implement change disagree with the needs, not much change will result. In this case, getting the change "on the books" (through new policy adoption) may be the most appropriate starting point.
6 The change, for instance, may not be sufficiently well developed to be "implementable."

ance and adoption. Such policies often do not indicate how implementation is to be addressed (see Weatherley, 1979; Sarason & Doris, 1979; Elmore, 1980). Curriculum guidelines in Canada have also suffered from vagueness of goals and especially of means of implementation (Downey et al., 1975; Robinson, 1982; and Simms, 1978).

There is little doubt that clarity is essential, but its meaning is subtle; too often we are left with *false clarity* instead. False clarity, as I indicated in chapter 3, occurs when change is interpreted in an oversimplified way; that is, the proposed change has more to it than people perceive or realize. For example, an approved textbook may easily become *the* curriculum in the classroom, yet fail to incorporate significant features of the policy or goals which it is supposed to address. Reliance on the textbook may distract attention from behaviors and educational beliefs critical to the achievement of desired outcomes. In Canada, new or revised provincial curriculum guidelines may be dismissed by some teachers on the grounds that "we are already doing that"; but this is another illustration of false clarity if the teachers' perception is based only on the more superficial goal and content aspects of the guidelines to the neglect of beliefs and teaching strategies. Similarly, many of the latest curriculum guidelines in Canada contain far greater specificity of objectives and content than previous guidelines, with the result that teachers and others welcome them as "finally providing direction" (see recent curriculum guidelines in Ontario and in British Columbia); however, these guidelines may be used in a literal way without the realization that certain teaching strategies and underlying beliefs are essential to implementing the guidelines effectively.

On the other hand, I have cited evidence above that not everyone experiences the comfort of false clarity. Unclear and unspecified changes can cause great anxiety and frustration to those sincerely trying to implement them. Clarity, of course, cannot be delivered on a platter. It is accomplished or not depending on the *process*.[7] Nor is greater clarity an end in itself: very simple and insignificant changes can be very clear, while more difficult and worthwhile ones may not be amenable to easy clarification. This brings me directly to the third related factor—complexity.

### 3. Complexity

Complexity refers to the difficulty and extent of change required of the individuals responsible for implementation. The actual amount depends on the starting point for any given individual or group, but the main idea is that any change can be examined in regard to the difficulty, skill required, and extent of alterations in beliefs, teaching strategies, and use of materials. Many changes such as open education (Bussis et al., 1976), systematic direct instruction (Gersten et al., 1981), inquiry-oriented social studies (Aoki et al., 1977), special education (Weatherley, 1979), and parent involvement (chapter 12) require a sophisticated array of activities, diagnosis, teaching strategies, and philosophical understanding if effective implementation is to be achieved.

---

7 The relationship to other factors in categories B and C is obvious. To take one example, staff development activities, if appropriate, contribute to greater clarity. The development of clarity about the value and means of implementing a change is obviously central to the development of meaning.

While complexity creates problems for implementation, it may result in greater change because more is being attempted. Berman and McLaughlin (1977, p. 88) found that "ambitious projects were less successful in absolute terms of the percent of project goals achieved, but they typically stimulated more teacher change than projects attempting less." Those changes which did occur were more thorough as a result of the extra effort which the project required or inspired. As Berman (1980) stated elsewhere, "little ventured, nothing gained." In the DESSI study, Crandall et al. (forthcoming) discovered that it was necessary to separate teachers attempting a major change from those attempting a minor change before discernible patterns of explanation could be found.[8] They also found, as Berman suggested, that those attempting major changes accomplished more—the more tried for, the more accomplished.

It is the case that simple changes are easier to carry out, but they may not make much of a difference. Relatively complex changes promise to accomplish more. Whether they do or not depends on all fifteen factors discussed in this chapter, but central to complexity is whether a complex change is introduced all at once or through more divisible or incremental components. Yin et al. (1977, p. 61) studied 140 technological innovations across the criminal, justice, fire, health, education, transportation, and planning sectors. They classified the innovations according to whether they could be used/tested on a limited basis. Those cases where divisibility existed were associated with a higher frequency of success (improvement plus eventual incorporation). Rosenblum and Louis (1979) examined divisibility in their study of comprehensive (complex) system-wide changes in the Experimental Schools (ES) program. Three of the four districts which scored high on implementation had undertaken changes with a greater number of components and these components were highly differentiated (Rosenblum & Louis, 1979, p. 269). Each component was targeted to a specific part of the problem (a grade level, a curriculum, etc.). On the other hand, districts undertaking changes with a small number of components, defined diffusely, fared badly. The authors suggest that complex district-wide changes should be differentiated into an array of specific components. In brief, difficult changes are attempted because they have the potential to achieve greater benefits, but they must be done in a way which maximizes clarity (through defining specific components and implementing them incrementally).

## 4. Quality and practicality of program

The last factor associated directly with the nature of change concerns the quality and practicality of learning materials, technologies, or other products. The history of product quality and its relationship to the other three variables (need, clarity, complexity) is revealing. To say that the importance of the quality of materials is self-evident is to underestimate how adoption decisions are made. Inadequate quality and even the simple unavailability of materials can be the result when adoption decisions are made on grounds of political necessity or perceived need without time for development. Put differently, when adoption

---

8 Degree of change was defined in terms of the individual starting points of teachers. Thus using the same innovation some teachers faced major change and others minor change depending on their starting points. Measuring change with reference to where individuals started, and how much change they were attempting, is an important conceptual and methodological contribution of the DESSI study, although several problems remain.

is more important than implementation, decisions are frequently made without follow-up or preparation time necessary to generate adequate materials (recall the short time lag between adoption and initial implementation in the DESSI case studies).

Aoki et al. (1977), Simms (1978), and Downey et al. (1975) all found that many teachers were not familiar with basic provincial curriculum documents. (Needless to say, familiarity is hardly implementation.) The quality of materials is another story. Teachers want, need, and benefit from tangible, relevant program materials which have been produced and tested in real classroom situations. Social studies teachers in British Columbia reported that the curriculum guides were not helpful and the lack of quality materials was a major problem in implementation (Aoki et al.). In Simms's case study of the use of the language arts guideline in Alberta, he found that nine of the fourteen teachers "indicated that the instruction materials which facilitators brought out to them were not relevant to what they were doing in their class at that particular time" (p. 160). Teachers in Ontario also find that lack of usable classroom materials is a frequent problem in dealing with provincial guidelines (Kormos, 1978). Curriculum guides can read well and seem clear, but the clarity is often related to the goals and content, not the "hows" of teaching strategies and instruction.

The findings are the same in the United States. The large-scale evaluation of innovations adopted through the National Diffusion Network (NDN) provides confirmation: "well articulated adoption materials, which ... are complete, well organized, comprehensive and detailed" and address "how-to" concerns are more effective at the implementation stage; at earlier awareness stages, concise overview materials are better (Emrick et al., 1977; Emrick & Peterson, 1978, p. 73). Learning materials especially at the time of initial implementation must pass the test of the "practicality ethic" of teachers (Doyle & Ponder, 1977–78). It is no accident that NDN innovations work in many cases because most of them have been developed by practitioners.

The Project Implementation Packages (PIPS) in the U.S., designed to be self-sufficient for those who adopted them, did not work well because they lacked detail on instructional methods (i.e., how to implement) and there was little provision for orientation or in-service training (see Stearns et al., 1977; Campeau et al., 1979; Horst et al., 1980).

The history of materials development, as I indicated above, is particularly instructive for understanding what turns out to be a very complex phenomenon. We have gone through phases from an emphasis on curriculum development in the 1960s to a de-emphasis during the 1970s to a renewed respect for product quality more recently. In the first phase the great curriculum development projects in the 1960s reflected a period of wanton materials production (Silberman, 1970; Welch, 1979). One can see in retrospect how these efforts were oblivious to the fact that implementation is a social process, not a delivery date. The failure of these programs gave materials development a bad name. In fact, much of the curriculum developed during this period did not address important needs, was theoretical in nature, and was of insufficient practical quality (Silberman, 1970; Sarason, 1971). As a result of rather massive failure at the implementation stage, product development was in disfavor during the 1970s.

The Rand study of Federal Programs Supporting Educational Change (FPSEC) is typical of the second phase. This study developed the theme that how school people went about implementation rather than the content of change dominated the educational change process (Berman & McLaughlin, 1976–79). These authors stressed that local material adaptation or development was essential to change in practice: "The exercise of 're-inventing the wheel' can provide an important opportunity for staff to work through and understand project precepts .... Without this 'learning by doing' it is doubtful that projects attempting to achieve teacher change would be effectively implemented" (1976, p. 361).

Berman and McLaughlin were right about the importance of implementation concerns, but it took a while longer to refocus on the importance of program quality and practicality. The latest research (RDU, DESSI) has demonstrated that program quality (especially proven materials demonstrating how to use a program) significantly influences change in practice (along with other factors in chart 2).[9]

The evolution of the use of computers in education provides another illustration of the importance of program quality and practicality. In the early period, computer-assisted instruction was first seen as a panacea, and then as a colossal waste of money when it failed to deliver; the failure was due among other reasons to the fact that the programs were not practically usable (see, e.g., House, 1974, ch. 5).[10] With the advent of more practical and available microcomputers the reputation of computers is rapidly changing for the better (Evans, 1979; Toffler, 1980), although new problems are emerging.

Our experience with computers marks one of the most prominent illustrations of "meaning" as the essence of change. Earlier classroom versions were impractical, mystifying, and frightening to teachers and students alike. The newer microcomputers are more practical, accessible, and usable, although some problems remain in relation to how microcomputers will be used in the classroom and what quality of software programs will be available. All serious change entails some anxiety and the microcomputer is certainly no exception; but the microcomputer allows individual users to work out the problem of meaning in assessing its educational potential.[11]

What conclusions can we derive from these uneven experiences with program quality? First, the rush for innovation in the early period (the 1960s)

---

9 See Louis and Rosenblum (1981) and Crandall et al. (forthcoming). The shift in emphasis on program quality can be interpreted in another way. The innovations examined in the FPSEC study were in fact not well developed (in the early 1970s); by the time the DESSI study was conducted (1980), the innovations examined were better developed. In this sense both studies were correct: the role of program quality was not evident in 1970; it is in the early 1980s— another example of the relatively short history of educational change and of the need to consider attempts at change in practice as still in their formative period.

10 It is revealing to note Yin et al.'s (1977, p. 60) findings: (1) that the computer-based innovations (compared to other technological changes in the sample) were more likely to fail to improve outcomes, and (2) a much higher proportion of computer-based innovations were adopted in education than in the other social agencies studied.

11 It is also noteworthy that familiarity with microcomputers is occurring outside the regular school system. In many ways, the school system is lagging behind the consumer market system in introducing microcomputers to students.

resulted in insufficiently developed or poor-quality changes. We are developing sounder innovations in some areas in 1982. Second, and more subtle, is what I have referred to elsewhere as "the dilemma of explicitness" (Fullan & Pomfret, 1977, pp. 368–69). To make innovations highly explicit at the development stage may mean that they are inappropriate for most of the variety of settings in which teachers operate. For many problems, the situational knowledge of teachers is essential to decisions about the specific form of change (see Connelly & Elbaz, 1980; Huberman, 1980; Roberts, 1980). On the other hand, to leave innovations unspecified results in great confusion about what to do in practice. One of the better resolutions is contained in Berman's (1980) later writings, in which he suggests that some educational problems are amenable to programmatic (or explicit) solutions, while others require more complex, adaptive resolutions over time. Be that as it may, many innovative efforts have suffered from the lack of high-quality, practical, usable resources. One of the more fascinating implications of this observation is to consider whether relatively unstructured innovations (e.g., open education) have failed because they have eschewed the cumulative development of practical, specific resources at the operational level. Bereiter and Kurland (1981) criticize the proponents of more unstructured education exactly on these grounds.[12] For implementation to gather any momentum, teachers and others must experience some sense of meaning and practicality relatively early in the process of attempting change; otherwise they will eventually abandon the effort.

In summary, the lack of a demonstrable need for change, the lack of a clear practical picture of the discrepancy between current practice and what is proposed, insufficient attention to the complexity of change in terms of extent and difficulty, and the lack of adequately developed and good-quality practical materials constitute one major set of barriers to implementation. While these can and should be assessed objectively, it is equally important to recognize that they must be understood *in relationship to individual implementers*—that is, in relationship to what they perceive as needs, as the extent of change, as difficulty, and as good quality/practicality. Implementation is a problem of individuals' developing meaning in relation to specific policy or program directions.

Providing innovation packages complete with a program to introduce the innovation to potential implementers can confront these barriers to only a limited extent. Concrete, demonstration-type materials stressing specificity may go a certain distance in improving meaning, but this emphasis misses the main point, unless one believes that people can learn complex change simply by being told and shown what to do. Greater specificity can be harmful if it overloads and overwhelms people with information. As with other aspects of change, clarification and skill in using new resources is a process in which demonstration materials may represent the starting point—but it is what *people develop* in their minds and actions that counts. Change is a difficult personal and social process of unlearning old ways and learning new ones (Marris, 1975; Sarason, 1981). Deeper meaning and solid change must be born over time; one must struggle through ambivalence before one is sure for oneself that the new version is workable and right (or unworkable and wrong and

---

12 There has been some provocative research on open education in primary schools in the United Kingdom (Bennett, 1976, 1979; Galton et al., 1980). See also Bussis et al. (1976).

should be rejected). Good change is hard work; however, we may find comfort in the realization that engaging in bad change or avoiding needed change may be even harder on us.

## B. Characteristics at the school district level

The remaining three categories in chart 2 focus on the social conditions of change. The setting in which people work—the planned and unplanned events and activities—influences whether or not given change attempts will be productive. The local school system represents one major set of situational constraints or opportunities for effective change.[13] The same program is often successful in one school system and an unmitigated disaster in another. Some districts have a track record of continual innovative achievement; others seem to fail at whatever they attempt. I have distilled a substantial amount of evidence about what makes school systems effective into six factors: the history of innovative attempts, the adoption process (if the change involves a district decision), central administrative support and involvement, staff development approaches, the time-line and information system, and board/community characteristics.[14]

### 5. The district's history of innovative attempts

I have suggested that adoption decisions are frequently taken without adequate follow-through, and that the difficulties (subjective realities) inherent in the process of change are not well understood. Most attempts at collective change in education seem to fail, and failure means frustration, wasted time, feelings of incompetence and lack of support, and disillusionment. The importance of the district's history of innovation attempts can be stated in the form of a proposition: the more the teachers or others have had negative experiences with previous implementation attempts in the district or elsewhere, the more cynical or apathetic they will be about the next change presented regardless of the merit of the new idea or program (see Sarason, 1971, pp. 219–22). Districts, provinces or states, and countries can develop an incapacity for change as well as a capacity for it (see Berman, McLaughlin, et al.'s 1979 case study of a district in a process of "decay," and Lambright et al., 1980, on coalition-building).

There isn't much direct research on the prehistory of innovative attempts, but it doesn't take a historian to conclude that history in the educational change field has been made with remarkable alacrity and intensity. And it is not good history. In general, teachers and others have become skeptical about the purposes and implementation support for educational change (and over the past fifteen years they would have been right more times than not—a "rational" response).

---

13 I do not consider every conceivable district factor. For example, the growing trend to more formal teacher/school-board relationships (management/union contracts) could be examined, but the issue is too broad and insufficiently researched to warrant any generalizations about its impact on change. I have confined the list of factors to those known to have an influence on implementation.

14 These are presented with enough detail to show how they operate, and are described more fully in the appropriate chapters in Part II (for example, the role of the district administrator is analyzed in chapter 10). District context or climate for change is crucial.

On the other hand, nothing is more gratifying psychologically than attempting a change that works and benefits students. If the subjective meaning of change is so central, it is worth stressing that people carry meanings from one experience to the next. This psychological history of change is a major determinant of how seriously people try to implement new programs. To predict and to understand individuals' and groups' responses to particular innovative programs, one must know their immediate past history.

## 6. The adoption process

The adoption process was discussed in chapter 4, but it was not explicitly related to implementation. I can be brief and specific by making two main observations. First, opportunistic and bureaucratically oriented adoption decisions (of which there are plenty of examples) are followed by limited implementation. As a consequence of the adoption process, subordinates become indifferent to implementation and senior management does not make serious follow-through attempts to provide resources, training, etc. On the other hand, if the decision to change has been carefully considered with appropriate commitment and follow-through by the district, implementation is much more likely to be taken seriously by principals or teachers. Berman, McLaughlin, et al.'s (1979) study of five school districts provides the clearest illustrations of how opportunistic and problem-solving districts differ in their day-to-day implementation follow-up activities (see also Miles et al., 1978).

Second, it may come as some surprise that participation in adoption decisions and/or development is not necessarily related to effective implementation.[15] In the ES study, Rosenblum and Louis (1979) found some evidence that the degree of community and staff participation in the early phases of the planning process turned out to be negatively related to successful implementation. (See also Giacquinta, 1973.) For most large-scale changes only a few district people make the big decisions. For example, the production of provincial guidelines or school district curricula usually involves selected teachers as participants in work groups or on committees. While these materials have been compiled by teachers, once they are ready for use they are no more meaningful to rank-and-file teachers (who are seeing them for the first time) than if they had been produced by publishers or central coordinators. It is the *members of the committee* who have developed their subjective meaning of the change, not anyone else.

The solution is not that everyone should participate in planning—a clear impossibility. Rather, it is the *quality* of the planning process which is essential: the degree to which a problem-solving approach at the adoption stage is combined with planning ahead for implementation (see Miles, 1980).[16] The quality of the adoption process already sets the stage for subsequent success or failure.

---

15 Whereas participation in decisions *during* implementation is essential (see below, factor 8: staff development and participation). Moreover, to say that effective implementation does not always require participation at the adoption stage does not mean that it is unimportant. Participation during the initiation phase may not always be essential, but it can increase the likelihood of implementation if done carefully (see Berman, 1981).

16 I am not recommending solutions at this stage, but rather explaining how change operates. If we were to consider solutions, the general gist of them would be to develop ways of addressing systematically the fifteen factors in chart 2 (see Fullan & Park, 1981).

Indeed, at the adoption phase sheer quantity in participatory planning can be harmful if it involves wasted time, disagreement, unclear needs assessment, frustrating meetings, and so on, without those involved having any program improvements to show for their efforts. If the planning process (regardless of whether it is participatory) results in a specific, high-quality, needed innovation, or in a broad-based flexible program whose general direction is compatible with the needs of the district, it will have been a sufficient start. More important for change in practice, however, is *implementation-level participation* in which decisions are made about what does work and what does not.

## 7. District administrative support

The role of the district administration and central staff is the subject of a future chapter (chapter 10); so it will be sufficient here to summarize the main findings. Individual teachers and single schools can bring about change without the support of central administrators, but district-wide change will not happen. Although it has always been said that the superintendent and the principal are critical to educational change, it is only recently that we are beginning to understand more specifically what that means in practice. All of the research cited in this chapter shows that the support of central administrators is critical for change in district practice (e.g., Emrick & Peterson, 1978, pp. 70–73). It also shows that support or endorsement in general of a new program has very little influence on change in practice (for example, verbal support without implementation follow-through). Teachers and others know enough now, if they didn't fifteen years ago, not to take change seriously unless central administrators *demonstrate through actions* that they should. Berman, McLaughlin, et al. (1979, pp. 84–95) give an excellent description of how one new superintendent with a mandate from the board "transformed the organization" by actively supporting new proposals, by visiting schools to see what was happening, by following through on decisions, and so on.

One of the more interesting analyses was carried out by Rosenblum and Louis (1979, p. 179). They investigated the relative effects on implementation of superintendent authority on the one hand and classroom autonomy of the teacher on the other hand. They found that superintendent authority (number of decision areas influenced by the superintendent) was *positively* associated with implementation of a new district-wide program, and classroom autonomy (number of classroom decisions that the teacher can make on his or her own) was *negatively* related to implementation. They suggest that a degree of centralization is necessary for implementing comprehensive changes across schools, and that strong norms of classroom autonomy in some districts may actually inhibit organizational and district-wide changes—a finding somewhat similar to Daft and Becker's (1978) conclusion about adoption of innovations directed to college-oriented students vs. high school terminating students.

The basic point, however, is that the chief executive officer and other key central administrators set the conditions for implementation to the extent that they show specific forms of support and active knowledge and understanding of the realities of attempting to put a change into practice. To state it most forcefully, the administrator affects the quality of implementation to the extent that he or she understands and helps to manage the set of factors and the processes described in this chapter.

## 8. Staff development and participation

Since the essence of educational change consists in learning new ways of thinking and doing, new skills, knowledge, attitudes, etc., it follows that staff development is one of the most important factors related to change in practice.[17] But, as with all the variables I am considering, the use of training can be grossly misapplied unless it is understood in relation to the meaning of change and the change process taken as a whole. One of the great problems in educational reform is that there is too much well-intentioned "ad hoc-ism"—the use of single, segmented solutions unconnected or unintegrated with their systemic realities. The result is more participation here, more materials production there, more in-service training everywhere—more, more, more. Well, when it comes to implementation, more is less.

The amount of staff training is not necessarily related to the quality of implementation, but it can be if it combines pre-implementation training with training during implementation, and uses a variety of trainers (see Louis & Rosenblum, 1981).[18] Pre-implementation training in which even intensive sessions are used to orient people to new programs does not work (Berman & McLaughlin, 1978, p. 27; Downey et al., 1975; Miles, 1978; Smith & Keith, 1971; and several others). One-shot workshops prior to and even during implementation are not very helpful (Rosenblum & Louis, 1979). Workshop trainers and program consultants are frequently ineffective. Consultants inside the district are unclear about their role and how to be effective consultants (Simms, 1978; Lippitt, 1979).[19] Teachers say they learn best from other teachers, but research shows that they interact with each other very infrequently (Lortie, 1975). When teachers are trained as staff developers, they can be very effective in working with other teachers (see Stallings, 1980). Teachers also say that they need direct outside help, if it is practical and concrete; and they find those qualities to be the exception rather than the rule. Researchers report that concrete and skill-specific training is effective, but "only for the short run" (McLaughlin & Marsh, 1978, p. 76).

The theory and meaning of change employed in this book explains why the above attempts at training are not effective. Simply put, most forms of in-service training are not designed to provide the ongoing, interactive, cumulative learning necessary to develop new conceptions, skills, and behavior. Failure to realize that there is a need for in-service work *during implementation* is a common problem. No matter how much advance staff development occurs, it is when people actually try to implement new approaches that they have the

---

17 Staff development is examined directly in chapter 14; the description of Jefferson County in chapter 10 provides a clear example of how effective staff development is integrated into a district-wide plan for implementing new programs. (For other very good sources see Joyce & Showers, 1980, 1981; Joyce, 1982; McLaughlin & Marsh, 1978; Little, 1981.)

18 Berman and McLaughlin (1978) found that amount of training was not related to implementation. Datta (1981) reinterprets Berman and McLaughlin's FPSEC findings to question whether the staff training was really based on "technical expertise" in most projects. But the basic point remains: it is the nature of in-service education, not the amount, that counts (see chapter 14). See also Joyce and Showers (1981), Louis and Rosenblum (1981), Crandall et al. (forthcoming) for further findings and discussion of this complex area of training and assistance.

19 Consultants must have at least two kinds of skills: content knowledge or expertise, and skill in facilitating the change process. The two do not always go together and may work at cross-purposes (see chapter 11).

most specific concerns and doubts. It is thus extremely important that people obtain some support at the early stages of attempted implementation. Getting over this initial critical hump represents a major breakthrough for working toward more thorough change (Huberman, 1981). Reflecting the problem of partial implementation, McLaughlin and Marsh stress that skill-specific training by itself has only a transient effect because the use of new materials and methods is often mechanical without the underlying ideas becoming assimilated. Similarly, the learning of new skills through demonstration and practice does not necessarily include the learning of the conceptual underpinnings necessary for lasting use (Joyce & Showers, 1980, 1981; Joyce, 1981; Bussis et al., 1976; Hall & Loucks, 1978; McLaughlin & Marsh, 1978).

The dilemmas and inconsistencies in trying to understand why the "obvious" strategy of staff development fails more often than it succeeds are easy to resolve. Implementation, whether it is voluntary or imposed, is none other than a process of *resocialization*. The foundation of resocialization is *interaction*. Learning by doing, concrete role models, meetings with resource consultants and fellow implementers, practice of the behavior, the fits and starts of cumulative, ambivalent, gradual self-confidence all constitute a process of coming to see the meaning of change more clearly. Once this is said, examples of successful training approaches to implementation make sense. They are effective when they combine concrete teacher-specific training activities, ongoing continuous assistance and support during the process of implementation, and regular meetings with peers and others. Research on implementation has demonstrated beyond a shadow of a doubt that these processes of sustained *interaction and staff development* are crucial regardless of what the change is concerned with.[20] People can and do change, but it requires social energy. School districts can help generate extra energy by developing or otherwise supporting continuous staff development opportunities for teachers, administrators, and others.

Participation in implementation decisions can be treated separately from staff development, but I consider it together, because good ongoing staff development programs involve decisions about the details of implementation.[21] Teacher participation in decisions about implementation is not just essential for program acceptance. The identification and solution of implementation problems *require* teacher decision-making. Very few new programs can fully prespecify all implementation details. For many innovations, implementation involves some further clarification, specification, and development or refinements in the program. Indeed, many programs are deliberately left flexible

---

20 The following studies, among others, support this statement: of federally funded change agent projects (Berman & McLaughlin, 1978; Louis & Rosenblum, 1981; Crandall et al., forthcoming); of school district program change (Melle & Pratt, 1981; Berman, McLaughlin, et al., 1978); of the implementation of provincial curriculum guidelines (Leithwood, 1978); of the National Diffusion Network (Crandall et al., forthcoming; Emrick et al., 1977); of Organization Development programs (Fullan, Miles, & Taylor, 1980); of staff development programs related to implementation (Hall & Loucks, 1978); of change in rural school districts (Herriott & Gross, 1979; Rosenblum & Louis, 1979); of the planning and implementation of new schools (Miles et al., 1978); of Head Start and Follow Through programs (Hodges et al., 1980; Stallings, 1979); of technological change (Yin et al., 1977).

21 The bigger decisions about whether to adopt or discontinue a program involve teacher input, but research indicates that this is not always essential or possible on a large scale. (See Hood and Blackwell, 1980, for a review of teacher participation, and Dawson, 1981.)

and general for the precise reason that specification should occur according to the different local situations. Provincial curriculum guidelines, new legislation, curriculum development projects, and the like are frequently based on this assumption (Elmore, 1980; Williams, 1980).[22]

Berman and McLaughlin (1978, p. 29) indicate why teacher participation is essential:

Teacher participation in decisions concerning project operations and modifications was strongly correlated with effective implementation and continuation. The reasons for this powerful effect were easy to uncover. Teachers, who are closest to the problems and progress of project activities, are in the best position to suggest remedies for perceived deficiencies. Moreover, where project activities and objectives reflected significant teacher input, the staff were more likely to invest the considerable energy needed to make the project work.

Limited teacher participation in decisions would be a good indicator that the subjective meaning of change is not developing, as would teacher decision-making which occurred without active involvement in staff development and other interaction-based activities.

### 9. Time-line and information systems (evaluation)

Time perspective is one of the most neglected aspects of the implementation process. Ten years ago, Sarason (1971) recognized time as a critical factor:

In practice, the desire of the agents of change to get started—not only because of internal and external pressures but also because of the awareness, sometimes dim, that the road ahead will not be smooth—results in bypassing the different aspects of the time perspective problem, a bypass that might have no immediately adverse consequences, but can be counted on to produce delayed, and sometimes fatal difficulties. (p. 219)

It was not just that reformers made incorrect decisions about time, but that they had *no* time perspective about implementation. The realization of the importance of conceptualizing implementation as a process which takes time has changed only slowly since 1971, and the reason is simple. The decision-makers for educational change have an adoption time perspective, not an implementation one. It is not politically wise to indicate that effective action will take several years to come to fruition, or to spend time and energy with implementation difficulties in programs X and Y when pressure exists for programs M, N, and O to be developed and adopted. More charitably, impatience arising from the desire to bring about much-needed educational reform results in hasty decisions, unrealistic time-lines, and inadequate logistical support during implementation because due dates arrive more quickly than problems can be resolved. Central decision-makers know the complexities of the adoption process; practitioners know the complexities of the implementation process. They live in two different subjective worlds. What appears to be rational plan-

---

22 We have seen, as with so many issues, that there are two sides to the problem—general programs increase ambiguity and anxiety about what is expected and opportunities for implementation evasion; specific programs delimit the options and preempt adaptations and learning. General programs require corresponding vehicles for participation during implementation to ensure that specification and clarification issues are addressed (see Miles, 1978).

ning to one world looks like resistance to change to the other (see Cowden & Cohen, 1979).[23]

Time is ignored, because it is a problem that cannot be solved. There will never be enough of it. Avoiding difficult problems creates even more serious ones, and time is no exception. Unrealistic time-lines add to the burdens of implementation: materials fail to arrive on schedule, orientation and training are neglected or carried out perfunctorily, communication is hurried and frequently overlooked or misinterpreted,[24] and people become overloaded with the requirements of new programs on top of carrying on as usual (see Charters & Pellegrin, 1973; Yin et al., 1977). Disillusionment, burnout, cynicism, and apathy come to characterize many people's orientation to every change that comes along. And yet open-ended time-lines are also problematic, because they create ambiguity about what is expected and when and a lack of clarity about what constitutes progress.

The complexities of the implementation process and the slow development of the meaning of change at the individual level make it obvious that change is a time-consuming affair. A time-line is needed which is neither unrealistically short nor casually long. The timing of events must be guided by an understanding of the process of implementation and by a plan for addressing the factors discussed in this chapter.

Whatever time-line is used, one of the major dilemmas faced is what kind of *information* to collect, when, and how best to use it. The information or evaluation component can range from highly elaborate accountability schemes (Wise, 1979) to no formal information system at all. Information can be gathered, for example, on the extent and problems of implementation, on student achievement, or on other desired outcomes. The issues involved in setting up a district-wide information system are too complicated to delve into at this point (see chapter 10) except for three observations. First, there is no evidence that information on student achievement by itself results in improved implementation. Such data provide little insight into the specific problems of implementation, such as teaching behavior or effective staff development activities. Second, information on implementation concerns can be very effective in facilitating change provided that it is linked to a system for acting on it. Melle and Pratt (1981) describe how this link works in one district; however, the research in general shows that most school districts do not have evaluation systems linked to instructional improvement procedures.[25] Third, it is at the school and class-

---

23 This difference helps to explain why each side feels misunderstood by the other, and why people are frequently surprised by how others completely misinterpret the best of their intentions and literally do not hear what they are saying. We often do not have much sympathy for the policy-maker or administrator. But it is just as important to appreciate their subjective worlds as it is to understand those of practitioners (see Parts II and III).

24 Our theory would tell us that it is not the intended communication of the sender that counts but the subjective interpretation of the receiver.

25 Two research programs have focused on identifying school districts which have evaluation systems, and especially have attempted to locate "exemplary districts" which integrate information-gathering with a plan to improve instruction using the information. See the work of the Center for the Study of Evaluation at the University of California at Los Angeles, reported in Bank (1981), Williams & Bank (1981), Lyon et al. (1978); and of the Huron Institute, reported in Kennedy et al. (1980), Apling & Kennedy (1981). Generally, these studies have found few districts which have adequate mechanisms for relating evaluative information to program improvement. Those districts which do link information to improvement do so by employing effective procedures of implementation similar to those described in this chapter.

room levels where information counts. I will be turning to the school level shortly, but it can be noted that an emphasis on collecting and using diagnostic information about student learning and other implementation problems has been found to be strongly related to school improvement (Cohen, 1981; Edmonds, 1979, 1982).

### 10. Board and community characteristics

It is very difficult to generalize about the role of communities and school boards vis-à-vis implementation. Corwin (1973) found that community support of the school was correlated positively with innovativeness. Smith and Keith (1971) and Gold and Miles (1981) tell the painful sagas of what happens when middle-class communities do not like the innovations they see in their schools. Demographic changes often put increasing pressure on schools to adopt, if not implement, new policies (Berman & McLaughlin, 1979). For example, a case study of the Toronto school system shows how the school board was central to the initial development of new multicultural policies and programs which were not necessarily welcomed by many schools (see Toronto School Board, 1976). Rosenblum and Louis (1979, p. 111) found that "the degree to which environmental changes external to the school were impinging on it to change" was one of four readiness factors related to subsequent implementation. Major conflicts, however, sometimes incapacitate districts in bringing about actual change; in a sense, certain adoption decisions have to be settled before energy can be turned to implementation. Whatever the case, as Miles (1980) asserts, attending to political stabilization in relation to the community is one of the primary tasks of planning and implementing new programs. In contemplating or introducing innovations, districts frequently ignore the community and/or the school board (see Gold & Miles, 1981; Smith & Keith, 1971).

There is also some evidence that rural districts not only have less access to innovations (House, 1974) but often are too distant geographically from needed sources of assistance during implementation. (Rosenblum & Louis, 1979, and Bass & Berman, 1979, 1981, analyze the situation of rural districts.)

I may tentatively suggest a few points: (1) most school communities are usually not directly involved in implementation; (2) they can become aroused against certain innovations; (3) neither highly stable nor highly turbulent school communities constitute effective environments for implementation.[26] The role of individual parents rather than community groups may provide one of the most powerful leverages to better implementation (see chapter 12).

## C. School-level factors

The meaning of the phrase "the school is the unit of change" (Goodlad, 1975) will become evident in this section.[27] Three main factors summarize the influence of the school on implementation: the role of the principal, peer relation-

---

26 There is no assumption that implementation is "a good thing." Turbulent communities need to resolve more basic problems regarding goals, purposes, and needed adoptions.

27 I do not separate elementary and secondary schools in this section. There is not enough research on their differences in relation to effective change to allow for clear conclusions. The generalizations I do describe have been found in schools at all levels (elementary, junior high, and secondary). Regardless of the level, school context and climate for supporting or ignoring needed change is the issue.

ships, and teacher orientations. Taken together they constitute the character and climate of the school as an organization.

## 11. The role of the principal

All major research on innovation and school effectiveness shows that the principal strongly influences the likelihood of change, but it also indicates that most principals do not play instructional leadership roles (see Fullan, 1981, and Leithwood & Montgomery, 1981, for reviews). Berman and McLaughlin (1977) provide some detail. They found that "projects having the *active* support of the principal were the most likely to fare well" (p. 124, their emphasis). Principals' actions serve to legitimate whether a change is to be taken seriously (and not all changes are) and to support teachers both psychologically and with resources. Berman and McLaughlin (1978, p. 128) note that one of the best indicators of active involvement is whether the principal attends workshop training sessions. If we recall the earlier dimensions of change (beliefs, teaching behavior, etc.), we might speculate that unless the principal gains some understanding of these dimensions (not necessarily as an expert or an instructional leader) he or she will not be able to understand teachers' concerns—that is, will not be able to provide support for implementation. Such understanding requires interaction.

There is an abundance of other evidence cited in chapter 8 which describes how and why the principal is necessary for effective implementation. To take one example, Emrick and Peterson's (1978) synthesis of five major projects (one of which was the Rand project, FPSEC) identifies administrative support as one of five factors common across all projects:

... utilization rarely occurred when building or district administrative components were indifferent and utilization was virtually impossible in the presence of administrative opposition. (p. 71)

While the principal can have a major impact on implementation, there is also considerable research which indicates that he or she frequently does not in fact play an active role. Berman and McLaughlin (1978, p. 131) report that one-third of the teachers thought that their principal functioned primarily as an administrator. Teachers rated these principals as ineffective and uninvolved in change. Similar findings come from studies of the use of provincial curriculum guidelines in Canada, which indicate that at best only about one-half of school principals provide active instructional leadership. (See Leithwood et al., 1978; Downey et al., 1975; Simms, 1978.) The subjective world of principals is such that many of them suffer from the same problem in "implementing a new role as facilitator of change" as do teachers in implementing new teaching roles: what the principal should do *specifically* to manage change at the school level is a complex affair for which the principal has little preparation. The psychological and sociological problems of change which confront the principal are at least as great as those that confront the teachers. Without this sociological sympathy, many principals will feel exactly as teachers do: other people simply do not seem to understand the problems they face (see chapter 8).

## 12. Teacher–teacher relationships

The theory of change which is evolving clearly points to the importance of peer relationships in the school (see chapter 7). Change involves resocialization.

Interaction is the primary basis for social learning. New meanings, new behavior, new skills depend significantly on whether teachers are working as isolated individuals (Lortie, 1975; Sarason, 1971) or exchanging ideas, support, and positive feelings about their work (Little, 1981; Rutter et al., 1979). The research I have been reviewing provides direct confirmation that the quality of working relationships among teachers is strongly related to implementation (e.g., Berman & McLaughlin, 1978, pp. 119-20; Rosenblum & Louis, 1979; Miles et al., 1978). Collegiality, open communication, trust, support and help, interaction, and morale are all closely related. How they come about is another question to be addressed later, but I have already suggested that the principal strongly influences the climate of the school. Berman and McLaughlin (1978), Galanter (1978), and others report strong correlations between principal support and peer relationships among teachers.[28]

### 13. Teacher characteristics and orientations

Research on teacher characteristics and effective change is inconsistent in its findings. Level of education (e.g., possession of a master's degree) and years of teaching experience are two variables frequently measured in research studies. The results vary, and it is not difficult to see why, given the other factors in chart 2. It is not level of education or years of experience that matter so much as under what district and school conditions teachers spend their time. Depending on the conditions, innovators and hard-core resisters are found among all ages and levels of education.

There is one teacher trait related to successful implementation and student learning which comes through strongly: *teacher sense of efficacy*. In the school effectiveness research, one of five generalizations related to improvements in student learning is concerned with whether teachers think and expect that all students regardless of family background can reach appropriate levels of achievement (Edmonds, 1979; Cohen, 1980). Similarly, the Rand FPSEC study found a strong relationship between teacher sense of efficacy[29] and positive impact of change on various measures of success, including percentage of goals achieved, reports of improved student performance, and teacher change (Berman & McLaughlin, 1977, p. 136).

While it is more difficult to explain how teachers get a sense of efficacy, it is encouraging to observe that the process is not idiosyncratic. In some schools there are much higher proportions of staff who have this orientation than in other schools, even when community and student characteristics are similar. This finding suggests that efficacy is more of an organizational feature of schools which come to have a *school-wide* emphasis and expectation that they can improve student learning—and they do! (Edmonds, 1979; Rutter et al., 1979).

---

28 I will always remember one of the first questionnaires we did, which asked teachers if the principal influenced the teachers to work closely as a team. One teacher wrote in: "Yes, against him!"

29 Defined as "a belief on the part of the teacher that he or she could help even the most difficult or unmotivated students." On the other hand, the DESSI study, using the same measure, did not find that sense of efficacy was related to better implementation (Crandall et al., forthcoming). Regardless of the general sense of efficacy, change in a specific program requires a sense of confidence that the program can and will work. See also Sarason's (1971) discussion of internal and external locus of control.

No words could sum up this section on school-level factors more accurately than those of Judith Little, based on her study of work practices in six urban schools:

School improvement is most surely and thoroughly achieved when:

Teachers engage in frequent, continuous and increasingly concrete and precise *talk* about teaching practice (as distinct from teacher characteristics and failings, the social lives of teachers, the foibles and failures of students and their families, and the unfortunate demands of society on the school). By such talk, teachers build up a shared language adequate to the complexity of teaching, capable of distinguishing one practice and its virtue from another . . . .

Teachers and administrators frequently *observe* each other teaching, and provide each other with useful (if potentially frightening) evaluations of their teaching. Only such observation and feedback can provide shared *referents* for the shared language of teaching, and both demand and provide the precision and concreteness which makes the talk about teaching useful.

Teachers and administrators *plan, design, research, evaluate and prepare teaching materials together*. The most prescient observations remain academic ("just theory") without the machinery to act on them. By joint work on materials, teachers and administrators share the considerable burden of development required by long-term improvement, confirm their emerging understanding of their approach, and make rising standards for their work attainable by them and by their students.

Teachers and administrators *teach each other* the practice of teaching. (1981, pp. 12–13, her emphases)

Only two of the six schools in Little's study evidenced a very high percentage of these practices, but no more convincing picture of the conditions for developing *meaning* on the part of individual teachers and administrators could be portrayed than in the passage just quoted. But see also Crandall's (1981) discussion of "emulation and replication" for elaboration on the idea of meaning in implementing new programs.

## D. The external environment

The last set of factors which influence educational change places the school or school district in the context of the broader society. In Canada this means primarily the offices of the department or ministry of education of each province. In the United States the main authorities consist of state departments of education and federal agencies. Other agencies such as regional R&D laboratories and centers also attempt to support educational implementation across the country. The relationship of the school to these various outside agencies is quite complicated, but necessary to analyze in order to understand the forces which impinge on school personnel. This section provides an overview of the influence of this outside set of forces defined as two broad factors: government agencies and external assistance.

### 14. Government agencies

I have already discussed the importance of unmet needs at the local level. But what does the larger society think of its educational system? Provincial/state and national priorities for education are set according to the political forces and lobbying of interest groups, government bureaucracies, and elected representatives. Legislation, new policies, and new program initiatives arise from public concerns that the educational system is not doing an adequate job of teaching basics, developing career-relevant skills for the economic system, producing effective citizens, meeting the needs of recent immigrants or handicapped children or cultural minorities, and so on. These "sources" of reform put pressure on local districts (sometimes to the point of force) and also provide various incentives for changing in the desired direction: new provincial guidelines are established as policy, new federal and state legislation is passed, new federally sponsored projects are developed. We have no reason whatsoever to imagine that these actions in their own right are related to implementation.[30] Whether or not implementation occurs will depend on the congruence between the reforms and local needs, and on how the changes are introduced and followed through.

Government agencies have been preoccupied with policy and program adoption. Until recently they vastly underestimated the problems and processes of implementation. We have a classic case of two entirely different worlds—the policy-maker on the one hand, and the local practitioner on the other hand. ("Divergent worlds" as Cowden & Cohen, 1979, call them.) To the extent that each side is ignorant of the *subjective* world of the other, reform will fail—and the extent is great. The quality of relationships across this gulf is crucial to supporting change efforts when there is agreement and to reconciling problems when there is conflict among these groups: between provincial ministries and local school boards, administrators, and teachers; between state departments and local districts; and between federal project officers and local authorities.[31]

The most straightforward way of stating the problem is to say that local school systems and external authority agencies have not learned how to establish a *processual* relationship with each other.[32] For example, Rosenblum and Louis (1979, p. 296) report that "respondents in several districts volunteered the information that they never recovered from the tensions and conflicts of the planning year and the process of negotiation with ES/Washington."

Lack of role clarity, ambiguity about expectations, absence of regular interpersonal forums of communication, ambivalence between authority and support roles of external agencies, and solutions which are worse than the original problems combine to erode the likelihood of implementation.

The difficulties in the relationship between external and internal groups are central to the problem and process of meaning. Not only is meaning hard to come by when two different worlds have limited interaction, but misinterpretation, attribution of motives, feelings of being misunderstood, and disillusionment on both sides are almost guaranteed.

But government agencies have become increasingly aware of the importance and difficulty of implementation and are allocating resources to establishing

---

30 This is not to say that they are unimportant or unnecessary in the long run (see chapter 6).

31 There is a growing literature in the United States on these problems. This research is used as the basis for chapter 13. (See Bardach, 1977; Berman & McLaughlin, 1978; Cowden & Cohen, 1979; Corwin, 1977; Elmore, 1980; Herriott, 1979; House, 1974; Kirst, 1979; McLaughlin, 1976; Rosenblum & Louis, 1979; Weatherley, 1979; Williams, 1980; Wise, 1979; and Yin et al., 1977.)

32 The relationship is more in the form of episodic events rather than processes: i.e., submission of requests for money, intermittent progress reports on what is being done—paperwork, not peoplework.

implementation units, to assessing the quality of potential changes, to support-ing staff development, and to addressing other factors discussed in this chap-ter.[33] Whether they will be successful is a relative matter, related partly to resources required to address problems and partly to the capacity of local school systems to use these resources effectively. It is ironic in the extreme that when money was freely available for innovation in the late 1960s we didn't have a clue about how to go about implementation; now that we know what makes for success, the money is increasingly unavailable. What school people would give today to have a fraction of the resources wasted on the big innovative flashes of the 1960s! We learned a great deal about educational reform, but it was a very costly experiment.

### 15. External assistance

Since governments are by far the major direct and indirect sources of exter-nal assistance to school systems, I need only extend a few ideas related to money and to technical assistance. The offer by governments of additional resources for educational reform is embedded in the U.S. educational system, even with recent major cutbacks in federal expenditures. These resources pro-vide the margin required for implementation support in many school districts. As one might predict, whether it is used for better implementation depends on the characteristics of local systems—that is, it depends on those factors just described in categories B and C of chart 2. The larger issue of compli-ance to federal and state policies raises a host of questions which are taken up in chapter 13. (See Elmore, 1980, for an excellent brief account of the problem.)

Technical assistance for implementation (materials, consultancy, staff devel-opment, etc.) is frequently available in federal or state-sponsored innovative programs.[34] This too involves a complicated set of issues. We have learned a great deal in the past few years about the conditions under which external help is needed and effective (see chapter 11; also Louis & Rosenblum, 1981; Louis, 1981; Crandall et al., forthcoming). The simplest observation at this juncture is that outside assistance or stimulation can influence implementation very greatly provided that it is integrated with the factors at the local level described above.

To conclude the discussion of external factors, major educational reform is not likely, but some success is achievable. The multiplicity of post-adoption decisions after educational legislation or new policy involves several layers of agencies. That success is achieved in many instances is a reflection that some people "out there" know what they are doing. Sharing and developing this knowhow should be a major goal of those interested in educational change.

---

33 Several provinces in Canada have established implementation units. Alberta recently allo-cated $2 million for staff development (for salaries for local resource teachers and for released time) related to the implementation of a new social studies curriculum guideline. The RDU and DESSI research studies in the U.S. indicate that government-sponsored programs are having some positive impact on implementation (Louis & Rosenblum, 1981; Crandall et al., forth-coming).

34 Programs which furnish funds to developers or to school districts to hire consultants/trainers from other school districts, labs, universities. Many programs fund the salaries of resource teachers or consultants at the school, district, regional, or state levels.

# Factors affecting continuation

Implementation is the big hurdle at the level of practice, but the question of the continuation of initiated reforms should be considered in its own right. In a sense continuation represents another adoption decision, which may be negative, and even if positive may not itself get implemented. Berman and McLaughlin (1978, pp. 166–83) found that projects which were not implemented effectively were discontinued (as would be expected), but they also found that only a minority of those which were implemented were continued beyond the period of federal funding. The reasons for lack of continuation were in the main the same ones which influenced implementation, except that their role became more sharply defined. Lack of interest or inability to fund "special projects" out of district funds, and lack of money for staff development and staff support for both continuing and new teachers, signaled the end of many implemented programs. Lack of interest and support at the central district office (e.g., of those who had taken on the project for opportunistic reasons) was another reason for non-continuation. Similarly, at the school level "the principal was the key to both implementation and continuation":

After the end of the federal funding, the principal influenced continuation in ... direct ways. Often because of turnover in the original cadre of project teachers, projects would have decayed without active efforts by principal to bring on new staff .... It was extremely difficult for teachers to go on using project methods or materials without the principal's explicit support. (Berman, McLaughlin, et al., 1977, p. 188)

Berman and McLaughlin identified a small number of cases in which continuation was sustained. In addition to the specific factors just cited (active leadership, staff development, etc.) the authors noted:

District officials paid early attention to mobilizing broad-based support for the innovation. And after federal funding ended, mobilization efforts were increased to pave the way for the project's transition from its special status to its incorporation into key areas of district operations: the budget, personnel assignment, curriculum support activities, and the instructional program. In short, the groundwork and planning for sustaining a change agent project had the early, active, and continued attention of school district managers. (Berman & McLaughlin, 1978, p. 20)

As a cautionary note, Berman, McLaughlin, et al. (1978, pp. 185–86) emphasize that the "meaning of continuation" can be misleading. For example, a district may officially decide to continue a project, but teachers may not implement it (e.g., in terms of the dimensions of implementation). Or a district may decide to discontinue the program, but many of the teachers have already assimilated it. In other words, the program may leave its mark on the district in ways which may be overlooked.

Direct assistance from external authorities may be helpful for initial implementation; but when it comes to institutionalization, the larger the external resource support, the *less likely* the effort will be continued after external funds terminate, because the district cannot afford to incorporate the costs into its regular budget (Yin et al., 1977, p. 16).

Miles, Fullan, and Taylor (1978, vol. III, p. 40) discovered a similar phenomenon in investigating the continuation of school district Organization Development programs which had been operating a minimum of eighteen months. Of those districts where no federal money supported the program, 57% had decisive institutionalization; but in cases where the program was supported by a *majority* of federal money, only 40% were institutionalized. It makes sense that school districts cannot afford the personnel, training, materials, and other budgetary resources necessary to continue a program that has been "added on" to their regular work, especially if they had originally adopted the program because they had to, or for opportunistic reasons. Unless the district is using a part of its own money, it is unlikely to be able or to be committed to continue a new program. (See also Corbett, 1982.)

The problem of continuation is endemic to all new programs regardless of whether they arise from external initiatives or are internally developed. The single most powerful internal factor which takes its toll on continued change is staff and administrative turnover (Louis, 1980; Berman & McLaughlin, 1977). Since effective change depends on interaction among users, removal of key users weakens the conditions that would incorporate or help new members. While this is obvious, very few new programs plan for the orientation of members who arrive after the program gets started. And arrive they do, chipping away, however unintentionally, at what is already a fragile process.

Probably the most discouraging prospect in understanding the implementation and continuation process is the realization that it is not linear and is never-ending. It does no good to take each of the fifteen factors in chart 2 and attempt to deal with them one at a time. They must be *continually* borne in mind and attended to when need be. It's like the balancing act of a juggler, but not so predictable and systematic.

While we are on the topic of institutionalization and continuation, it will be useful to conclude this section with some discussion on the question of *outcomes* of change efforts. There are in fact a variety of types of outcomes of attempted change which require careful conceptualization and measurement. After all, innovations are supposed to accomplish something worthwhile. But there are short-term and long-term outcomes, as well as outcomes of different types. The most helpful examination of the area of outcomes of change efforts is contained in the DESSI study (Crandall et al., forthcoming). Five different kinds are identified and measured roughly in order from intermediate to more long-term effects.

1 Degree of implementation
2 Attitude toward innovation
3 Impact (a) students' benefits
          (b) teachers' benefits
          (c) organizational benefits
4 Continuation or institutionalization
5 Attitude toward school improvement

Degree of implementation assesses the degree of actual change on the part of teachers. Attitude toward the innovation concerns perceptions of the strengths and weaknesses of the change. Impact involves an assessment of student learning, teacher benefits (e.g., professional development), and organizational change (e.g., increased interaction, teaming). Continuation, as we have discussed, involves such matters as incorporation in the budget, staffing, and extent of durability of the change. Attitude toward school improvement is a kind of meta-variable related to whether the experience with the change effort increases or decreases people's attitude toward engaging in new school improvement programs—in brief, whether the experience has led people to conclude generally that it is worthwhile to try and implement changes.

The DESSI study did find significant and lasting changes on most of its measures (see Crandall et al.).[35] The more general contribution, however, resides in the much needed conceptualization and pinpointing of different kinds of outcomes in the chain of consequences. While to attribute simple causation is unwarranted, there is a logic to the change process in which factors affecting adoption and implementation result in (1) more or less implementation (degree of implementation), which affects (2) attitudes to the innovation and (3) the quality of impact—and attitudes and impact in turn contribute to the likelihood of (4) continuation. The entire process influences (5) our attitude to school improvement. It is by no means that straightforward, and certainly there are other reasons why any one of the five outcomes could occur. But the idea of carefully specifying and interrelating the different consequences of attempted innovations is extremely important.[36]

# Perspective on the change process

Despite the length of this chapter, it contains only an overview of the implementation process. It presents a way of thinking about change, and an organizing framework rather than a detailed blueprint. True to the theory of meaning, any given set of details must be developed from where one is located. There is no assumption in this chapter about who should initiate reform or on what scale. The principal interested in bringing about or coping with change starts at factor 11 in chart 2, and must figure out how to contend with the other fourteen sets of factors. The teacher, the consultant, the government policy-maker, and the district administrator all have different vantage points and corresponding issues to confront and manage. Whether it is big change or small change, whether one is the initiator or the receiver, the implications of coping with change can be systematically derived from the general framework. But the details do vary, and these must be taken up in the specific chapters in Parts II and III.

The broad implications of the implementation process have several interrelated components. The first is that the crux of change involves the develop-

---

35 The question of measurement is a serious one, because much of the information depended on retrospective perceptions. The interested reader should examine the study directly.

36 The RDU study also makes a major contribution to the study of outcomes of adopted programs. Six different outcomes were assessed: organizational change, scope of implementation, incorporation of the product, incorporation of a problem-solving process, problem resolution, and personal impacts (Louis & Rosenblum, 1981, p. 149). The six outcomes are not seen to be in any particular causal order or relationship.

ment of meaning in relation to a new idea, program, or set of activities. But it is *individuals* who have to develop new meaning, and these individuals are insignificant parts of a gigantic, loosely organized, complex, messy social system which contains myriad different subjective worlds.

The causes of change also become more easily identifiable and understood once we possess an underlying conception of what constitutes change as a process over time. The factors of implementation and continuation reinforce or undercut each other as an interrelated system. Single-factor theories of change are doomed to failure. Arguments that product quality is more important than teacher attitude, or that external factors are more important than internal ones, or that teachers are more central than administrators, are pointless. Effective implementation depends on the *combination* of all four sets of factors described in this chapter. The characteristics of the nature of the change, the make-up of the local district, the character of individual schools and teachers, and the existence and form of external relationships interact to produce conditions for change or non-change. It takes a fortunate combination of the right factors—a critical mass—to support and guide the process of resocialization which respects the maintenance needs of individuals and groups and at the same time facilitates, stimulates, prods people to change through a process of incremental and decremental fits and starts on the way to institutionalizing or discontinuing the change in question.

Moreover (as if we could stand more quandaries), there is frequently no definitive "change in question" at the beginning of the process of implementation. Situations vary, and we never fully know what implementation is or should look like until people in particular situations attempt to spell it out through use. Implementation *makes* further policy; it does not simply put predefined policy into practice (see Farrar et al., 1979; Majone & Wildavsky, 1978; Berman, 1980).[37]

We understand that not all change is progress, or even meant to be. As individuals react incorrectly to pressures, so do schools, school districts, and societies. There are many motivations and origins for educational change, and in retrospect only a fraction of them seem to be based on the identification of a clear and important educational need and on the development of a quality idea and program. Even if we get the need and the idea right, the sheer complexity of the process of implementation has, as it were, a sociological mind of its own which frequently defies management even when all parties have the best of intentions. After fifteen years of ripping off and ripping into the system, we have learned "the pathos of implementation":

Faithful implementation is sometimes undesirable (because the idea is bad), sometimes impossible (because power won't permit), and often unforeseeable (because it depends on what people bring to it as well as what's in it). (Majone & Wildavsky, 1978, p. 25)

---

37 Some changes are more programmatic than others, as the earlier discussion of fidelity and adaptive perspectives indicates. And some developers have been able to define and implement programs relatively precisely for certain basic educational objectives even under conditions of initial resistance (see Emrick & Peterson's 1980 case study of the Direct Instruction Follow-Through Program, Gersten et al., 1981, and Rhine, 1981).

The odds against successful planned educational change are not small. Increasing our understanding of implementation may alter them. We will see examples of how change can work when the factors of adoption, implementation, and continuation are combined in certain ways. The theory of the meaning of change and the change process provides us with an underlying conception of what should be done. This guide to change enables us to locate very specific factors, to observe how they work in concrete situations, and to explain why they function as they do, with what consequences for school improvement.

The "solution" to the management of educational change is straightforward. All we need to do in any situation is to take the fifteen factors described in this chapter (and all their subvariables and interactions), change them in a positive direction, and then orchestrate them so that they work smoothly together. The mind may be excused for boggling.

If the theory of change emerging at this point leads us to conclude that we need better implementation plans and planners, we are embarking on the infinite regress which characterizes the pursuit of a theory of "changing." To bring about more effective change, we need to be able to explain not only what causes it but how to influence those causes. To implement programs successfully, we need better implementation plans; to get better implementation plans, we need to know how to change our planning process; to know how to change our planning process, we need to know how to produce better planners and implementers; etc.; etc. Is it any wonder that the planning, doing, and coping with educational change is the "science of muddling through" (Lindblom, 1959)? But it is a *science*. All of which is another way of saying that chapter 6 is ready to begin.

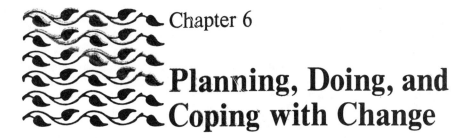 Chapter 6

# Planning, Doing, and Coping with Change

*When I remember how many of my private schemes have miscarried . . . how the things I desperately strove against as a misfortune did me immense good—how while the objects I ardently pursued brought me little happiness when gained . . . I am struck with the incompetence of my intellect to prescribe for society. There is a great want of this practical humility in our political conduct.*

— Herbert Spencer, *"Over Legislation,"* The Westminster Review, *July 1853*

For the growing number of people who have attempted to bring about educational change, "intractability" is becoming a household word. Being ungovernable, however, is not the same as being impervious to influence. And the inability to change *all* situations we would ideally like to reform does not lead to the conclusion that *no* situation can be changed. (To complicate matters even further—to conclude that a situation can be changed in a certain way does not mean that it should be.)

The picture of change which has been evolving in the previous chapters needs to be considered from the point of view of what, if anything, can be done about it. To do this, I treat four major aspects of the problem of planning educational change: "Why planning fails," "Success is possible," "Guidelines for planning and coping," and "Scope of change."

# Why planning fails

Understanding why most attempts at educational reform fail goes far beyond the identification of specific technical problems such as lack of good materials, ineffective in-service training, or minimal administrative support. In more fundamental terms, educational change fails partly because of the assumptions of planners and partly because some "problems" are inherently unsolvable. These two issues are explored in the next two subsections.

### Faulty assumptions and ways of thinking about change

In a word, the assumptions of policy-makers are frequently *hyperrational* (Wise, 1977, 1979). One of the initial sources of the problem is the commitment of reformers to see a particular desired change implemented. Commitment to *what should be changed* often varies inversely with knowledge about *how to work through a process of change*. In fact, as I shall claim later, strong commitment to a particular change may be a barrier to setting up an effective process of change, and in any case they are two quite distinct aspects of social change.[1] The adage "Where there's a will there's a way" is definitely not an apt one for the planning of educational change. There is an abundance of wills, but they are *in* the way rather than pointing to the way.

Lighthall's (1973) incisive critique of Smith and Keith's (1971) famous case study of the failure of a new open-concept elementary school provides strong support for the hypothesis that leadership commitment to a particular version of a change is negatively related to ability to implement it. Lighthall states, as I do throughout this book, that educational change is a process of coming to grips with the *multiple* realities of people who are the main participants in implementing change. The leader who presupposes what the change should be and acts in ways which preclude others' realities is bound to fail. Lighthall describes Superintendent Spanman's first speech to the Kensington school faculty:

Spanman's visit to Kensington School was to make a "presentation" to the twenty-one member faculty. It was not for the purpose of discussing with them their joint problems of creating a whole new kind of education. His purpose was to express to the faculty parts of his reality; it was not to exchange his for theirs. Inasmuch as it was the faculty who were to carry the educational goals and images of his reality into action, that is to make much of his reality their realities too, and inasmuch as no person responds to realities other than his own, Spanman's selection of a one-way form of communication was self-defeating. In order for his reality to become part of theirs he would have to have made part of theirs his. (p. 263)

Innovators who are unable to alter their realities of change through exchange with would-be implementers can be as authoritarian as the staunchest defenders of the status quo. This is not to say that innovators should not have deep convictions about the need for reform or should be prepared to abandon their ideas at the first sign of opposition. It is to say that, for reasons which should be very clear from chapters 2 to 5, innovators need to be open to the realities of others: sometimes because the ideas of others will lead to alterations for the better in the direction of change, and sometimes because the others' realities will expose the problems of implementation which must be addressed and at the very least will indicate where one should start.

Lighthall clearly documents how the superintendent and principal at Kensington continually imposed only their own realities and how their stance led in a relatively short time to disastrous results. Lighthall observed:

The tendency is widespread for problem solvers to try to jump from their private plans to public implementation of these plans without going through the [number of realities] necessary to fashion them in accordance with problems felt by the adult humans whose energy and intelligence are needed to implement the plans. (p. 282)

---

1 This point is somewhat overstated in order to emphasize that zealous commitment to a change is not sufficient, and may get in the way if it results in impatience, failure to listen, etc. A certain amount of vision is, of course, required to provide the clarity and energy for promoting specific changes. A more balanced summary of the basic point is that promoters of change need to be committed to the change *process* as well as to the change.

Sarason (1971, p. 29) states it another way: "An understandable but unfortunate way of thinking confuses the power (in a legal or organizational chart sense) to effect change with the processes of change." In short, one of the basic reasons why planning fails is that planners or decision-makers of change are unaware of the situations which potential implementers are facing. They introduce changes without providing a means to identify and confront the situational constraints, and without attempting to understand the values, ideas, and experiences of those who are essential for implementing any changes.

But what is wrong with having a strong belief that a certain aspect of schooling should be changed? Is it not appropriately rational to know that a given change is necessary, and to make it policy, if one is in a position to do so? Aside from the fact that many new programs do not arise from sound considerations (chapters 2 and 4), there are other more serious problems. The first problem is that there are many competing versions of what should be done, with each set of proponents equally convinced that their version is the right one. Forceful argument and even the power to make decisions do not at all address questions related to the process of implementation. The fallacy of rationalism is the assumption that the social world can be altered by seemingly logical argument.[2] Sarason comments on the experiences of social scientists when they attempt to apply their knowledge to social action:

The social scientists who entered the world of social action after World War II, armed with their theories and scientifically tested knowledge, found a world that would not bend to their paradigms. They had entered a world governed by values, not facts, where persuasion and power were in the service of different definitions of age old questions .... Many social scientists reacted either with petulance or bewilderment. They had not been content to study and explain the social world; they had wanted to change it. They fared poorly. (1978, p. 370)

Wise (1977) also describes several examples of excessive rationalization, as when educational outcomes are thoroughly prescribed (as in competency-based education) without any feasible plan of how to achieve them. Wise characterizes the behavior of some policy-makers as wishful thinking:

When policy makers require by law that schools achieve a goal which in the past they have not achieved, they may be engaged in wishful thinking. Here policy makers behave as though their desires concerning what a school system should accomplish, will, in fact, be accomplished if the policy makers simply decree it. (p. 45)

Wise goes on to argue that even if rational theories of education were better developed—with goals clearly stated, means of implementation set out, evaluation procedures stated—they would not have much of an impact, because schools, like any social organization, do not operate in a rational vacuum. Some may say that they should, but Wise's point is that they do not, and wishing them to do so shows a misunderstanding of the existing culture of the school (see Sarason, 1971; Lortie, 1975).[3]

---

2 As George Bernard Shaw observed: "Reformers have the idea that change can be achieved by brute sanity."
3 The question of what is rational is too complicated to discuss in detail. My point is that focusing on the technical rationality of a change (goals, means, evidence) is not sufficient. We must also attend to the personal and social conditions of change. Indeed, it is eminently irrational to ignore these conditions. Moreover, these social conditions are frequently "rationally" predictable if we take an implementation perspective.

The other faulty approach alluded to above is that planners (whether they be policy-makers or developers of innovations) have not been sensitive to the need for a theory of *changing*. We could have at our disposal the best expert in the world in the field of reading—one who is clear about the goals of reading and how to teach to achieve them. We can leave aside the fact that we do not have enough such experts to go around, and the fact that different teaching strategies will be needed in different classrooms. These problems notwithstanding, our expert would fail, if he or she did not possess knowledge and theory about the process of social change—knowledge which is entirely independent of his or her curriculum expertise. More specifically, effective educational planners and policy-makers have to combine some expertise and knowledge about the direction or nature of change with an understanding of and an ability to deal with the factors in action which characterize the processes of adoption (chapter 4) and implementation (chapter 5).

## Unsolvable problems

More disturbing is the conclusion reached by several people who have attempted to understand or combine theory and practice in their daily work: that some problems are so complex that in the final analysis and final action they are simply not amenable to solution.[4] This is not to say that our efforts to solve them cannot be improved. But let us admit the hypothetical possibility that some social problems in a complex diverse society contain innumerable interacting "causes" which cannot be fully understood. Nor can we necessarily change those factors which we do understand as causes.[5]

Wise refers to the ways in which statements of goals for education frequently ignore this more basic question of whether the goals can be attained:

To create goals for education is to will that something occur. But goals, in the absence of a theory of how to achieve them, are mere wishful thinking. If there is no reason to believe a goal is attainable—as perhaps evidenced by the fact that it has never been attained—then a rational planning model may not result in goal attainment. (1977, p. 48)

Social science is not natural science. As sophisticated and impressive as natural science has become in regard to some problems, it is not dealing with objects which have hidden motivations and diverse values which are constantly being activated and frequently change in unpredictable ways. It *is* easier to put a person on the moon than to attain the goal of raising reading levels across the country, because the factors keeping reading at its current levels are innumerable, different in different situations, constantly changing, and not conducive to altering on any wide scale. In solving educational problems, it is not just the number of factors to be understood but the reality that these factors sometimes change during the process: for example, people's attitudes change. Sarason reviews the expectation for social science:

Just as the natural sciences had developed laws about the nonhuman world, the social sciences would seek the laws of human society, not only for the purposes of

---

4 See Lindblom and Cohen (1979); Schon (1971); Sarason (1978); Sieber (1979).
5 Further, there may be such an overload of problems that it is not possible to solve very many of them with the time, energy, and resources at our disposal.

explaining the workings of society but for controlling it. They would be the embodi-ment of Plato's philosopher-kings. Apparently, they were not impressed with the fact that Plato saw the problems of social living as so difficult to understand and cope with, requiring of philosopher-kings such a fantastic depth of learning and wisdom that one could not entrust social responsibility to them until they were well along in years. (1978, p. 375)

Of course, Plato's solution was a "theory of change" which claimed that the world would be better off *if* we could develop and install philosopher-rulers with certain characteristics. It was not a theory of *how* to arrive at and maintain such a state.

Lindblom (1959) also claims that it is patently impossible to manage social action by analyzing all possible alternatives and their consequences:

Although such an approach can be described, it cannot be practical except for rela-tively simple problems and even then only in a somewhat modified form. It assumes intellectual capacities and sources of information that men simply do not possess, and it is even more absurd as an approach to policy when the time and money that can be allocated to a policy problem is limited, as is always the case. (p. 156)

There are two issues running through the above comments. The first is that with complex social problems the total number of variables (and their inter-active, changing nature) is so large that it is logistically infeasible to obtain all the necessary information, and cognitively impossible for individuals to com-prehend the total picture even if the information is available (see Schon, 1971, p. 215).[6] The second is that even if some experts were able to comprehend the total picture themselves, our theories and experiences with meaning and implementation suggest that they would have a devil of a time getting others to act on their knowledge—partly because others will not easily understand the complex knowledge, and partly because the process of implementation contains so many barriers which have nothing to do with the quality of knowledge avail-able.

In sum, to return to the opening paragraph of this section, planning fails partly because of the assumptions of planners (policy-makers, developers) and partly because the problems may not be solvable. In a perverted twist of Greek mythology the hubris of the change agent becomes the nemesis of the imple-menters and others affected by new programs. The first form of hubris occurs when policy-makers assume that the solutions that they have come to adopt are unquestionably the right ones. We have seen that those solutions are bound to be questioned on grounds of competing values or technical soundness.

The second and related form of hubris, which compounds the problem, occurs when planners of change introduce new programs in ways which ignore the factors associated with the process of implementation—factors which are only partly controllable, but which are guaranteed to be out of control if ignored. The more the planners are committed to a particular change, the *less* effective they will be in getting others to implement it if their commitment represents an unyielding or impatient stance in the face of ineluctable problems of implementation. Commitment to a particular program makes it less likely that they will set up the necessary time-consuming procedures for implementa-

---

6 It is also the case that the "right combination" of variables has not been vigorously addressed—for example, the factors affecting implementation in chapter 5.

tion, less likely that they will be open to the transformation of their cherished program and tolerant of the delays which will inevitably occur when other people begin to work with it. If we react to delays and transformations by assuming that they arise from the incompetence or bullheadedness of those implementing the program, we will add one more major barrier to the considerable number already operating. The solution is not to be less committed to what we perceive as needed reforms, but to be more sensitive to the possibility that our version of the change may not be the fully correct one, and to recognize that having good ideas may be less than half the battle (compared to establishing a process which will allow us to use the ideas).

# Success is possible

Recognizing the limitations of planning is not the same thing as concluding that effective change is unattainable. But in order to conclude that planned educational change is possible, it would not be sufficient to locate situations where change seems to be working. We would need to find examples where a setting has been *deliberately transformed* from a previous state to a new one which represents clear *improvement* on some *criteria*. We need to know about the causes and dynamics of how change occurs.

There are several good examples of how school districts radically transformed and improved the quality of education through a process of deliberate change. Berman, McLaughlin, et al.'s (1979) description of Lakeville district (pseudonym) represents a concise but comprehensive account of how major changes transpired over a several-year period. Among the reasons: hiring a new superintendent, creating a new role for central district personnel, transferring school principals and establishing new expectations and training for the role of principals, creating incentives and opportunities for teachers to obtain resources for changes which they proposed, establishing a teachers' center and other activities to stimulate teacher interaction and professional development, obtaining added resources through federal innovative programs. Adam's County District 12 in Colorado underwent a similar process during the 1970s (Fullan, Miles, & Taylor, 1978, vol. IV). The descriptions in chapter 10 of Jefferson County in Colorado and Kamloops in British Columbia also show how central administrators can move toward improving the leadership roles of principals, professional development programs for teachers, and the overall instructional system in district schools. The large-scale DESSI (Crandall et al., forthcoming) and RDU (Louis & Rosenblum, 1981) research studies on implementation found numerous examples of successful change efforts. (See Appendix.)

A second area of success can be found in some of the Follow Through programs (Appendix; see Rhine, 1981; Hodges et al., 1980). While the evaluation of Follow Through models has been very controversial, there are a number of successes, all the more impressive because the programs deal exclusively with disadvantaged children and their parents. Stallings (1979, p. 175) summarizes the reasons why Follow Through training has been more successful than other forms of staff development: it is continuous and developmental; it is concrete, relevant, and keyed to specific needs; it is integrated with processes of monitoring, evaluation, and creation of materials; it is designed to change the way people relate to each other and work together; it uses demonstration, observation, and practice. Using the same principles, and adding an emphasis on training teachers to train other teachers, Stallings (1981) documents how the difficult problem of improving reading levels in secondary schools can be addressed with considerable success. The Direct Instruction Follow Through program (one of twenty-two programs) seems to have been frequently successful even in cases where the start-up was botched and teachers initially resistant (Emrick & Peterson, 1980). The reasons for success: explicitly structured program and procedures, and intensive follow-up support, training, etc.[7]

The Urban/Rural School Development project in California is a federally sponsored program to involve community members and school staff from 25 extremely poor neighborhoods in equal decision-making focused on the use of staff development to improve the quality of education. Joyce (1978) describes how and why it was successful: a collaborative identification of needs and on-site, hands-on, in-service experiences which were integrated with the teachers' daily job.

The school effectiveness research shows why some individual schools are quite successful in the face of some of the most intransigent educational problems. This research demonstrates that schools and classrooms have a positive impact on student learning in situations where (1) there is strong program leadership in the school on the part of the principal; (2) administrators and teachers make instruction a high priority and there is a high proportion of "time on task" by students; (3) administrators and teachers expect (believe) that virtually all children can improve their achievement; (4) the school's atmosphere or climate is orderly and supportive of instructional emphases; and (5) there is a means to monitor pupil progress through diagnostic data collection and use of data for instructional improvement (Edmonds, 1979; Denham & Lieberman, 1980; Lezotte et al., 1980; see also D'Amico, 1980). There is also a growing body of research which indicates that programs for parents can be implemented and can produce significant results (see chapter 12 for a review).

The point of all this is that successful change is possible in the real world, even under difficult conditions. And many of the reasons for the achievements can be pinpointed. By and large, the reasons for success relate to the fifteen factors analyzed in the previous chapter. I am not by any means implying that these factors can be inserted like pieces in a puzzle. However, there are classrooms, schools, communities, and districts which have altered the conditions for change in more favorable, workable directions. Not every situation is alterable, especially at certain periods of time; but it is a good bet that many situations are amenable to constructive change.

The central, practical question is how best to plan for and cope with change in settings which are not now enjoying success. This takes us into the vicissitudes of a theory of changing and contingency theories in which improvement rather than resolution is the name of the game.

---

7 It should go without saying that I am not advocating particular programs. I am less interested in the programs than in the underlying common reasons for their success. For any given program, value and ideological issues would have to be considered in relation to the content of the objectives and methods of implementation. (On the Direct Instruction model see Bereiter and Kurland, 1981; Gersten et al., 1981; Rhine, 1981.)

# Planning and coping

*Many have dreamed up republics and principalities which
have never in truth been known to exist; the gulf between
how one should live and how one does live is so wide that a
man who neglects what is actually done for what should be
done paves the way to self-destruction rather than self-
preservation.*

— *Machiavelli,* The Prince *(1514)*

We have come to the most difficult problem of all. When all is said, what can we
actually do to plan for and to cope with educational change? This question is
pursued in the following subsections.[8] First, I introduce the topic by indicating
some of the basic issues and by noting that advice will have to vary according to
the different situations in which we find ourselves. Second, I provide some
advice for those who find that they are forced to respond to and cope with
change introduced by others. Third, the bulk of the section is addressed to the
question of how to plan and implement change more effectively. Three interrelated sets of issues are investigated: What assumptions about change should
we know? What knowledge and skills will be necessary? What guidelines for
action can be formulated?

Change is full of paradoxes. Being deeply committed to a particular change in
itself provides no guidelines for attaining it, and may blind us to the realities of
others which would be necessary for transforming and implementing the
change effectively. Having no vision at all is what makes for educational band-
wagons. In the final analysis, either we have to give up and admit that effective
educational change is impossible, or we have to take our best knowledge and
attempt to improve our efforts. We do possess much knowledge which could
make improvement possible. Whether this knowledge gets used is itself a problem of change, part of the infinite regression which, once we have gained some
knowledge of the process of change, leads us to ask how do we get that
knowledge—of the process of change—used or implemented.

A framework for planning and/or coping with educational change has been
implicit throughout this book. It does not lead to an optimistic scenario,
because there are too many deep-rooted factors keeping things the way they
are. I do not think that a detailed technical treatment on how to plan for change
is the most profitable route to take, although such a treatment may have some
benefit.[9] The most beneficial approach consists in our being able to understand
the process of change, locate our place in it, and act by influencing those factors
which are changeable and by minimizing the power of those which are not. All
of this requires a way of thinking about educational change which has not been
characteristic of either planners or victims of past change efforts.

---

8 This section contains an overview of the assumptions, elements, and guidelines for action.
Additional specific implications for particular roles and agencies (teacher, principal, superintendent, federal or state/provincial agencies, etc.) are left for the appropriate chapters in Parts II
and III.
9 See, for example, Zaltman et al. (1977); Rothman et al. (1976); Havelock (1973).

Figure 3    Change Situations According to Authority Position
             and Relation to the Change Effort

Authority position

|  | | YES | NO |
|---|---|---|---|
| Relation to change effort | Initiator or promoter | I<br>Planner<br>(e.g., policy-maker) | II<br>Planner<br>(e.g., developer) |
| | Recipient or responder | III<br>Coper<br>(e.g., principal) | IV<br>Coper<br>(e.g., teacher) |

In general, there are four logical types of change situations we could face as individuals. These are depicted in figure 3. There are many different specific roles even within a single cell which cannot be delineated here, but people generally find themselves in one of the four situations depending on whether they are initiating/promoting a change or are on the receiving end and whether or not they are in authority positions. I start with coping or being on the receiving end of change (cells III and IV).

## Coping with change

Those in situations of having to respond to a particular change should assume neither that it is beneficial nor that it is useless; that much is clear from the previous analysis. The major initial stance should involve *critical assessment* of whether the change is desirable in relation to certain goals and whether it is "implementable." In brief, assess whether it is worth the effort, because it will be an effort if it is at all worthwhile. Several criteria would be applied. Does the change address an unmet need? Is it a priority in relation to other unmet needs? Are there adequate (not to say optimal) resources committed to support implementation (technical assistance, leadership support, etc.)? If the conditions are reasonably favorable, knowledge of the change process outlined in previous chapters could be used to advantage: for example, push for technical assistance, opportunities for interaction among teachers, and so on. If the conditions are not favorable or cannot be made to be favorable, the best coping strategy consists of knowing enough about the process of change so that we can understand why it doesn't work, and therefore not blame ourselves, and/or we can gain solace by realizing that most other people are in the same situation of non-implementation. We can also realize that implementation, in any case, cannot be easily monitored; for most educational changes it is quite sufficient to *appear* to be implementing the change such as by using some of the materials. In sum, the problem is one of developing enough meaning vis-à-vis the change so that we are in a position to implement it effectively or reject it as the case may be.

Those in authority positions who are confronted with unwanted change (cell III in figure 3) will have to develop different coping mechanisms from those in non-authority positions (cell IV). For the reader who thinks that resisting change represents irresponsible obstinacy, it is worth repeating that non-implementable programs probably do more harm than good when they are attempted. The most responsible action may be to reject certain innovations which are bound to fail and to work earnestly at those which have a chance to succeed.[10] Besides, in some situations resistance may be the only way to maintain sanity and avoid complete cynicism. In the search for meaning in a particular imposed change situation, we may conclude that there is no meaning, or that the problem being addressed is only one (and not the most important or strategic) of many problems which should be confronted. The basic guideline is to work at fewer innovations, but do them better—the reason being that it is probably not desirable, certainly not humanly possible, to implement all the changes expected, given what we know about the meaning, time, and energy required for effective implementation.

We should feel especially sorry for those in authority positions (middle management in district offices, principals, intermediate government personnel in provincial and state regional offices) who are responsible for seeing to implementation but do not want or do not understand the change—either because the change has not been sufficiently developed (and is literally not understandable) or because they themselves have not been involved in deciding on the change or have not received adequate orientation or training. The psychiatrist Ronald Laing captures this situation in what he refers to as a "knot":

> There is something I don't know
>     that I am supposed to know.
> I don't know what it is I don't know,
>     and yet am supposed to know,
> And I feel I look stupid
>     if I seem both not to know it
>     and not know *what* it is I don't know.
> Therefore, I pretend I know it.
>     This is nerve-wracking since I don't
>     know what I must pretend to know.
> Therefore, I pretend I know everything.

> — R.D. Laing, "Knots" (1970)

A ridiculous stance to be sure, as painful as it is unsuccessful.[11] Teachers know when a change is being introduced by or supported by someone who does not believe in it or understand it. Yet this is the position in which many intermediate managers find themselves, or allow themselves to be. Those in authority

---

10 There are those who will say that this advice gives a license to anyone who wants to reject a change even though the change might be necessary to benefit, for example, a disadvantaged group. This may be the case in a particular instance. But let us remember two things. First, many inappropriate and/or insufficiently developed changes have been introduced in the last fifteen years which should have been rejected or delayed. Second, promoters of change also will receive guidelines (indeed, quite elaborate ones in the next subsection). Unless we assume that all change being promoted is good, it would be myopic to think that only the promoters need advice.

11 It can, of course, be successful in the sense of maintaining the status quo. Depending on one's capacity for self-deception, it can be more or less painful as well. It is also a very general phenomenon. Teachers pretend they know more than they do with students and with parents; university professors with students, colleagues, and the public; men with women; etc.

have a need for meaning too, if for no other reason than change will be unsuccessful if they cannot convey their meaning of the change to others.

## Planning and implementing change

The implications for those interested in planning and implementing educational change (cells I and II in figure 3) are very important, because we would all be better off if changes were introduced more effectively. It is useful to consider these implications according to three interrelated sets of issues: What *assumptions* about change should we note? What *knowledge and skills* will be necessary? What *guidelines for action* can be derived?[12]

### Assumptions about change

The assumptions we make about change are powerful and frequently unconscious sources of actions. When we begin to understand what change is as people experience it, we begin also to see clearly that assumptions made by planners of change are extremely important determinants of whether the realities of implementation get confronted or ignored. The analysis of change carried out so far leads me to identify ten "do" and "don't" assumptions as basic to a successful approach to educational change:[13]

1 Do not assume that your version of what the change should be is the one that should or could be implemented. On the contrary, assume that one of the main purposes of the process of implementation is to *exchange your reality* of what should be through interaction with implementers and others concerned. Stated another way, assume that successful implementation consists of some transformation or continual development of initial ideas. (Particularly good discussions of the need for this assumption and the folly of ignoring it are contained in Bailey, 1975; Lighthall, 1973; Marris, 1975, ch. XVIII; Schon, 1971, ch. 5.)
2 Assume that any significant innovation, if it is to result in change, requires individual implementers to work out their own meaning. Significant change involves a certain amount of ambiguity, ambivalence, and uncertainty for the individual about the meaning of the change. Thus, effective implementation is a *process of clarification*.
3 Assume that conflict and disagreement are not only inevitable but fundamental to successful change. Since any group of people possess multiple realities, any collective change attempt will necessarily involve conflict.
4 Assume that people need pressure to change (even in directions which they desire), but it will only be effective under conditions which allow them to react, to form their own position, to interact with other implementers, to obtain technical assistance, etc. Unless people are going to be replaced with others who have different desired characteristics, resocialization is at the heart of change.
5 Assume that effective change takes time. It is a process of "development in use." Unrealistic or undefined time-lines fail to recognize that implementation occurs developmentally. Expect significant change to take a minimum of two or three years.[14]

---

12 I will not address issues of how to get changes "adopted." The focus is on what it means to plan for effective "use."

13 For a somewhat similar set of assumptions applied to planning for school system curriculum implementation, see Fullan and Park (1981, pp. 24–26).

14 The time, of course, varies with the complexity of the change and the size of the system in question. The DESSI study found that teachers can reach routine levels of use of an innovation in a shorter period (such as within one school year), with conceptual integration taking longer (Crandall et al., forthcoming). This evidence should remind us that change is incremental—progress can start very early and develop over time.

6 Do not assume that the reason for lack of implementation is outright rejection of the values embodied in the change, or hard-core resistance to all change. Assume that there are a number of possible reasons: value rejection, inadequate resources to support implementation, insufficient time elapsed.

7 Do not expect all or even most people or groups to change. The complexity of change is such that it is totally impossible to bring about widespread reform in any large social system. Progress occurs when we take steps (e.g., by following the assumptions listed here) which *increase* the number of people affected. Our reach should exceed our grasp, but not by such a margin that we fall flat on our face. Instead of being discouraged by all that remains to be done, be encouraged by what has been accomplished by way of improvement resulting from your actions.

8 Assume that you will need a *plan* which is based on the above assumptions and which addresses the factors known to affect implementation (see the section below on guidelines for action). Knowledge of the change process is essential. Careful planning can bring about significant change on a fairly wide scale over a period of two or three years (see chapter 10).

9 Assume that no amount of knowledge will ever make it totally clear what action should be taken. Action decisions are a combination of valid knowledge, political considerations, on-the-spot decisions, and intuition. Better knowledge of the change process will improve the mix of resources on which we draw, but it will never and should never represent the sole basis for decisions.[15]

10 Assume that change is a frustrating, discouraging business. If all or some of the above assumptions cannot be made (a distinct possibility in some situations for some changes), do not expect significant change *as far as implementation is concerned*.[16]

### Knowledge and skills

Assumptions, whether consciously or unconsciously held, comprise our philosophy of change. The realization of change is furthered (or not) according to the knowledge and skills of those leading or managing change. It would be onerous and none too productive to attempt an inventory of all of the leadership and change agent skills which might be needed (see Havelock, 1973; Lippitt & Lippitt, 1979; Katz & Kahn, 1978, ch. 16). It is possible, however, to clarify the types of knowledge and skills required, and to classify them in three categories: (1) technical expertise related to *substantive content* area, (2) *interpersonal* skills, and (3) conceptual and technical skills pertaining to *planning and implementation*.

Technical knowledge and skills in the substantive area of the change require little elaboration. Those interested in promoting a given change should possess

---

15 See especially Lindblom and Cohen (1979) and Lindblom (1959). Again the issue is that the complexity (e.g., the number of variables and contingencies) is so great that complete authoritative knowledge is a myth. We can increase the amount of good knowledge, but we will always have to rely on what Lindblom and Cohen call "ordinary knowledge" which comes through experience, interaction, and so on. It is not so much that the latter type of knowledge inevitably gets in the way, but that it is vital to making effective decisions. (See also Corcoran, 1982.)
16 Recall that I am concerned with the question of whether new changes happen *in practice*. For certain types of reform which will be strongly resisted by some groups (e.g., desegregation and other issues which involve hard-core value conflict), the best long-term strategy may be to concentrate in the short run on getting new legislation adopted, and monitored. This will not represent implementation in the sense that implementers will pursue the intended outcomes of the policy, but it may be the best that can be done. These types of changes often take decades before real implementation becomes even partially evident. The assumptions represent a guide for action when there is some possibility of change.

some technical understanding of what the change is and how to use it.[17] Otherwise, they would not be able to support its use effectively. (Indeed, lack of such knowledge raises the question whether they should be supporting it in the first place.)

Interpersonal or human relations skills have also been frequently acknowledged as essential. The abilities to communicate, listen, motivate, gain trust, and the like are all critical interpersonal skills necessary for effective leadership for change. So much has been written about these and other interpersonal skills that I need not repeat it here (see, e.g., Lippitt & Lippitt, 1978).

On the other hand, and generally not adequately recognized, are the technical and conceptual knowledge and skills which relate to the ability to comprehend and organize the process of educational change and our own and others' places in it. This is unfortunate, for our cognitive ability to *conceptualize, understand, and plan the social processes* of educational change represents the most comprehensive and generative resource for dealing with change. In order to engage in successful change, we need to develop a way of thinking about change based on a thorough understanding of the processes analyzed in chapters 4 and 5.

It can also be seen that such knowledge, once obtained, is far more powerful as a resource than a memorized list of specific steps that we should follow. For this reason I consider Sarason's (1971, 1982) difficult-to-grasp treatment of educational change in terms of practical implications much more important than Zaltman et al.'s (1977) seemingly more comprehensive formulation of the steps. Sarason talks about the importance of understanding the culture of the school, people's relationship to the change process, the murky areas of values and motivations, and the ubiquitous problems of communication. (See also Miles's 1980 discussion of eight basic dilemmas in planning.) Zaltman et al. provide a more bloodless step-by-step set of recommendations. But change is never a wholly rational process. The fundamental goal for planners in my view is to achieve a feel for the change process and the people in it, which entails a blend of research knowledge and experiential knowledge. Lindblom and Cohen (1980) make a similar and more complete argument for the necessity of combining knowledge from "professional inquiry" with what they call "ordinary knowledge." Both types of knowledge are necessary for solving problems.

In other words, change is not a fully predictable process. The answer is found not by seeking ready-made guidelines, but by struggling to understand and modify events and processes which are intrinsically complicated, difficult to pin down, and ever changing. Sarason explains that change agents do not confront their own conceptions of how to go about change, and thus do not learn to improve their approaches:

I confess that I find it somewhat amusing to observe how much thought is given to developing vehicles for changing target groups and how little thought is given to vehicles that protect the agent of change from not changing in his understanding of and approach to that particular instance of change. (1971, p. 217)

---

17 The degree of technical knowledge and skill required will vary by role. Curriculum consultants will need more detailed knowledge than the superintendent of schools.

The conceptual factor, far from being an abstract exercise in theorizing, represents a way of thinking about the process of change which in a practical way helps us plan and coordinate an approach to change. It helps us identify which factors need to be addressed. It helps us recognize that concentrating on one or two sets of factors while neglecting others is self-defeating. It provides ideas for formulating a "plan" designed to address and review how these factors are operating in a given instance. I have frequently stated that good ideas, while necessary, are not sufficient for influencing others to change. To the extent that good ideas or visions of change are not combined with equally good conceptualizations of the process of change, the ideas will be wasted. Just as meaning about the substance of change is necessary, so is the development of a sense of meaning and competence about how best to approach it.

It should be evident that *all three* sets of skills are essential. Most of us could probably identify change projects in which leaders possessed only one or two areas of skills—the curriculum consultant who is a renowned expert. in the subject area but a disaster interpersonally and a failure in conceptualizing/planning on any scale which would allow work with larger numbers of people; the principal who is great with people but has few ideas when it comes to deciding on particular educational programs; the superintendent who endorses a certain change but has little knowledge of the change process and thus cannot anticipate what might be needed to plan for and support implementation.

If we accept the premise that conceptual and technical planning knowledge and skills are essential to promoting effective educational change, two other issues immediately arise. First, how can we be sure that our conceptualizations are accurate and complete? Second, if we agree that better conceptualizations and skills are needed in planning for implementation, how can they be nurtured? That is, the need is not just to identify better conceptions and skills but to go about *changing* people's conceptions and skills. In answer to the first question, a great deal of knowledge has been developed during the 1970s. The conceptualization of change in this book is based on a large body of fairly consistent research evidence and descriptions of how change works. As such, it can contribute substantially to the conceptual knowledge we need to increase our effectiveness as participants in change.

The second question brings us back to the problem of regression. A "theory of change" says that people *should* be able to conceptualize the change process in order to be more effective. A "theory of changing" questions whether it is possible to alter (i.e., to increase) people's conceptual and organizational abilities merely by telling them what the concepts should be. Just as implementing the conceptual or philosophical basis for curriculum changes (see chapter 3) is one of the most difficult dimensions of change to achieve, so is implementing new conceptions and beliefs among leaders and other participants concerning how to plan for and approach change. Some of the ways in which this might be attempted include (1) hiring or promoting new leaders who possess these conceptual abilities, and who will in turn develop them in others; (2) adding training in the processes of implementation to in-service workshops and other project training activities directed at program change; (3) adding courses in the theory of practice of change to pre-service programs for teachers, principals, and other administrators; (4) carrying out action-oriented research as a collaboration between researchers interested in the process of change and practitioners interested in promoting and evaluating specific change projects; and (5) encouraging practitioners to reflect on their experiences by making available to them research knowledge on the change process. The most fundamental problem, of course, is that administrators and other planners of change frequently do not have adequate formal or on-the-job preparation to be change leaders (see chapter 14).[18]

It should be clear that I am not advocating conceptual thinking for the sake of theoretical elegance. Conceptualization must be integrated with the appropriate technical steps and human relations processes if it is to be useful; that is, it must be grounded in actual change events. Practical conceptual formulations can only be developed through experience *and* reflection. The ever-elusive nature of this process is described by Schon:

> The learning agent must be able to synthesize theory, to formulate new projective models out of his experience of the situation, while he is in the situation. He cannot operate in an "after-the-fact" mode, taking as given or as *a priori* applicable, theory which is already formulated. And as often as not, his projective methods come apart. He must be willing for them to come apart, and to synthesize new theory in process as the old explodes or decays. (1971, pp. 235–36)

Implicit in Schon's observations is that social change should never be treated solely as a rational, predictable phenomenon. Intuition, learning from experience, formulation and reformulation, getting something to work without necessarily knowing why it works — all have their place in planning and coping with change.

In summary, leaders of educational change to be effective must possess all three types of knowledge and skills, and use them in a way that allows learning from specific change attempts. Preoccupation with the content of proposed changes has resulted in neglect of the interpersonal and conceptual/organizational aspects of planning for change, which turn out to be the most potent barriers to progress. The most difficult factors also tend to be the most neglected, as Lindblom and Cohen remind us:

> Practitioners of PSI [Professional Social Inquiry] often incorrectly assume that policy makers want help from PSI on the substance of policy under their jurisdiction. A study of roughly a hundred different problems facing thirty policy makers disclosed that their PSI needs, in their own eyes, converged on problems in organization and interpersonal relations rather than on the substance of policy. (1979, p. 55)

In short, knowledge and skills about how to plan for implementation are just as needed as ideas about the content of reform.

## Guidelines for action:
## theories of changing and contingencies

In the final analysis, the bottom line for many people is what can we actually do to introduce change more effectively. Basically, this involves attempting to incorporate the assumptions and knowledge and skills about change into our ways of thinking and acting. The specifics present us with some problems, since

---

18 Argyris and Schon (1974) analyze just how fundamental the problem is. Professionals' "theories in use" are often discrepant from their "espoused theories"; and the discrepancy is frequently not recognized.

it is difficult to alter the forces of change. Sixteen years ago, Bennis criticized theories of social change in the following words:

> They tend to identify and explain the dynamic interactions of a system without providing a clue pertaining to the identification of strategic leverages for alteration. They are theories suitable only for *observers* of social change, not theories for *participants* in, or practitioners of, social change. They are theories of *change* and not theories of *changing*. (1966, p. 99)

Thus, the practitioner interested in planning and bringing about educational change requires a theory of changing. In the rest of this section, I take up the question of how to approach change in order to influence the direction of events more effectively. Essentially, the process involves being able to identify "strategic leverages for alteration" (i.e., an orientation to changing) and being able to match strategies with situations (i.e., an orientation to contingencies).

### Theories or ideas of changing

Given the number of variables which interact and potentially affect implementation, it would get us into a hopeless quagmire to attempt to spell out all the factors and contingencies which would need to be addressed. It is more fruitful and practical to provide an overview of the possible steps to be taken.

A theory of changing suggests that we determine to what extent factors conducive to implementation can be altered in favorable directions. In chart 2 (chapter 5) fifteen factors affecting change in practice were listed according to four major categories: (1) *characteristics of the change* (need, clarity, complexity, quality of materials); (2) *school system characteristics* (history of change, adoption process, administrative support, staff development approach, timeline and information, and school board/community support); (3) *school traits* (principal involvement, teacher/teacher relations, teacher characteristics); and (4) *extra-local characteristics* (role of government agencies, external assistance). These fifteen factors can be taken as a checklist for analyzing existing change efforts or for planning new ones.[19] To illustrate, let us comment briefly on how factors from each of the four main categories can be used.

Whether or not a potential need is perceived by those who would have to implement a particular change should be tested early in the process. Several different outcomes could arise: (a) the need may be readily confirmed and an agreed-upon plan formulated; (b) the need may be generated through peer influence or other information (e.g., student achievement data); (c) the need may not be confirmed or it may be of low priority compared to other needs. Such a process may or may not operate as a decision-making forum, but it is essential to know what situation is being faced. Situation (c) may lead the proposers of the change to abandon the idea in favor of another one, to redouble efforts, or to adopt a longer-term strategy. The point is that some explicit work should be done on ascertaining and/or creating the felt need for moving in a particular change direction.[20]

---

19 See Fullan and Park (1981) for a number of action-oriented recommendations for planning and implementing change.

20 An alternative strategy is to attempt to create the need during implementation. This may be effective if the participants do not reject the idea at the outset because they have not been consulted in the initial decision. If the decision-makers are in tune with the felt needs of teachers, they may accurately decide on change programs or directions which turn out to be well received.

Whether the district- and school-level factors (categories 2 and 3) can be influenced will depend on several factors. There are three possibilities: (a) we are blessed with favorable existing conditions; (b) we alter the conditions by replacing existing personnel, especially leaders; or (c) we influence existing personnel development through some organizational or staff development program. If condition (a) prevails, it is not a question of changing, since the favorable conditions already exist. Approach (b) represents the most powerful leverage for change, but depends on other conditions. It is a fact that the most successful examples of change occur when leaders are *replaced* with new leaders with different characteristics and a mandate for change. The Lakeville (Berman & McLaughlin, 1979) and Adam's County (Fullan, Miles, & Taylor, 1978) examples referred to earlier involved major changes at the top (new board members, new superintendent, new central office personnel in key coordinatorship roles).

Condition (c) represents the usual situation. It is neither ethically nor practically possible to make wholesale replacements of school personnel. Professional development for existing staff is the only realistic approach when large numbers of principals and teachers are involved. If my analysis is correct, a number of school people (not all) are interested in change, but the conditions do not favor or otherwise facilitate or stimulate constructive change. The best combination seems to occur when there is a new person in the top leadership position (in the district or the school), who then provides the coordination, opportunity, and support for staff development and other activities likely to stimulate implementation of needed programs. Professional development of teachers and administrators, in fact, represents one of the most effective strategies for implementation, if combined with other factors listed in this section. (See chapter 14 for an account of staff development.)

Factors associated with the external environment—category 4—are by definition extremely difficult to influence. For example, political pressures for reform in schools which come from the larger political arenas (states, provinces, the federal level, the media, etc.) will be almost impossible to influence. The best that we can do is take advantage of financial and other resources which these external agencies provide, and attempt to establish a supportive relationship with those agencies with which we have the most contact. Schon suggests other strategies for influencing and coping with those external sources he refers to as "central" (as distinct from local):

Propose what central wants to hear, but do what you want to do. Develop a rhetoric compatible with central policy.

Play funding agencies off against one another.

Seek minimum federal control over the use of money.

Take advantage of the surplus of information about what is going on at the local level, and the high cost of finding out for central.

Bring pressure to bear on the funding agency, exploiting its political insecurities.

Attempt to gain central's commitment over time, so that it develops a heavy investment in the local venture and finds it difficult to back out. (1971, p. 154)

Manipulative, of course—but no more so than what central planners do in figuring out what to do with local systems.

Thus, a theory of changing consists in formulating specific approaches to improving schooling, using our research and practice-based knowledge about what makes for success and failure. Effective approaches to change must include procedures for addressing and coping with issues related to characteristics of the change, the school district, the school, and the broader environment. I have not set out a complete list of procedural steps for two reasons: such a list is already implicit in the fifteen factors and need not be repeated; and specific applications of the ideas must be embedded in—and to an important extent generated by those in—*particular roles in particular situations.*[21] For example, a superintendent interested in stimulating improvements in elementary school science teaching will have to assess and draw on the expertise and commitment of central office staff to assist in developing the direction of the change; directly or indirectly establish orientation programs to involve principals as program facilitators; provide teachers access to resources and assistance and some say in the direction of the change; and so on. The fact that these activities do not constitute a linear sequence of steps—rather, the various factors must be attended to continuously—illustrates the futility of relying too heavily on a step-by-step checklist.

In summary, a theory of changing concentrates on those factors in a situation which are thought to be alterable. The extent to which certain factors cannot be altered is the extent to which we cannot go beyond explaining change and into the realm of bringing it about. We may also be discouraged to realize that identifying seemingly alterable factors is only one layer in the regress of change. For example, if our theory of changing leads us to develop an in-service training plan to change principals' leadership effectiveness, it is only the first layer, since the plan may not work. In other words, the plan itself has to be effectively implemented and have its desired outcome before any progress can be claimed.

It is important to dwell on these subtleties because what appears to be a theory of changing (a theory stating how to go about change) may turn out to be only a theory of what *should* change. In keeping with the theme of this book, a theory of changing should be judged only in terms of whether *it is successfully implemented*—whether it actually alters factors it sets out to change—not for what it claims to be. Otherwise, there is no real difference between those who claim that educational problems would be solved if only schools would adopt this or that *program change*, and those who argue that problems would be solved if only schools would follow this or that *process of change*. Both are engaged in wishful thinking—the former on the substance of change and the latter on the form.

## Theories or ideas of contingencies

Many of those who have been immersed in large-scale change efforts have concluded that it is next to impossible to alter situational characteristics at the district and school level when large numbers of schools and school systems are involved. Contingency theory is an extension of the theory of changing, but

---

21 More targeted guidelines are stated at the end of each chapter in Parts II and III. For a short basic list of procedural steps compatible with the ideas in this section, see Howes and Quinn (1978), who suggest six steps in preparing for change under the category "setting up adequate orientation," and a further six steps for "setting up adequate support networks for implementation."

instead of focusing on changing conditions which might not be changeable (except perhaps through prodigious effort), it suggests that the most effective approach is to use different strategies in different situations. What we do is *contingent* on the characteristics of the change being attempted and the situations at hand. In answer to the question "Where do you start?" Sarason states:

I suggest that where one starts has to be a problem that is presented to and discussed with the target groups—not as a matter of empty courtesy or ritualistic adherence to some vague democratic ethos but because *it gives one a more realistic picture of what one is dealing with. An obvious consequence of this is that in different settings one may very well answer the question of where to start rather differently*, a consequence that those who need to follow a recipe will find unsatisfactory because there is no one place to start. Still another consequence is that one may decide *to start nowhere*, that is, the minimal conditions required for that particular change to take hold, regardless of where one starts, are not present. The reader should note that the decision not to proceed with a particular change, far from being an evasion, forces one to consider, *what other kinds of change have to take place before the minimal conditions can be said to exist*. (1971, pp. 217–18; his italics)

At this general level, a number of implications for planning change can be noted. First, it is clear that it is unrealistic to expect all situations to change. We may, depending on the circumstances, decide to work intensively with those schools or school districts which are interested in the particular change effort.[22] Many federal programs in the United States are based on this approach. It is a testimony to the complexities of implementation that even programs which involve apparently voluntary groups frequently fail. Put another way, even if we work with such groups, we will need most of our skills and knowledge about change in order to be effective. The first possibility, then, suggests that we might as well expend the energy where we will have at least some chance of success.

A second contingency possibility is to encourage different users to select different programs according to their own goals and interests. The Follow Through project is based on such a "planned variation" design. Potential implementers can select among 22 different educational programs, many of which are radically different from each other in philosophy, structure, goal focus, and so on (see Rhine, 1981). Again, it will take much of our best knowledge of change to support effective implementation, even when implementers can choose in this fashion.

A third contingency would involve using quite different approaches depending on the readiness conditions in different settings. For example, the leadership and climate in one school may be so well developed that the provision of adequate resources (curriculum materials, consultants, etc.) will be sufficient; in another school the priority may be to replace the principal; in still another a

---

22 Basically, the strategy is to work only with voluntary populations, since it will be extremely time-consuming to change involuntary ones, and since working effectively with the former probably will take all the time and energy at our disposal. (Recall that effective implementation is extremely difficult, even with districts or schools who volunteer.) It is important to emphasize that this is only one of several possible approaches. It will not be acceptable politically, for example, if the change effort concerns a major problem of equity (e.g., desegregation). In the latter case, in a sense, people are still working at the adoption and early implementation stages. It is considered important enough that longer-term struggles are warranted.

program of leadership and staff development may be the most effective starting point. Educational leaders, of course, make these types of contingency decisions all the time. The suggestion here is that knowledge about the process of change be used more systematically to inform the choices.

Berman (1978, 1980) has developed an initial promising framework along these lines. He suggests that there are at least five major situational parameters which vary and which must be taken into account in designing a change strategy. He states that there are two distinct implementation approaches which could be used depending on the five sets of conditions.[23] The following framework resulted (Berman, 1980, p. 214):

| Situational Parameters | Implementation Approach | |
|---|---|---|
| | **Programmed** | **Adaptive** |
| Scope of change | minor | major |
| Certainty of technology or theory | certain (within risk) | uncertain |
| Conflict over policy's goals and means | low | high |
| Structure of institutional setting | tightly coupled | loosely coupled |
| Stability of environment | stable | unstable |

Berman argues that change situations vary in terms of whether the scope of change is major, whether the theoretical/technical soundness of the idea is established, whether there is serious conflict among potential implementers, whether the institutional setting is loosely or tightly organized and controllable, and whether or not the environment is relatively stable or turbulent. He claims that programmed approaches are more effective under some conditions, while adaptive ones are necessary under other conditions. (See also Berman, 1981.) For example, compare the problem of improving reading skills with that of integrating special education children in regular classrooms. The technology (the programs) for improving reading is relatively well developed and specified, and the goal is almost universally endorsed. By comparison, the proven programs to facilitate mainstreaming are not available, and consensus by no means exists. Contingency theory would suggest quite different approaches in the two cases. In the case of reading, the selection of a program, specific staff development activities, and the like can be established relatively quickly. With mainstreaming a much slower, experimental, developmental strategy would be called for.

Contingency theories of implementation are only at an early stage of development. A word of caution is in order, because they do not have infinite value. The more we attempt to spell out all the details and contingencies pertaining to implementation, the more we become overloaded with complexity and fall into the trap of overrationality. The details of change *are* overwhelming. As before, the only manageable route is to develop a way of thinking about contingencies which can provide a framework and basis for generating ideas about where it might be best to spend our time and energy.

---

23 The guidelines for action discussed in this chapter do not adequately distinguish between programmed and adaptive approaches, because this would get us into too fine detail. This brief illustration of contingency approaches by Berman partly addresses the distinction; but more would have to be done at the level of specific implications.

# The scope of change

Are we better off in the long run if we attempt very small changes, or should we go big in the hope of reaching more people? The reader who by now has concluded that the theory of educational changing is a theory of unanswerable questions will not be too far off the mark.[24] It is a theory of probing and understanding the meaning of multiple dilemmas in attempting to decide what to do. The question of scope is no exception.

Sarason, as usual, identifies many of the underlying issues:

A large percentage of proposals of change are intended to affect all or most of the schools within a system. The assumption seems to be that since the change is considered as an improvement over what exists, it should be spread as wide as possible as soon as possible. The introduction of a new curricula is, of course, a clear example of this. What is so strange here is that those who initiate this degree of change are quite aware of two things: that different schools in the system can be depended on differentially to respond to or implement the proposed change, and that they, the sources, ... do not have the time adequately to oversee this degree of change. What is strange is that awareness of these two factors seems to be unconnected with or to have no effect on thinking about the scope of the change. This is like a psychotherapist who, after listening to a patient present many serious personal problems affecting his life, decides that he will attack, simultaneously, all of these problems even though in another part of his head he is quite aware that the symptoms will not be equally vulnerable to change and that within the time he spends with the patient it will literally be impossible to deal with all of the symptoms. (1971, pp. 213–14)

Several additional points put the problem of scope in perspective. First, in some situations it may be more timely or compatible with our priorities to concentrate on getting a major policy "on the books," leaving questions of implementation until later. In other words, the first priority is adoption, not implementation. Major new legislation or policies directed at important social reforms often fit this mode—for example, new legislation on desegregation, special education, multicultural educational programs, or decision-making councils. There is no answer to the question of whether this is more effective than a more gradual approach to legislation, but it should be recognized that implementation is then an immediate problem.[25] Much social policy legislation is vague on implementation; some vagueness may be essential in order to get the policy accepted, but nonetheless it means that implementation can be easily evaded (see Weatherley & Lipsky, 1975; Williams, 1975; Sarason & Doris, 1979, ch. 19). In the face of major value or power resistance, it is probably strategically more effective in the short run to concentrate our energies on establishing new legislation, hoping that in the long run the pressure of the law and the emergence of new implementers in future years will generate some

---

24 Harry Truman (and later Pierre Trudeau) said, "We need more one-armed economists," because he was frustrated at the advice he kept getting: "on the one hand ... on the other hand." The same can be said about the scope of educational change efforts. No one knows for sure what is best.
25 Sarason and Doris (1979) in commenting on special education legislation warn us: "To interpret a decision ... as a 'victory' is understandable but one should never underestimate how long it can take for the spirit of victory to become appropriately manifested in practice" (p. 358).

results. The only implementation guidelines are to realize that implementation will not be forthcoming in the short run, and to stress the need for specifying implementation criteria and resources (see Bardach, 1978; Elmore, 1980). Many new policies in education are not clear about what implementation would look like, and do not contain reference to planning for the requirements of implementation. In short, those who decide to devote their energies to establishing new policies would be well advised to incorporate more deliberate implementation analysis into their thinking.

Second, it does seem to be the case that the reputation of innovation has suffered badly precisely because grandiose schemes were rampant in the 1960s and early 1970s—open education, large-scale curriculum projects, computer-assisted instruction, and the like (see Silberman, 1970). It is no criticism of the intentions of reformers to observe that faith and optimism in the power of big dreams, new technologies, and large-scale resources have little to do with the likelihood of successful implementation. The number of teachers, parents, and others who have turned against innovation because of negative experiences with previous change attempts is indeed a large price to pay for the wishful thinking of those who wanted to accomplish the big change. (See Smith and Keith's 1971 case study, and Sarason's 1971 discussion of the consequences of non-implemented proposals.)

Third, most change theorists and practitioners agree that significant changes should be attempted, but they should be carried out in a more incremental, developmental way. Smith and Keith (1971) compare the "alternative of grandeur," which was a colossal failure, to the "alternative of gradualism," which might have been attempted at Kensington school. (See also Etzioni, 1966.) The issue is not to eschew large-scale change but to decide whether the problem is important enough, and the resources adequate, to warrant the attempt. In such an attempt, concreteness and incrementalism of implementation are important ingredients.[26] Large plans and vague ideas make a lethal combination.

Significant change can be accomplished by taking a developmental approach, building in more and more components of the change over time. Complex changes can be pursued incrementally by developing one or two steps at a time. Such a strategy is crucial when implementers are faced with major changes (see Huberman's 1981 case study; Crandall et al., forthcoming). The question of how widespread a change effort should be is a difficult one. Dissemination could be made more manageable if we concentrated early efforts on parts of the system (e.g., several schools, several districts) instead of the entire system. Given that universal reform cannot succeed (and may do more harm than good), Sarason wonders: "Why not pick one's spots, learn from the experience, and then take up the tactics of extension? What if the schools that were not to receive service were part of an ongoing group to discuss and evaluate what was going on in the schools receiving service?" (1971, p. 214). Depending on the problem at hand, this approach may not be advisable (for example, in a question of legislative equity); but most field-based researchers now agree that it is essential to concentrate on more manageable portions of the problem

---

26 Van den Berg et al. (1981) contains a very useful discussion of "large scale strategies for supporting complex innovations in schools." Suggestions include materials development, trainer of trainers, peer networking, demonstration sites, technical assistance systems, etc.

and to build in ways of extending these critical efforts. (See especially Rothman et al., 1976, ch. 2, "Promoting an Innovation"; Baldridge, 1975. The relatively successful National Diffusion Network is built on this assumption—see Far West Laboratory, 1976; Crandall et al., forthcoming.)

Even changes which are quite explicit and clear face the problem of scope of coverage when they are attempted with larger numbers than the support system (such as staff development and one-to-one assistance) can handle.

# The problem of change

I am sometimes asked for specific recipes for how to implement particular programs. I usually respond by listing the major things that must be done: opportunity (time) for training and interaction during implementation, good program development or selection, allowance for redefinition of the change, a two- or three-year time perspective, supportive principals, and the like. The response to the list is frequently along the lines that it is impossible to do this or that because of lack of time, lack of resources, and so on. I then say, "Well, don't expect much implementation to occur." Needless to say, this answer is found to be unsatisfactory, but one cannot expect change to come easy or even to be possible in some situations. I say this not because I am a cynic but because it is wrong to let hopes blind us to the actual obstacles to change. If these obstacles are ignored, the experience with implementation can be harmful to the adults and the children directly involved—*more harmful than if nothing had been done*.

Understanding the central importance of "meaning" for those who are implementing change gives us hints about the processes which may be required, and makes sense of the assumptions, knowledge and skills, and guidelines for action formulated above. It also reveals why the usual approaches to change fail. Many of those concerned with educational reform have been preoccupied with developing and advocating the goals of change, as if all that is needed are good intentions. Even good programs are not enough, if it is simply expected that others will easily accept them or could be forced to.

It is easier—more tangible, clear, and satisfying in the short run—to concentrate on *developing* a new program than to enter the conflict-filled, ambiguous, anxious world of seeing what others think of the idea. But what is understandable is not necessarily right. Ideas about meaning, changing, and contingencies help to explain the perils of putting all our marbles into development. Curriculum development over the past fifteen years provides the best examples of developers and planners who lost their marbles. The subtleties of change are once again evidenced when we point out that these efforts failed regardless of whether they were engineered by university professors, federal or state/provincial departments of education, or local teacher committees. The main reason for failure is simple—the developers went through a process of acquiring *their* meaning of the new curriculum. And once it was presented to teachers, there was no provision for allowing them to work out the meaning for themselves of the changes before them. Innovations which have been succeeding have been doing so because they combine good ideas with good implementation support systems.

Planning and coping with change is not peaceful, because we can never let up for long. The implications for agents of change are well stated by Marris:

They must listen as well as explain, continually accommodating their design to other purposes, other kinds of experience, modifying and renegotiating long after they would like to believe that their conception was finished. If they impatiently cut this process short, their reforms are likely to be abortive. (1975, p. 167)

Recognizing the problem of educational change for what it is should help us bring about more effective implementation in some situations. While complex to use skillfully, the planning principles and guidelines contained and implied in Part I reflect more than anything else "organized common sense." Improvements in success rates seem achievable, if by success we mean attaining more and better implementation than in the past and reducing the number of wasted and ill-advised attempts. We should not underestimate the extent to which the latter would represent progress.

Success, however, depends on people. Understanding the orientations and working conditions of the main actors in schools and school systems is a prerequisite for planning and coping with educational change effectively. The chapters in Part II portray the social realities of those most directly involved in attempting to balance stability and change in education in their daily work lives.

# Part II

# Educational Change at the Local Level

# Chapter 7

# The Teacher

*If a new program works teachers get little of the credit;*
*if it fails they get most of the blame.*

— *Anonymous*

Educational change depends on what teachers do and think—it's as simple and as complex as that. It would all be so easy if we could legislate changes in thinking (Sarason, 1971, p. 193). Whether significant educational change is possible is a moot point; easy it certainly isn't.

The quality of working conditions of teachers is fundamentally connected to the chances for success in change. And these conditions have deteriorated steadily over the past two decades. Leaving aside the question of blame, it is a fact that teachers are valued less by the community and the public than they were even a short time ago. Teacher stress and alienation from the profession as discussed later in this chapter appear to be at an all-time high, judging from the increasing demand for workshops on coping with stress and the numbers of teachers leaving or wanting to leave the profession. The range of educational goals and expectations for schools and the transfer of family and societal problems to the school, coupled with the ambivalence of youth about the value of education, present intolerable conditions for sustained educational development and satisfying work experiences (see Kratzmann et al., 1981, and Flanders, 1980). Yet the mental health and attitude of the teacher are absolutely critical to the success of any serious change effort.

If educational change is to happen, it will *require* that teachers understand themselves and be understood by others. As Nisbet (1969) has effectively argued, in order to consider change, we must first understand stability and order. For this reason, I start with a sketch of where teachers are. From there I move to the phenomenon of the introduction of change—in nine cases out of ten a gross mismatch, as far as the world of the teacher is concerned. Third, I focus on the question of whether and in what respects change is indeed needed in the classroom and the school. In the final section of the chapter—"Change is possible"—I make recommendations for how teachers might assess and cope with wanted and unwanted change.

## Where teachers are

It is clearly not possible to describe in a few pages the school lives of two and one half million teachers in diverse settings across North America. Not even a sociologist could do that. However, there has been enough firsthand research over the past ten years to allow for a description of the main themes which appear in the daily work of most teachers.[1] Let me hasten to add that this section says nothing about whether teachers *should* think and act in the way they do, or whether their actions are amenable to change, or should be changed. My first purpose is to describe the existing order of things, as a precondition for understanding why change attempts fail and how they can be improved.

One of the most respected and widely quoted studies of what teachers do and think is the one conducted by Lortie (1975). Lortie based his study on 94 interviews with a stratified sample of elementary and secondary school teachers in the greater Boston area (called the Five Town sample), questionnaires to almost 6000 teachers in Dade County, Florida, and various national and local research studies by others. His findings can be best summarized in point form.

1  Teacher training (see also chapter 14) does not equip teachers for the realities of the classroom. Nor could it be expected to do so in light of the abruptness of the transition. In September, the young teacher (who has typically been a student in June) assumes the same responsibility as the 25-year teacher veteran. For both the beginning and experienced teacher, issues of classroom control and discipline are one of their major preoccupations. Lortie claims that for most teachers there is always a tension between the task-oriented controlling aspect of a teacher role and the relational reaching-the-students aspect.[2]

2  The cellular organization of schools means that teachers struggle with their problems and anxieties privately, spending most of their time physically apart from their colleagues.

3  Partly because of the physical isolation and partly because of norms of not sharing, observing, and discussing each other's work, teachers do not develop a common technical culture. The picture is not one of "colleagues who see themselves as sharing a viable, generalized body of knowledge and practice" (p. 79). In many ways student learning is seen as determined either by factors outside the teachers' control (family background) or by unpredictable and mysterious influences. According to Lortie, the lack of a technical culture, an analytic orientation, and a serious sharing and reflection among teachers creates ambiguity and ad hoc-ness: "The teacher's craft ... is marked by the absence of concrete models for emulation, unclear lines of influence, multiple and controversial criteria, ambiguity about assessment timing, and instability in the product" (p. 136). You are either a good teacher or a bad one; you either have a good day or a bad one. It all depends.

4  When teachers do get help, the most effective source tends to be fellow teachers, and secondly administrators and specialists. Such help is not frequent and is used on a highly selective basis. For example, teachers normally do not relate objectives to principles of instruction and learning outcomes of students. Rather, "they describe

---

1 One caveat is that the vast majority of this research has been at the elementary school level. Many of the findings about classroom concerns of teachers would seem to apply to the secondary level, and there is some indication that this is so (Lortie, 1975). However, we do need more studies of the phenomenologies of secondary school teachers. Lieberman and Miller's (1982) chapter on "life in secondary schools" is a recent valuable contribution.

2 This is not to say that they are incompatible. It is much too large an issue to get into the question of teaching style and effectiveness—formal versus informal, child-centered, etc. Some of these issues are raised in a later section of this chapter in relation to whether change is needed. In the meantime, it does seem safe to conclude that all teachers face the problem of classroom control, and for many it is a constant concern.

the 'tricks of the trade' they picked up—not broader conceptions that underlie class-room practice" (p. 77). As to the frequency of contact, 45% of the Five Town teachers reported "no contact" with other teachers in doing their work, 32% reported "some contact," and 25% "much contact" (p. 193). There is some indication that teachers desire some more contact with fellow teachers—54% said that a good colleague is someone who is willing to share (p. 194). Again, this refers more to 'tricks of the trade' than to underlying principles of teaching and to the relationship of teaching to learning.

5 Effectiveness of teaching is gauged by informal, general observation of students—59% of the teachers in Dade County responded in this vein; the next most frequent choice related to the results of tests—a very distant 13.5%. In short, teachers rely heavily on their own informal observations.

6 The greatest rewards mentioned by teachers were what Lortie labels "psychic rewards"—"the times I reached a student or group of students and they have learned" (p. 104). Over 5000 (86%) of the 5900 teachers in Dade County mentioned this source of gratification. The next most frequent response—respect from others—was selected by 2100, or 37% of the sample.

7 Lortie also found that "striking success with one student" here and one student there was the predominant source of pride (as distinct from raising test scores of the whole group) (p. 121). For secondary school teachers, the success stories often did not become visible until one or more years after graduation when a former student returned to thank a teacher. In comparing single successes with group results, it is revealing that 64% of the Five Town teachers mentioned the former category, and only 29% mentioned the latter, as a major source of satisfaction.

8 One of the predominant feelings that characterize the psychological state of teachers and teaching is *uncertainty*—"teachers are not sure that they can make all students learn" (p. 132), nor are they sure whether they have made any difference at all.[3] Intangibility, complexity, and remoteness of learning outcomes, along with other influences (family, peer, and societal) on the students, make the teacher's assessment of his or her impact on the student endemically uncertain (ch. 6): 64% of the Five Town teachers said that they encountered problems in assessing their work, and two-thirds of the 64% said the problem was serious (p. 142).

9 Of particular relevance to innovation, when Lortie asked teachers how they would choose to spend additional work time, if they received a gift of 10 hours per week, 91% of the almost 6000 teachers in Dade County selected classroom-related activities (more preparation, more teaching with groups of students, more counseling). "It is also interesting," writes Lortie, "that 91 percent of the first choices are *individualistic*; they are all tasks which teachers normally perform alone" (p. 164, my emphasis). Secondly, the lack of time and the feeling of not having finished one's work is a perennial problem experienced by teachers. Unwanted or unproductive interruptions, Lortie observes, "must be particularly galling" (p. 177). Among the Five Town teachers Lortie found that 62 of the 98 reasons of complaints given by teachers "dealt with time erosion or the disruption of work flow" (p. 178).[4]

---

3 Philip Jackson (1980) quoted Henry Adams as writing, "A teacher affects eternity, he can never tell where his influence stops." As the title of Jackson's article ("The Uncertainties of Teaching") indicates, and as Lortie and others have so clearly demonstrated, the obverse is also true. Teachers can never tell when or even whether their influence *starts*, or whether or not it will ever become evident after the student leaves them.

4 The implications of this finding for educational change will be taken up in the next section. In the meantime, we get a sense of how some educational innovations intrude on teachers, and can understand how many teachers resent the extra (voluntary as well as paid) time and energy required. It is also clear why innovative projects which provide teachers with release time from the classroom are reacted to with ambivalence.

There are many other details one could add concerning what teachers do, particularly if we could examine differences between grade levels, types of communities, and so on; but as a basic characterization of common problems faced by most teachers, Lortie's description seems amazingly accurate and complete in light of confirmation in numerous other studies of his main conclusions. House and Lapan (1978), Clark and Yinger (1977), Jackson (1968, 1980), Smith and Geoffrey (1968), Huberman (1978, 1980), and Leithwood and MacDonald (1981) all corroborate Lortie's analysis. For example, House's description of his first year of teaching is reminiscent of Lortie's findings:

The other striking feature of my first year of teaching, besides the strong feelings of my own failure and despair, was that I was entirely alone. There was no senior partner in the firm from whom I could solicit advice on my first case .... Professionally I was alone. It was sink or swim by myself. There were some people who might have helped. I was teaching in a combined junior and senior high school so both the principals theoretically were supervisors of instruction .... Of course this is far removed from the truth. Help from sources where one might have expected it—from the common culture of teachers, from discussions in the teachers' lounge, from talks with a few colleagues—was almost totally absent .... The information [that was] transferred tends to be more personal than professional. (House & Lapan, 1978, pp. 16–17)

There is no need to repeat the details of House and Lapan's other observations; they represent a litany of the issues raised by Lortie—uncertainty and guilt about whether what they are doing has any value, the isolated joys of reaching individual students, the lack of reflexivity on either an individual or a collective basis, the perennial frustration of lack of time and unwanted interruptions, the complexity of the teaching act in a crowded classroom with management problems, interacting with one or more students while others are waiting, and the unpredictability of a well-planned lesson falling flat, an unplanned session connecting, and so on.

Observational research studies show just how astonishingly variable and difficult teaching is. On variability, research on "time on task" consistently finds that time allocated to subject areas, and student time actively engaged in a task, is all over the map. (See Denham and Lieberman, 1980, and Karweit, 1981, for good reviews.) For example, researchers in the Beginning Teacher Evaluation Study (BTES)[5] examined 25 second-grade and 21 first-grade classrooms. They found that average classroom time allocated to mathematics varied from 25 minutes a day in some classes to 60 minutes in others and that to reading from 60 to 140 minutes (Fisher, Berliner, et al., 1980, p. 15). Other studies confirm that, depending on the school and the classroom, students can spend up to 100 hours a year more (or less) on given basic subjects (Karweit, 1981, p. 81). Similarly, the "engaged time in instruction" is remarkably variable among classrooms and students, ranging from less than a third of allocated time to over three-quarters in a day (Karweit, 1981). These studies find that the engaged time on task is highly related to student learning.

The difficulty and complexity of teaching as described by Lortie have been portrayed more fully in observational studies. Bussis et al. (1976) and Carew and Lightfoot (1979) describe how the choices of teaching are extremely intri-

---

5 Despite its label, the study investigated regular classroom teachers, not beginning ones. The focus of the study changed after it was initiated, but the original title was retained.

cate. In the United Kingdom, Galton et al. (1980) carried out detailed observations in 58 classrooms (in 19 schools) and found several different patterns of teaching and pupil behavior. (See also Bennett's 1976 and 1979 work in the U.K.) On a more substantive note, Galton et al. (1980, p. 157) discovered that teaching was "overwhelmingly factual and managerial" and that the idea of engaging students in more interactional higher-order cognitive tasks in a class of 30 was highly impractical, if not impossible. Some teachers do succeed, but it requires an enormous amount of skill and energy if they are left to find the way on their own. Huberman (1980), in updating and elaborating on Lortie's (1975) and Jackson's (1968, 1980) analyses, concludes that much teaching is a question of "finding and using recipes for busy kitchens."

Nor does teaching necessarily become more rewarding with experience. Those who have the most trouble leave teaching; many of those who stay adjust to a routine. After discussions with numerous elementary school teachers over a period of years, Sarason had this to say:

Without exception those who have been teaching for five or more years admitted that they no longer experienced their work with the enthusiasm, excitement, sense of mission, and challenge that they once did. (I should make it perfectly clear that these teachers were *not* saying that they disliked being a teacher, although in a minority of instances I felt that to be the case.) For the most part they felt as competent as they ever were going to feel, and they verbalized no expectation that they would be teaching or thinking differently sometime in the future .... In one way or another these teachers indicated that they rarely experienced anymore the sense of personal or intellectual growth. (1971, pp. 163–64)

Sarason also indicates that many of these teachers had considered moving out of the classroom—a trend and finding only too strongly confirmed in national opinion polls of teachers in the U.S. conducted by the National Education Association. Polls conducted in 1967 and 1979 found the following:

| Suppose you could go back and start over again. Would you become a teacher? | *1967* | *1979* |
|---|---|---|
| Certainly would become a teacher | 53% | 30% |
| Probably would | 25% | 29% |
| Probably would not become a teacher | 7% | 22% |
| Certainly would not | 2% | 10% |
| Not sure | 13% | 10% |

In 1967 over one-half the teaching force were positive that they had made the right choice. In 1979 the proportion had declined to less than one-third. Most striking is the finding that in 1979 one out of every three teachers "probably" or "certainly" wished that he or she had never become a teacher.

Teacher stress and burnout have become common terms in the professional and public media. Cherniss's (1980) characterization of burnout among professionals (teachers were included in his sample) concisely captures the pervasive malaise associated with the phenomenon, which if it continues is bound to lead to the extirpation of client-oriented professional service. (See also Truch, 1980.)

Burnout involves a change in attitude and behavior in response to a demanding, frustrating, unrewarding work experience. The dictionary defines "to burn out" as "to fail, wear out, or become exhausted by making excessive demands on energy, strength, or resources." This term all too aptly describes the experience of many human service professionals. However, the term "burnout" has come to have an additional meaning in recent research and writing on the topic; it refers to negative changes in work-related attitudes and behavior in response to job stress. What are these negative changes? A major one is loss of concern for the client and a tendency to treat clients in a detached, mechanical fashion. Other changes include increasing discouragement, pessimism, and fatalism about one's work; decline in motivation, effort, and involvement in work; apathy; negativism; frequent irritability and anger with clients and colleagues; preoccupation with one's own comfort and welfare on the job; a tendency to rationalize failure by blaming the clients or "the system"; and resistance to change, growing rigidity, and loss of creativity . . . .

In addition to these negative changes in thought and behavior related to the job, there are physical and behavioral signs. These include chronic fatigue; frequent colds, the flu, headaches, gastrointestinal disturbances, and sleeplessness; excessive use of drugs; decline in self-esteem; and marital and family conflict. Of course, not all of these symptoms need to be present to say that a person is burning out. Some may be present and some not in any particular case. However, when there are several of these signs and changes in a professional, the work situation is all too likely the source of this burnout. (pp. 6–7, cited in Sarason, 1982)

A commission was established in Alberta (Kratzmann et al., 1981) to analyze and make recommendations on how to alleviate the deep-rooted conflict between teachers and administrators in the Calgary Board of Education arising from a collective bargaining dispute. The commission found the issues of conflict so widespread in the province (and in the broader media and research literature) that it decided that a more basic report was needed covering the profession as a whole. It describes "the quality of working life" of teachers, as indicated by attitude, stress levels, relationship to decision-making, and access to support systems, as in critically bad shape.[6] Kratzmann et al. contend that the conditions of work for teachers must encompass two notions: that the teacher, like any worker, has a right to expect that work conditions be supportive of rewarding activities and accomplishments; and that, correspondingly, employers have the right to expect quality in the work life to result in heightened morale and commitment and in increased effort and productivity. Their recommendations place equal responsibility on the teaching profession and on school board and provincial authorities for addressing the problem. The underlying point for our purposes is that effective educational change in practice cannot occur without improvements in the teachers' work life.

Under the conditions described in the past several pages, change can be a two-edged sword. It can either aggravate the teachers' problems or provide a glimmer of hope. Judging from the history of educational change over the past fifteen years, it is much easier to do the former than the latter.[7]

# Enter change

Although educational change is all around the teacher at any given time, each new policy or curriculum, psychologically speaking, does "enter" when it is

6 A study commissioned by the British Columbia Teachers' Federation (Flanders, 1980) also focuses on working conditions and reports similar findings.

7 As a later section shows, this is not to say that only changes that teachers want should be introduced. It does say that strategies of change which ignore the working conditions of teachers are bound to fail.

first proposed or arrives on the scene. This is true *even when innovations are voluntarily undertaken or are developed by other teachers.*

One of the great mistakes in North America in the late 1960s and 1970s was the naive assumption that involving *some* teachers on curriculum committees or in program development would facilitate implementation, because it would increase acceptance by *other* teachers. Of course, it was such an automatic assumption that people did not use the words "some" and "others." It was just assumed that "teachers" were involved because "teachers" were on major committees or project teams. Well, they were not involved, as the vast majority of classroom teachers know.[8] Once again there was a failure to distinguish between "the change" and "the change process." As far as most teachers were concerned, when the change was produced by fellow teachers it was just as much *externally experienced* as if it had come from the university or the government. In fact, it could be more aggravating if teachers who had developed the change were seen as getting special rewards and recognition, or if the teacher developers saw themselves as innovative and their colleagues as somewhat resistant or slow to catch on to the great new ideas they had produced. Change is a highly personal experience—each and every one of the teachers who will be affected by change must have the opportunity to work through this experience in a way in which the rewards at least equal the cost. The fact that those who advocate and develop changes get more rewards than costs, and those who are expected to implement them experience many more costs than rewards, goes a long way in explaining why the more things change the more they remain the same. If the change works, the individual teacher gets little of the credit; if it doesn't, the teacher gets most of the blame.

The problem of the meaning of change for teachers can be understood most directly if we examine the criteria teachers use in assessing any given change. This pertains to the balance of rewards and costs, or, more simply, "Why should I put my efforts into this particular change?" The research in the previous section, as well as some to be introduced shortly, shows that teachers use three main criteria:

1 Does the change potentially address a need? Will students be interested? Will they learn?
2 How clear is the change in terms of what the teacher will have to do?
3 How will it affect the teacher personally in terms of time, energy, new skill, sense of excitement and competence, and interference with existing priorities?[9]

Doyle and Ponder (1977–78) refer to these aspects as "the practicality ethic" of teacher decision-making:

The essential features of this ethic can be summarized briefly as follows. In the normal course of events teachers receive a variety of messages intended to modify or

---

8 I am not suggesting that all teachers should participate in development—a clear impossibility. I am saying that the fact that they have not been involved cries out for radically different approaches to the way implementation is conceived and carried out.

9 A fourth criterion—how intellectually rewarding will the experience be in terms of interaction with peers or others—will emerge in a later section; however, teachers have had little opportunity to believe that intellectual rewards will be forthcoming. A fifth criterion—chance for promotion—has sometimes been cited as an important motivator; but I discount this, because by definition it cannot apply to very many teachers (especially these days). My interest is in the motivation to implement for all teachers, not just the few who see it as a stepping stone.

improve their performance. If one listens carefully to the way teachers talk about these messages, it soon becomes clear that the term "practical" is used frequently and consistently to label statements about classroom practices. (pp. 1–2)

The label "practical" in Doyle and Ponder's terms is an expression of "the taken-for-granted world of the practitioner." They suggest that there are three aspects to this ethic, which they designate as congruence, instrumentality, and cost. These three criteria parallel the three suggested above: need, procedural clarity, and personal costs and benefits.

Congruence refers to the teachers' best estimate (based on the evidence presented) of how students will react to the change (student interest, learning, etc.), and how well the innovation appears to fit the teachers' situation. Instrumentality concerns the procedural content and clarity of the proposal (i.e., the hows of implementation). Statements of theory, philosophy, general principles, or even clearly specified student outcomes "are not practical because they lack the necessary procedural referents" (p. 7). As is central to the theme of this book, teachers have to have some understanding of the *operational meaning* of the change before they can make a judgment about it.[10] For example, curriculum guidelines are the major policy documents in each of the ten provinces in Canada, but they are rarely clear about what a teacher would have to do to implement them (i.e., the procedural content). The assumption is that local school districts or teachers will make procedural decisions; but by and large they don't do this adequately, because there is little incentive or effective support for doing it.

Finally, the question of cost can be defined as the ratio of investment to return as far as the individual is concerned. Money is a very small part; personal costs in time, energy, and threat to sense of adequacy, with no evidence of benefit in return, seem to have constituted the major costs of changes in education over the past twenty years. On the other hand, when the changes do involve a sense of mastery, excitement, and accomplishment, the incentives for trying new practices are powerful (see Huberman, 1981).

In sum, the balance of incentives and disincentives from the perspectives of individual teachers helps explain the outcome of change efforts. Need, clarity, and the personal benefit/cost ratio must be favorable on balance at some point relatively early during implementation. Ambivalence about whether the change will be favorable is nearly always experienced prior to attempting it. It is only by trying something that we can really know if it works. The problem is compounded because first attempts are frequently awkward, not providing a fair test of the idea. Support during initial trials is critical for getting through the first stages, as is some sign of progress.

The above notions have been further confirmed through the extensive work of Hall, Loucks, and colleagues at the University of Texas on the reaction of teachers to innovations. Building on the earlier work of Frances Fuller, Hall and others have found that different teachers have different "concerns" in relation to innovations, as well as concerns about an innovation's impact on or benefit to students (Loucks & Hall, 1979). Depending on how the innovation is introduced, these concerns may be abated or exacerbated.

---

10 To repeat an earlier point, clear specification of an innovation at the outset does not seem to resolve the problem. Clarification is a process. Full understanding can only come after some experience with the change.

Let us now see how the history of innovative attempts measures up to this practicality ethic. Not very well. In chapter 2, I have already suggested that educational innovations are as unreliable at least as often as they are reliable— that is, they do not work out either because they have been ill conceived (they are inappropriate or underdeveloped), or because resources to support implementation are missing, or too frequently for both reasons. House (1974, p. 73) summarizes the situation of teachers viewing most innovations: personal costs are high, and benefits are unpredictable.

In other words, teachers get the worst of all three criteria worlds—student benefit and procedural clarity are low, and personal costs are high. Moreover, House claims that there is a strong tendency to "oversell" innovations in order to obtain funding or to get them adopted by policy-makers, teachers, and others.[11] The gap between the benefits promised and those received is usually very large, even in situations where good intentions exist. The difficulty of learning new skills and behavior and unlearning old ones is vastly underestimated. As we have seen in chapter 3, changes in educational beliefs, teaching styles, and other practices represent profound changes affecting the teacher's professional self-definition. The "oversold" innovation, however, may often be promoted on the basis of an oversimplification of what implementation involves, and the supporting resources provided on a scale suited to the oversimplification—as though the change for the teacher consisted of no more than a superficial alteration in routine activities.

In any case, changes are often introduced to teachers with the emphasis on the wonderful benefits of the innovation in general or on long-term goals. Yet even when the innovation is thoroughly "explained" at the beginning, it cannot be absorbed, for teachers like anybody else do not learn new ideas all at once. Change is a process, not an event. On top of all this, even potentially good changes do not fare well because far too many changes are in front of teachers at any one time. Regardless of the reasons (such as policy-makers' treating innovations as products) there are more changes being proposed than are humanly possible to implement—if by implementation we mean changes in behavior and thinking. Nor does giving teachers the opportunity to develop their own innovations work, unless they are also given some support and external assistance (Charters & Pellegrin, 1973).

In summary, the strategies commonly used by promoters of changes, whether they be legislators, administrators, or other teachers, frequently do not work because they are derived from a world or from premises different from that of the teachers. Innovations are "rationally" advocated from the point of view of what is rational to the promoter, not the teachers. Sometimes innovations (particularly from university professors) are rationally sold on the basis of sound theory and principles, but they turn out not to be translatable into practice with the resources at the disposal of teachers. Or innovations may contain many good ideas and resources, but they assume conditions different from those faced by teachers. Other times, innovations are strongly advocated in terms of the supposed benefits for students, without clear evidence that the particular

---

11 George Santayana's definition of fanaticism may not be too far off the mark in some cases: "Fanaticism is redoubling your effort when you have forgotten your aim." Even innovators who have remembered their aim often redouble their effort in order to overcome resistance—a strategy long since discredited by Kurt Lewin in his use of force-field analysis.

teacher's particular students would share the benefit.[12] Other proposals are not clear about the *procedural* content (the how to implement). Others fail to acknowledge the personal costs, the meaning of change to teachers, and the conditions and time it will take to develop the new practices. Stated another way, teachers' reasons for rejecting many innovations are every bit as rational as those of the advocates promoting them. Wise (1977) has called the promoters of change "hyperrational" in their assumptions, an idea which accurately captures what proposed changes look like from the vantage point of the everyday teacher (although I am sure that a few other adjectives more readily come to teachers' minds).

# Change is necessary

Are we to conclude that all teachers are saints, and that if we only left them alone educational problems would be largely reduced? Aside from this being a practical impossibility from the point of view of educational authorities, it is as far from the thesis in this book as we could get. However, there are other equally far positions, such as the conclusion that more resources should be allocated to forcing teachers to implement what they are supposed to. Implementation is a process of working out the meaning of change with those directly responsible. But to what extent are changes in schools necessary?

There are many indications that educational change is sorely needed. First, many of the more fundamental aspects of the new curricula of the 1960s and 1970s have not been implemented. It is true that many of these changes probably should not be implemented. But the fact remains that innovative teaching practices aimed at the higher-order cognitive skills (decision-making, problem-solving, inquiry learning) and personal and social skills (communication skills, ability to work in groups, multicultural understanding, attitudes and skills in preparation for the job market) have also not been implemented despite their endorsement in national, regional, and local policy statements. Joyce and some colleagues have carried out intensive observation studies in a number of classrooms in order to determine the nature of teaching. In one school (typical of others) they catalogued 22,228 observations. Of these, over 18,000 or 80% of the teaching activities were directed at the learning of specific "facts" rather than skill or concept development (McNair & Joyce, 1978–79, pp. 18–19). The domination of "teacher talk" in the classroom is a well-known phenomenon. See also Galton and Simon's (1980) careful observation study of teachers' classroom behavior.

Similarly, studies of elementary schools (Goodlad & Klein, 1970) and of specific curriculum (Social Studies in Alberta, Downey et al., 1975) and reviews of curricular fields (Welch, 1979) have concluded that changes assumed to have been implemented had not been. Even teachers who had received special training in summer institutes over several weeks showed wide variation in their use of curricula and still tended to emphasize factual knowledge acquisition.

---

12 It is the credibility of the claim for student benefits that is at stake. The DESSI study found that if another teacher or some other trusted person vouches for the benefits of the innovation, teachers are willing to try it out. But even then, some early success or progress must be experienced (Crandall et al., forthcoming).

Welch's review of twenty years of science teaching shows that little significant change has come about despite massive inputs of money for curriculum development and in-service training of teachers.

Now, the problem in deciding whether the above changes are *actually needed* is a difficult one. The decision depends on the answer to two questions. First, are the educational objectives of the change wanted, needed, *valued* by society? Second, are the programs effective in accomplishing these objectives? The former is a value (political) question rather than an educational one; but judging from the curriculum policies in Canada and the United States, the answer is a definite yes—higher-order cognitive, personal, and social goals are stated in policy as major educational goals. The latter question—the educational one—cannot really be answered with confidence, because we *don't really know* what are the most effective teaching approaches when it comes to these kinds of objectives. We only "hypothesize" that student involvement, interaction, learning by doing, and other aspects of inquiry-based curricula are more effective for achieving these objectives than teacher dominance and concentration on "facts." More work is being done on the relationship between teaching styles and student behavior (Bussis et al., 1976; Bennett, 1976; Galton et al., 1980). Increasingly sophisticated research is examining the relationship between teacher time spent on subjects and student learning in the basics (math and reading). But we still do not have a good overview of the "balance of the curriculum" in relation to espoused goals. What we do know suggests that (1) concentration on factual knowledge and basic skills predominates; (2) we may be on the road to getting better at teaching basic skills; (3) the preoccupation with basic skills, while they represent an important goal, may be preempting or crowding out other priorities; and (4) there is no evidence that we are attending to (or improving performance in) higher-order cognitive and personal/social-development objectives.

A second and partially related reason why change is needed concerns the almost arbitrary variation and emphasis in classrooms on some subjects over others. The BTES study, as mentioned in the previous section, discovered wide variations in how much time (and how much effective time) was spent on mathematics and reading. To take another example, in a detailed observation study of four primary teachers, Carew and Lightfoot (1979) found that two teachers spent over 75% of their instructional time on reading, while one spent 47% and the fourth only 29%. Other studies of science curriculum, social studies, language arts, career-based education—you name it—have found similar wide variations: some teachers leave out entire components, while others devote enormous amounts of time to those same components. Moreover, partly because of declining enrollments and corresponding shifts in teaching assignments at the secondary school level, and to multiple subject areas at the elementary school level, many teachers are teaching in subject areas for which they have limited preparation.[13] I cannot say whether any given teacher is right or wrong; but the fact that there are wide variations in effective time spent in

13 For example, at the elementary level, Aoki et al. (1977, p. 10) found that over 60% of the teachers had taken one or fewer social studies methods courses. Tuinman and Kendall (1980, p. 136) report that 30% of the elementary school teachers had taken less than one course in the teaching of reading. The science background of elementary school teachers is also limited. Increasing numbers of secondary school teachers are teaching some subjects for which they have little prior training.

specific subject areas, variations that are certainly related to what students learn, raises serious questions about what different students are being exposed to and how this relates to students', parents', and society's goals.

Third, teachers, as we have seen, do not have time for (or their culture does not support) reflection or analysis either individually or collectively about what they are doing. Teachers seldom invite each other into their classes. Being private has a long tradition (see Lieberman & Miller, 1982). For this reason, teachers are not likely to recognize or develop needed changes—changes which they themselves might identify if they were engaged in such reflection and exchange. The lack of analysis and interaction among teachers concerning the planning of lessons, teaching behavior and style, underlying principles, impact of teaching, and needed changes probably accounts for the large individualistic variations in what is taught. When such interaction does take place on a regular basis, as it does in some schools or among some teachers, it has a positive effect on learning conditions and outcomes (Rutter et al., 1979; Little, 1981). In other words, change is needed to promote critical interaction among professionals about what they are doing. Huberman (1981, p. 217) touches on this need when he notes:

One of the intriguing findings in our field study was that the introduction of a new practice or product obliged collaboration between teachers within a building, as well as between teachers and administrators, who had previously had virtually no substantive contacts. This was even the case for teachers at the same grade level working next door to one another and between whom relations were cordial, but in professional terms, frivolous.

Interaction about a change is necessary, even when a new program is highly structured (programmed vs. adaptive in our terms). Teachers who feel reassured when the program seemingly tells them exactly what to do may be victims of false clarity. Most changes worth their salt involve some significant alterations in what teachers do and think. The lack of opportunity for teachers to reflect, interact with each other, share, learn, develop on the job makes it unlikely that significant changes will occur. Whether the change is relatively programmed in the first place or more adaptive, many valuable ideas and resources go unutilized. Change in the current situation is needed, for many teachers have no opportunity to stop and question their practices.

Fourth, although there is no thorough research on the topic, there is every reason to believe that the textbook industry dominates the teachers' field of choice in many states in the U.S. and in several provinces in Canada (see Boyd, 1978, for one discussion). Teachers frequently take and "teach the textbook." Textbooks probably reinforce the tendency to cover the content and use tricks of the trade, rather than grapple with underlying beliefs and teaching styles. Whatever the case, publishers are more interested in selling books than in improving classroom practice, especially if the latter is impractical. A more critical assessment of the role of textbook *selection and use* is needed, whether carried out by committees, administrators, or individual teachers.

Fifth, change is needed because many teachers are frustrated, bored, and alienated. Good change processes which foster sustained professional development and lead to student benefits may be one of the few sources of revitalization and satisfaction left for teachers. It may be too late for many of the one out of three who think they made a mistake in choosing teaching as a career (NEA, 1979); it may be impossible to overcome the polarization between teachers and school boards which has developed in some situations where bitter strikes have occurred; and it may be extremely difficult to establish the conditions which allow teachers to reevaluate their own role and responsibility in student learning.[14] As Dewey indicated many years ago (1916), and as Sarason reiterates, "If teaching becomes neither terribly interesting nor exciting to many teachers, can one expect them to make learning interesting and exciting to students?" (Sarason, 1971, pp. 166–67). Yes, change is needed.

The main message is not that teachers should make learning more exciting to students, desirable as that goal is. Rather, I refer to a much more pervasive problem, so clearly recognized earlier by Sarason—that those who introduce change (policy-makers, university professors, administrators) treat teachers in precisely the same way as they criticize teachers for treating the students. New curricula emphasize the importance of being sensitive to where students are, what they think and why; but these curricula are often introduced in a way which ignores what teachers think and why. Proponents prefer to take the more direct and rational route: *telling* teachers what is the right way to act and think. In short, *"Those who want change do exactly that for which they criticize teachers"* (Sarason, 1971, p. 193). Such a change process is simply not conducive to increasing teachers' skills, excitement, or interest in the value of change. Ergo, teachers cannot implement those changes in a way which transfers the learning to students. It seems like such an obvious pedagogical principle, that the only reason that promoters and managers of change miss it must be that they do not see implementation as a *learning process* in which they and the teachers are *adult learners*. When it comes to change, we have a lot to learn.

Sixth and finally, because of their cultural conditions and practicality concerns, most teachers do not take the initiative to promote changes beyond their own classroom. As Lortie and others have found, teachers want smaller classes, more time, fewer interruptions, and fewer clerical and other duties. In short, they want more time to do more of what they are already doing as *individual* teachers.[15] Lortie, as sympathetic as anyone to the plight of teachers, concludes that most individual teachers are not interested in major shifts or changes in pedagogical practice or wider school and school-community reforms. Teachers have limited access to information about innovation, or limited time to look into information they do receive (House, 1974, ch. 4). When school or school district program or policy changes are advocated, they more frequently come from district administrators, school boards, or federal or state/provincial authorities,

---

14 Witness the teacher response to the NEA question of where the blame lies regarding poor performance by students—81% selected "the children's home life," 14% said the child, 4% the school, and only 2% the teachers. Change is needed in supporting teachers to diagnose school- and classroom-related sources of problems, and to obtain ideas and programs for addressing these problems.
15 Interestingly, when teachers do experience good peer or other professional interaction, they recognize and value the benefits (Clark & Yinger, 1980; Elliott, 1977; Little, 1981). It is as if most teachers have not had enough exposure to know whether peer interaction around needed changes in practice can be valuable.

as Rosenblum and Louis (1979), Daft and Becker (1978), Crandall et al. (forth-coming), and many others have found. Even curricular changes which come from other teachers and focus on the individual classroom are unlikely to be disseminated effectively by and among teachers because of their relative class-room isolation, lack of time to reflect and discuss the meaning of changes, and lack of a culture which promotes or sanctions teacher–teacher exchange. For these as well as other reasons cited above, teachers should not be left alone; nor should they leave each other alone.

It should be clearly understood that I am not saying that teachers are *intrin-sically* uninterested in serious educational change. The truth of the matter is that the culture of the school, the demands of the classroom, and the usual way in which change is introduced do not permit, point to, or facilitate teacher involvement in exploring or developing more significant changes in educational practice. Fortunately, the usual way of introducing change is not the only way, and there are cases which indicate guidelines for how educational change can be more effectively carried out.

# Change is possible

When I talk about *improvement*, I mean just that: what can be done to introduce change which will increase the numbers of successes and decrease the numbers of failures. Even a modest increase and decrease in these respective numbers may make it better for thousands of teachers and students. Depending on the circumstances, some people will still be frustrated about the thousands of other teachers and students and administrators who do not seem to be reachable. Nonetheless, improvement and progress do seem possible by virtue of the fact that success does happen in some settings and does happen as a result of delib-erate planning, not just by chance.

The general principles and the cases of success described in chapter 6 repre-sent the underlying guidelines for doing and coping with change, and the reader should refer back to these suggestions as a foundation. The current chapters (Part II) are intended to extend and specify change guidelines for those who are in the roles being analyzed. That is, the guidelines are from the point of view of the person in the role. Thus, guidelines for teachers working with others are discussed in this section, while guidelines for principals working with teachers are contained in chapter 8. In the wider view, an understanding of teachers will clearly generate ideas for those in whatever role who deal with teachers. The message to everyone outside the role under review is: *Understand the subjective world—the phenomenology—of the role incumbents as a necessary precondition for engaging in any change effort with them.*

In the remaining part of this chapter, I first review what makes change work with or among teachers. I then make recommendations related to the three situations in which individual teachers typically find themselves: namely, (1) as someone on the receiving end of change, (2) as someone interested in advocat-ing or promoting change, and (3) as a member of a teacher federation or union. In the concluding section I reflect on teachers' interest or lack of interest in educational change.

# What makes change work
# at the teacher level

Chapter 5 was devoted to an explanation of what makes change work and not work. It may be recalled that at the teacher level the degree of change was strongly related to the extent to which teachers *interact* with each other and others providing technical help. Within the school, collegiality among teachers as measured by the frequency of communication, mutual support, help, etc. was a strong indicator of implementation success. Virtually every research study on the topic has found this to be the case.[16] And it does make eminent sense in terms of the theory of change espoused in this book. Significant educational change consists of changes in beliefs, teaching style, and materials which can *only* come about (except for the odd religious-type conversion) through a process of personal development in a context of socialization. As Werner (1980) observes in explaining the failure of social studies curriculum in Alberta:

Ideally, implementation as a minimum includes shared understanding among participants concerning the implied presuppositions, values and assumptions which underlie a program, for if participants understand these, then they have a basis for rejecting, accepting or modifying a program in terms of their own school, community and class situations. To state the aim another way, implementation is an ongoing construction of a shared reality among group members through their interaction with one another within the program. (pp. 62–63)

There is no getting around the *primacy of personal contact*. Teachers need to participate in skill-training workshops, but they also need to have one-to-one and group opportunities to receive and give help, and more simply to *converse* about the meaning of change (for further discussion see House, 1974; House & Lapan, 1978, ch. 10; Werner, 1980).

Under these conditions teachers learn how to use an innovation as well as to judge its desirability on more information-based grounds; they are in a better position to know whether they should accept, modify, or reject the change. Sometimes teachers cannot answer this question until they have had a chance to try out the new program and to discuss it. For example, as I will describe in chapter 14, in-service education pertaining to an innovation must take this into account by moving from the concrete to the abstract, from the practical procedures and activities to a discussion of underlying principles, rather than the other way around, as is the more frequent order (see especially Elliott, 1977, 1980; Clark & Yinger, 1977).

It is essential to recognize that I am not referring only to innovations developed externally to the school. Innovations decided on or developed by teachers

---

16 We do not have adequate knowledge to analyze elementary, junior high, and secondary school teachers separately. The description in this section refers to all three levels of teachers, but further specification is needed to identify possible differences and their implications. Some of the obvious differences relate to the stronger subject-discipline training of secondary school teachers, the teaching of one or two subjects versus several subjects, and school size and organization. (See Lieberman & Miller, 1982.) None of these would seem to gainsay the basic principles formulated here, but more specific knowledge and guidelines are definitely needed for teachers at different grade levels.

within a school also require teacher–teacher interaction, if they are to go any-where. Whether external or internal, the more teachers can review and interact concerning their own practices, the more they will be able to bring about improvements that they themselves identify as necessary. It will be recalled from chapter 3 that even wanted changes have costs and create ambivalence. Social support is necessary for reducing costs and resolving the ambivalence in terms of how much change is needed and what can feasibly be accomplished. Thus, whether the source of change is external or internal to the school (and either may be good or bad, feasible or infeasible), it is teachers as interacting professionals who should be (and in any case as individuals are) in a position to decide *finally* whether the change is for them (see Schulz, 1979).

This is not to imply that teachers have the time to analyze every potential change. In many circumstances teachers may quite accurately conclude at the outset there is no need or time for interaction, and that no change is needed or possible. This outcome will occur in situations where teachers are relatively satisfied with their current program and/or when they perceive that administrative support for change is low. We have seen that change is not necessarily progress. Not attempting to change may be the most appropriate response, in some situations, if there is disagreement about the innovation, or if the mini-mal conditions for change do not exist; for example, there may be no resources to support implementation, or a major conflict may exist within the school or between the school and community which must be resolved first. There is a constant tension between the legitimate rights of governments (society) to pro-pose program changes and the legitimate rights of teachers to decide whether changes are or are not needed. Both are legitimate sources of decisions, and they will continue to coexist.

When teachers have had the opportunity to analyze their work under sup-portive conditions, they have found such reviews to be productive and reward-ing. Establishing conditions for teachers to interact represents an important untapped resource for reducing the personal costs of change. Clark and Yinger's (1980) research on teacher thinking reports that when teachers were helped to reflect, they found it an enjoyable and powerful experience for their profes-sional development. Cohen and colleagues' analysis of open-space schools (Cohen, 1973; Cohen 1981) shows that increased teacher–teacher collaboration occurs in some cases and is strongly related to job satisfaction. Elliott's (1980) extensive work in England also demonstrates that teacher reflection and inter-action can substantially increase teacher ability to analyze and improve class-room practice. Furthermore, a much larger body of research clearly proves that when teachers do use resources beyond their own ingenuity, it is other teachers and in some cases district specialists whom they find most helpful (see Aoki et al., 1977; Berman & McLaughlin, 1976; Fullan, 1981b; House, 1974; Little, 1981; Loucks & Melle, 1980; Stallings, 1980). Under the right conditions, pro-ductive and satisfying changes have resulted.

The more teachers experience the rewards of interaction the more they will use the criterion of professional contact and development—satisfaction from the intellectual and practical benefits of helping, getting help, and sharing with other teachers—as a measure of whether to become involved in innovation. And make no mistake about it, focused teacher interaction is essential to large-scale successful change.

Once teachers are involved, there can be considerable opportunity to alter or further develop the innovation, depending on the approach taken. Berman and McLaughlin (1976) found that local materials adaptation was an important factor related to teacher change. On the other hand, if the process is characterized by teacher isolation, the innovation may well get adapted right out of existence or used in a perfunctory way. Teachers need to help each other decide, and when they do, dealing with change may become more productive and less costly. At least, we know these more positive experiences are happening in some situations.

The DESSI research findings help to clarify the role of teachers in relation to materials adaptation. The DESSI researchers found that having teachers spend time on materials development inhibits change in practice, if it takes time away from attempting changes in the classroom (Crandall et al., forthcoming). If working with materials stimulates interaction with other teachers, and is done in a context which includes early application, it can be quite beneficial. Thus, it is not materials adaptation per se that is important, but interaction with other users and the application of ideas, with or without modification of materials. The latter may be necessary depending on the congruence of available materials with the problem at hand; but time spent on materials development—on re-inventing the wheel, for example—takes time away from classroom application.

## On being on the receiving end

Governments have a legitimate role to play in formulating policy and program changes (and in democratic societies they usually obtain input from teacher groups as well as from many other interest groups). Local school boards and administrators also have the right to set up procedures to develop new programs, including the option of encouraging individual schools to establish their own priorities. Wherever the priorities are set (at the district or school level or a combination of the two), administrators have a right to know if they are being implemented.[17] Within the system, there is much flexibility at the local district and teacher level for making major decisions on many of the implementation details (such as choice of materials or teaching methods). But by and large most *individual* teachers are still on the receiving end of new policy and program directions, either from governments, the local district, or the school, many more times than they are on the initiating end. Indeed, many individual teachers ask for more direction and clarity from external authorities as to exactly what they should be teaching. In any of these cases, however, the individual teachers can and should become more adept at assessing, and in some cases influencing, whether the necessary conditions exist for dealing effectively with the change. At least three types of questions should be answered before the teacher decides to throw his or her energies into a change effort (or totally reject it).

First, and by no means self-evident: Is the change needed? Does it address an important educational goal which is currently not being achieved adequately, and does the particular change offer some potential for accomplishing the goal

---

17 At this point I am not taking up the question of how governments and administrators do and should approach these roles. Subsequent chapters address these problems.

more effectively (is it procedurally practical)? Being self-critical (analytic) is necessary in order to avoid the problem of false clarity, when a teacher super-ficially *assumes* that the goal is already being addressed but in reality is not employing teaching resources and behaviors which would maximize attain-ment. Related to this issue is the current tendency for many teachers to reject all external changes (particularly if they come from certain sources, such as governments). Rejecting *all* proposed changes out of hand may be just as regressive as accepting them all. However, even if the change is desired and needed, it will also be necessary to determine its *priority*. Since teachers are often faced with too many changes at once, they individually or jointly must choose where to put their efforts. If everything is attempted (or rejected), noth-ing will succeed. In one sense, the best a teacher can do is work hard on one or two of the most important priorities at one time, and cope with the others as well as possible.

Second, an attempt should be made to ascertain if the administration is endorsing the change, and why, because some form of active commitment by administrators will be necessary for freeing up necessary resources (reducing the cost) for the innovation to succeed. It may be still possible to go it alone, if the specific change is highly valued by the teacher, but it will be difficult unless there is some support from adminstration. It is also important that teachers should not automatically accept apparent lack of interest on the part of an administrator at face value. Administrators have their own worlds of pressure, which they frequently keep private. They are still learning how to cope with their roles as change managers (see chapters 8 and 10). It may be that indi-vidual or group-based teacher initiative and negotiation with administration could lead to significant changes in support in some cases. Untested assump-tions are fertile ground for false attribution of motives and intentions. Apparent lack of attention by the administrator may or may not mean lack of interest.

Third, the teacher should assess whether fellow teachers are likely to show an interest in the change. If collegiality among teachers in a school is already strong, the degree of teacher interest can usually be found out quite quickly. As before, one should not assume lack of interest. Because of the isolation of teachers from each other, there may be a lot of "pluralistic ignorance"—that is, each one assumes that no one else is interested, everyone is making the same assumption, but no one bothers to test it out. In any case, if peer interest exists or can be stimulated, it can represent one of the most satisfying (and necessary) aspects of the change process.

In brief, the answers to the above three questions and their different patterns will tell the individual teacher—or teachers, if there has been a collective dis-cussion—what is in store, and whether the change is worth taking seriously.

## Teacher as advocator

Similar assessments have to be made by the teacher who has participated in the development of or the decision to promote a particular change. If the teacher is the primary mover of the change, obtaining support from administration will be one of the essential tasks (see House & Lapan, 1978, p. 173—"advocacy is the key"). Whether the teacher is the main advocate or part of a development/decision-making committee, the way in which fellow teachers are approached is crucial. Too often teachers on curriculum development teams fail to recognize that they have benefited from a process of learning which others have not experienced. If these teachers try to sell the product without recognizing that it may not be the most important thing on other teachers' minds, and without being sensitive to the need for other teachers to come to grips with the sense of the innovation (and to modify in some ways the cherished ideas of the developers), they will be doing exactly what most developers or advocates of change do— confuse the change with the change process. It is this tendency which led me to form the proposition that the more an advocate is committed to a particular innovation, the *less* likely he or she will be effective in getting it implemented. The opposite is not true: commitment is needed; but it must be balanced with the knowledge that people may be at different starting points, with different legitimate priorities, and that the change process may very well result in transformations or variations in the change. It is extremely difficult for advocates to maintain balance between their knowledge of and commitment to the change and their knowledge of the change process, especially because they do not often realize that these two different aspects of the problem coexist and must be addressed with equal care. If the teacher as advocate can become skilled at integrating the change and the change process, he or she can become one of the most powerful forces of change, as House states:

Here the teacher leader has an advantage over other people trying to implement new programs. The teacher leader can attain access to the classroom much more easily than anyone else. In fact, the idea of teachers working with one another on actual teaching behavior, as opposed to writing curriculum guides, opens up a whole new approach to improving instruction that has not really been pursued. (House & Lapan, 1978, p. 179)

The teacher leader's task, of course, is not easy, because teachers have not been used to viewing and helping with each others' work. In some situations mentioned earlier, where collegiality has developed, it has become a significant "practical" benefit from getting involved in an innovation. According to House and Lapan (1978, p. 179), "Satisfaction derived from cooperatively improving one's skills in the view of one's fellow teachers offers professional rewards, heretofore untapped." At least, such a development offers some potential for not only improving classroom practice but also remedying some of the burnout, alienation, and lack of excitement that blights the working day of many teachers. Such changes, however, will not come quickly. Nor do I envisage teachers having to spend great amounts of time sitting around observing and talking with each other. A modest amount of exchange on some regular basis in the context of coping with particular innovations could have enormous benefit. The DESSI study, for example, found that with good materials available, bringing together teachers with like interests for short periods of time (such as the equivalent of two or three days over a school year) in structured sessions focusing on one program area resulted in significant changes in practice (Crandall et al., forthcoming). The number of contact hours in formal sessions was not large, but in the isolated world of teaching modest contact on some continuous basis among people attempting the same change can have large residual benefits if it results in greater informal interaction among small groups of teachers.

# Teacher as group member
## (unions and professional associations)

As they say, volumes could be written on the emergence of collective bargaining in teaching, but sections on program innovation would be rather thin.[18] Most teacher unions have been preoccupied with salary, fringe benefits, and job security issues. When they have become involved in innovation, it has been in relation to those issues, and rightly so. More recently, teacher groups in some locations have begun to specify what teachers may or may not do in relation to innovations (such as resources for staff development). In other cases teacher unions or subgroups within them, such as subject specialist associations, have participated in hot debates about what should and should not be in new policies or curricula. Never to my knowledge have they bargained for procedures that would allow innovations to be implemented collectively by teachers.[19] This is a radical notion and fraught with political difficulties which may not be resolvable. The underlying idea, however, is that teachers formally (through collective bargaining) or less formally (in local teacher associations, among subject specialists, within one school) *negotiate* the whats and hows of an innovation. Many innovations are complex and cannot be entirely programmed or agreed-upon in advance. Negotiation should recognize that adaptation and further specification will and should occur during implementation. Agreement on how this should be done is more fruitful than endless arguments about the content of change, which never get resolved except by policy fiat. Teachers will always have tremendous power during implementation. It might as well be put to good use. House and Lapan (1978, p. 186) summarize:

In negotiated innovation those to be affected by the innovation would bargain with the innovators over the terms of implementation. How far would the innovation go? What would the teachers get out of it? What would be the rewards to innovators? What resources are available to implement? In this scheme both the costs and rewards are distributed by a deliberate bargaining process between the concerned parties.

The process could be more or less formalized, but at the current time and more so in the years ahead, the cooperation of local and non-local teacher groups for educational reform will be essential. The long-term goal would be to increase the professional self-responsibility of teachers. Within this development, teachers and teacher groups would have to show much more willingness to view and help each other's work. They will have to take responsibility for supporting interaction and review on matters of classroom practice regarding agreed-upon innovations. If they do not, the technology of measuring implementation and student achievement may be imposed on them in ways which will be counterproductive for all (Wise, 1979).

---

18 The thinness is because the topic has not been studied, not because policy innovations in collective agreements have been nonexistent. Agreements have contained direct or indirect implications for program change, although it is safe to say that they have rarely included procedures for implementation. (See Bickel & Bickel, 1979.)

19 A recent exception is the American Federation of Teachers' (1982) "educational research and dissemination program." Under a grant from NIE, the project is designed to deliver educational research on classroom management and effective teaching to local teachers using the structure of the local union as the mechanism. The program, in its early stages, includes pilot sites in three cities: New York, San Francisco, and Washington.

# Are teachers interested in change?

Many teachers do want changes in their own work and in that of colleagues. They do not like the way in which change is currently being introduced; but most are not against change per se. In the U.S. nationwide poll of teachers (NEA, 1979) 65% of the respondents said that "to try more innovations" was needed in the schools where they taught; 85% said that teachers and administrators should be required to update their skills periodically through training.

There is no "typical" teacher in terms of what teachers want in curriculum or program change. I have frequently asked individuals and groups of teachers what role, if any, they as individuals would like in curriculum change. I have nearly always received four types of responses. One group—a small minority—said that they wanted to be left alone to make their own choices. They would pick and choose outside materials, if those met their needs. A second group, also a minority, said that they wanted to play a role in curriculum development. They did not necessarily see themselves as writing the curriculum, although sometimes they did perform this role; but they wanted to participate in decisions and development of new materials. The assumption was that these materials would be used by other teachers. This group tended to exhibit various degrees of advocacy; they wanted curriculum change and were willing to put their energies into the development and decision-making phase. The third and fourth groups were the largest and about equal in proportion. The third type of response I received was from teachers who did not have the time or interest in curriculum development, but were willing, in fact wanted, to have good external materials developed and presented to them. They used "the practicality ethic" to criticize unclear and difficult-to-use existing materials that came with district or government curriculum change programs or projects. The fourth group, equally large, strongly emphasized the desire for more opportunities to interact, share, and discuss with fellow teachers what they were doing in relation to a particular new curriculum. They were quite interested in receiving outside input and help in this process from district specialists or other external resource people. Lack of time, limited support from administration, and absence of opportunities for such exchanges were seen as the main problems.[20]

It is obvious that teachers have different interests and needs. But the range of responses reflects potential interest among many teachers in becoming engaged in productive change efforts, the kinds of efforts which current conditions do not permit. The first small group—the autonomous teachers—probably cannot be forced to be involved, and may very well be doing a good job. Provision of good new materials may be the most appropriate help for them; but they will decide. Some of these teachers may be seen as doing an incompetent job. In teaching, as in any group, there are incompetent people. The problem of incompetence is a special one, and this is not a book on how to handle it; however, one way of mishandling it is to assume that most teachers are incompetent and have to be forced to change. It is a book on how to and how not to introduce

---

20 To label the four groups of teachers is to run the risk of reifying what is a loose classification system and implying that teachers might not change from one orientation to another. However, for ease of communication we might think of the four clusters as representing (1) the autonomous teacher, (2) the developer/participator, (3) the receiver, and (4) the interactor.

change; and how change is introduced will increase or decrease the degree to which school improvement Ís realized for the *majority* of teachers involved.

The second group of teachers already participate in curriculum work; their main need seems to be to find ways to relate more effectively to fellow teachers— that is to say, to learn how to work with the change and the change process in a more balanced way. The main difference between the third and fourth responses is that the former teachers, on the surface, are not calling for inter- action with other teachers. They want better help as *individuals*. Many of them say, "Tell us what to teach and give us the appropriate materials to do it, and we will do it." In these instances false clarity may raise its ugly head. It would be easy to provide good materials, which might end up being used superficially. We could see, however, that there would be ways in which these teachers could begin to use new materials and subsequently be interested in discussing impli- cations with fellow teachers and district specialists. Their interest in exchanges could be stimulated. The fourth group, who are interested in more exchange among teachers, would constitute a much better forum for teachers to influence each other in examining issues of practice and principles.

I am not trying to typecast teachers, but trying rather to illustrate two points. One is to emphasize that it is unrealistic to expect all teachers to be interested in change, or to participate in the same way if they are interested. The other point is to realize that there is a basis of interest in change among a large number of teachers.[21] If effective educational change is a process of personal learning and socialization, improvement will come to the extent that individual teachers can be helped, and particularly to the extent that they can be brought in contact with each other and with external resources in a focused way around a given change.

There will never be enough time and resources to do all that is desired, but it is essential to recognize one of the basic truths about educational change. Inno- vation is not something that can be added on as an afterthought to be covered in a workshop or through voluntary work after hours. *It must be part and parcel of the job.* If change in education consists of an ongoing social process, and if teachers are central, that process must be a regular part of their daily work. Again, the DESSI research shows that time spent on an innovation is strongly related to change in practice (Crandall et al., forthcoming).[22] More time for teacher meetings, planning, skill training, and trying out the change in the class- room should be built into the weekly schedule, and more imaginative ways of creating additional time should and can be found.[23] The implication is clear that some additional money, even small targeted amounts, will have to be allocated to support the types of implementation activities described in this book. More time in itself, of course, is not sufficient. On the contrary, there is considerable evidence which shows that additional time is wasted unless many of the other factors supporting implementation (see chapter 5) are also in place. Proper

21 I did not affix percentages to the different responses, because the proportions would vary from district to district, or region to region, depending on local conditions and history.
22 Five distinct areas of time spent were identified: time on materials preparation, classroom application, training, evaluation, and discussion/interaction with other teachers.
23 It can be done. Many schools and school districts have supported and arranged for time for training and interaction. In the process most teachers also contribute many hours of time vol- untarily.

planning involves taking into account the *system* of variables which are known to affect change.

Time for change, then, is a critical missing factor in the schedules of most teachers. Small increases in regular interaction and skill training could make a very great difference. The basic point is that the consideration of *change* must be just as much a regular part of the job as is emphasis on *routine*. Politicians, policy-makers, administrators, and those among the general public who are not willing to recognize this fact cannot realistically expect much change to occur. Teachers must learn to take advantage of opportunities which enable them to interact with other teachers in examining instructional practices. One of the most pressing needs in education is for teachers to have the opportunity to restore their sense of confidence, meaning, and efficacy in making improvements through carefully considered changes in instruction.

The final conclusion that should be crystal clear in the descriptions of this chapter is that school improvement is related not just to what the teachers do and think. Equally important is what those around them at the school, district, provincial/state, and federal levels do. Too often we think of the need for change only in terms of the teacher. If there is any changing to be done, *everyone is implicated* and must face it in relation to his or her own role. In this network, because of closeness to the classroom situation, probably the most powerful potential source of help or hindrance to the teacher is the school principal.

 Chapter 8

# The Principal

Mother calling upstairs in the morning:
Mother: *It's time to get up for school.*
Chris: *I'm not going to school!*
Mother: *Why not?*
Chris: *Because everybody at the school hates me—the teachers, the kids, the janitor—they all hate me!*
Mother: *You have to go. You're the principal.*

Forget about the principal as head of the school for a moment and think of him or her as someone just as buffeted as the teacher is by wanted or unwanted and often incomprehensible changes—and, what is more, *expected to lead these very changes.*[1] Change is only one small part of the forces competing for the principal's attention and usually not the most compelling one. Yet some principals are actively engaged as initiators or facilitators of program change in their schools. The principal is in the middle of the relationship between teachers and external ideas and people. As in most human triangles there are constant conflicts and dilemmas. How the principal approaches (or avoids) these issues determines to a large extent whether these relationships constitute innovations' Bermuda triangle.

An understanding of what reality is *from the point of view of people within the role* is an essential starting point for constructing a practical theory of the meaning and results of change attempts. This phenomenology is social science's contribution to addressing the frequent lament "No one understands me."[2] In the field of educational change, everyone feels misunderstood. One of the most revealing and frustrating indicators of the difficulties in educational change is the participants' frequent experience of having their intentions not only misunderstood but interpreted exactly opposite to what they meant. Principals should have no problem claiming their fair share of frustration, since the role of the principal has in fact become more complex, overloaded, and unclear over the past twenty years. On the optimistic side, very recent research has identified

---

1 I do not describe the vice-principal separately, although many of the same issues apply. More research is needed on the role of the V-P and his/her relationship to the principal and staff regarding change.
2 Life is full of ironies, since many social scientists write such that no one can understand them in turn.

some specific change-related behaviors of principals who deal effectively with educational change. It is time to go beyond the empty phrase "The principal is the gatekeeper of change."

While research on educational implementation is barely twelve years old, systematic research on what the principal actually does and its relationship to stability and change is (remarkably) only two or three years old—and much of this research is still in progress. Some of the earlier implementation research identified the role of the principal as central to promoting or inhibiting change, but it did not examine the principal's role in any depth or perspective (nor was that its purpose: e.g., Berman & McLaughlin, 1978). Almost the entire body of more thorough research has just recently appeared in unpublished and published papers, and a sizeable proportion are interim reports of "work in progress." The National Institute of Education in the U.S. has a program of research on the role of the principal (see Baltzell, 1981; Crowson & Porter-Gehrie, 1980; Van Cleve Morris et al., 1981; Peterson, 1981). At least two studies of Teacher Corps (see Appendix) have focused on the role of the principal (Rosenblum & Jastrzab, 1981; Reinhard et al., 1980). Hall and associates at the University of Texas are currently conducting a firsthand study of the role of the principal in three districts in different regions of the U.S. Leithwood and Montgomery at the Ontario Institute for Studies in Education have just embarked on a major investigation of the role of the principal in program improvement. The role of the principal in the DESSI study is also highlighted and explored in terms of his or her contribution to educational change and implementation (Crandall et al., forthcoming). Several other useful studies cited later contribute to a growing (but by no means complete) understanding of the complexities of the world of the principal. Principals' associations, school districts, and researchers are all taking a closer look at what the school principal's role has and should become.

In the next section I start with a description of where principals are. I then turn to that part of their role which interests us most—what principals do and don't do in relation to change. In the last section of the chapter, I discuss the dilemmas of change faced by principals, and outline some guidelines for how they might cope with change.

# Where principals are

If change is everywhere in the air, we would think that the greatest pressure a principal feels is to bring about some major transformation of the school. But the air is not the ground, and on the ground many principals experience (and some people may say too easily accept) precisely the opposite—pressures to *maintain stability*. As we shall see in the next section, this does not say that all principals do work to maintain stability. But there is often great pressure on them to do so. How this pressure is handled depends on the conception that the principal has of his or her role[3] and on the expectations that the school district administrators have—that is, what they *really* want principals to do. Nearly all school district role descriptions (and courses in educational administration

---

3 Over 90% of principals are male (e.g., Byrne et al., 1978).

theory, which nearly all principals take) stress the instructional leadership responsibilities of the principal—facilitation of change, helping teachers work together, assessing and furthering school improvement, etc. However, how principals actually spend their time is obviously a better indicator of their impact on the school. If we were to follow principals around on a typical day, what would we find out (other than that they would get somewhat paranoid)? The anthropologist Harry Wolcott (1973) did just that for an entire school year with one elementary school principal. He found that virtually all Ed's (the principal's) time was taken up in one-to-one personal encounters, meetings, and telephone calls. As House and Lapan (1978, pp. 141–42) summarize:

About one-fourth of his time is spent in prearranged meetings, another one-fourth in deliberate but not prearranged meetings, and another fifteen percent in casual, unplanned encounters. *The principal has only fifteen percent of his time to spend in his office alone.* He can hardly be an instructional leader with that much thinking time. (their emphasis)

Weldy (1979) also describes how high school principals spend their days. He presents a time log for a typical day of one principal which shows a continuous stream of one-to-one interactions, telephone calls, and administrative details which occur in one-minute to fifteen-minute clips all day long.

Sarason (1971, ch. 8) also shows that most of the principal's time is spent on administrative housekeeping matters and maintaining order. Many principals expect or feel that they are expected to keep everyone happy by running an orderly school, and this becomes the major criterion of the principals' ability to manage—no news is good news, as long as everything is relatively quiet. House and Lapan summarize the problem nicely:

Another facet of trying to please everyone and to avoid any trouble that might reach central office is to deal with any problem that arises. The principal has no set of priorities except to keep small problems from becoming big ones. His is a continuous task of crisis management. He responds to emergencies daily. He is always on call. All problems are seen as important. This global response to any and all concerns means he never has the time, energy, or inclination to develop or carry out a set of premeditated plans of his own. Containment of all problems is his theme. The principal cannot be a change agent or leader under these conditions. (1978, p. 145)

Other studies confirm these central tendencies in the principals' role. Crowson and Porter-Gehrie (1980) carried out a detailed observation study over a period of time of 26 urban school principals in the Chicago area. The overwhelming emphasis in their daily work was oriented toward maintenance, specifically (1) student disciplinary control, (2) keeping outside influences (central office, parents, etc.) under control and satisfied, (3) keeping staff conflicts at bay, and (4) keeping the school supplied with adequate materials, staffing, etc. (See also the final report of the study: Van Cleve Morris et al., 1981.) It is noteworthy that this "natural" description of what principals do rarely mentions attention to program changes.

Martin and Willower's (1981) and Peterson's (1981) observations of principals also found that principals' work days were sporadic, characterized simultaneously by brevity, variety, and fragmentation. For example, Martin and Willower report that secondary school principals perform an average of 149 tasks a day with constant interruptions—over 50% of their observed activities were interrupted. Most (84%) of the activities were brief (one to four minutes). Principals "demonstrated a tendency to engage themselves in the most current and pressing situation. They invested little time in reflective planning" (p. 80). Instruction-related activities took up 17% of their time.

Recent large-scale national and regional surveys of principals in the United States and Canada provide another useful context for viewing the problem. In a study of the senior high school principalship, Byrne et al. surveyed a representative sample of 1131 principals in the U.S. The respondents were asked to rate how essential certain types of pre- or in-service courses were to their work. The authors were able to compare the results with those of a similar survey carried out twelve years earlier and report the following (Byrne et al., 1978, p. 10):

| Course | 1977 Rated essential | 1965 Rated essential |
| --- | --- | --- |
| School law | 77% | 32% |
| Curriculum and program development | 76% | 41% |
| School management | 74% | 26% |
| Supervision of instruction | 71% | 56% |
| Human relations | 71% | 45% |
| Administrative theory and practice | 32% | 41% |

Two aspects are worth highlighting for our purposes. First, the overall amount and range of essential knowledge as seen by principals has increased dramatically: five of the six categories show major increases.[4] The increased knowledge requirement reflects what some principals see as the problems of role overload and the need for role clarification in the contemporary principalship. Second, curriculum development, which is closest to our concern with program change, shows a major increase: from 41% who said it was essential in 1965, to 76% in 1977.

Even more interesting in the same survey is the rank ordering of how principals "do spend time" compared to how they think they "should spend time." Program development was ranked 5 out of nine tasks in terms of "do" and 1 out of the nine in terms of "should."

In a subsample of the 60 most "effective" principals, as identified through reputational criteria, Gorton and McIntyre (1978) found that these principals focused more on program development than did the sample as a whole. They ranked program development 1 out of the nine tasks for time actually spent during the previous two weeks, and 3 out of the nine for time spent over the whole year (compared to 5 out of the nine among the larger sample).

Generally similar findings on time spent are reported by Eastabrook and Fullan (1978) in their representative Ontario sample of principals: 44% of the principals said that they actually spend a great deal of time on curricular tasks, while 76% indicated that they would ideally like to spend a great deal of time on such tasks. The percentages were reversed for administrative tasks (paperwork, meetings, etc.).

---

4 We can only speculate on the reasons why the one category "administrative theory and practice" showed a decline. It is perhaps related to dissatisfaction with the practical value of courses in educational administration.

Similarly, Hill et al.'s (1980) exploratory study of how federal programs affect the principal's role found that paperwork took up 25% of the principal's work week (ranging from 10% to 50% among the 55 principals in the sample). Principals reported that their roles had become more demanding, busier, less autonomous, and more complex than they had been five years ago: administrative work, consultation with parents (required by many federal projects), and non-instructional involvement with students (e.g., discipline) had all increased significantly. Nothing had decreased except that they spent slightly less time on supervising the instructional process. They spent less time on instructional issues than they wanted to.

The skeptical reader may question the sincerity of principals who say that they do want to spend more time on the program side of their responsibilities.[5] But there should be no doubt that unless special steps are taken (by the principal and by others), the principal has no time for being an educational leader. More and more responsibilities have been added to the role without any being taken away.

It should also be noted in passing that the preoccupation with organizational stability is not always or even usually a bad thing. Aside from providing the advantages of a stable working climate, the principal helps to protect the school from ill-conceived or unrealistic change projects. Since change is not always progress, some tempering is needed. On the other hand, the predominance of order effectively screens out changes which are needed. The importance of the principal in change is highlighted when we realize that many things must be done by the principal even in cases where he or she and the majority of teachers are in favor of a particular change—that is, even when there is a favorable climate, many things in addition must be done to bring about changes in actual practice.

# The principal and change

The above conflicting demands and problems notwithstanding, one of the greatest barriers to the development of a more effective change agent role for the principal is that hardly anyone knows what that means. Generalities, such as "The principal is the gatekeeper of change," or "The principal and the school is the unit of change," provide no practical clarity about what the principal could or should do. We have seen the complexities of the change process, and general exhortations only create obscure, impossible expectations. Given the other demands on the role, it is no wonder that most principals do not approach their change responsibilities with enthusiasm. In the best of times very few of us go out of our way to do something that is both complex and unclear. Stated another way, principals are being asked *to change their role* and become more active in curricular leadership in the school. This role change is a far more important innovation to the principal than any specific program innovation. Role changes, as we have seen with the teacher, have their costs and presumed benefits which create ambivalence even among those who are willing to try.

---

5 And I will formulate a set of guidelines at the end of this chapter which principals could use to move in directions consistent with greater program involvement.

The principal has had little preparation for managing these dilemmas of change, and even less time to reflect on this aspect of his or her work while on the job (see chapter 14 for a discussion of the preparation of principals; and Sarason, 1971, ch. 8).

What do principals specifically do about potential changes in their schools? All the evidence at our disposal confirms that the majority of principals play a limited role in educational change. Those who do become involved have a strong influence on how well the change progresses; those who don't show an interest have an equally powerful influence on how poorly it goes.[6]

## The principal's role in change

The Rand study of Federal Programs Supporting Educational Change followed up the results of several types of federally sponsored educational programs in almost 300 school districts. Berman and McLaughlin report that one-third of the teachers in their study thought that their principal functioned primarily as an administrator. Teachers rated these principals as ineffective and uninvolved in change. The authors do not say how many of the other two-thirds were directly involved in change, but they describe what "successful" principals did. They found that "projects having the *active* support of the principal were the most likely to fare well" (Berman & McLaughlin, 1977, p. 124; their italics). They claim that the principal's *actions* (not what he or she "says") carry the message as to whether a change is to be taken seriously and serve to support teachers. They note that one of the best indicators of active involvement is whether the principal attends workshop sessions with teachers. Emrick and Peterson's (1978) synthesis of five major research studies in the U.S. also identified direct administrative interest and support as one of five major generalizations common to all the studies.

In a series of interviews we carried out in Ontario on what principals were doing with provincial curriculum guidelines (policy), one of the secondary school principals provided a good description of what active involvement means to him:

The principal has to become directly involved. He may not know mathematics per se or science or history; but he can [be] and the teachers can see him as an expert in curriculum planning. That's the one thing he has to do is develop and acquire some expertise in this area. I think he has to work with the departments in helping them plan what they are going to do with that guideline. He has to meet with them, he has to sit down with them, he's got to be familiar enough with the document that he can discuss it. He has to be prepared to give some of his time to that particular group of teachers, let's say the English department, and be involved in not all of their meetings, but some of them, keeping informed, being knowledgeable about what they are doing. I think he's got to help them plan what they are going to do and then help them measure whether they're doing it or not. *But if the principal detaches himself from it, and says, "Go ahead fellows," and that's what happens too often, then I don't think it will happen effectively.* (interview, June 1980; my italics)

---

6 Those statements are oversimplified, and their full meaning will become clearer over the next few pages. At a later point I will compare the principal as initiator of change and as facilitator, and also compare the elementary and secondary school principal.

The principal goes on in the interview to say it is necessary to establish priorities about which subjects will receive attention at any one time, so that the time demands are manageable. The main point, however, is that serious problems at the implementation stage will likely go unresolved if the principal is uninterested, or even if he or she verbally supports the change but does not participate in some fashion.

Hall, Loucks, and others were involved in a three-year project in Jefferson County, Colorado, in which the district attempted to revise the teaching of science in grades 3 through 6 in the 80 elementary schools in the county. They were able to monitor implementation over the three-year period, during which they assessed the levels of implementation of the curriculum in each classroom. They found that the degree of implementation by teachers in a school was a direct function of what the principal did. From their field research they give the following descriptions:

Principals in [certain schools] did not get personally involved with teachers and their use of the science innovation. Rather these principals delegated responsibility or made major decisions with little follow-up on the results. For example, in School 1, the principal assigned the administrative assistant to handle anything related to science, and in School 3, the principal assigned a teacher to handle science materials and never checked to see what happened. The principal in these schools seemed to be more concerned with general issues rather than specifics and left teachers on their own to determine how to implement the innovation. (Hall et al., 1980, p. 24)

In other schools in which better implementation resulted, principals

were concerned about supporting and helping teachers in their use of the innovation, so on a weekly and daily basis they were monitoring what teachers were doing with science. They set policy within the school that clearly indicated that science would be taught. They worked on teacher specific implementation problems. They also served on the district-wide principals committee for science. (p. 24)

The authors conclude that "the single most important hypothesis emanating from these data is that *the degree of implementation of the innovation is different in different schools because of the actions and concerns of principals*" (Hall et al., 1980, p. 26; their italics).

Reinhard et al. (1980) contribute a similar set of descriptions in their field-based research on what happened with Teacher Corps projects (see Appendix). The sample included six elementary schools, four middle schools, and four high schools in rural, suburban, and urban settings. They found that in the most successful projects the principals were intensely involved at the initial stage. What was done at this stage by the principal drastically affected later success or failure of the project. At later stages, in very small schools principals had to stay very much involved if the project was to proceed. In larger schools the principal normally did not stay involved on a day-to-day basis, but "a pattern observed in successful projects was for the principal to remain interested and ready to problem-solve around obstacles the project might encounter" (Reinhard et al., 1980, p. 9).

Rosenblum and Jastrzab's (1980) case studies of the role of 13 principals in four Teacher Corps projects reinforces the validity of the findings I have been describing. Projects were more successful when principals gave general approval, allowed access to teachers, *and* took an active role in the project (p. 32). Active did not always mean direct. In some cases, the principal delegated day-to-day responsibilities to an assistant: "As long as the principal was actively involved and interested in getting feedback from the assistant, the project did not suffer—all of the staff were aware that the principal was committed to the project and to follow up on their participation in it" (p. 39). Direct involvement was more likely in elementary schools, but Rosenblum and Jastrzab, in reflecting on the indirect but active facilitating role, observe: "Secondary school administrators can play much more of an educational leadership role than is often presumed" (p. 39). The most recent large-scale research studies (DESSI and RDU) also have something to say about the role of the principal. In preliminary analysis the DESSI study shows that when teachers perceive that the principal is supportive of a change and willing to provide or arrange for assistance, teachers are much more likely to change their classroom practice (Crandall et al., forthcoming).[7] The RDU project found that direct principal influence was not a powerful influence on change, but in many of the most successful schools the principals "facilitated" a process which was led by other staff.

The research focusing on the link between evaluative information and the use of such information for program improvement at the school level also stresses the role of the principal. Not many principals or school districts utilize testing and other program information to plan and implement specific changes, but in two recent studies of "exemplary" school districts known for their use of evaluation information, principals were seen to be important agents (see Kennedy et al., 1980; Neumann, 1981; Williams & Bank, 1981).

It seems, then, beyond question that the principal's interest in instructional matters and program and organizational planning is critical. The school effects research corroborates this finding. Wellisch et al. (1978) carried out an in-depth study of 22 elementary schools in which they correlated principals' leadership in instruction to school success in raising reading and mathematics achievement. The sample was part of a national evaluation of school districts supported through the Emergency School Aid Act. In brief, the schools in which principals showed a direct interest in instruction were significantly more likely to show gains in student achievement.[8]

## The extent of principal involvement in change

The list goes on—but perhaps we should pause to consider two of the more basic questions. First, what percentage of principals in our schools show an

7 The DESSI research also found some examples of successful change in situations where the principal was not at all involved. In those cases project directors or other local program leaders provided the daily support and direction. The general point is that someone with some authority who is close to the scene must actively facilitate the process because there are so many inevitable problems that crop up and require attention. The principal is usually a key figure in facilitating (or preventing) change; but it is possible for significant change to occur when there is an alternative program leader *and* the principal is content to allow it to proceed.

8 Clark's (1980) review of 40 research studies on school success, Edmonds's (1979) description of effective schools in disadvantaged areas, and Moore et al.'s (1981) study of effective reading programs also single out the principal. See also Venezky and Winfield (1979), Leithwood and Montgomery (1981), and Fullan (1981b) for reviews of the role of the principal in effective change, and Greenfield (1982).

active interest in instruction? Second, when they do participate in instructional matters, do they always do good? (Or, stated another way, are there different *types* of change roles played by principals?)

I have indicated earlier that the majority of principals in North America do not operate as instructional coordinators or leaders in their schools. The question, of course, is an empirical one; the answer varies from district to district depending on whether the district has emphasized and supported principals in this role, as some districts recently have (see chapter 10). When teachers are asked who influences their curricular decisions, very few mention the principal or rank the principal very high (e.g., Aoki et al., 1977; Leithwood & MacDonald, 1981). More direct examinations of any given group of principals show that administrative management is the modal category. Leithwood et al. (1978) observed and interviewed 27 principals from three school districts. They discovered four types of leaders—administrative (50%), facilitative (31%), directive (12%), and interpersonally oriented (8%). In other words, when it came to curriculum change, one-half the sample operated basically as administrators. In the words of the authors:

The administrative leader is essentially a passive observer of the curriculum process in his school. He keeps track of what is going on and may make suggestions on an infrequent basis; he becomes directly involved only if there is a visible problem. (Leithwood et al., 1978, p. 66)

Equally interesting apropos of the comments by Rosenblum and Jastrzab above is the distinction between facilitative and directive leaders, because *both* play an instructional change leadership role. The facilitative leaders were "highly involved in the curriculum decisions of teachers" (Leithwood et al., p. 70). They used a variety of strategies to organize and influence teachers. They established priorities, but "relied heavily upon teachers to influence other teachers" (p. 71). By contrast, the more directive leaders decided themselves on the nature of change and attempted to get their teachers to follow their decisions.

Thomas (1978) identified essentially the same three main roles as Leithwood in her study of principals in alternative school programs in Alum Rock, California, in Minneapolis, Minnesota, in Cincinnati, Ohio, and in Eugene, Oregon. In those projects principals were observed and described as either directors, administrators, or facilitators. Of the 68 principals in the study, 49% acted as administrators (identical to Leithwood's finding), 26% as directors, and 25% as facilitators. Schools which had administrative-oriented principals did not implement the alternative programs as effectively as the others. For example, in Minneapolis "the five schools where either a majority of the teachers did not follow the same classroom practices, or where the teachers were following classroom practices not consistent with their program label, were headed by principals who behaved primarily as administrators" (p. 60). The directive and facilitative principals were equally effective in implementing the alternative programs that they had set out to.

The distinction between directive and facilitative principals may be important, for research on the principal which lumps together all principals who are involved in an innovation may result in misleading or inconsistent findings. There is some other evidence that strong directive principals under certain conditions may do more harm than good. Smith and Keith's (1971) now famous case study of a new elementary school provides abundant description of the massive failure of the innovation and the role of the principal in the process. Lighthall's review and critique of the book forcefully brings home the point in discussing the principal (Eugene Shelby):

Again and again it was the images of Eugene's reality, not the images of others' realities, that had to determine actual events .... Shelby appeared from the data to use every possible occasion to bring others' behavior in conformity with his reality. He knew best. What he did not know was that what he knew best was a small fraction of the total social reality of his staff. (Lighthall, 1973, pp. 277–78)

Miles's (1978) case studies of two new open-space schools raise similar issues about the subtleties of the principal's role in change. It *appeared* that in one school the principal was actively endorsing the open-education change with his staff and that the other principal was not. Yet it was in the latter principal's school where most implementation was achieved. In probing for possible explanations, Miles discovered that the so-called active principal was continually endorsing the innovation in public (with parents and central office administrators) but his actions (or absence of actions) with staff conveyed to them a lack of endorsement on his part. Teachers felt the general pressure for change but no clear or specific support from the principal as to what they were supposed to do. Consequently, low implementation resulted. In the other school, although the principal did not actively intervene, Miles found that he was indirectly supportive of the teachers' work. The principal's support affected the extent of the "help given" by teachers, and "help received" among teachers, with the latter being directly related to better program implementation (see Galanter, 1978, for the details). Thus, the meaning and influence of principal endorsement of change is not always clear and requires close examination.

Blumberg and Greenfield's (1980) in-depth study of eight "effective" principals throws further light on how administrative matters are managed. The eight principals were identified through reputational criteria and were selected to represent male/female, elementary/secondary, and rural/urban differences. There were a great many differences among the eight, but some common elements stood out, most notably "their individual commitment to the realization of a particular educational or organizational vision" and "their ability to satisfy the routine organizational maintenance demands in a manner that permits them to spend most of their on-the-job time in activities directly related to the realization of their personal mission" (p. 208). The reference to the management of routine matters is particularly revealing in light of the frequent finding that many principals are preoccupied with administrative detail and routine.

To summarize what is known about the role and impact of the principal on change, four main conclusions can be stated.[9] First, a large percentage of principals (at least one-half) operate mainly as administrators and as ad hoc crisis managers. These principals are not effective in helping to bring about changes in their schools. Second, those principals who do become involved in change do so either as direct instructional leaders or as facilitative instructional leaders. Both styles of leadership can be effective. It seems that the direct leader can be

---

9 Very recent research describes different facilitation styles of principals. See Hall et al. (1982); also Huling et al. (1982); Hord et al. (1982); Rutherford et al. (1982).

effective only if he or she is clear about the purpose of change and has (or can select) teachers who agree with the direction of change. Third, the principal cannot become an expert in all subject areas, and has great demands on his or her time, especially in larger schools. Being a facilitator or coordinator of change is probably the more effective role under these conditions. Fourth, none of this research says that change is impossible without the principal, or that the principal is always the most important person. There are many instances of teacher leaders or project leaders having had a strong impact on implementation, but they usually had supportive principals; if they did not, the results of their initial efforts tended to disappear before long. As Reinhard et al. (1980, p. 9) say, "In almost every instance in which we studied a project that was near the end of its life or had ended, the principal decided what was to remain." Whether it is direct or indirect, the principal plays a fateful role in the implementation and continuance of any change proposal; the evidence is very strong on this point.

# The principal's dilemma: coping with change

I have strayed from the question of what might be going on in the minds of principals as they deal with change. It is necessary to return to this way of thinking in order to understand the actions of principals.

Change may be of two kinds—that which the principal initiates, or, more typically, that which is initiated external to the school (by the district or the government) and is applied to all or most schools. I start with the latter because it is the more frequent experience for principals.

## The principal as the person in the middle

Educational changes of various sorts are constantly before the principal as reformers or reactors try to right the educational system. Whether a particular change is seen as a backward or forward step depends on our point of view, but all reforms including "back to the basics" are proposals for change. The principal is constantly being admonished to ensure or support implementation of this or that new policy or project. In Canada, revised provincial curriculum guidelines are always on the doorstep as the cyclical revision process continues ad infinitum. Legislation for special education, community-based programs, and work–school options are added to the list along with any other project deemed important by school trustees or central district administrators. In the United States, it is all the more chaotic because more levels are involved. In addition to the local and state demands, the federal government, unlike in Canada, has had a strong indirect presence in local innovation. (How much this will change with President Reagan's orientation to decentralization remains to be seen.) Categorical grants, federal legislation, supreme court rulings, and voluntary projects on every conceivable topic are being perpetrated on the educational system. It would not be unusual for a school district to be participating in twenty or more federally sponsored programs at any one time, all of which have implications for the principal.

What do school principals think of all this ferment? If we were able to get inside their minds, the following script would probably come close to the truth:

*Here is another change which is politically and not educationally motivated, and which will probably be reversed in two years anyway. The teachers are not interested in it, or don't have the time to deal with it. They will groan and bitch about it. I hate to even present it to them. I really don't understand the program. It seems so abstract and full of nice generalities. The one-half-hour orientation we received at the last principals' meeting only confused me further. I doubt if the superintendent or the board members know what it means either, judging by their comments. The superintendent wants it in order to look good. I will put it on the agenda of the next staff meeting and get it over with. I worry about any future meetings we might have to have on it. I hope nobody follows up on it. My annual principal report will describe that the new program has been introduced.*

Of course, a single fragment cannot capture the variety of change projects and reactions. Some projects have new staff positions, district project directors, and specified resources which will require the principal to make certain decisions and to hold meetings and workshops to monitor how the change is going. If the project is not a sound one or the principal for whatever reason is not confident about the change and his or her role in it, these meetings (even if the principal does not have to participate) will be a painful, visible reminder of an undesirable anxiety-producing side of the job. Many principals will also have strong pangs of guilt and questions about their own adequacy and competence in managing such a crazy thing as a school. They will know that many new policies are attempting to address important educational goals which are currently not being met, and that some students and their parents are not getting a fair deal. When they do make a sincere effort to bring the issues to the attention of teachers, countless more questions will emerge about how to address the problem. Each proposed solution seems to raise more new problems than it remedies. The veteran principal eventually learns to take all this with a grain of salt.

A number of things are implicit in the above descriptions. First, the principal is usually not helped by central administrators in how to deal with the change. On the contrary, he or she is given a brief description in a meeting where it is difficult to say in front of peers or superiors, "I don't understand it," or "I have serious concerns about whether we ought to be doing this," without feeling stupid or being seen as reactionary.

Second, the principal will experience all these feelings and concerns *privately*.[10] Principals do not have much opportunity or create much opportunity to interact professionally with other principals, although there is some desire to do so (see Blumberg & Greenfield, 1980, p. 168). As Sarason (1971, p. 117) observes, the principal "escaped from one kind of role loneliness [as a teacher] to another."

It is ironic to think of principals surrounded by people all day long as lonely. But they do not have much opportunity to exchange ideas under constructive conditions. Rosenblum and Jastrzab (1981, p. 46) identified the positive side of interaction in their case studies: "One of the most important benefits ... in the project is the *opportunity to meet with other principals and discuss common problems and frustrations*" (their italics). In one of the four sites in-service training was

---

10 See also Sarason (1972, chs. 9–11) on leadership. The chapter "Leader's Sense of Privacy and Superiority" contains a fresh and insightful account of this unrecognized but deeply important phenomenon.

specifically designed for administrators, and principals stated that this was one of the most successful project activities, even though they were at first not eager to participate in the training sessions.

Third, the principal does not share concerns with teachers either. The tradition among teachers (which the principal learned as a teacher) and the history of relationships between principals and teachers are more based on keeping a distance and respecting each other's professional autonomy. The principal's supervisory/evaluative role creates another barrier to confronting the problems of change openly:

> He quickly learns that telling a teacher what is wrong or insisting upon a change is a far from effective means for changing attitudes and practices. The power to legislate change is no guarantee that the change will occur—a principle the principal learned when as a teacher he was confronted with changing the behavior of children. From the standpoint of the principal there is little he feels he can do about what goes on in the classroom, particularly if the teacher has tenure or has been a teacher for a number of years. (Sarason, 1971, p. 120)

In situations where interaction is awkward or painful for one or both parties (or presumed to be so) most people do the obvious, if they have the choice—*they minimize contact*. Without personal contact there is no significant change.

We are talking about the existence of historical norms in schools, according to which it is assumed that people want to be left alone to carry out their professional responsibilities. For many this is no doubt true, but *many other teachers and principals desire more social contact around professional matters, if it can be done in a supportive climate*. Unless all teachers and principals are isolates, it could hardly be otherwise. The problem with norms is that people sometimes mistakenly assume that they are held by others. For example, the principal who talks infrequently with teachers about recent changes, because he or she sees the teachers as "professionals," may be perceived by some teachers as not interested in the change or in them—a perception which could be far from the truth.

Fourth, few things could be more uncomfortable or more undermining of our confidence than being expected by our superiors to lead the implementation of a change (1) which we do not understand, (2) in which subordinates are not interested, or (3) in which they are interested but it is unclear how they are to obtain necessary resources and assistance.

The fifth implicit aspect is that the principal is in the middle of a highly complicated personal and organizational change process. Knowledge, understanding, and skills in the change process are essential in sorting out the potentially good from the bad changes, and in getting the good ones implemented.

## What to do

We can never know absolutely what are the good changes, but we do know a fair amount about how to set up a process of change which makes it more likely that better decisions will be made and that fewer negative change experiences will occur. There are two ways in which a social system changes: either those in the system change their behavior for whatever reasons, or new system members with different characteristics are added and replace some existing members. In most social systems, both types of change are going on simultaneously in different degrees. So it is with the principalship. Many principals, particularly in school districts which emphasize principal leadership and provide principals with professional development and support, are becoming more involved in implementing educational innovations. At the same time, some principals are retiring, and newer ones are being appointed with (in many cases) explicit change-related attitudes and skills among the criteria for their selection. It is not an attack on old age per se to recognize that thousands of principals were promoted in the late 1950s and 1960s with little thought given to their roles as implementers of change. Even when change was considered, innovativeness rather than ability to lead implementation—which is quite a different thing— was the main criterion. Nor could it have been otherwise, with the need to rapidly staff hundreds of new schools and with the lack of knowledge at the time about what it means to implement changes. Be that as it may, even today it is not clear how principals are selected. The only reasonably systematic study I know of is just being conducted (Baltzell, 1981). The results are not in yet, but we can wager that the selection process varies a great deal from district to district, uses unclear criteria, and applies those that are used unevenly. Knowledge and ability as managers or facilitators of organizational implementation should be a primary criterion for selection.

In the meantime every principal has a conception of his or her role; and these conceptions vary as we have seen, in that some principals are actively engaged in leading or facilitating change, while others are not. Certainly different systems (school districts, states, provinces) limit or facilitate change in different ways, but the starting point from the individual principal's point of view should be a reflection on how his or her own *conception* of the role of the principal has built-in limitations regarding change. Sarason captures this problem in the following words:

While I do not in any way question that characteristics of the system can and do have interfering effects on an individual's performance, it is the major theme of this chapter that "the system" is frequently conceived by the individual in a way that obscures, many times unwittingly, the range of possibilities available to him. Too frequently the individual's conception of the system serves as a basis for inaction and rigidity, or as a convenient target onto which one can direct blame for almost anything. (1971, p. 134)

Thus, principals within the same system operating under almost identical circumstances will work with change, or avoid it, depending on *their* conception of the role. Just as the teachers' sense of efficacy is important in bringing about school improvement, so is the principal's—perhaps more significant, because it affects *the whole organization*. Rosenblum and Jastrzab (1981, p. 46), among others, found that many principals were unaware of the extent of influence they could have over the projects. We could also speculate that many principals are diffident about their change leadership role because they do not feel prepared or clear about how to carry it out. Principals as much as anyone need to develop meaning about change and the change process. Opportunities for interaction and professional development about the role of the principal in change are very much needed, and only recently are being established (see Leithwood & Montgomery, 1981; Rosenblum et al., 1981, district descriptions in chs. 10 and 14).

The individual principal interested in increasing his or her capacity for coping with externally initiated changes, or in planning internal changes, should seek out those opportunities. In so doing many principals may discover that they can have more influence in leading change than they had assumed. At least part of the limitations of their roles may be self-imposed.

# Guidelines for coping

Drawing all this together into a set of suggestions for how the principal might cope with change proposals coming from outside the school is a difficult task, but I offer the following general guidelines in assessing particular changes:

1 Critically reflect on whether your own conception of the role is placing unnecessary limits on what can be done. This kind of reflection is difficult to undertake unaided. Get feedback from teachers and other principals whom you trust.

2 Determine the extent to which the district administration supports and really expects the principal to play a major role in the implementation of change.

3 For any given change, assess whether it potentially addresses a program need (an educational goal that is currently being met inadequately), as seen by teachers, parents, district administrators, etc.

4 For any given change, attempt to determine *why* the district administration is proposing it. One of the most important indicators is whether there are resources allocated to implementation—not unlimited resources, but enough to indicate that the administration is serious about the change and has some knowledge of what implementation entails. Lack of resources may not reflect lack of seriousness; so test the possibilities (negotiate).

5 In considering 3 and 4, determine whether the change is a priority among other changes. There is a limit to how many innovations can be handled at once, but *some* change priorities can and should be selected for any time period.

6 In assessing the need for change, talk with teachers about their views. If many teachers recognize the need, or if you observe that there is a serious problem, set up a change process built on the assumptions in chapter 6, the concerns of teachers described in chapter 7, and the knowledge in this chapter of what effective principals do. Knowledge and conceptions of the change process and corresponding planning are a necessary foundation to which must be added some knowledge or familiarity with the content of the change and communication and interpersonal skills. It would be repetitive to review all those things which effective principals did, but two things stand out. They showed an active interest by spending time talking with teachers, planning, helping teachers get together, being knowledgeable about what was happening. They all figured out ways of reducing the amount of time spent on routine administrative matters; they made sure that change had an equal priority. It may take some time to overcome teachers' historical experiences with principals, but the evidence shows that many teachers want to interact with fellow teachers around an innovation, and want direct support from principals.

7 Seek out some opportunities for personal/professional development and informal/formal exchanges with fellow principals about what principals are and should be doing.

8 In reacting to some particular changes which seem unrealistic or meaningless, do what you always do (keep it from getting out of hand), but discuss the meaning of change with teachers and fellow principals.

9 If all changes seem senseless, or if you have no interest in program change, go back to guideline 1.

# The principal as initiator

Nearly all of the same guidelines apply to the principal who has personally initiated or developed a proposal for change. The only major additional guideline is a reminder that our personal commitment to a particular change should not blind us to the necessity of setting up a process of change within the school. Commitment to a change, along with the assumption that authority to legislate it is the same as power to implement it, is often a lethal combination (unless the principal has the power to replace all the teachers who disagree). The principal as initiator can have a powerful influence on teachers provided that he or she is willing to work with teachers over a period of time, be open to modifications in the idea, and be sensitive to the need for teachers to develop their own sense of meaning in relation to the change.

The reader should be reminded that the above guidelines refer to the principal's role *as an agent of change*. There are many other aspects of the role—community relations, scheduling, security and safety, staffing, the law, etc.—which are contained in more basic books on the principalship. Nor has there been space to consider the different kinds of community and school conditions faced by principals. The chapter, however, was written with these things in mind. It says that principals must (and many do) carve out a role in leading and facilitating educational change proposals, if effective implementation is to happen. The details of this aspect of their role will differ according to the size and type of school.[11]

It should be noted that the research cited in this chapter comes equally from studies of elementary and secondary school principals. There are differences which should be examined in greater detail than I have done. (See Lieberman & Miller, 1982, for chapter on the life of the secondary school principal.) Their role in change also differs by virtue of the fact that the secondary school principal is running a much bigger operation. However, their ultimate responsibility for leading organizational and program changes designed to bring about improvements does not differ. The elementary school principal can work more directly with individual staff members, but the secondary school principal needs to work with, and influence the role of, department heads and other administrative staff to promote positive change.

Principals will vary in terms of how directly they will get involved as instructional leaders; but if change is as important as maintenance, principals as heads of the organization should play a leadership role in the planning and coordination of new or revised programs in the school. As with teachers, the management of change must become a regular, ongoing part of the principal's job, if the organizational factors which affect change are to be confronted. In other words, the principal has to learn to manage the implementation process at the school level, taking into account all those factors known to influence change in practice (chapter 5).

It was not long ago that many innovators (project directors, teachers, superintendents, university professors) used to figure out ways of bypassing the principal in an attempt to get changes implemented directly in the classroom. The

---

11 I have also left out any discussion of the role of the vice-principal or department head. These would have to be examined in any full treatment of the administration of a school.

assumption was that the principal was more of an obstacle than a help, and that anything that would neutralize his or her role would be a good thing. Many soon found out that the principal still ended up being a powerful force in whether the change went anywhere—all the more powerful by dint of his or her reaction to being ignored in the process.[12] If these innovators concluded (as many did) that principals were incorrigible blockers of progress, they did not learn their lesson. There are no doubt principals who should not be in their positions, or who cannot manage or tolerate change; but by far the more important lesson of these failed efforts is that implementation, as we have seen throughout the previous chapters, is an *organizational process*, with all that that entails both within the school and in relation to external contacts. Once that is said, it should be self-evident that the principal as head of the organization is critical regarding any proposed change. As long as we have schools and principals, if the principal does not lead the development of an effective organizational process, or if he or she leaves it to others, it will normally not get done. That is, change will not happen.

---

12 The initial Teacher Corps regulations, for example, ignored the principal. Later regulations added the principal as an important element, although the role of the principal is still not explicit, and in-service training for administrators not widely available (Rosenblum & Jastrzab, 1981).

 Chapter 9

# The Student

*Why in a democratic society, should an individual's first real contact with a formal institution be so profoundly anti-democratic?*

— *Bowles and Gintis, 1976, pp. 250–51*

In the field of educational innovation it is surprising how many times a teacher will finally shout out of desperation, "But what about the students?" Innovations and their inherent conflicts often become ends in themselves, and students often get thoroughly lost in the shuffle. When adults do think of students, they think of them as the potential beneficiaries of change. They think of achievement results, skills, attitudes, and jobs. *They rarely think of students as participants in a process of change and organizational life.*

In this chapter I continue to pursue the main theme of the book. Educational change, above all, is a people-related phenomenon for each and every individual. Students, even little ones, are people too. Unless they have some meaningful (to them) role in the enterprise, most educational change, indeed most education, will fail. I ask the reader not to think of students as running the school, but to entertain the following question: *What would happen if we treated the student as someone whose opinion mattered in the introduction and implementation of change in schools?*

I start with a look at where students are, followed by a consideration of the student and change, and guidelines for coping with change.

## Where students are

Tremendous numbers and diversity of students, combined with minimal research from the students' point of view, make it impossible to do justice to the question of where students are. Instead, I will present a summary of some of the main issues that seem to concern students. This will be used as a context for considering the student and change.

In the seven-year period 1970–77 I was involved in a large-scale and smaller-scale intensive research project on the role of students in Ontario schools (see Fullan & Eastabrook, 1973; Fullan, Eastabrook, & Biss, 1977). We started with a survey of students in 46 Ontario schools representing a range of large-city, medium-size-city, suburban, and rural settings. Information was gathered from a random sample of students in grades 5 through 13 (Ontario high schools go to grade 13). The information was collected directly by us in classrooms using a questionnaire. The original sample was 3972, from which we obtained 3593 returns, or a 90% response rate. Questions included both fixed-choice formats and open-ended questions asking for comments. We categorized the responses according to three levels: elementary school (grades 5–6, or 5–8 in some schools), junior high (grades 7–9), and high school (grades 9–13, or 10–13 in some schools). The following summarizes our main findings:

1  A minority of students think that teachers understand their point of view, and the proportion decreases with educational level—41%, 33%, and 25% from elementary, junior high, and high school respectively.
2  Less than one-fifth of the students reported that teachers asked for the opinions and ideas of students in deciding what or how to teach (19%, 16%, 13%), a finding which we consistently replicated in subsequent work in a large number of classrooms in other schools.
3  Principals and vice-principals were not seen as listening to or being influenced by students.
4  Substantial percentages of students, including one out of every two high school students, reported that "most of my classes or lessons are boring" (29%, 26%, 50%).

Written comments on open-ended questions elaborate the meaning of the fixed-format responses. About one thousand students (of the total of almost 3600) wrote comments about the school. Of these about 30% reflected positive attitudes such as:

"Teachers are friendly." (elementary)

"This school is great." (junior high)

"I think the school I go to is good the way it is now. It doesn't need any changes." (junior high)

"I like my school because it has modern techniques, teaching methods and facilities. It is a clean and up to date school. I think they should keep the school just the way it is." (high school)

The other 70% of the comments are indicative of what we labeled generally as "the alienation theme":

"I think schools should make students feel comfortable, and not tense." (high school)

"I feel that teachers don't really care about what happens to students as long as they get paid." (elementary)

"I know that school is important to me and that I need it to get anywhere in life. But I'm beginning to realize that this reason is not good enough. I don't enjoy school at this point. It is the last place I want to be. If I wasn't so shy I imagine I could express these feelings to a teacher, but I've never spoken to one, not even about extra help." (high school)

"I'm only in school so I can go to university so as to make more money than if I quit school now. I do not particularly like school, in fact sometimes I hate it, but I don't particularly want to be poor." (high school)

Our questions on principals and vice-principals stimulated many comments from junior high and senior high students along the following lines:

"I have never spoken to the principal, and I don't even know who the vice-principal is."

"It's hard to say anything about the principal. He's always hiding."

"We never see him and I think the only kids he knows is the head boy and the head girl. He seems like a nice man, but who really knows, when he is always in his office."[1]

Finally, we asked students an open-ended question about what they thought of the questionnaire and the project. This opened a floodgate. Over one-third of the students wrote responses, nearly all of which indicated that students were interested in the topics and had something to say. Typical of these 1200 responses were the following:

"I think this project is very interesting in many ways. It asks many questions that I have never been asked before." (elementary)

"I think its great that grown-ups want our opinion. I feel that they treat us like babies." (elementary)

"It brought me to thinking about things I had never thought much about, and is giving you at the institution, knowledge of what we students think about the school." (junior high)

"No comment. Only that this may help the teachers or planning board realize what lousy classes and subjects we are taking." (high school)

"I think this is an excellent project. It gives the man at the bottom of the ladder a chance to unleash his feelings and say something about this damn school." (high school)

We followed up this research with some intensive work in two high schools in which we worked in over forty classrooms over a three-year period (Eastabrook & Fullan, 1978; Fullan et al., 1977). With the classroom as the unit, we met with students and teachers, developed a new questionnaire based on their input, had the questionnaires filled out, and reported and discussed the results with students and with teachers and students together. In addition to their corroborating the earlier findings, a number of more specific issues emerged:

1  While we found that students did not think that teachers understood them, there was even more of a communication gap among students (except those who were close friends or in one's own group). While 41% of the students felt that teachers did not understand their point of view, 63% indicated that fellow students did not know or understand their point of view. Most students had two or three close friends in a class; some were isolates. There was virtually no communication inside or outside of class with *the vast majority of other students* (i.e., outside of one's own small friendship group).

2  Only a small number of students participated regularly in classroom discussions (typically 5 to 8 students out of a class of 25–30). In response to a fixed-choice question, 86% of the students said that most fellow students do not participate in class discussions or ask questions. Lack of familiarity with other students, combined with extreme sensitivity and self-consciousness in the presence of peers, strongly inhibited classroom participation.

---

1 Of course, students who get in trouble frequently see the principal or vice-principal.

3 Students who were not interested in going to college or university were impatiently waiting for the day when they could leave the school and get out and make money. They were not at all interested in the curriculum. Interaction with close friends provided the only satisfaction at school.

4 College- or university-bound students were interested in discussing curriculum participation and had many ideas to suggest. However, their predominant orientation was to "cover the course topics" and "get good grades." These students valued teachers who were fair in their grading practices, knowledgeable in their subject areas, and friendly and helpful.

The limited amount of other research on the views of students provides confirmation for most of the above findings and helps us to understand further what students think. At the elementary school level, Sarason (1971) did an informal observational study to see how the rules of the classroom were formed (what he calls the constitution of the classroom) and what assumptions about students were implicit in the process. In Sarason's words, "the results were quite clear": the rules were invariably determined by the teacher; teachers never solicited the opinions and feelings of students in developing rules. In making explicit the assumptions underlying the observed behavior, Sarason suggests several: (1) teacher knows best; (2) children cannot participate constructively in the development of rules; (3) children are not interested in such a discussion; (4) rules are for children, and not for the teacher (rules state what children can and cannot do, but not what a teacher could or could not do); and so on (pp. 175–76). Sarason also observed that teachers rarely, if ever, discussed their own thinking about planning and learning. Issues pertaining to teachers' assumptions and theories of learning and thinking, whether children were interested in these matters, and whether they were able to talk about them, never came up.[2] Rather, the task of the student was to get the right answer and know the facts. Sarason comments that teachers "unwittingly [created] those conditions that they would personally find boring" (p. 182).

The central issue, however, is contained in the following passage:

The point I wish to emphasize is that it appears that children know relatively little about how a teacher thinks about the classroom, that is, what he takes into account, the alternatives he thinks about, the things that puzzle him about children and about learning, what he does when he is not sure of what he should do, how he feels when he does something wrong. (Sarason, 1971, p. 185)

Sarason states that he is only raising the question of whether children would be curious about what the teacher plans and thinks, and whether it might be helpful to children to know this. But he also makes clear his own position:

If my experience with school children—in fact, with all levels of students, from elementary through graduate school—is any guide, that large part of a teacher's "thinking about thinking" which is never made public is precisely what children are interested in and excited about on those rare occasions when it becomes public. (p. 187)

---

2 These very issues of thinking, learning, and problem-solving are exactly the higher-order cognitive objectives fundamental to inquiry learning, which most people agree do not get adequately taught in schools.

These same issues could be stated in another more direct curricular way. When teachers plan a lesson or unit, do they discuss their ideas and concerns with students? Would it be helpful (regarding modification of the curriculum, achievement of objectives, etc.) if they did? The former question has been answered by our own research and that of others. Teachers do not discuss these issues with students. Clark and Yinger's (1980) close look at "the hidden world of teacher planning" confirms this finding and suggests (pp. 21–22) an answer to the second question of whether it may be beneficial:

No matter how elaborate and complete a plan may be, it cannot be carried out successfully unless the students are brought rather fully into the knowledge of what to do and how to do it, and brought to a commitment to cooperation in the process . . . . But communication of plans to students is almost never addressed.

Sarason's and Clark and Yinger's research was based on elementary school teachers, although the main findings about the role of students in schools holds true at all levels. Additional aspects of the life of secondary school students have been documented in several other studies.[3] For example, House and Lapan (1978) discuss student views of teachers under the chapter heading "Credibility with Students." Using taped interviews with 211 high school students from three schools and a more extensive secondary analysis of other research findings, they identify five main factors that make teachers credible in the eyes of students. In order of importance, they are (1) *teacher openness* (is willing to accept suggestions; encourages students to express their ideas, likes, and dislikes about the subject area or methods), (2) *teacher qualification* (subject matter knowledge and expertise), (3) *communication effectiveness* (ability to communicate clearly and to make material understandable), (4) clarity in *defining expectations* (about what is expected of students), and (5) *teacher objectivity* (gives fair and objective evaluations of all students equally). Our own study cited above tends to corroborate these findings, and indicates that most students do not perceive these characteristics in most student–teacher relationships.

Cusick (1973) spent an entire school year carrying out a participant observation study of students in one high school. He too found that students were relegated to the role of passive listeners in class and that student group-life rather than classroom interests dominated the school day.

For any single senior, the time spent actively engaged with some teacher over a matter of cognitive importance may not exceed twenty minutes a period for five periods a day. That is a high estimate. I would say that if an average student spent an hour to one and a half hours a day in school involved in subject matter, that was a good day. (p. 56)

During the rest of the time the student is not paying attention (yawning, looking about, doodling, looking at pictures, chatting, etc.). Commenting on class discussion, Cusick (p. 180) notes that in one typical lesson he observed, only 5

3 More studies of student role have been conducted at the secondary school level than the elementary level. Could it be that this relative emphasis reflects a tacit assumption that secondary school students are old enough to have some opinions while elementary school students are not?

of 22 students in the class participated (virtually identical to our finding). Regarding what interests students most, Cusick writes:

More and more, as I continued in the school, I saw that the students' most active and alive moments, and indeed the great majority of their school time, was spent not with teachers and subject-matter affairs, but in their own small-group interactions which they carried on simultaneously with their class work. (p. 58)

Cusick concentrates a great deal in his writing on student relationships, and he suggests that having friends "may have been the single most important thing in the school" (p. 66). He found, as we did, that students are very clearly distinguished as members of small groups, or as isolates with little contact across groups:[4]

If I were talking to a member of one small group and a friend of mine who was in another group approached, I might find myself in two isolated conversations, since the two students would not even recognize each other's presence. (p. 67)

The consistent theme in Cusick's observations is that only a minority of students are really involved in basic educational processes, with the rest being passive watchers and waiters who pay a minimal amount of attention to formal classroom work while channeling their energy and enthusiasm into their groups of close friends (p. 222).

Research on "time on task," it may be recalled (chapter 7), confirmed Cusick's observations on a more systematic basis. It showed that active learning time in general, and in relation to specific subjects, varied across classrooms and was related to academic achievement. That is, individual students have different degrees of exposure to and involvement in different aspects of the curriculum. If we think of this difference in terms of student behavior, it can be very revealing. An observational study conducted in Britain (Galton et al., 1980; Galton & Simon, 1980) is one of the few projects which examined types of student behavior directly. The authors identified four types, which they labeled attention seekers (19.5% of the total), intermittent workers (35.7%), solitary workers (32.5%), and quiet collaborators (12.3%). The middle two groups of students (i.e., 68.2%) had very little contact with the teacher.

Student behavior differed markedly with teaching style. Galton et al. had identified six main teaching styles (infrequent changers, class inquirers, group instructors, individual monitors, habitual changers, and rotating changers). Differences among pupil types is striking in some cases. For example, the percentage of intermittent workers ranged from 9.2% (in classrooms with teachers having a class inquiry style) to 47.6% (with teachers who had an individual monitor style). The other three student-to-teacher patterns showed similar ranges. Galton and Simon (1980) also observed teacher and student behavior from one year to another. Every teacher observed in the second year displayed the same basic teaching style as in the previous year. However, 70% of the students changed their patterns of behavior on moving to a new teacher in ways compatible with the style of the new teacher. Thus, individual students behave differently, and they do so in response to different teaching styles.

---

4 The experience of the number of individuals who had no friends is particularly heartrending (see Cusick, ch. 6).

The relationship to learning outcomes is complicated, and depends on the educational objective (see Galton & Simon, 1980). Generally, however, the amount of teacher–student contact, particularly contact involving challenging and open-ended questions, was related to student achievement. Some students get exposed to more intensive academic learning activities than others. Little is known about personal/social-development goals mentioned in chapter 1, except that there seems to be little explicit emphasis on them. Whatever the case, students have quite different experiences and show different patterns of behavior in schools, sometimes from teacher to teacher. We do not yet know enough beyond Galton and Simon's pioneering work about (1) how valid the observed patterns are in other schools and what other patterns may be found, (2) what students think about their own behavior and that of other students, and (3) what impact these patterns have on academic and social learning outcomes.

Willis's fascinating account of how working-class youth in a British high school "learn to labour" adds another dimension of what students learn while they are at school (and it ain't the curriculum). Willis conducted a case study of working-class youths in a comprehensive high school in an industrial community in England. He found that the school provided working-class youths with the opportunity to develop and extend their own working-class value structure. Far from providing mobility, the school ironically enabled these youths to consolidate their own system of values precisely counter to the school's formal values:

"The lads" of this study have adopted and developed to a fine degree in their school counter-culture specific working class themes: resistance; subversion of authority; ... and an independent ability to create diversion and enjoyment. (Willis, 1977, p. 84)

The predominance of the informal small groups (as Cusick also found), the working-class values of their parents, the irrelevance and oppression of the middle-class academic values of teachers and other students, and the preoccupation with getting out to make real money permitted the students to develop the values which came most naturally to them. These students literally learn in school how to cope with the kind of conditions and menial jobs which they inevitably will find themselves in as laborers on the shop floor—a deep, hidden, and unconscious social self-fulfilling prophecy. As Willis (1977), Apple (1980), Sharp and Green (1975), and Eggleston (1977, ch. 6) all contend, progressive and liberal educational innovations often enable teachers and working-class students themselves to use the freedom to avoid the curriculum, or to lock themselves into patterns of activities which run counter to the intended goals of the formal curriculum.

The above review of where students are by no means captures all aspects of the students' thoughts and experiences at school. For many students, especially in urban centers, personal safety at school, hunger, racial fights, and unhappy home lives are far more preponderant on their minds. Moreover, it is necessary to separate and compare the different experiences of boys and girls in the culture of the school (see Gaskell, 1981, and Connell et al., 1981, for two examples in a neglected but growing area of research). Both the types of innovations being introduced and the way in which they are implemented should be investigated from the point of view of potential differential impact on boys and on girls. Sexism in the curriculum has received a certain amount of attention, but not enough attention has been paid to the role of girls as participants in the classroom and organizational life of the school in terms of academic and personal/social outcomes.

Despite the need to examine the differences just mentioned, we can be fairly confident in our main conclusions: students are not treated in schools as people whose opinions matter;[5] basic issues on how the classroom is run are rarely discussed; the central satisfaction for the majority of students derives from their relationship with a small circle of friends; there are distinctly different types of student behavior and these vary at least partly with teaching style; academically oriented students are preoccupied with getting good grades; the curriculum has little interest for non-academically oriented students; and social-development goals (independence, interpersonal skills, etc.) do not get adequately taught. As students move from elementary through secondary grade levels they become *increasingly bored and alienated from school.*

*Does and could educational innovation have any meaning for these people?*

# The student and change

As I have indicated, we hardly know anything about what students think about educational change because no one ever asks them. If we were to attempt to infer what some of the experiences with change meant to students, several images come to mind. Four such images which seem to have some basis in fact concern (1) indifference, (2) confusion, (3) temporary escape from boredom, and (4) heightened interest and satisfaction with school.

*Indifference* is closely tied to the claim that the more things change in education the more they remain the same. There is a great deal of evidence which indicates that many changes in curriculum materials have not resulted in any real change in how the classroom operates. To the extent that this is true, students would not notice any significant change. As they move from one grade level to another, their experience in the classroom would be pretty much the same (a good teacher here, a bad teacher there, etc.). For many students the classroom is not the most interesting aspect of schooling anyway. For them the main benefit of the school is the opportunity it provides to interact with close friends on a daily basis. In short, a certain percentage of innovations adopted in schools are reacted to with indifference by students, simply because *the changes in fact do not make a difference to them.*

Non-change is one form of failed implementation. But misdirected change resulting in *confusion* is something else, because "something" does change. Consider the changes undergone by students over the past fifteen or twenty years. At the elementary level, open education, non-grading, individualization, team teaching, and all their associated educational objectives dominated the 1960s and early 1970s. Secondary school students were treated to inquiry learn-

---

5 For a different look at this issue, see our study of high school student reactions to recent teacher strikes in their school district (Fullan & Eastabrook, 1979). What comes through loud and clear in our sample of 1100 students who had experienced strikes was that they had strong feelings about the strike, and that no one cared about their thoughts or bothered to acknowledge them as people involved in a serious situation which affected them deeply.

ing in science and social studies, flexible scheduling, independent study time, free choice in subjects, work study programs, and so on. It does not seem out of line to suggest that the extent to which these programs were not clear in the minds of administrators and teachers would be closely related to *confusion on the part of students*. Smith and Keith's (1971) detailed case study of a new open-education elementary school provides indirect evidence on this point:

The possibility that students might not yet be able to work in a program that emphasized considerable pupil responsibility had not yet been fully taken into account.
When the staff spoke of changing pupil roles, they seldom considered equipping the students with techniques that would insure facility in performing the new roles. (p. 140)

Students were described as "running around a lot" (p. 141), "wandering and milling" (p. 156), "restless" (p. 156), and not knowing how to work in small groups (p. 141). As with other research, no one (including Smith and Keith) asked students about their experiences, but the description strongly indicates massive confusion.[6]

Some preliminary evidence from a project in Britain which directly examines the perceptions of pupils indicates that student expectations are a neglected yet crucial aspect in relation to the success of some innovations. Hull and Rudduck (1980) report on interviews with students involved in a new humanities curriculum project. The authors claim that pupils' interpretations of their traditional roles in the classroom "may well constitute a barrier to change [which] could be crucial" (p. 1). As one student expressed it:

"You suddenly get dumped in the deep end. Suddenly they say they are going to teach us as adults after teaching us as babies for years." (p. 2)

Curriculum innovations vary according to how much change in student roles and activities might be involved, but all innovations by definition involve something new for students. The main argument is very simple. Any innovation that requires new activities on the part of students will succeed or fail according to whether students actually participate in these activities. Students will participate to the extent that they are clear and motivated to try what is expected. We have every reason to believe that, whatever the causes, students' experiences with innovations are not conducive to increasing their clarity and motivation. Nor could we expect it to be otherwise, if teachers, principals, and other administrators are having similar problems.

The third pattern of response—*temporary escape*—concerns the possibility that some innovations provide a welcome change of pace in the routine and boredom of schooling. This response is seen most clearly in Farrar et al.'s investigation of the large-scale Experience Based Career Education (EBCE) program at the high school level in the United States. The authors state:

Students tend to see EBCE as an alternative to the regular high school program, and so many use it as a way to get out of regular school. A large percentage of EBCE students seem to dislike or to be bored with school, or want to experience something more before graduation. So they join EBCE as a way to get out of regular classes.

---

6 Of course, students were likely further bewildered as individual teachers vascillated about student autonomy and as they themselves went from an open-education grade or school to a more traditionally organized classroom or school.

Although their motives vary widely, many students interpret EBCE as an escape from school. (Farrar et al., 1979, p. 50)

Innovations within classrooms which enable students to spend more time talking with friends, watching TV, playing on their own, or daydreaming are also candidates for the escape-from-boredom pattern.[7]

A fourth logical outcome for students—*heightened interest*—suggests that the innovation "works." It engages them in more interesting educational activities and increases the attainment of desired educational objectives. I know of no research which has actually interviewed students about this possible result, but it seems reasonable to suggest that students would experience satisfaction in situations of successful innovation.[8]

Whatever the case, the basic problem remains that little research has been undertaken which has examined the reactions of students to innovations. We can speculate that reactions will vary by social class, type of innovation, teaching style, and approach, and probably by age and sex. And these reactions are important to success for many if not all classroom changes. Certainly, innovations which call for changes in teacher–student relationships, as many do, would require involvement of students and knowledge of their thoughts, attitudes, and skills regarding the new behavior. For example, innovations directed at personal and social development (e.g., listening skills, tolerance, cooperative decision-making) would seem to require student involvement in order to work. Students learning new behavior are in the same boat as teachers learning how to use a new practice; they need to be involved in a process in which they are assisted as well as listened to concerning the difficulties of implementing the new behavior. Even innovations at the lower grade levels which focus on basic skills would benefit from knowledge of student views. More fundamental to this whole argument is the suggestion that treating students as *people* comes very close to "living" some of the personal and social educational goals which are stated as objectives in much of the curriculum. It is in this sense that school is not just preparation for life: *it is life* for a significant proportion of the lives of young people (see Dewey, 1916).[9]

# Guidelines for coping

Since the student is at the bottom of the heap, he or she has only limited power except to conform or reject (see Eggleston, 1977, ch. 6). Students could test out whether individual teachers or the school administration would be interested in some discussion about the advantages and disadvantages of specific innovations being considered or introduced in the school. Students would have to learn to give feedback without being overly negative. However, it is likely the adults who will have to initiate this process. Their motivation for so doing should lie in the recognition that the absence of a role for students in educational change

---

7 I am not implying that these are necessarily valueless; I am only *describing* types of outcomes.
8 That these situations are in the minority only says that students do not frequently get much satisfaction from educational changes.
9 For another view of the neglect of non-cognitive educational goals see Wynne (1980), who claims that schools need to put more emphasis on developing "student character." Greater student interaction and responsibility is a major part of Wynne's argument.

weakens in a profound way the impact of potentially valuable innovations, especially concerning personal- and social-development goals.

Of course, there are other more basic problems over which students and parents normally have exercised little control. The Designs for Change group in Chicago have been carrying out some significant analysis and training on problems related to student need in schools. In one study on student classification and its relationship to reading they found large numbers of disadvantaged students misclassified and consequently receiving inadequate services (see Moore et al., 1981). They have developed a set of guidelines and resources to support parents and other public interest groups focusing on "child advocacy and the schools" (Moore et al., forthcoming). These activities are directed at adults on behalf of children, but there is no reason to believe that students could not work with parents and their schools in specific program areas (see Moore et al., forthcoming, for some basic guidelines).

Effective change in schools involves just as much cognitive and behavioral change on the part of students as it does for anyone. Earlier I said that implementation frequently involves role change by the teacher in the classroom. The more sociologically accurate statement is that implementation actually comprises a change in the *role relationship* between teachers and students. We could take any number of innovations (a new social studies curriculum, mainstreaming, basic instructional systems in reading and math, microcomputers, parent involvement, career education, etc., etc.) and identify the kinds of student activities and teacher activities which make up the change. Critical to understanding educational change is the recognition that these changes in students and teachers must go together—that is, students themselves are also being asked to change their thinking and behavior in the classroom. Most students will not or cannot change simply by being lectured to or ordered to, any more than the rest of us would. The reason that this issue is critical is that student motivation and clarity regarding a change are directly related to whether and how they engage in what we might call implementation activities, which are the *means* to achieving the learning outcomes in question. If these assumptions are correct, we should stop thinking of students just in terms of learning outcomes and start thinking of them as people who are also being asked to become involved in new activities.

Another problem is that information is negligible as to what students think of specific innovations which affect them. To say that students do not have opinions and feelings about these matters is to say that they are objects, not humans. Those responsible for innovations (whether they be teachers, principals, or others) would be well advised to consider explicitly how innovations will be *introduced* to students and how student reactions will be obtained at that point and periodically *throughout implementation*. Hull and Rudduck have launched a project in four schools in England to experiment with and develop ways in which the introduction of curriculum innovation might be done:

In each case our aim will be to assist in mounting induction courses for pupils who will be involved in the planned change. The courses will centre on audio-visual representation of the new form of working, which will provide the starting point for group discussion. (Hull & Rudduck, 1980, p. 6)

I am not for a moment implying that teachers should all of a sudden step in and start a conversation with students on the meaning of a new curriculum unit.

But the possibilities for thinking along these lines have not been considered at all. Testing these possibilities could turn out to be a powerful untapped resource for improving the success rate of educational change.[10]

This chapter can be more fundamentally summarized in other words. *Effective educational change and effective education overlap in significant ways.* Involving students in a consideration of the meaning and purpose of specific changes directly addresses the knowledge, skills, and behaviors that relate to the educational objectives in question. It is not so much that teachers and students should spend time away from the curriculum in order to do this. It is more that this can be *part of the curriculum.*[11]

Teachers who blend education and change, and periodically discuss the meaning of activities with students, and consider the relationship between old and new, will be going a long way in accomplishing some of the more complex cognitive and social educational objectives contained in the policy statements and curricula of most school districts.

---

10 It will be exceedingly difficult to develop and implement these possibilities because they involve a new and complex role (role relationship) for the teacher and students, and because there has been little prior training or current time and opportunity to establish the new skills and behaviors required. I also recognize that the conditions for students to become involved in discussions of the curriculum and change do not exist in some schools and classrooms. As I have said before, change may be impossible in some situations at some times, but we can do a lot better in more situations more of the time.

11 For example, participating in discussions about the value and nature of a new activity or a new way of doing things requires talking and listening skills directly related to important educational objectives. In the areas of communication skills and social studies, talking about how to do something, doing it, and discussing how it went is tantamount to implementing parts of the curriculum.

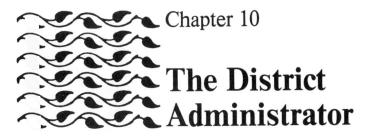 Chapter 10

# The District Administrator

*To get the whole world out of bed,*
*and washed, and dressed, and warmed, and fed,*
*Believe me, Saul, costs worlds of pain . . . .*

— *John Masefield, "The Everlasting Mercy," 1911*

Chapter 5 described the factors which determine whether educational change gets implemented. The conclusion was that there are many different ways in which change can and does go wrong. The task of the district administrator is to lead the development and execution of a plan which explicitly addresses and takes into account *all* these causes of change at the district, school, and classroom levels.[1] No wonder there is such a high turnover rate among superintendents! This is a great expectation, and failure to meet it in some cases may have more to do with the impossibility of the odds than with the skills of the administrator. As the quote beginning this chapter suggests, just getting the kids and teachers through a school day without incident costs worlds of pain and represents a major accomplishment. But some school districts do establish effective change processes, while others follow a disastrous pattern. The district administrator is the single most important individual for setting the expectations and tone of the pattern of change within the local district. (This statement, of course, does not deny that change can occur at the school level without central office involvement.)

I follow the standard sequence in this chapter: commencing with a discussion of where district administrators are, then reviewing what is known about the administrator and change, and concluding with a set of guidelines for the district administrators interested in managing change more effectively. The main vehicle for presenting the guidelines will be through actual descriptions of two district change efforts.

---

1 By district administrator I mean the chief executive officer and those immediate subordinates who are in *authority* line positions at the district level. The chief executive officer is called Superintendent in most school districts and Director of Education in some jurisdictions in Canada. Immediate subordinates are variously called Assistant Superintendent, Area Superintendent, Superintendent of Program, Director of Instruction, Director of Curriculum, etc. District curriculum consultants (who are in staff positions) are discussed in the next chapter.

# Where district administrators are

As with principals, nearly all district administrators are men.[2] They work in school systems ranging in size from fewer than 1000 students to more than 200,000. As we could imagine, the conditions and tasks vary tremendously across these situations; but in one way or another all district administrators face big problems. In smaller districts they frequently carry out several functions with few resources, and in larger districts they are constantly dealing with conflicts and crises and large financial and personnel issues through an elaborate bureaucracy of specialists.

Although there is a fair amount of evidence about the role of the administrator and change (which is the subject of the next section), there is little representative information on what administrators do and think in their total roles. Goldhammer (1977) reviewed the changing role of the American school superintendent from 1954 to 1974. Goldhammer suggests that the major change over the twenty-year period has been away from the role of educational spokesperson and executive manager of a relatively homogeneous system, toward one where negotiation and conflict management of diverse interests and groups predominate. School boards have become more politically active, as have teacher unions and community and other special-interest groups. Communities have become more heterogeneous. Declining enrollments present unfamiliar management problems. Federal government agencies and federal courts in the U.S. have become major participants in educational programming through financial and legislative means (see chapter 13). The superintendent, says Goldhammer (p. 162), has become more of a negotiator than a goal-setter, a reactor to and coordinator of diverse interests, and a person who must learn to lead and involve teams of specialists. (See also Campbell, 1977.)

In a few cases, superintendents in the U.S. have been asked for their perceptions of their role and important issues therein. Volp and Heifetz conducted a recent (1980) survey of school superintendents in New York State. Part of the problem in interpreting the results is that the survey obtained only a 45% response rate (96 from a total sample of 212), with none of the six major metropolitan areas represented. In a listing of the "most pressing issues locally," the most frequent responses (the percentage mentioning each issue) concerned fiscal matters (99%), declining enrollment (44%), curriculum issues (39%), and student attitudes/achievement (36%). The growth of teacher unionism was the most frequently mentioned major change over the ten-year period 1969–79; 39% of the sample identified this issue. The next most frequently stated change was cited by only 20% of the sample—the emergence of a more vocal citizenry. In commenting on needs in university-based training for administrators the

---

2 In Ontario, a whopping 97.8% of all administrators from the principal level upward are males (no province goes much below 90%). In the U.S., most states (there are seven exceptions) have over 95% male superintendents and assistants, and over 85% male principals and assistants. Aside from the waste of human talent in this situation, it is unknown whether women would turn out to be different kinds of administrators from men.

respondents stated personnel relations (41%), business and finance (19%), and law (14%). None mentioned management of change or curriculum issues.

An earlier study (State of New York, 1974) in the same state found that 79% of the superintendents' work week was spent on fiscal and administrative matters. The most time-consuming activities included fiscal management, professional participation, public relations, preparation of board meetings, and labor negotiations and grievances.

Holcomb, a school superintendent in Colorado, states:

Instead of educational leaders, public school superintendents have become meeting-attenders, form filler-outers, public relations experts, and specialists at coordinating advisory committees. (1979, p. 34)

In an informal survey of 17 fellow superintendents, Holcomb asked, "How have you spent the last three days?" (Respondents could list more than one activity.) One-half answered that they had worked on federal programs or guidelines, almost one-half named state education meetings, and four or five mentioned legal hearings, finance hearings, and grievance disputes. Holcomb also asked how many had worked on curriculum or on staff in-service programs. The answer was three.

Similarly, Keidel (1977), a superintendent in Michigan, reports on a survey of all superintendents in that state. (Of the total of 511, 70% or 355 responded.) Insufficient financing and labor relations were identified as the two most significant issues faced by school superintendents.

Martin and Zichefoose (1980) carried out a 1979 survey of board members and superintendents in West Virginia concerning their views of "what qualities a superintendent needs to be 'successful'" (p. 4). Board members and superintendents differed. Board members emphasized business, financial, political, and communication skills, but superintendents stressed knowledge of the curriculum and communication skills (that is, the latter representing the only area of agreement).

In one of the few Canadian studies, Duignan (1979) conducted a more detailed observation study of eight school superintendents in Alberta:

The superintendent averaged 26 discussion sessions each day, and these talks accounted for approximately 70 percent of his daily working time. Specifically, 70 percent of this discussion time was spent with school trustees, central office staff members, and building-level administrators. *Less than 7 percent of the time he spent in conversation was with teachers and less than half of 1 percent with students.* (p. 34, emphasis in original)

Duignan goes on to report that much of the time spent was unscheduled and in reaction to situations and events. Superintendents rarely had time or allocated time to think and plan. Consequently, superintendents said that "the pressure of time" was the most frustrating aspect of their job.

Also in Canada, Partlow et al. (1980) in Ontario surveyed 850 school system administrators and interviewed 222. Ten competencies were identified as most important (communication skills, human relations skills, organizational skills, knowledge of the curriculum, knowledge of law, etc.). Respondents indicated that neither present training nor selection criteria for supervisory personnel adequately addressed most of the competency areas.

The final reality of the superintendent, and one which radically affects the fate of programs of change, relates to the length of term in office. In the United States, a typical term seems to be three years. Gaines (1978, p. 5) states that the average tenure of a superintendent is "a short two years and three months." In Michigan, superintendents typically have two- or three-year contracts (Keidel, 1977). In West Virginia, Martin and Zichefoose (1979, p. 5) found that the superintendent "failure rate" was 90% over a six-year period (defined as superintendents who were fired, not rehired, or forced to resign, or who fled to a parallel or lesser position in less than six years). For Canada we do not have comparable figures, and the situation is somewhat different, since most chief executive officers are appointed on longer-term contracts—five years or more.

By and large, then, school superintendents seem to be a harried lot. As we shall see, some are able to wrestle the sundry social forces to the ground and lead effective district change efforts, but it seems to take a great amount of skill and stamina.

I have only been discussing the role of the *chief* district administrator. Second-level administrators (assistant superintendents, curriculum directors or superintendents, etc.) are directly responsible for program development and improvement. Research studies of these roles are almost nonexistent, perhaps because of their diversity and because of the preoccupation with the role of the superintendents. However, since the main responsibilities of these other administrators concern program change, it will be possible to examine their roles along with that of the superintendent by turning directly to the district administrator and change. It is only by considering change as part of the everyday reality of district administrators that we can learn more fully where they are and, more important, where they should be.

# The district administrator and change

Anytime you get two or more people together to pursue some goal over a period of time, whether it be in marriage or in the organization of schools, conflict and problems of communication are inevitable. Whenever you have more than one person with values, ideas, and minds of their own, you have difficulties. Attempting change magnifies these difficulties. The larger the social system, the greater the chances for disagreement and misunderstandings. District administrators are in the center of this social system, and unlike the eye of the hurricane, it is not calm. What distinguishes effective from ineffective administrators is not whether they can obliterate conflict, but how they anticipate it and deal with it as an inevitable and natural part of change and stability. (See Lambright et al., 1980, for discussion of coalition-building.)

All superintendents and district administrators with program responsibilities are involved in some manner with change. The variation comes into play in relation to how change is approached and reacted to, not whether change is considered. A quick review of the evidence shows conclusively how important district administrators are.[3] What they do at each of the three main phases of change—the initial decision or mobilization, implementation, and institutionalization—significantly affects the destiny of the proposed change.[4]

## Initiation phase

The concept of initiation or mobilization refers to two phenomena. One concerns the question of the *need* for the particular change; the other already sets into motion *planning for implementation*. Both of these aspects are captured in Berman and McLaughlin's discovery that decisions taken by district administrators regarding federally sponsored educational innovations were characterized by one of two patterns, which they labeled *opportunistic* versus *problem-solving*:

Projects generated essentially by opportunism seemed to be a response to available funds and were characterized by a lack of interest and commitment on the part of local participants—from district administrators to classroom teachers. As a result, participants were often indifferent to project activities and outcomes, and little in the way of serious change was ever attempted—or occurred.

The problem-solving motive for projects emerged primarily in response to locally identified needs and was associated with a strong commitment to address these needs. (Berman & McLaughlin, 1976, pp. 351–52)

In another article, McLaughlin and Marsh (1978, p. 72) explain:

The attitudes of district administration about a planned change effort were a 'signal' to teachers as to how seriously they should take a special project. The fieldwork offers numerous examples of teachers—many of whom supported project goals—who decided not to put in the necessary extra effort simply because they did not feel that district administrators were interested.

It makes such obvious sense that there is no need to report the large number of other studies which support this finding, other than to say that it is a more subtle point than appears at first glance. There is an exact correspondence to the earlier discussion of the principal, except that the reference is now to what happens district-wide instead of within one school. Thus, the district administrator who sincerely gives verbal support to a proposed change will not do that change any favor unless he or she has also determined whether the change in its present form meets a priority need in the schools, and especially whether he or she sets up a process *to deliver specific implementation support*.[5] As with the principal, *general* support doesn't amount to much.

---

3 In the following description I am talking about the *function* of district administrators in relation to change. Depending on the size of the district, the superintendent may be centrally directing change efforts or may be a facilitator of an assistant superintendent who is the main program leader.

4 See Berman (1981) for an excellent overview of the three phases of change.

5 See Emrick and Peterson (1978) and Rosenblum and Louis (1979) for two (among many) sources of support for the importance of the active role of the central administrator. See also Crandall et al. (forthcoming).

The district administrator can change the system through a combination of replacing key support staff and helping others develop.[6] As Sarason contends, it is exceedingly difficult for strong leaders to support other people's growth, because the leader must help others develop in *their* way:

One of the most frequent complaints of ... members is that they have little or no opportunity to experience the sense of autonomy, learning and growth. The tendency for a leader to give precedence to his needs and goals, to see them as identical with the success of the setting, adversely instead of positively affects the general welfare of the setting. (1972, p. 214)

The fact that the leader is continually pressed for time and has a tendency to keep things in his or her own mind, and that the complexity of communication in large school systems is extreme, makes it very likely that the sincere leader will not feel appreciated and understood by others. But the primary reason that the leader is not appreciated is that he or she does not make *other people* feel appreciated and understood. Even sincerity can be a barrier, if it prevents our thinking about others and planning about what must be anticipated and addressed next. Yet the leader must establish credibility early in the change process.

The further aspect of the initiation phase concerns the question of who the primary promoters of change proposals are. The answer has to be ambiguous for the very reason that change comes from a number of sources depending on the innovation and the circumstances. I will also contend in a moment that the answer of who initiates change is not nearly as crucial as what happens from that point onward. The primary impetus to innovation sometimes comes from school boards, sometimes from government agencies, sometimes from teachers, and other times from district administrators. The majority of changes of any scope appear to be initiated by central office staff or other agencies external to the school. Hood and Blackwell (1980) review several studies and conclude that teachers as a group are not responsible for most innovations which get initiated. This finding is consistent with the problem of teachers' lack of time and limited access to information, noted in chapter 7. The DESSI research also found that extra-school personnel were the key advocates in nearly all cases (Crandall et al., forthcoming). Even in the RDU project, in which participatory problem-solving (problem identification and solution selection) was a basic part of the design, decisions were in fact often made by administrators (Molitor, 1981; Louis et al., 1981). On the other hand, Daft and Becker (1978) report that many of the curriculum changes in the high schools they surveyed were initiated by teachers. Certainly, individual teachers and small groups can be instrumental in launching important changes, and they often do participate along with administrators in deciding on the details of new programs.

---

6 New superintendents often use the strategy of gradually (or not so gradually) replacing other central district administrators and principals who they feel are not changeable (at least, according to their image of change). They rarely publicly announce this strategy. It can be powerful, but also self-defeating to morale, if the administrator is not firmly and first committed to individual growth and development, using replacement as a last resort, and using it sparingly. See the account of Adam's County for one good example of the premise of development at work (Fullan et al., 1979; Bailey, 1980).

To summarize: all change requires an advocate or advocates; the advocates can and do come from any level of the system; district administrators and boards tend to be the initiators of major changes (when the initiating is internal to the district); government agencies initiate change external to the district; and teachers as a group (but only a small percentage of individual teachers) are a source of some curriculum change proposals.

A final issue at the initiation phase concerns the difficulty of deciding whether a potential change actually meets a need, especially if there are many contending forces. There is a certain amount of needs assessment and conflict confrontation which the administrator must do with district staff in order to determine what changes to adopt and whether the timing is right. Any mobilization at this phase is already setting in motion the conditions for implementation. Ironically, widespread and time-consuming participation at the initiation stage is sometimes counterproductive, but there must be enough participation so that people can contribute to the procedures or plan for change, and so that there is some confirmation that the change is needed. In some cases participatory input can be so great that no one recognizes his or her own contribution once more specific decisions have to be made. Participation can also prolong the preliminary stage and burn people out. For example, in some provincial curriculum guideline development procedures the initial phase has been so prolonged and taken so much energy that, now that the document is distributed for use, people are sick of it or more confused than they ever were.

The district administrator then must contend with several forces during the mobilization phase. In some cases this may involve coping with an unwanted or low-priority externally imposed change. In other situations the district administrator's skill at obtaining outside resources (e.g., from state or federal governments) for needs identified within the district will be the issue. Getting the need right, mobilizing support or responding to requests for support, establishing initial conditions conducive to implementation, and developing a momentum for change are all at stake during the initiation phase (see Berman, 1981).

All of this says that needs assessment represents another dilemma of change. There must be some assessment as to whether the innovation potentially addresses a priority, but it must be part of a continuous process (i.e., a plan) which moves to initial implementation or pilot testing within a relatively short time. Large-scale needs assessment surveys, which gather too much information to be readily used and which require large amounts of energy before implementation can be considered, create more barriers than they remove. In brief, need should be partially tested at the initiation stage but more fully specified during implementation. Opportunities for disagreements to be confronted must be provided at both the initiation and implementation phases.

Regardless of the source of change, the single most important factor is *how central office administrators take to the change*. Put another way, once a change is at the point of initial decision in the district, the attitudes and behavior of the district administrators are crucial. If they take it seriously, the change stands a chance of being implemented. If they do not, it has little chance of going beyond the odd classroom or school.

## Implementation and institutionalization

The crunch of whether a change has been taken seriously by the district admin-istration comes forcefully at the implementation stage. Participation during implementation is more important than participation at the initiation phase, because *every implementer must be actively involved* at the implementation phase if the change is to happen (even though every implementer cannot participate in the development). It is essential that the implementation procedure be set up in a way which permits new decisions, adaptations, redevelopment, etc., and gives participants the opportunity to make specific decisions about the change, if they wish. Implementation dynamics are central to the process of social change.

In the districts where implementation has worked on any scale, it has worked because district administrators have been able to put together a plan which possesses the three main characteristics referred to in chapter 6: it addresses technical knowledge needs related to the *substantive content area* of the change; it embodies the *conceptual and sociotechnical* requirements for addressing prob-lems inherent in implementation; and it is *communicated* in an active two-way collaborative manner with system members.[7]

Our knowledge of what effective district administrators do and must do in incorporating the three elements into a plan for improving implementation is fairly good. They must lead a process which (1) tests out the need and priority of the change; (2) determines the potential appropriateness of the particular innovation for addressing the need; (3) clarifies, supports, and insists on the role of principals and other administrators as central to implementation; (4) ensures that direct implementation support is provided in the form of available quality materials, in-service training, one-to-one technical help, and opportu-nity for peer interaction; (5) allows for certain redefinition and adaptation of the innovation; (6) communicates with and maintains the support of parents and the school board; (7) sets up an information-gathering system to monitor and correct implementation problems; and (8) has a realistic time perspective.[8] This is no doubt a tall and impossible order in some situations. But it is precisely what effective districts do whether they be in rural, medium-size-city, or large-city systems. If it cannot be done, then I say again, *do not expect much change*, unless you are in a position to make wholesale replacement of district staff.

The above set of factors does not occur by accident. Someone at the district level must know what he or she is doing, and plan for them to happen. The

---

7 Two further points of clarification: this formulation does not say that the administrators develop the plan by themselves—only that they must be centrally involved; it also should be noted that I am referring to the chances for change across schools in the district. For any indi-vidual school, certain teachers and principal can bring about major changes within the school on their own, although it is infinitely easier if they are receiving help from the district administrator.
8 Chapter 5 explains in more detail how these factors work. I have also said that this process is not one of providing support and letting people do what they want. It does put tremendous pres-sure on people to confront change in themselves, with peers, and with others. The process can vary in the degree to which it creates and maintains insistent pressure for change. Chart 2 in chapter 5 contains the list of fifteen factors which the district administrator must address (or ensure that someone addresses).

leader's *conceptual understanding of the dynamics of organization, the processes of change, and the people in his or her jurisdiction* represents the most *generative* (or degenerative, if it is missing) source of ideas about what goes into a plan and what steps have to be taken when things go wrong. Sarason comments on the failure of leadership in new organizations in this respect:

> A major source of control missing in the leader in this situation is an organized conception of the nature of the process in which he and others are engaged, a conception based on knowledge of the dynamics of group interaction, of the inevitability of conflict, of the strength of fantasy and the tendency to deny the obvious, of the distinctions between overt and covert behavior, and the fact that he is perceived as a model of how one should think and act. In short, he needs to possess—literally to feel that he "owns"—a theory that tells him what he is assuming and what variables he is dealing with.
>
> Leaders of new settings have no theory about the nature of the process they are engaged in and the complications of their relationship to it. They do not come to the task with a theory which, so to speak, has a status independent of them and is formulated in a way that it can act as a guide to and control of their thinking and actions. (1972, pp. 245–46)

Mostly, central administrators keep their conceptions or misconceptions to themselves, but we can infer and in some cases can obtain direct explanations of the thinking behind district leaders. These inferences and descriptions tend to confirm that successful administrators operate from a basic set of principles— a theory of changing.[9] A theory of changing, as stated in chapter 6, combines knowledge about factors which inhibit or facilitate change and knowledge about how to influence or alter these factors (the latter is crucial to changing) in more favorable directions. And, when we come to think of it, it makes preeminent sense to say that effective administrators possess knowledge and ability concerning principles of changing. No technical checklist, even if religiously followed, can come close to matching the power of knowing the dynamics of social change. Dealing effectively with the implementation of educational change more than anything else involves a way of thinking—a feel for the change process.

No amount of good thinking by itself will address the ubiquitous problem of *faulty communication* (Sarason, 1972, p. 206). Because change is a highly personal experience, and because school districts consist of numerous individuals and groups undergoing different (to them) experiences, no simple communication is going to reassure or clarify the meaning of change for people. A cardinal fact of social change is that people will always misinterpret and misunderstand some aspect of the purpose or practice of something that is new to them. Of course, the administrator who has adopted an innovation without being aware of or interested in implementation needs aggravates the problem; that is, the worst suspicions of subordinates may be correct. But even the administrator who thinks of "everything" will still face the problem of communication, because it is not possible to transfer all his or her thoughts instantly to the

---

9 For a fuller description of how this works in practice see our case study of Adam's County School District No. 12 (Fullan et al., 1978) and the superintendent's own article on "management of change" (Bailey, 1980). Berman and McLaughlin's (1979) account of the successful transformation of Lakeville school district also depicts the assumptions and key role of the superintendent. See also the description of the two school districts in the next section of this chapter.

minds of others (not to mention the fact that the administrator has to learn what others think, know, and can contribute to improving the change). The effective district administrator is one who constantly works at communication, not because he or she thinks that people are resistant or dense, but because he or she realizes that difficulties of communication are natural and inevitable. The administrator's theory of change will have told him or her that frequent, personal interaction is the key to implementation, and his or her interpersonal skills as a communicator (to communicate concisely and clearly, and to listen perceptively) will determine the effectiveness of confronting this perennial problem.[10]

Two-way communication about specific innovations that are being attempted is a requirement of success. To the extent that the information flow is accurate, the problems of implementation get identified, and each individual's personal perceptions and concerns—the core of change—get aired. The district administrator more than any other individual in the district sets the pace and tone of the climate of accuracy of communication. Sarason's comment about the leader is again on target:

There can be no question that the leader plays the most crucial role. He is the most visible and influential model of how one should think and talk, what one should talk about, how one deals with reality, and how one anticipates and deals with problems. (1972, p. 206)

In summary, the district administration mainly determines whether district-wide change gets implemented. Whether central administrators are equal to the task is sometimes beyond their control but less often than many administrators have shown. Being equal to the task, as stated above, means integrating three things: addressing *technical knowledge* requirements; possessing a *conceptual and technical understanding of the dynamics of change* which guides and generates one's actions and reactions; and having the *interpersonal skills* and behavior of an active communicator, who gets around and demonstrates the sincerity of one's intentions as well as knowledge of the problems of change faced by system members.

The thinking and skills which I have been discussing do not just "show up" at the implementation stage. They are intrinsic to the district administrator's basic approach to change, from the early exploration or initiation phases, through implementation, to the question of longer-term continuation or institutionalization.

The continuation stage does not require extensive discussion except for two points. If the change project depends on external funds (as many, if not the majority, do in the United States), what the administrator does and does not do to plan for continuation is crucial. Berman and McLaughlin (1978) have examined this aspect of change most closely. In most of the 293 school districts they studied, only a small proportion of projects were effectively institutionalized. In those projects which did become institutionalized, district officials paid early and continuing attention to how the program could be incorporated into the

---

10 Partlow et al. (1980) report that communication skills headed the list of competencies thought essential for the supervisory role in Ontario school systems.

budget with respect to personnel support needs. See Berman and McLaughlin (1978, p. 20) and Crandall et al. (forthcoming) for the importance of the district administration to institutionalizing new programs. Berman (1981) discusses the institutionalization phase more completely than I do here.

In addition to the question of incorporation in the budget, the second longer-term phenomenon which takes a heavy toll on change is *turnover*. It is so difficult to get change started and so easy to get it stopped. Turnover can facilitate change, if it is used to bring in administrators and others favorable to and skilled in the change, and many districts do just that. It can also be positive when career-related motives generate energy and enthusiasm for the extra work required at the early stages of a change effort. (Recall the discussion of career motives in the DESSI study program changes, referred to at the end of chapter 4.) But the unseen hand of destruction of enthusiastic or heavily promoted change efforts over time is the changeover of personnel.[11] Change is a continuous process, and district administrators or school administrators who know change will also know that systematic provisions for orientation and follow-up with new members must be part of the plan. When administrators turn over, this need applies in spades. When a school district experiences frequent changes in its chief executive officer, it is virtually impossible to establish an effective change process.[12]

The district administrator must make many choices initially about what innovations to back, and secondly many more decisions about how to guide implementation and follow-through. District officials are frequently dealing with changes that they themselves did not initiate. They are even more frequently attempting to implement several innovations at once, all of which may seem important to them or to their superiors. In either case, this section has confirmed the importance of district administrators as leaders of change or non-change, depending on how they respond to the task. Guidelines and illustrations of successful response to school district change are addressed in the concluding section of this chapter.

# Guidelines for coping

Guidelines for change are clearly implied in the preceding section, but it is more practically helpful to draw them together in one place. The main vehicle that I will use is brief descriptions of two school district efforts in which change appears to have been successful. District One—Jefferson County, Colorado—provides an illustration of how a large school district brought about significant change in the elementary science curriculum across the district. District Two—Kamloops, British Columbia—describes how a medium-size school district plans and implements curriculum guidelines and programs. After the two dis-

---

11 Researchers have not paid attention until recently to the hidden impact of turnover, and managers of change have not made provisions for continuous reorientation of new members (see especially Louis, 1980; Yin et al., 1977; Crandall et al., forthcoming).

12 The ultimate goal is for a district to develop a capacity for change throughout the system, which then can stand the loss of its central leader. It takes a special leader in the first place to build this capacity (see next section).

tricts' plans are described, I conclude the chapter by suggesting eight general guidelines for the district administrator.

## District-wide change of an elementary science curriculum: Jefferson County, Colorado

Jefferson County is a suburban school district which serves 80,000 students. The district carried out a survey of teachers which confirmed that revisions in the science curriculum, grades 3 to 6, were needed. A planned change effort was designed collaboratively between Jefferson County central staff and the Texas Research and Development Center (see Hall et al., 1980; Loucks & Melle, 1980; Melle & Pratt, 1981). The combined effects of external assistance and internal commitment were very substantial. Let us see what they did over a three-year period, and with what results.

An overview of the steps taken can be approximately summarized as follows:

1 The need for revision was confirmed in a needs survey of teachers and principals.
2 District curriculum staff using teacher input revised the curriculum, which "combined a 'hands-on' inquiry approach to science instruction with behavioral objectives and techniques" (Loucks & Melle, 1980, p. 3). A detailed teacher's guide with materials and equipment was also developed.
3 A deliberate plan of phased-in implementation was formulated, based on assumptions and knowledge of effective implementation processes.
4 Central consultants and 23 resource teachers (seconded part-time) were trained as helpers.
5 Because the central staff and other resources could not support all 80 schools at once, the schools were divided into three groups of equal size and commenced the innovation at six-month intervals (that is, the innovation was first introduced to one-third of the schools; six months later, to the second third). Thus, it took 12 months to introduce the innovation to all 80 schools.
6 Principals received one half-day orientation three months before teachers, so that they would have some time to familiarize themselves with the curriculum before they had to deal with teachers.
7 Teachers received a brief introduction, at *each* school, two to three months prior to in-service, in order to allow for a period of initial thinking and familiarization.
8 Teachers received three full days of in-service training, one day at a time, with three-month intervals between sessions.
9 In between sessions central consultants and the 23 resource teachers provided one-to-one follow-up support with individual teachers. These informal contacts ranged from saying hello, through discussions of experiences with the revised curriculum, to more technical problem-solving sessions.
10 Information was gathered on five occasions regarding the concerns of teachers and the levels of implementation in the classroom in a sample of 19 schools. In other words, implementation was monitored and the information used to address implementation problems.

The implementation results showed the following distribution over the three-year period for the first one-third group of teachers.

Levels of Use (Implementation)[13]
(percentage of teachers at each level)

|            | Non-use/ preparation | Mechanical use | Routine/ refined use | No. of teachers |
|------------|------|------|------|------|
| Fall '76   | 97%  | 1%   | 1%   | N = 75 |
| Spring '77 | 13%  | 53%  | 33%  | N = 74 |
| Fall '77   | 11%  | 38%  | 51%  | N = 63 |
| Spring '78 | 7%   | 42%  | 52%  | N = 62 |
| Spring '79 | 8%   | 23%  | 69%  | N = 52 |

The Jefferson County case contains a number of lessons. The importance of district-wide support and emphasis on program planning and implementation clearly stands out. The superintendent and the curriculum director made a commitment to plan the development and implementation of the science curriculum according to principles of planned change. It was very much a *process*. Originally, they had intended to develop the curriculum, hold a three-day workshop at the beginning for all teachers, and assume that implementation would follow. In short, they had intended to follow the usual recipe for introducing educational innovation. It was as a result of thinking about and applying knowledge of implementation as a process over time that they changed their approach. It was not abstract theory but *very specific steps* that followed from their revised thinking. The innovation was phased in with one-third of the schools at a time, so that the process could be adequately supported. Principals were given advance warning. Teachers were carefully provided with skill training, material resources, and informal help over a period of time instead of receiving everything at once and wondering what hit them. It was a central assumption of the approach that teacher change was an individual, developmental experience. Implementation was monitored, and was seen as something that occurred over time. The three-year period of implementation was understood as a natural requirement of working with a large number of people.

Five other interesting results and questions emerge from the experience. In chapter 8, I indicated that some school principals in Jefferson County played a strong follow-up role during implementation, while others did not. Level of implementation in the schools varied directly in relation to whether principals did become actively involved. Furthermore, having recognized the crucial role of principals for implementation, the district has now established an Instructional Improvement Plan which provides more intensive training for principals. In the new approach, five or six schools are selected each year to participate in an extensive year-long effort designed to help the principal improve his or her role as an instructional leader. The result is that implementation (measured in terms of 12 components) has "increased dramatically" in the district's current attempts to establish the new curriculum (Melle & Pratt, 1981, pp. 11–12).

Second, the results tell us that common use of a new curriculum across classrooms can be achieved, but the achievement itself also raises some questions.

---

13 Adapted from Loucks and Melle (1980, p. 8). Actually the CBAM model contains eight levels of use ranging from non-use to renewal. I have collapsed these levels into three categories. The methodology for assessing levels of use for any innovation has been quite thoroughly (reliably and validly) developed and employed with a wide range of innovations (see Hall & Loucks, 1977).

Is homogeneous use desirable? Different teachers and different classrooms might benefit from permission and support to develop variations.[14] Put another way, perhaps some of the 8% who were non-users of the particular curriculum under review were great teachers who had developed or used other science curricula which were more effective. Or perhaps subject areas other than science were more important priorities in some classrooms.

Third, what is the relationship between levels of use and student achievement? We do not know enough about this question. Generally, tests conducted by the Texas group have shown the expected relationship between use up to the refined level and achievement on tests. However, only a small amount of research on this relationship has been conducted, and it indicates possible complications. For example, Pratt, Winters, and George (1980) examined the relationship between use and student achievement in Jefferson County in a sample of 12 of the schools. They selected the schools to represent each of the three phases, and they tested a total of 198 students. They found that longer use of the new science program led to increased achievement, but only for students of high ability (measured by standard reading ability tests) to begin with. Thus, high-ability students in phase 1 schools (who had been taking the program for three years) did better than phase 2 and 3 students. But for low-ability students, the reverse was true: those who were in the program longer (phase 1 students) did less well than phase 2 and 3 students. The results are only exploratory, but they remind us never to get complacent about the meaning and impact of educational change.

Fourth, notice in the table above the decline in the number of teachers over the three-year period. In the fall of 1976, there were 75 teachers in the cohort. By the spring of 1979, only 52 of the original set of teachers remained.[15] A sizeable turnover rate (in this case one-third) over a three-year period seems to be standard even in these days of declining enrollment. Orientation and incorporation of new teachers vis-à-vis the innovation must be built into the process. Change is an ever ongoing process, as perpetual as stability.

Fifth, and a point to which I return at the end of this chapter, Loucks and Melle found that the length of time in moving from non-use to routine implementation was shorter for phase 3 than phase 2 than phase 1 teachers. There could be a number of explanations (e.g., lateral dissemination of information). One possibility is that those managing the change (district administrators and coordinators) got more skilled at providing support for implementation. It is possible that *capacity for change* can be developed through practice and experience. People internalize principles that work as well as practical techniques and activities.

The Jefferson County case certainly provides an example of relative success among a great many failures. The implementation plan is not presented as a recipe for change, but as an illustration of a way of thinking about district-wide implementation that is different in concrete ways from the vast majority of its predecessors.

---

14 The approach did allow for this in the sense that "renewal" or higher levels were encouraged; but the weight of the process clearly favors routine or refined use.

15 Since the researchers were interested in following levels of use over time, they did not test replacement teachers.

# District-wide coordination of school-focused change: Kamloops school district, British Columbia

Kamloops is a medium-size school district in the interior of British Columbia which serves 18,000 students. As is the case in each province of Canada, the provincial department of education is responsible for developing curriculum guidelines in each of the subject areas. Those guidelines allow for and encourage local-district adaptations and further development. School districts are responsible for implementation. What follows is a short description of the assumptions, design, and main implications of the approach to change used by the Kamloops district.[16] The district-wide approach is used to implement the various curriculum guidelines, which are continually being developed and revised on a cyclic basis at the provincial level and assessed at the district and school levels in relation to local goals.

Kamloops district bases its planning for change on certain explicit assumptions which it has publicly stated and attempts to follow:

1 The school is the unit of change.
2 Teacher learning, self-development, and growth are critical.
3 The principal is a key leader of change.
4 District guidelines are necessary; the main role of the district is to coordinate change by helping schools to identify their own needs, by gathering materials and resources to meet those needs, by providing in-service training support and opportunities, and by monitoring the change process.
5 Provincial guidelines are legitimate vehicles for testing the goals and needs of teachers and schools in each of the subject areas. District priorities (as distinct from individual school priorities) are kept at a minimum, although most frequently school and district priorities coincide because of the process followed (see below).

The implementation strategy used combined two elements—district coordination of resources, and school self-analysis and program planning. A typical design in examining a new provincial guideline proceeds roughly along the following lines:[17]

1 An ad hoc committee in the curriculum area, chaired by a principal, and containing mostly teacher members, is established.
2 A teacher contact person at each school is identified.
3 A survey is conducted at each school regarding existing practices, need for change, and concerns of teachers. Each school is given guidelines and training as to how to conduct a self-evaluation.

---

16 This description is based on various documents provided by Tarry Grieve, Director of Instruction. His paper "The Role of a Curriculum Director at the School District Level" (1980) is one good source which is available in published form. Note, however, that the description is more of an "official version." It does not contain the independent objective-data confirmation that we have for the Jefferson County study.
17 See chapter 13 for a description of the Canadian provincial system. A typical guideline contains a statement of goals, content to be covered, suggestions for methods, resource materials, and evaluation.

4 Holdings of the district learning resource center are reviewed. Additional materials are developed, gathered, or otherwise obtained to meet the needs of teachers and to bring materials in line with the new curriculum.

5 A materials list is distributed to aid schools in purchase of support materials. A subcommittee of school librarians is established to develop a proposed library purchase plan.

6 The involvement of principals is maximized in four ways. First, all principals receive supervisory skills training with a view to equipping them with the ability to work with staff in planning individual and group staff development. Second, curriculum projects are planned with input from principals. Third, direct in-service training on each specific new curriculum is provided for principals with respect to the knowledge, skills, understandings, and attitudes that they must possess to lead the implementation process at the school level. Finally, district administrators follow up all these efforts by monitoring and providing additional support (and pressure) to ensure that principals are carrying out a curriculum leadership role. These expectations and nature of the principal's role in change are stated in district policy (and followed in district practice).

7 Workshop opportunities are developed and identified for teachers. Curriculum coordinators and principals and teachers on curriculum committees develop and are available to lead workshops, but the individual school formulates its own staff development plan (see below). The district workshops are only used if they meet the needs of the school staff, as decided by the staff itself.

8 Schools are provided with a budget and released time over which *they* have control to decide what will be done, and how it will be done, in their particular school. Each school develops its own plan for staff development in relation to the change.

9 The district curriculum director and supervisory staff continually interact with principals and teachers to find out what they are doing and to facilitate further work. The interaction is based on the assumptions cited earlier.

10 The district does not collect direct (formal) data on levels of implementation. Student tests are being considered, but the district curriculum director is reluctant to use them extensively for fear that they will interfere with school development. Implementation of any new curriculum is assumed to be a two- or three-year process, in which early formal evaluation would be a barrier.

A number of other related features should be noted. Through the efforts of the Superintendent and the Curriculum Director, the school board allocates budgetary support for implementation activities.[18] There is an annual substitute teacher account of 1500 days. Of these, 1200 days are awarded directly to the schools on a formula basis (1½ days per year for each elementary teacher), and 300 days are held centrally to support particular curriculum development efforts. These days are in addition to the standard quota of professional development days provided by the province (6 days annually). Each school is given one full-time-equivalent teacher above formula, whom they can use as they see fit. Each school is also given a budget to purchase materials. Additional money is available centrally and allocated on the basis of proposals from schools. All

---

18 Always a revealing question at any level (district, province) is the proportion of the budget which goes to support implementation (as distinct from development). The allocation is often an arbitrary process, as the group of board members (elected every two years in Canada) decide on the annual budget. The superintendent has to have a very clear and specific notion of what is involved in change, if he or she is to (a) develop an appropriate budget in the first place, and (b) be able to present it to the board in a convincing and defensible way in the second place. The superintendent's knowledge of change is critical.

materials for the district learning resource center are purchased from a central account. Thus, considerable resource support is available centrally; but most important, each school develops its own individualized plan for implementation, which incorporates staff development and materials use.

The Curriculum Director sees his role as continuously attending to the communication network, ensuring the predominant role of teachers and principals, assessing how the change process is going, and screening the need and timing of change to avoid unrealistic overload situations. I have already dwelt on the ubiquitous problem of communication. In the words of the Curriculum Director:

The Director must be familiar with the network and must be appreciative of its limitations. I have identified the parts of our district's communication network as the local teachers' association; the school district's learning resources centre, which serves as a meeting place and service centre for curriculum coordinators and committees; the district's educational programs advisory committee, which has representation from all major interest groups in the district; numerous curriculum committees each of which is chaired by a principal; the principals and trustees who are asked to comment on and react to proposals .... To ensure a common understanding and level of awareness about proposed implementation plans, I try to ensure that all parts of the communication network are used to exchange messages and to generate ideas. (Grieve, 1980, pp. 2–3)

In short, he perceives his role to involve constant attention to communication with all parts of the system, primarily through personal contact and discussion. All supervisory personnel, including the Curriculum Director, purposely spend three days a week out of the office in the schools talking and meeting with the people in the district.

In ensuring the predominant role of teachers and principals, he makes clear the expectations that they are responsible for forming plans for evaluation and development for the school, and that the district will provide materials, workshops, release time, guidance if requested, etc. to help the school in this work.

In monitoring the process of change, he and other supervisory staff spend time in schools asking principals and teachers about their plans, being prepared to assist in and insist on planning.[19]

Screening the need for and timing of change is the fourth main role of the Curriculum Director in Kamloops. Some curriculum guidelines are unclear about the nature, need, and justification of the change. He sees his function as setting up a procedure for assessing and clarifying the need. Second, he recognizes that more than one major change at a time cannot be handled by any one teacher or group of teachers and principal. He therefore stresses the importance of priorities and encourages and supports schools to set their own priorities, to take changes one at a time, and to work them through.

Unlike the Jefferson County case, there is no *formal* information-gathering procedure on levels of implementation (although student achievement tests appear to be coming); but it should be evident from the process, particularly

---

19 The content of the plan is not the issue; the insistence is that each school (with the principal as leader) should be spending time on thinking, interacting, and developing *some* plan which addresses its needs.

from the amount of personal interaction, that supervisory personnel get to know to a certain extent what principals are doing in planning with teachers, and principals know what teachers are doing. Informal, sustained interaction, planning, skill training, and review constitute the district's implementation assessment system. With such a system we cannot determine objectively whether it is a "success." The people in the district are convinced that it is working. I for one am not prepared to deny it, when I take a close look at the elements of implementation which they have institutionalized in their way of planning and managing curriculum change.

The Kamloops School District's approach to curriculum implementation is again not offered as an ideal model. The purpose of the description is to depict concretely an implementation process—a set of specific assumptions and procedures which incorporates the elements of successful implementation: assessment and clarification of the need for change, district implementation support, availability of materials, the key role and training of principals, staff development by and for teachers, plenty of lateral and vertical interaction, sustained pursuit of change over a period of time, and a curriculum director (supported by a superintendent) who has an explicit and well-worked-out theory of change and changing which forms the foundation for the district plan and guides daily decisions in dealing with implementation events.

The reader may well ask whether the Jefferson and Kamloops school districts are typical. They are certainly not typical in that the majority of school districts in North America do not plan for change so deliberately, thoughtfully, and resourcefully. But what about differences in circumstances? One is a large sub-urban district; the other is a medium-size city. Other examples of success confirm that these districts are not unique. Adam's County in Colorado, with 18,000 students, employs similar strategies of change with equal success (see Fullan et al., 1978; Bailey, 1980). Berman and McLaughlin's (1979) case studies of five school districts describe two "successes"—one in a very large district of 125,000 students, the other in a city in which the school's minority population increased from 6% to 20% (the size of the district is not specified). The successful school districts in the DESSI and RDU studies also represent numerous instances of positive school improvement efforts. Joyce's (1978) study shows the success in shared governance and change in some California school systems. Hyde and Moore's (1981) analysis of staff development expenditures among three school districts shows great differences in support for professional development of teachers (see chapter 14).

Another range of variations in district success is evident in the extremely complicated area of using evaluation information to bring about school improvement. In a survey of all districts in the U.S. with enrollments over 10,000 students, Lyon et al. (1978) found that only 43% had a central office responsible for program evaluation, and three-quarters of these districts concentrated primarily on testing and student achievement data. Little attention was paid to questions of using program and testing information to help instructional personnel bring about program improvement.

Since the Lyon et al. study, two groups have received contracts to locate and study districts which are "exemplary" in integrating evaluative information with a procedure for program improvement. Both found such districts to be very much in the minority. Nonetheless, there were some which were quite successful in gathering and using evaluative information, and they were of different sizes and circumstances. The first study is being conducted by the Center for the Study of Evaluation at U.C.L.A. The researchers identified 40 districts with reputations for linking testing and other data to instructional decision-making, and in the six they selected for case studies they found some common characteristics. These relatively successful districts had "idea advocates" — a small group of key people who possessed the beliefs, goals, and knowledge of how to set up and use an evaluative information system; they had an effective "technical delivery system" for gathering testing information and for providing in-service education and assistance for teachers and principals on how to diagnose and use the information; and they had a strong "communication and coordinating system" in which the curriculum division, school principals and teachers, and the evaluation unit were brought together for communication and decision-making purposes (see Bank, 1981; Williams & Bank, 1981). In short, it is no coincidence that the characteristics of these exemplary districts are remarkably similar to the characteristics of school districts which are effective at implementing change. Gathering information and using it for altering the program is central to effective change (see chapter 5; also Estes, 1982; Carnie, 1982).

The second study, conducted by the Huron Institute, found similar results (described in some detail in Kennedy et al., 1980, and Apling & Kennedy, 1981). The researchers managed to identify 111 districts reported to use testing and other information for program improvement, from which they selected 18 for closer study. They found several subpatterns depending on the type of issue, the availability of information, and the decision-making system. Other studies (Alkin et al., 1979; Fullan, 1982) also review the orientation and capacity of school systems to use evaluative information. The simple message in this research is that a system or procedure for information gathering and use is part and parcel of an effective change process.

In summary, there are comparatively small numbers of successful districts, but they do cover the range of sizes and circumstances experienced by the vast majority of districts in North America.[20] Some districts no doubt experience frequent turmoil and face impossible odds for bringing about constructive change. But for most districts, the main difference appears to be that the successful ones had central office administrators who enjoyed or were able to gain the support of the board, and who had very clear views and sets of ideas and skills which determined how they confronted and managed change; in the management of change they provided the support and training to increase the willingness and capacity of principals and teachers to deal with change.

---

20 We do not know enough about the very small rural school districts (26% of the school districts in the U.S. have fewer than 1000 students). Rosenblum and Louis (1979) provide one thorough description of 10 rural school districts which indicates that many implementation problems are similar. However, lack of resources, geographic spread, absence of a proximate job market, and distance from urban information centers are bound to make some differences (see Bass & Berman, 1979, 1980). Also, very large districts (e.g., above 150,000 students) face particularly difficult problems (see Bassin & Gross, 1980).

# Guidelines for the
# district administrator

The most important guidelines are grounded in the descriptions in this and the previous sections, and they will not be repeated. A highly condensed version of the main guidelines which the administrator should consider can be set forth as follows:[21]

1 *Choose a district in which change has a chance of occurring or do not expect much change.* George Bailey, the Superintendent of Adam's County, best summarizes this guideline in a recent publication (Bailey, 1980). He cites research evidence and his own experience, which essentially shows that some communities are dominated by a power structure which is more interested in the status quo; other communities are so fractious that the superintendent is the inevitable victim; others are pluralistic and expect administrators to lead change. Although the classification is somewhat oversimplified, the main message is sound—the interest in change, or leverage for change, in a district must be minimally present. Without that the chief executive officer is as powerless as anyone else, and in fact will likely become the convenient scapegoat.

   Other district administrators (below the level of the chief executive officer) will have to make similar choices, with the addition that they will also have to determine whether the superintendent with whom they will be or are working is knowledgeable and actively supportive of change—ideally someone who can teach them something about how to implement change effectively.

2 Once in a district, *develop management capabilities of administrators—other district administrators and principals—to lead change.* Using a combination of in-service training emphasizing development and growth, and replacement of administrators through attrition or forced resignation (in extreme cases), the goal is to develop gradually the district's administrative capability to manage and facilitate change. Among other things, the administrator must require and help principals to work with teachers, which means that he or she, as district administrator, must have the ability and willingness to work closely with principals.

3 *Directly and indirectly (e.g., through principals) provide resources, training, and the clear expectation that schools (teachers, principals, etc.) are the main units of change.* District administrators, at the early stages of their appointments, will have to convince and prove to teachers and principals that "this time it will be different." Put differently, they will have to understand the local history of innovation experiences; and overcome the barriers by their actions in helping to determine the specific need for change, and in supporting the implementation efforts at the school level for those innovations which are adopted. The district approach must address the practicality concerns of teachers and the role concerns of principals described in chapter 7 and 8. Helping to provide more positive experiences with change would be a fundamental accomplishment.

4 *Develop with other administrators, school boards, and teachers a clear procedure for dealing with change.* The main components of the procedure have been stated repeatedly in this book. They embody the three phases of initiation, implementation, and continuation. The plan must incorporate conceptual knowledge and assumptions about the change process, technical resources and assistance in clarifying and supporting imple-

---

21 For other guidelines applied directly to the role of districts in Canada in working with provincial curriculum guides see our recent resource books written for the British Columbia Ministry of Education (Fullan & Leithwood, 1980) and the Ontario Ministry of Education (Fullan & Park, 1981).

mentation, and a thorough communication system modeled by the district administrator. The district administrator also must continually analyze and learn from his or her experience with previous innovation attempts in building his or her own generative knowledge.

5 *Recognize that implementing the implementation plan is itself a fundamental implementation problem* (Williams, 1980, p. 103). The ultimate irony would be for a district administrator to formulate a plan for change and to introduce it into the system in exactly the same self-defeating way as most curricular innovations have been introduced (that is, in a top-down manner, having foreign meaning to participants, and providing little opportunity to develop skills in the change process). Developing a new implementation procedure means working with system members over a period of time in which they increasingly come to understand, modify, become skilled in, and believe in the effectiveness of the approach to change being used. As with innovation, negotiating the plan for innovation is necessary.

6 *Monitoring the implementation process is a never-ending requirement.* Actually, this guideline is a basic part of guideline 4, but it warrants separate emphasis. The information-gathering system to assess and address problems of implementation must be institutionalized. The more horizontal and vertical two-way communication that exists, the more knowledge there will be about the status of change. Williams (1980, pp. 90–91) claims that the need is not for formal research methodologies but for "competent, reasonable people" in the system to be concerned about implementation through careful observation, questioning, and discussions. This is none other than the systematic social interaction referred to so frequently as the core ingredient of developing knowledge and meaning about change. More formal information-gathering systems can also be very effective, if they are integrated with procedures for instructional improvement (Kennedy et al., 1980; Bank, 1981).

There can be no one recipe for change, because unlike ingredients for a cake, people are not standard to begin with, and the damned thing is that they change as you work with them in response to their experiences and their perceptions. The paramount task of the district administrator is not to get this or that innovation put into practice, but *to build the capacity of the district to handle any and all innovations* (which is not to say to implement them all). The administrator who tries to deal with innovations one at a time will soon despair, or be victimized. The one who works over a four- or five-year period to develop the district's and schools' core capacity (that is, teachers', principals', other administrators', and the school board's capacity) to process the demands of change, whether they arise internally or externally to the district, *may find change easier as time goes by*. More important, people in the district may find innovation easier and maybe even rewarding. If anyone has the opportunity to lead the way, it is the district administrator.

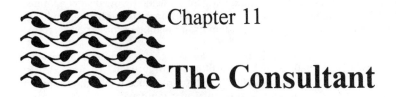Chapter 11

# The Consultant

*... the omnibus portfolio ...*

Subject consultant, curriculum coordinator, program adviser, resource teacher, organization development specialist, change agent, project director, linkage agent—the educational consultant comes (and goes) in many different shapes and sizes. In Canada, school district consultants primarily work on subject or grade-level curricula arising from provincial and local policies and programs. In the United States, district curriculum staff also exist, but layered in are a host of other consultants and program directors paid for through federal and state special project grants (see chapter 13).

In addition to these local or internal district consultants, there are numerous types of external consultants. Some work in provincial/state or federal education departments, others in regional educational laboratories or centers (in the U.S.), and still others in universities and private consultancy firms. Within those various agencies, some are on permanent staff, while others' positions are due to major special projects which frequently last for only two or three years.

Because my primary interest at this point is in what happens at the local level, I will start with a discussion of district consultants. In the subsequent section, I will expand this discussion to include external consultants. In the last section of the chapter, I will formulate some conclusions about the role of internal and external consultants in the conduct of educational change from the perspective of the local district.

# Internal district consultants

In keeping with the theme of this book, we should like to know how effective district consultants are in introducing and responding to new ideas and, more important, in following through with new programs to support implementation and continuation. The truth of the matter is that very little specifically is known about the role of district support staff. School districts, even those of the same size and with similar total budgets, are organized very differently in terms of the extent, nature, and duties of support staff. Districts focus on different parts of the change process: some are preoccupied with adopting externally produced programs, while others work more at facilitating exchanges or development internal to the district. In addition to (or because of) this confusing variety, there simply is not much thorough research on the topic. It is dangerous to generalize from any one case study, or even a general survey, because so many conditions may be either unique (the case study) or left unspecified (the survey). What we can do is to examine some findings and attempt to understand them in terms of what we know about the theory and practice of change described in previous chapters.

In one of the few larger-scale studies, Regan and Winter (1980) obtained responses from 630 school district consultants in Ontario concerning how they spent their time. Of the 10 highest-ranked tasks (out of a total of 28), only two (in-service workshops and explaining curriculum guidelines) involved group activities. Most of the high-ranked activities involved one-to-one interaction. As the researchers observe:

When consultants deliver materials to teachers and counsel them about classroom program, the interaction is one-to-one with consultants providing much individualized and personal assistance to the teachers involved. As a means of influencing teacher decisions, however, these tasks by their very nature limit the number of teachers whose needs/requests can be accommodated. (pp. 11–12)

A second major finding of the Regan and Winter research was that the consultants "have had no other training/experience preparing them for consulting" beyond basic teacher training and classroom teaching experience. Given the complexities of facilitating educational change with large numbers of teachers, this lack of preparation undoubtedly creates major problems in carrying out the role. There is some evidence that there are serious problems, and other evidence that district consultants can be quite effective under certain conditions.

On the negative side there are a number of cases where district consultants experienced severe problems in their role as coordinators or facilitators implementing given programs or policies. In 1976 the Vancouver school board in British Columbia embarked on a comprehensive three-year district-wide project to further the language competencies of all students in the system. The impact of Project Build, as it was called, was assessed by an external evaluator. Despite strong motivation and commitment on the part of district consultants assigned to the project, one of the major problems in implementation concerned their role. As the evaluator sums up the interviews with consultants and teachers:

Frequently the consultant team felt the tasks that faced them were overwhelming. They were expected first to be authorities in the acquisition of language at all grade levels, then to be curriculum developers, staff developers, and change agents. (Rayder, 1979)

In a case study of two schools attempting to implement a provincial language arts policy in Alberta, Simms (1978) identifies a litany of problems associated with the lack of orientation and effective support to teachers by 15 district "facilitators" who functioned as full-time consultants.

Similarly, Lippitt (1979) sums up the lack of clarity in the roles of district consultants in the U.S. federally sponsored Experimental Schools (ES) project in rural districts:

Staff members who were assigned to coordinate, facilitate, train or support were almost always carrying a combination of supervisory, administrative, monitoring and consultative duties. Overlapping responsibilities made it difficult to gain trust or credibility or legitimacy as a consultative helper or supporter. (p. 262)

In one of the few studies asking district consultants what they think about problems of implementing curricular change, Dow and Whitehead (1980) discovered that the 44 consultants who participated perceive "organizational" factors at the school level as most problematic. In particular, consultants perceive lack of program knowledge and leadership on the part of the principal, as well as difficulties in establishing ongoing communication with teachers in the school, as presenting the greatest barriers to implementation.

When internal consultants have been effective, it has been where districts have set up a deliberate, organized system of support for implementation. For example, as I have described in chapter 10, Jefferson County, Colorado, has effectively used 23 resource teachers to introduce and provide follow-up support for implementing a revised elementary science curriculum (see Pratt et al., 1980; Loucks & Melle, 1980; Melle & Pratt, 1981).

Daft and Becker's (1978) study of innovativeness in several high schools, referred to earlier, is one of the few which have highlighted the critical role of district support staff:

The presence of a special group playing a coordinating role in the high school districts seems to make a real and positive difference to the number of innovations adopted.

They proceed to explain why district support staff were so important:

The coordinators arranged frequent meetings with small groups of teachers and department heads to exchange ideas and information. The coordinators also did the research work and proposal preparation for ideas the teachers wanted approved by the district superintendent and school board. Coordinators seldom proposed their own ideas for adoption. Coordinators also did extensive research work and proposal preparation for top administrators, thereby facilitating the trickle-down of administrative changes as well. (p. 156)

The DESSI study, especially the 12-site case studies, describes the important role of ongoing internal district assistance for implementation. In the short run, assistance contributed to the development of support, reassurance, and clarity about the innovation. In the longer run, assistance developed confidence and ownership in the innovation (see, for examples, Miles's 1981 case study of Perry-Parkdale; Huberman's 1981 study of Masepa; Loucks & Cox, 1982).

Berman, McLaughlin, et al. (1979) elaborate on the importance of school district "infrastructure for change," which they describe in one of their case studies of "successful" school district change:

Their district curriculum specialists' primary tasks are to assist teachers and principals by providing pedagogic leadership, being on call to deal with special problems, and stimulating grass roots innovation. Specialists are expected to keep abreast of the latest research and theory developments and to share these developments with Sandwood staff. The assistant superintendent for the Programs Division summed up the role of the specialists in the following way: "We expect them to be in tune with national developments; they're supposed to stir things up. This whole operation is geared toward destroying the status quo and the specialists are critical to this effort." (p. 53)

In their larger study of federal programs (FPSEC), Berman and McLaughlin report that the *amount* of assistance by district resource staff is not at all related to achievement of project goals, but that specific kinds of assistance are helpful. When district resource staff could help with demonstrating or making suggestions for classroom implementation, they were very effective. When they offered only general or abstract advice, they were not effective—in fact, "Numerous visits to the classroom by district or project staff do more harm than good when teachers do not feel they are being helped" (Berman & McLaughlin, 1977, p. 109).

Fullan, Miles, and Taylor's (1978) case study of Adam's County, Colorado, confirms the importance of the establishment of a resource unit within the district which is integrated with ongoing program needs. External consultants are used, but mainly to train inside resource people (i.e., trainer-of-trainers approach). The resource system is clearly under the control of the district. Schmuck, Runkel, and colleagues at the University of Oregon have developed an integrated and well-documented approach to Organization Development (OD) in school districts and schools in which the external consultants (Schmuck et al.) train internal "cadres" of personnel to be relatively self-sufficient in developing the internal problem-solving capacities of the district. (See Schmuck et al., 1975, 1977; Runkel et al., 1978. Fullan, Miles, & Taylor, 1980, review the research on the role of both internal and external consultants in OD programs.)

Organized and coordinated district efforts, however, seem to be the exception rather than the rule. Howey and Joyce (1978) in the United States, and Nash and Ireland (1979) in Canada, both found that there was a distinct lack of planning, coordination, job focus, and use of knowledge and principles of program planning and implementation in district in-service programs.[1] For example, Nash and Ireland found only three cases out of 40 districts in Ontario in which there was any relationship between stated curriculum priorities and in-service programs for curriculum implementation, and found only two school systems which had a planned sequence at the district and school levels to facilitate the use of a selected curriculum change. On a different but related aspect of the problem, Lyon et al. (1978) at the Center for the Study of Evaluation at U.C.L.A. conducted a comprehensive survey of how the 750 districts in the U.S. having 10,000 students or more go about program evaluation. Among their findings: (1) only 43% of the districts have a central office for program evaluation; (2) in those districts with evaluation units, achievement testing is the dominant topic; and (3) in those districts there are limited attempts to use evaluative data for instructional improvement. In a parallel study of the activities of school district evaluators, Bank et al. (1979) found that only a small percentage (20%) of evaluation units are involved in implementation assessment, and that there is very limited coordination or integration between district evaluators and district consultants and between district evaluators and external consultants. (See also Bank, 1981, for a brief summary of what successful districts do.)

In summary, the amount and specificity of research on the role of district consultants are limited. We can piece together some of the main issues by using

---

1 The role of in-service is examined in chapter 14.

the information that is available in combination with the practical theory of change described in earlier chapters. If district consultants work just on a one-to-one basis, they will likely have limited impact, because they will reach only a minuscule percentage of teachers, although they may have a very strong effect on those teachers. If they are in a district which has no coordinated plan for introducing and implementing change and yet attempts numerous innovations, they will be in an even worse no-win situation, for it will be extremely difficult for them to set up a program of continuous assistance and follow-through so necessary to support change in practice. On the other hand, if the district or project personnel set up a program of ongoing assistance, implementation will be greatly facilitated. Because of the numbers of teachers and principals and the scarcity of time, consultants and other district staff need to figure out how to work with groups of people, not just one individual at a time.

Until I have taken up the role of external consultants, I will leave a consideration of what characteristics of the role of consultants seem to be most effective. But essentially effectiveness involves combining expertise in the *content* of a new program with knowledge or expertise in the *change process* in working with schools and districts as organizations and social systems. The role of district consultant in educational change represents a significant resource which has not received the attention it deserves. The continued development of this group's supportive role in program implementation is an important priority.

# External consultants

In Canada the structure of external assistance is fairly simple. There are provincial ministry of education[2] personnel (sometimes including regional offices) whose main job is to disseminate new policies and programs and get feedback on the quality and impact of programs. Outside of these "official agents" the main other external consultants come from professional development activities of university faculties of education and teacher unions or associations. The only national presence of any note has been the Canada Studies Foundation, which has supported the development and dissemination of Canadian curriculum materials, primarily in history and geography, although the dissemination role especially with respect to providing assistance has been neither clear nor effective (Anderson & Benoit, 1978).

Again, there are few studies in Canada which examine closely the impact of these external forces on educational change. The general-survey type studies have placed these external agencies near the bottom of any list of helpful or influential resources. For example, Aoki et al. surveyed 1488 teachers in British Columbia regarding their teaching of social studies. Teachers placed teacher federation professional development staff, university faculty of education personnel, and ministry of education consultants at the very bottom of a list of 13 support services (school librarians, fellow teachers, and district resource centers were at the top). The researchers found:

---

2 Some provinces use the style "Ministry of Education" and others "Department of Education." For simplicity I shall use "ministry" as the general term.

Although the services of Faculty of Education personnel and Ministry of Education consultants are unavailable to 68 to 80 percent of teachers respectively, assistance from these two groups is rated as "inadequate" by teachers for whom these services *are* available. (Aoki et al., 1977, p. 41; their italics)

Other studies in Canada have confirmed this finding: Kormos and Enns (1979) in a survey of 500 teachers in 90 school boards in Ontario found that ministry of education staff and faculty of education professors were "not at all helpful" in curriculum implementation. Leithwood et al. (1978) found the same response in a more direct study of teachers in three school boards in Ontario.

The situation in the United States is considerably more complicated. There have been numerous federally sponsored programs involving "linkage agents": the Pilot State Dissemination Program, the National Diffusion Network, the R&D Utilization Project, the State Capacity Building Project, the R&D Exchange, the Documentation and Technical Assistance Project, and Technical Assistance Groups, as well as several large-scale research studies on these and other programs.[3] There are also state departments of education, regional educational laboratories or R&D centers, and intermediate agencies in which several school districts band together to create a regional unit that provides certain types of resource services. Fortunately, there has been a fair amount of documentation and evaluation of the efficacy of these various efforts. Emrick and Peterson (1978) analyzed the common findings from five of the above major projects: the Pilot State Dissemination Program, the Federal Program Supporting Educational Change, the Project Information Packages, the National Diffusion Network, and the Technical Assistance Groups. In synthesizing the findings from the projects, the authors draw five major overall conclusions:

1 Meaningful change occurs as a process, not an event.
2 Direct personal intervention is by far the most potent technical resource, and may be a necessary condition for many forms of utilization.
3 Continuous personal participation of the implementation staff (e.g., teachers) is needed to firmly root and sustain the utilization.
4 Administrators occupy a crucial role in supporting the utilization process.
5 Material resources at the "how to" level are needed, particularly for utilizations involving organizational or instructional change (Emrick & Peterson, 1978, pp. 51–87).

All five meta-findings relate directly to the role of external agents or consultants. Findings 1 and 3 say that external agents have to have some continuous contact with school district people if they are to have an impact. Findings 2 and 5 state that personal contact is essential and that such contact should offer some directly useful technical assistance at the "how to" level. Finding 4 says that the external consultant not only has to have some technical expertise but

---

3 See chapter 13 for descriptions of these projects and their impact. The main large-scale studies are Berman and McLaughlin (1978), Crandall et al. (forthcoming), Emrick and Peterson (1978), and Louis and Rosenblum (1981). See also the Appendix for brief statements on the nature of the projects.

also has to be knowledgeable about the process of organizational change, especially in relating to key district administrators and school principals.

Other studies of external agents reinforce and elaborate on these findings. In evaluating the R&D Utilization Project, Louis and Rosenblum (1981) found that external "linkers" associated with the projects were seen by schools as valuable in identifying needs, selecting solutions, and facilitating the implementation of validated R&D projects. The projects possessed characteristics similar to the five cited above by Emrick and Peterson—that is, R&D utilization was seen as a process, involving direct personal interaction over time with teachers and administrators, and using validated material resources which could be practically used.

As Louis and Rosenblum (1981, p. 7) report:

The *amount of training* received by the site staff prior to implementation has a strong positive effect, and this impact is augmented by having *training provided by a variety of types of people*.

The *time that the linking agent* spends with local site committees or "problem solving teams" is predictive of several dependent measures. Our site visits revealed that much of the importance of the agents can be attributed to the role that they played on site in both stimulating committee members to stay active and to reach decision points, and also of providing logistical support to ensure that the meetings were scheduled regularly, that suggestions for consultants were obtained etc. Thus, the actual presence of the agent on-site was important. (their italics)

The large-scale DESSI survey (Crandall et al., forthcoming) and the 12 case studies (e.g., Miles, 1980; Huberman, 1981) also investigate the role of external assistance at each of the three stages of change referred to in previous chapters: mobilization (helping in needs assessment, writing proposals, selecting programs); implementation (training, demonstration, identifying resources, keeping attention focused on implementation); and continuation (identifying decisions about resources and personnel for continued change).[4] The complete analysis on the role of external assistance from the DESSI research is not yet available, and so it is not possible to make any firm generalizations. There is some indication that the main role of external consultants is at the "front end" (providing information, getting a program started, etc.) with the question of follow-through depending on other factors such as commitment of the district and presence of internal advocates; or, to state it negatively, external consultants may disappear after introducing something new and be unavailable for follow-through. However, the opportunity for training or other forms of assistance from an external resource person during implementation can have a major impact; but, of course, someone internal has to coordinate the use of such assistance (see Huberman's 1981 case study; Cox & Havelock, 1982; Hergert, 1979). The importance of the on-site presence of the external agent *during* implementation should be noted, because earlier research showed that many "linkers" attended primarily to getting programs adopted without following through on these decisions (Bank et al., 1979).

Miles's (1979) review of the linkage aspect of the Documentation and Technical Assistance Project provides a somewhat negative example of attempts to

---

4 The DESSI study makes the useful distinction between "event specific" assistance and "ongoing" assistance.

make external assistance work. The project attempted to link knowledge from nine urban school districts, which had been awarded local problem-solving grants, to two "user" sites interested in developing their own problem-solving capacity.[5] The overriding reason why not much effective external assistance materialized was that the linkers had great difficulties in transferring a complex problem-solving model to new situations. The goals of assistance were diffuse and unclear, and the information to be transferred was complex, not validated, and not coherent—that is, not in a form in which it could be understood, adapted, and used (Miles, 1979, p. 27).

In their study of Federal Programs Supporting Educational Change, Berman and McLaughlin (1977) found that outside consultants had positive effects on project goals achieved, but only under certain conditions. They found, for example, that the degree or frequency of employment of outside consultants was not related to achievement of goals. They comment that "when consultants were good they were very good; when they were bad, they were an obstacle" (p. 109). They explain:

Good consultants can help by providing concrete, practical advice to project teachers—showing them, either in their classrooms or in "hands-on" workshops, how to adapt project methods or materials to their own situations. Good consultants help teachers to solve problems for themselves rather than solve problems for them. Ineffective consultants often furnish advice that is too abstract to be useful. (pp. 109–10)

Datta (1980) provides a useful critique of FPSEC's generalization that the amount of external assistance is unrelated to achievement. As she points out, assistance in most FPSEC projects seemed to consist of "nearby university professors." She emphasizes that one-shot (e.g., workshop) or ongoing "general" assistance is a far cry from "extensive technical assistance from a recognized authority in the subject area who had experience in program development, implementation, and dissemination" (p. 109). Even one-shot or event-linked assistance can be helpful if it provides clear demonstration and active involvement and if internal district personnel take the responsibility for follow-through (see Miles, 1980, p. 68).

In summary, in order to understand more fully the role and effectiveness of external agents in any given set of circumstances, we would have to know a number of specific facts pertaining to their training, the project and organizational conditions under which they are working, the type of change with which they are dealing, and the kind of role they are expected to perform (e.g., implementing a specific product vs. facilitating information-seeking).[6]

---

5 The activities at the nine sites varied, of course, but included various programs for involving parents, students, and staff, development of alternative schools, school-community programs, and so on.

6 There is a growing body of research on these details. The number of variables and the contingencies are too complex and the space is too limited for me to systematically describe in this chapter the variety of external agent roles. See Crandall's (1977) comprehensive conceptualization of the roles of linkers, and Louis's recent review (1981) of external change agent roles. See also Butler and Paisley (1978); Firestone and Wilson (1981); Harris (1979); Hood and Cates (1978); Louis and Kell (1981); Madey et al. (1979); Research for Better Schools (1981); Taylor (1979); section on external assistance in Crandall et al. (forthcoming); Cox and Havelock (1982).

# The role of internal
# and external consultants
# in perspective

In drawing together the main conclusions about the separate and combined roles of internal and external consultants, it is useful to consider the following aspects: phases in the change process, types of consultancy roles, and internal/external use of consultants.

## Phases in the change process

As an overlay to the whole problem, let us recall that we are interested in the entire process of educational change, which has been defined as including three phases: mobilization/adoption, implementation, and continuation. Thus, the consultant, whether internal or external, who gets a new program "adopted" may do more harm than good if little effective implementation follows. Put differently, in deciding on or in assessing the role of consultants, we should have in mind not only whether they obtain or provide good information on given occasions (e.g., a workshop), but also whether they or someone else follows through to provide support for the use of that information. Effective implementation involves the development of individual and organizational meaning vis-à-vis a particular change. Consultants, if they are to be effective, must facilitate the development of that meaning as they interact with school and district personnel.

## Types of consultancy roles

A second and interacting aspect of the role of consultants is the question of what is the nature of the role itself. Although there are a variety of roles, as we have seen, there have been some very useful conceptualizations of the main roles.[7] More than a decade ago, Havelock established some of the basic ideas for change agents in his reviews and conceptualization of their roles in planned change. He described a six-stage model, starting with the need for the change agent to "build the relationship" with a client group and ending with the "stabilization of the innovation and self-renewal" (Havelock, 1973). Within these stages he identified a number of skills and corresponding training needs for change agents (Havelock & Havelock, 1973).

---

7 I do not attempt to present an inventory of consultancy skills. For general treatments of the topic see Lippitt and Lippitt (1978); Lippitt (1979); Blake and Mouton (1976); Crandall (1977). I tend to focus in this chapter on the consultant's role in influencing specific changes in practice. It is not always easy to assess the actual impact of consultants. Moreover, Weiss (1979) claims that the role of knowledge (such as research and program knowledge in the field of innovation) is "to enlighten" practitioners in a diffuse, undetermined process of "knowledge creep and decision accretion." So it is not that easy to measure the effectiveness of consultants who are in more general-information-providing roles. (See also Lindblom & Cohen, 1979.)

Crandall (1977) developed a very comprehensive analysis of the roles, skills, and training needs of "linking agents." He identified ten different roles (information linker, technical assister, process enabler, etc.) and nine skill clusters (skills in planning, communication, implementation, evaluation, etc.). Crandall's 90-cell matrix (p. 256) is as good a summary as any of the "omnibus portfolio" of the linkage agent. While no single person is expected to be all things to all people, most linkage roles involve a wide range of the functions and skills he described.

Building on Havelock's and Crandall's work, Butler and Paisley (1978) suggest four types of linking roles: resource finder, process helper, solution giver, and generalist. Madey (1979) identified empirically three slightly different types: resource finder, facilitator, and communicator. Perhaps the main issue for our purposes can be simplified if we distinguish between consultants who act primarily as *solution givers* and those who act more as *facilitators*. The solution giver is the kind of consultant (e.g., as a writer or developer of a program) who has expertise in a specific program. The facilitator is the kind of consultant who, as the name implies, helps clients identify and select (or develop) their own solutions—or, if a program has already been adopted, works in a facilitative way to adapt the program during implementation. There are advantages and disadvantages to each role. If the solution is the right one, the solution giver has greater expertise to offer in substantive matters; the facilitator may not be able to offer practical assistance. On the other hand, we have seen that decisions to adopt programs (i.e., solutions) are not always the best ones. Even if a program is needed, the technically expert consultant, as Berman and McLaughlin discovered, sometimes creates overdependency or overreliance to the detriment of teachers' learning to use the program for themselves (1977, p. 110). But the external consultant who combines content expertise with intensive strategies for training and support can be very effective in bringing about change in practice.[8]

The resolution to the problem, as one might suspect, is not to choose between supplying content expertise and facilitating; both kinds of help are needed and may be offered by the same person or by a combination of people. The ideal internal consultant would be able to provide both, being a good internal facilitator of the change process and being able to contribute and/or arrange for content assistance. External consultants can provide content assistance, but the internal consultant must possess enough technical knowledge to provide follow-through support.

Whether internal or external, it is possible for content expertise to blind us to the necessity of change process skills, as when the expert sees only one solution (i.e., his or her solution) or ignores key administrators, teacher anxieties, and follow-through support systems. In any case, the internal consultant to be effective with large numbers of teachers must essentially plan or influence the planning of the *process* of adoption, implementation, etc.—and that involves much more than content expertise with the program in question.

---

8 Two programs exemplify this point: the Direct Instruction follow-through program (see Emrick et al., 1979; Gersten et al., 1981; Rhine, 1981) and the NDN ECRI program on reading (Huberman, 1981).

Of course, it may not be possible for the individual consultant to have a great influence on the district's approach to educational change. As I have stated in the previous chapter, the district administration can go a long way in making it more likely or less likely that district consultants operate as effective change agents; but even with this constraint the individual consultant has some leeway in how he or she works with teachers and principals.

## Internal/external use of consultants

If internal district consultants are to operate in this blended fashion, combining content and change-process expertise, what is the place of external consultants? To answer this question, we must consider both perspectives: the district looking out and the external consultant looking in.

As a context, consider the following. At the beginning of the chapter we saw that school districts do not seem to use external assistance to any great extent. In the Lyon et al. survey of 750 school districts, 50% of the districts do not spend *any* money on consultants. Miles (1978, 1980), studying the planning and implementation of new schools, identifies the dilemma of "expertise-seeking vs. self-reliance." He found that school districts did not seek much external knowledge. Even when confronted with the opportunity to take advantage of matching funds from the project to bring in external consultant help, districts refused on the grounds that "district resource staff could provide all the help that was needed." Yet, in analyzing the planning and implementation process, Miles et al. (1978) found that the internal help was not used or was not adequate to the tasks. Butler and Paisley (1978) also note that large school districts are not good prospects for external consultancies.

In fact, a large district is a discouraging assignment for an external linking agent in three respects: (1) the district's dynamics can be understood only after a long period of observation; (2) the district's internal capacity duplicates the general set of external linkage services; (3) progress in the district's attainment of its goals is inertia-bound and uneven. (p. 28)

And Lippitt (1979) reports that outside consultants were ineffectively used in rural districts in the experimental schools (ES) project.

In order to make some sense of all this, let me return to the two perspectives—looking out and looking in—starting with the former. Looking out, as Miles (1980) has said, the district faces the dilemma of expertise-seeking vs. self-reliance. And it is a dilemma. Some consultants are not good; others offer "solutions" which may or may not be appropriate; and still others are inspiring, but nothing comes of the ideas once they leave. But not to seek any outside help is to be more self-sufficient than the demands of educational change would allow. The primary task of the school district should be to develop its own internal capacity to process needed educational change, relying on external assistance to train insiders and to provide specific program expertise in combination with internal follow-through (see Fullan & Park, 1981). Lippitt captures several of these points in his review of the ineffective use of outside consultants in the rural experimental schools (ES) project:

In all cases local administrators lacked skill in recruiting consultants, working out meaningful contractual understandings with them, and bringing local personnel into the working relationship. The consultants were typically seen as limited tools of the administrator or as mechanisms to carry through a restricted training function for a group of teachers. No one knew why, when, or how to use a consultant . . . .

Both ES/Washington and local administrators failed to differentiate between a consultant's expertise on particular education innovations or procedures . . . and his expertise in the area of educational change. The methodology of stimulating and facilitating change and helping to cope with resistance to change is a specific area of competence quite different from competence in various educational subject matters or procedures . . . .

In most of the consultative situations, the consultants and consultees failed to recognize that a consultant-trainer, after introducing and advocating new ideas and procedures and behaviors, must have a specific design for follow-through and must support the effort to apply the skills and procedures on the job. (Lippitt, 1979, p. 261)

It is an undeveloped art to know how best to select and use external consultants. Indeed, the whole linking-agent syndrome is itself an innovation in education. As with all innovations, people must learn how to use it effectively. Both external resource people and internal personnel are faced with the problem of how to define and implement new internal/external relationships in ways which are most effective for bringing about change in practice.

There are, as we have seen, several recent *positive* examples of the use of external consultants. The RDU research, the DESSI survey and case studies, the linkage-agent work of The Network (Harris, 1979; Taylor, 1979), and Datta's reinterpretation of the Rand FPSEC research all show the same finding: that districts which select (through wisdom or blind luck) consultants who possess technical competence, plus the commitment, knowledge, and energy to spend time on-site to assist during implementation, are rewarded with more thorough and longer-lasting change.

Finally, the local district should set out to develop its own content and change-process expertise (among consultants, administrators, teachers). When external consultants are used, they should be used in combination with some internal team or personnel with some specific design or plan for following through on the ideas.[9]

The perspective of the external looking in is the other side of the same coin (with one added twist which I will take up shortly). Most research shows that external consultants are effective only when there is an internal consultant or team which supports their activities. All the major research we have been reviewing shows that effective educational change occurs when there is the *combined* involvement of internal and external members.[10] External change agents who are interested in facilitating real educational change, therefore, should establish some ongoing relationship with internal district administrators, consultants, and teachers who will act collectively to follow through on the

---

9 Schmuck et al. (1975) describe and document very clearly the process of developing internal "cadres" in school districts and schools. Our case study of Adam's County, Colorado, also provides a good illustration of internal-capacity-building using external resources (Fullan, Miles, & Taylor, 1978).
10 See the discussions presented in Crandall et al. (forthcoming); Emrick and Peterson (1978); Fullan, Miles, and Taylor (1980); Harris (1979); Louis (1981); Louis and Rosenblum (1981); Taylor (1979).

change. More so than other participants, external agents need both technical and change process expertise.

The twist I referred to is that many external agents (e.g., in provincial/state or federal agencies) have mandates to ensure the implementation of "official policy." What does an external agent do when a district shows no interest in policies or programs which are required to be implemented? I take up the question of compliance with government policies in chapter 13. At this point, it is sufficient to say that there may be cases in which districts can be forced to comply with certain categorical requirements, but that effective implementation of most programs needs the kind of external–internal relationships referred to above (see Elmore, 1980). To put it more positively, external agents probably have more willing school districts with which to work than they can currently handle, *given the requirements of an effective change process from initiation through implementation and continuation.*

Indeed, the dilemma faced by both internal and external consultants is one of scope vs. intensity (see Louis & Sieber, 1979; Louis's 1981 review). Although effective change requires intensive, ongoing contact, the number of clients is far beyond the available time and energy of consultants. Like most dilemmas, it is not solvable; but by employing principles of social change including the setting up of peer support systems, consultants whether internal or external can reach and respond to more people more effectively than they currently do. (See Louis, Rosenblum, Molitor, et al., 1981; Joyce & Showers, 1981.)

The variety of internal and external consultancy roles and the range and complexity of skills required make it very difficult to draw fine-grained conclusions about these roles. Some roles do primarily emphasize program expertise, while others are established essentially to provide general facilitation and capacity-building. There are some very useful guidelines and training materials available focusing on both basic and special skills, such as Bank and Sniderman's *The Guidebook for Evaluating Dissemination Activities* (1981), The Network's *Linking Agent's Tool Kit* (Crandall, 1979), and the Northwest Regional Educational Laboratory's *Preparing Educational Training Consultants* (NWREL, 1976). As with all innovations, the effective use of consultants will take much more than materials. Individual consultants should think through their role as change agents—and their clients should do the same—in light of the phases and dilemmas in the change process. With declining resources, we cannot afford to squander the potential assistance consultants represent.

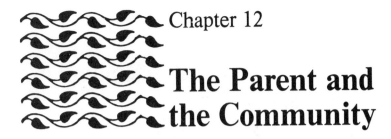 Chapter 12

# The Parent and
# the Community

*Whose school is it, anyway?*

*— Gold and Miles (1981)*

If teachers and administrators who spend forty or fifty hours a week immersed in the educational world have trouble comprehending the meaning of educational change, imagine what it is like for the parent. Highly educated parents are bewildered; what of the less educated ones who have always felt uncomfortable in dealing with the school?

The question of parent and community involvement in schools has been the subject of hundreds of books and articles over the past twenty years. At first glance this literature appears to be a mass of contradictions, confusion, and hopelessness for understanding—let alone coping with—the relationship between communities and schools. Yet, emerging from this research is a message which is remarkable in its consistency: *the closer the parent is to the education of the child, the greater the impact on child development and educational achievement.* Of course, it is not quite that simple, because such a statement encompasses a multitude of variables which make it more possible or less possible that closeness will occur. And certainly we can imagine situations in which closeness per se could be harmful to the growth of the child. Moreover, decisions about the precise nature of parent involvement must take into account cultural, ethnic, and class differences as well as variations related to the age of students. Most of the research has been on elementary schools, although many of the principles I will identify are applicable at the secondary school level.

In determining under what conditions parent and community involvement is most beneficial, we have to understand the different forms of parent participation and their consequences on the student and other school personnel. Stated another way, why do certain forms of involvement produce positive results while others seem wasteful or counterproductive?

I start with the big picture by considering the role of school boards and community influence in adopting/rejecting and implementing new policies or programs. The purpose is to obtain an overview of how or when change gets started or stopped in school districts. In the second section I turn to the more interesting, specific, and powerful issue of the ways in which parents relate to their local schools, and with what results for changing (improving) education. In the final section, as with other preceding chapters, I formulate some general guidelines as to how parents and school people might better cope with educational change together.

# School boards, communities, and change

Communities can either (a) put pressure on district administrators "to do something" about a problem, (b) oppose specific innovations which have been adopted, or (c) do nothing (passive support or apathy). Although there are several dramatic individual examples of the first two types of situation, by far the most prevalent case is that school boards and communities do not initiate or have any major role in deciding about innovative programs; that is, administrators and teachers develop or make recommendations about most new programs, or governments legislate new policies. That this is the case can be seen from the recent national large-scale DESSI study in the U.S., in which a number of major categories of innovations adopted by school districts were investigated (Crandall et al., forthcoming). The study was comprehensive in its coverage. While the initial sampling design called for interviews with chairpersons of school boards about particular major innovations adopted in their districts, this part of the design had to be soon abandoned when interviewers found out that the chairpersons knew virtually nothing about the innovations.

Boards and communities can be radically powerful in the smaller number of cases where, for whatever reasons, they become aroused. One of the more typical pressures for change over time comes as a result of population shifts. Berman, McLaughlin, et al.'s (1979) study of five school districts undergoing change illustrates that major demographic changes (rapid growth or decline in population, changes in ethnic or class composition) lead to the development of demands for change. In one of the cases, for example, rapid growth led to community activism in a previously stagnant school system, election of new board members, hiring of an innovative superintendent, wholesale restructuring of central staff roles and activities, facilitation of school-level involvement in change on the part of principals and teachers, and so on. The district became transformed in a short time with many new programs successfully implemented. It would be easy to locate other case studies which show similar patterns of cumulative community pressure leading to successful change or to endless conflicts between the community and the central administration. My point is twofold. First, such cases do occur, are dramatic, and can lead to positive change (good new programs implemented) or to negative change (continual conflict). Second, these cases of community pressure leading to change are very much in the minority.[1]

Boards and communities, if ignored, can also bring an end to innovations adopted without their informed consent. Gold and Miles (1981) describe the painful history of what happens when middle-class communities do not like the innovations they see in their schools. In this case study, the school attempted to

---

1 See, for example, Tucker and Zeigler (1980), who found that administrators usually dominate the school board and the public when it comes to decision-making.

implement open education (a notoriously undefined and ambiguous innovation) without involving the community. Parents became increasingly concerned about whether the innovation was an appropriate one, as teachers did not seem to be able to explain why they were doing what they were doing. The concern mounted, and before long the parents did not have any trouble putting the innovation to rout.

Schaffarzick's study of 34 San Francisco Bay area districts provides additional evidence for the pattern we have been discussing. He found that in 62% of the major curriculum decisions he examined, there was no lay (community) participation (cited in Boyd, 1978, p. 613). However, in those cases which involved conflict and bargaining, the community groups nearly always prevailed. Similarly, the two case studies in the late 1960s which launched the focus on "failed implementation" are classic examples of disregarding the community, adopting progressive undefined innovations, and paying the price— failed and eventually abandoned innovation, poor morale, and attrition of administrations and teachers (Gross et al., 1971; Smith & Keith, 1971).

On the positive side, what these experiences say, in effect, is that communities can rise to the occasion to reject ill-conceived innovations—what some impolite observers refer to as the "crap detector" capacity of those on the receiving end of change. Unfortunately (and this gets us to the negative side), confidence, insight, and power to crap-detect are not evenly distributed. Communities in which parents are less educated are not as able to translate their doubts into concerted efforts to combat change for the sake of change (see chapter 2). In other words, middle- and upper-class communities are more able to keep school districts honest. As Bridge (1976) says:

The unfortunate fact is that "disadvantaged" families are usually the least informed about matters of schooling and the result is that advantaged clienteles will have the largest impact on school innovations unless extraordinary efforts are made to involve others. (p. 378)

Given that boards and communities whether lower or middle class do not have an influential role in determining change, one can ask, "How many inappropriate innovations have been perpetrated on the educational public over the past two decades?" The simple answer is "Far too many," which is another way of saying that the importance of the role of parents in educational reform has been both sadly neglected and underestimated. More broadly, those interested in effective educational reform will have to deal with school boards and with community members in a way which confronts the fact that these groups are essential for the eventual implementation of many reforms: the school board for its endorsements, provision of resources necessary to support implementation, and ability to ask the right question about results; parents for their support, reinforcement, and modification of the change at the family and classroom levels.

There may, of course, be certain kinds of reforms (e.g., some secondary school curricular innovations) for which parent involvement is irrelevant or inappropriate. In other cases, teachers may need time to develop their capacity to implement a new approach before parents become actively involved in questioning the change. Some buffering may be needed in situations where small groups of parents might dominate decisions. On balance, however, parents are more likely to defer to the professionals and therefore need encouragement to become involved. In any case, deciding whether, when, and how to approach parents in educational reform represents a major dilemma—what Gold and Miles (1981) refer to as the problem in "environmental contact versus withdrawal" (p. 30). The review of some of the basic research on parent involvement in the following section indicates that it is important for educators and parents to confront this dilemma actively rather than ignore it.

# Parent involvement in schools

Let us now zero in on the local school and parents. I would like to suggest at the outset that here the issue is not just keeping schools honest but the *necessity* for parent involvement (at the elementary school level at least) with innovations if they are to have a significant impact on students. There is no need to take my word for it, for the evidence is becoming as impressive as any in the field of educational change. I examine this evidence in two broad sets: the first set concerns forms of parent involvement and their consequences; the second set describes the main barriers to parent involvement.

## Forms of involvement and consequences

There are different forms of parent involvement, and we must identify them in order to sort out and understand their consequences. Fantini (1980), one of the principal authors in community involvement research since the 1960s, has recently brought the literature together in delineating different types of parent involvement and their consequences on educational attainment of students. Drawing on Fantini and some other research to be introduced shortly, we can list the main forms of parent involvement.

1  a) Instruction: at school (e.g., parent aides)
   b) Instruction: at home (e.g., parents as tutors)
2  Governance (e.g., parent advisory councils)
3  Home–school relations (e.g., projects to increase community support)
4  Community service (e.g., adult education, use of facilities)

One of the reasons research on parent involvement is so confusing is that what is meant by involvement is frequently not specifically defined, nor is it carefully linked to particular outcomes. To anticipate the main finding from recent research which has become more focused, it turns out that only forms 1a and 1b—direct parent involvement in instructional activities designed to contribute to child development—consistently influence educational achievement of students. Once stated, this is an eminently understandable finding, but perhaps some facts should be presented. The other forms of involvement, as I will suggest, may have benefits other than on student achievement or may be potentially effective in conjunction with involvement in instruction. The simplest way of summarizing the findings on the impact of parent involvement is to subdivide the forms of participation into two categories—those pertaining to instruction (forms 1a and 1b) and those relating to non-instructional forms of participation (forms 2, 3, and 4).

## Involvement in instruction

Clark (1980) carried out a literature search to identify those studies which presented evidence on "exceptional performance in urban elementary schools." His purpose was to discover the main school-related factors which seemed to account for educational success. After a thorough search, 40 reports were retained for analysis. Of the 40 studies, 13 involved the relationship between parent involvement and achievement, and 11 of the 13 reported a positive relationship. Clark includes excerpts from some of the studies:

Perhaps the most unexpected result is the recurrent finding that parental involvement is important .... (McLaughlin, 1977, p. 69)

Among the characteristics common to the more successful programs in the basic skills is the active involvement of parents in instruction. (Chase, 1978, p. 28)

Successful schools were more likely to have parents in the classroom as aides, visitors, and as volunteers ... involvement in the *classroom* rather than in the school in general, is related to academic success ... that *parent* involvement specifically, and not the use of instructional aides in general, is associated with school success. (Wellisch et al., 1976, pp. iv–9)

Similarly, Fantini (1980) cites several other studies which draw the same conclusions. Among many examples:

Masoner reports that educators in St. Paul, Minnesota have developed an ongoing home-based program involving parents as tutors for their own children. Mothers, fathers and grandparents of over 50% of the students in participating schools have been trained to assist their youngsters in mathematics as a supplement to the normal school curriculum. As a result, student achievement has jumped significantly. (Fantini, 1980, p. 14)

The list goes on: Berlin and Berlin found that Head Start remedial programs showed no lasting effect "except for children whose mothers became directly involved in the classroom process" (Fantini, 1980, p. 14). Armor et al. (1976) investigated the impact of a reading program on the reading gains of students in 10 minority (black and Mexican-American) Los Angeles schools; they found that "greater number of parent visits to the classroom ... were associated with higher levels of reading progress" (p. 25). They also found that in the black communities, overall level of involvement by parents in the school (e.g., being in the school, space provided for parents in the school) was related to reading gains (but no such relationship was found in the Mexican-American communities). In Ontario, Hedges for a number of years has found that the training and use of parent volunteers in the classroom is consistently related to gains in achievement levels of students (see, e.g., Cussons & Hedges, 1978). Other reviews of research on parent involvement in instruction tell the same story (Gordon, 1978; Center for Equal Education, 1977).

There is no need to burden the reader with much additional information, but there is more. Barth (1979) carried out a review of programs using "home-based reinforcement of school behavior." In a review of 24 studies using the approach (i.e., parents and teachers together targeting specific academic skills and scheduling specific reinforcement practices for the home and the class-room), Barth found significant improvement on even the most difficult learning problems.

Most compensatory programs in the U.S. mandate parent participation in decisions, although very few require parent involvement in instruction. The System Development Corporation (SDC) conducted a major evaluation of parent involvement programs for the Office of Program Evaluation, U.S. Education Department (see Keesling, 1980; Melaragno et al., 1981). Four major federal programs were evaluated: Title I, Title VII bilingual, Follow Through, and the Emergency School Aid Act (ESAA).[2] The study consisted of two parts: one a survey of 369 districts and 869 schools participating in the four programs; the other a detailed on-site investigation of 57 projects (selected approximately equally from the four programs). Five forms of parent participation were investigated: governance, instruction, parent education, school support, and home–school relations. In this section I take up the question of parent participation in instructional activities—as paid aides and as home tutors. The researchers found the following patterns across the four programs:

|  | Title I | ESAA | Title VII | Follow Through | Total |
|---|---|---|---|---|---|
| Sites with parents as paid aides | 12 | 5 | 3 | 14 | 34 |
| Sites with parents as home tutors | 2 | 0 | 3 | 12 | 17 |
| No. of sites | 16 | 12 | 13 | 16 | 57 |

Source: The four site reports respectively: Melaragno et al. (1981); Robbins and Dingler (1981); Cadena-Munoz and Keesling (1981); Smith and Nerenberg (1981).

Thus, most Title I and Follow Through sites had parent aides (while most of the other two did not). The majority of Follow Through sites had formal parent home tutoring activities, compared to only a total of 5 of the 41 sites in the other three programs. Keesling suggests that the reason for such high involvement in Follow Through is related to two main factors: federal regulations which require hiring of parents where possible and which tie refunding to proof of implementation; and the more comprehensive philosophy of parent participation in Follow Through. (See also Rhine, 1981; Hodges et al., 1980.)

Neither the survey nor the site studies collected formal student achievement data. Secondary data (existing data, interviews) were collected at the sites. In those cases where there was parent involvement, positive outcomes were found regarding student learning, student attitudes, and parent attitudes. The authors also note that where home tutoring programs were used, they involved many more parents in an active, ongoing way than did any other form of parent activity in their study. The successful "parent as tutor" programs had four common features: "they were centrally coordinated by project staff; they included procedures for developing instructional plans for children; they provided individualized training to parents in those plans; and they included mechanisms for

---

2 See the Appendix for definitions of these programs.

monitoring parents' and children's progress in the home instruction'' (Smith & Nerenberg, 1981, pp. 9–11).[3]

The use of parents as paid aides was also related to positive outcomes. Parents who served as aides report many positive personal benefits (as other studies have found). And Melaragno et al. (on Title I) emphasize:

Undoubtedly the most striking outcome of an institutional nature was that students developed better attitudes toward their work when their parents were involved with the school's instructional program. (p. 7)

This carry-over effect on students occurred as a result of parents' familiarity with the school and the instructional program, and was not confined to the situation where parents were working in their own children's classroom. In the site studies, the SDC researchers also found some negative outcomes of a logistical nature: teachers' needing extra time to coordinate the work of aides; doubts in some cases about the skill and commitment of parent aides; and some parents' reporting that some teachers were intimidating. These negative cases, according to the researchers, were "exceedingly rare." In three of the four programs the researchers concluded unequivocally that the programs affected the quality of education positively in the several sites in which parents were active. ESAA was the exception; the researchers felt that they could not make such an overall statement. The size of the financial grant was unrelated to proportion of parents involved in any of the four programs.

There are other programs in addition to the four studied by SDC which mandate or encourage parent involvement. The most prominent example concerns special education legislation in the U.S. (PL 94–142) and in Canada (at least four provinces have such legislation). The problems of implementing special education legislation are enormous. Careful training and support for implementation are required. In few other programs is the need for parent cooperation and involvement so necessary. (See Stearns et al.'s 1980 study of local implementation issues in PL 94–142.) Hauser-Cram and O'Leary (1981) describe one attempt to implement PL 94–142 in Massachusetts. "Project partnership" provided funds to promote and train for parent/professional collaboration in the education of special-needs children. Three pilot sites involving 37 families were evaluated (there are now over 500 families participating). For each classroom, a paid parent leader is appointed who is trained in how to organize and conduct parent–teacher activities and in how the "system" works (e.g., various special education forms and procedures). Although the project is in its early stages, some interesting findings are emerging from the pilot study and a control group of families not involved. The findings indicate greater initiative, interest, and involvement in instructional issues on the part of "partnership parents." For example, the most frequent type of contact between parents and teachers in the partnership classrooms involved "discussions about methods of instructing a student" (35.7%); this type of contact was much less frequent in the control classrooms (10.2%). More dramatic was the finding that the most frequent occasion of contact in the partnership classes was the school visit (62.0%), whereas this was the least preferred occasion (9.1%) in the control classrooms (Hauser-Cram & O'Leary, 1981, p. 11).

---

3 Note the similarity to good implementation principles (chapter 5).

We do not have the space to specify the relationship between parent involvement and different types of learning outcomes at all levels of the elementary and secondary schools. There are some areas of fundamental controversy (e.g., sex education, busing for desegregation) where it may be that no amount of exchange will resolve differences. Moreover, parent–teacher involvement in instruction should also be examined more systematically for different areas of instructional objectives: for example, basic skills, problem-solving skills, independence. Most of the research relating to student achievement concerns basic skills at the elementary school level. An exception is the work of Epstein (1982), who is doing some very interesting research on patterns of student participation in family decision-making, in school decision-making, and in classroom decision-making and the effects on student self-reliance or independence over time. Epstein observes that regardless of the particular patterns of decision-making, her findings stress the importance of families and schools working together to produce decision-making capabilities. However, the complexities of how to do this can be appreciated when we consider the nature of objectives such as self-reliance, the ethnic and other cultural differences in families, and the student at age levels ranging from pre-teen to mid-adolescence. Nonetheless, the fact remains that several research studies have found that parent involvement in instruction is beneficial.

Those familiar with the theory of change being developed in this book may have formed at least one major impression from the above findings consistent with that theory: it is intuitively if not theoretically obvious that direct involvement in instruction in relation to their own child's education is one of the surest routes for parents to develop a sense of specific *meaning* vis-à-vis new programs designed to improve learning. Jobs as paid aides provide this opportunity for some parents. Experience as home tutors provides the opportunity for every parent at the elementary grade levels.

The future adds other possibilities for the role of parents in instruction through the rapid expansion and availability of home microcomputers. It may seem far off, but Toffler (1980) and Evans (1979) make a compelling case that microcomputers will, without great financial expense and in an easily usable format, pervade society in a way which will make the family more of an educational center complementary and supplementary to the school. Not the least form of the change will involve parents and children interacting and working together in educationally related activities.

## Non-instructional forms of parent involvement

As the following pages indicate, there is little evidence to suggest that other, non-instructional forms of parent involvement directly affect student learning in the school; however, there may be indirect effects, and there is some evidence that there are positive benefits for the adults who participate. Many studies on the impact of parent–school relations on student achievement have come up empty. The School–Community Relations Group at the University of Wisconsin–Madison conducted a series of case studies in five very different settings (rural, urban, elementary, secondary, varying on social class). In every case they found virtually no relationship between amount of parent participation on advisory councils and student achievement. (They did not examine parent involvement in instructional activities.) The main positive finding in the study concerned the relationship between school–community communication and perceived effectiveness of school–community relations (see Bowles, 1980).

Fantini in his review suggests that the research on governance forms of involvement clearly supports the generalization that for "parents as decision-makers, no direct evidence was found to confirm or reject the basic hypothesis about impacts on children, although there is evidence of benefits in participating adults" (Fantini, 1980, p. 10). Another study of parents' participation as decision-makers on advisory councils found that school principals dominated information and decisions. The title of the paper tells it all: "The Myth of Parent Involvement through Advisory Councils" (Paddock, 1979).[4]

In the same vein, legislation in Quebec mandates parent advisory councils for every school. Lucas et al. (1978–79) looked into what was happening in ten elementary and five secondary schools by doing a content analysis of committee minutes during the school year. These researchers found: (1) pedagogical issues were infrequently discussed; (2) whatever was discussed was mainly of an informational nature (as distinct from a recommendation role, which occurred less than 4% of the time); and (3) topics of discussion were mostly initiated by administrators or teachers (67.2% at the elementary level, and 78% at the secondary level) rather than by parents (27.6% at the elementary level, and 17.9% at the secondary level).

The SDC research contains the most comprehensive information on parent involvement in governance, since it covers four major programs. All four programs mandate district and/or school parent advisory committees. The survey findings indicate that nearly all districts and schools have set up advisory committees. Most are reported as serving in an advisory capacity; some are indicated as having joint decision-making responsibility with the district or school. For our purposes, however, the survey does not tell us much. We know very little about how the committees function. No information is presented on their impact.

The site studies are more informative with respect to committee effectiveness. The findings tend to confirm other studies on parent participation in governance: namely, that when advisory committees are mandated, they work in a very small proportion of cases. For example, of the 16 Title I sites, only three district advisory committees were found to be actively involved.[5] Of the other 13, one had no committee at all, seven had committees but no involvement, and five had "token involvement" (Melaragno et al., 1981, pp. 5–38). Similarly, for school-level advisory committees, Melaragno and his colleagues found that only three of 31 school committees played an active role in project governance. Of the others most played a token role; in fact, in 12 of the 31 schools the committees had never been formed, existed only on paper, or met so seldom that there was no opportunity for any involvement.

The site studies also provide information on factors associated with effective committees. The most active councils occurred (1) where federal or state legislation was precise and monitored regarding the specific forms of involve-

---

4 For a further litany of problems of implementing parent advisory councils relating to Title I programs, see Brown (1980).
5 Four of 16 ESAA committees, three of 13 Title VII and "less than a majority" of Follow Through parent committees were active.

ment; (2) where state departments were committed to parent involvement and actively pursued that goal through providing assistance, frequently visiting districts, etc.; and (3) where local districts specified parent roles, provided training for parents, and had active parent coordinators who facilitated the involvement of other parents.

As to outcomes, both personal benefits (e.g., personal growth, knowledge) and project benefits (e.g., better delivery of instruction) were reported by parents and district staff in the cases where councils were active. The main finding, however, remains: very few councils at either the district or school levels were implemented in a manner that resulted in more than token participation.

Nor do most parents seem to want to be involved in advisory committees or councils. A 1979 Canada-wide survey of over 2000 parents asked such a question. Overall, 63.4% of the respondents indicated that they would not like to serve as a member of a home–school advisory committee (Canadian Education Association, 1979).

On the other hand, part of the problem may be that many advisory councils and other forms of parent participation in decision-making do not have a clear focus and are not well implemented—that is, they do not address the needs of parents, are inefficient, are not productive, and the like. For example, Joyce (1978) in a study of councils in California presents convincing evidence that a large number of parent–school advisory councils can be very effective when they have a clear task and are carefully developed. Similarly, the Designs for Change (1981) organization in Chicago has demonstrated that parent groups can be very effective in influencing decisions and improving schools *provided* that they are assisted in developing three major areas of skills: (1) the capacity to gather accurate information about the system they are trying to change; (2) mastery of a variety of techniques for intervening skillfully; and (3) the capacity to ensure that their own group functions effectively as a group (see Moore et al., forthcoming). Also, involving parents in the school can result in support for obtaining additional resources and in dealing with problems in relations with the district office and other agencies outside the local community.

These significant exceptions, along with the apparent success in many of the Follow Through programs, suggest several guidelines (see Huguenin et al., 1979; Joyce, 1978; Lyons et al., 1982; Moore et al., forthcoming). Such guidelines are very much needed in light of the fact that many federal projects, some states (California, Florida), at least one province (Quebec), and many school boards across North America have mandated parent–school councils.

It is important to be clear about what is and is not being said in this chapter. First, the focus is on parent involvement in educational matters. Thus, I have not wandered into the rather large separate literature on adult education, community use of schools, and "community schools." Second, as I have indicated, to discover that there is no relationship between parent participation in governance and student achievement leaves a number of unanswered questions. Is the lack of relationship due to poorly implemented governance councils? That is, if they worked as intended, would there be a positive impact? (The Designs for Change work and Joyce's research indicate that this might be the case.) Does parent participation have positive impacts on other important outcomes (other than student achievement), such as parents' knowledge and support of the school, skill development for those parents on councils, a restraining influence in adopting possibly inappropriate changes, budgetary responsibility, and so on? Third, for reasons just stated, the findings do not lead to the conclusion that advisory and other forms of parent involvement in governance should be abandoned. The more accurate conclusion is that advisory councils by themselves probably do not make much of a difference on achievement. It is quite likely that *multiple* forms of involvement have a synergistic positive impact: involvement in instructional activities helps to establish a knowledge base for advisory recommendations; frequent contacts within the school provide knowledge and confidence for those who have always felt daunted just walking into a school; frequent involvement in the school gives parents an appreciation of the real-world problems of teachers, principals, and students and increases school accountability. In short, parent involvement has a number of important functions.

Be that as it may, if I had to single out the most significant conclusion from the research on parent involvement, it is that *most parents are concerned and interested in programs and changes relating to their own children*. The vast majority of parents find meaning at this level rather than in school or system-wide advisory councils. Given their interest, given its potential impact on student learning, and given the fact that this vast resource is largely untapped for educational purposes, it is a crying shame there are so many barriers to parent involvement. But then again, neither the barriers nor the potential has been properly recognized and worked on in most schools and communities.

## Barriers to parent involvement

Barriers to parent involvement can be divided into two broad categories—phenomenological and logistical. Phenomenological barriers relate to the lack of knowledge and understanding that administrators and parents have of each others' subjective worlds. Logistical or technical problems concern lack of time, opportunity, and know-how about what activities or forms of parent involvement would be most effective. The phenomenological obstacles are the greatest, because they are more fundamental (thus reinforcing the logistical barriers) and because they often go unrecognized. Stereotyping is easier and more efficient than empathizing.

### Phenomenological barriers

Phenomenology, of course, is at the heart of the theory of meaning espoused in this book. Given what has been said in previous chapters about the complexities and unknowns concerning changes in education, parents should be forgiven if they wonder what is going on in schools. The phenomenological barrier represented by the different worlds of the parent and the teacher makes it extremely difficult for questions of wonderment and concern to get expressed constructively or even at all. Lightfoot states the problem in two words in the title of an insightful book on family–school relationships in black communities: *Worlds Apart* (1978). In a recent paper she elaborates on some of the key points:

In order to fully capture family-school interactions, families need to be seen as educative environments .... In order to effectively attend to children in one setting, the adult sponsors would have to be aware of life in the other, see the child's experience as continuous, and seek an integration of educational realms. (1980, p. 2)

She goes on to say that most forms of contact between parents and teachers are either ritualistic (e.g., parent–teacher conferences) or specially requested on account of a particular incident or dissatisfaction. She contrasts this reality with other studies which show "overwhelmingly that blacks universally view education as the most promising means for attaining higher socio-economic status" for their children (p. 10). Incidentally, other studies in Canada and the U.S. have shown that students and parents of minority groups (Italians, Greeks, blacks) have higher educational aspirations than do their non-minority counterparts (Marjoribanks, 1979; Calliste, 1980).

Lightfoot brings together the argument in a compelling way:

Despite the passionate and often unrealistic dreams of black parents, teachers continue to view them as uncaring, unsympathetic and ignorant of the value of education for their children and unconcerned about their children's academic success in school. Often they perceive the parents' lack of involvement in ritualistic school events and parent conferences as apathy and disinterest and rarely interpret it as the inability to negotiate the bureaucratic maze of schools or as a response to a long history of exclusion and rejection at the school door .... Parents' and teachers' perceptions of each other as uncaring about children and as devaluing the education process lead to distance and distrust and the need to blame one another. Misconceptions, rarely articulated and confronted, always nurtured by hostile stereotypes, lead to increasing disregard for each other's place in the lives of black children. Rather than search for the origins of conflict and find effective strategies for real (rather than contrived) participation of parents and teachers in a collaborative task, schools develop more sophisticated methods of exclusion; parents draw farther and farther away from parental responsibilities in the schooling process, and children fail. (1978, pp. 166–67)

Lightfoot (1978) makes a number of other fundamental points, which are not well recognized or addressed and which she claims (with some supporting evidence) are essential for improving student learning (see also Carew & Lightfoot, 1979). First, she argues that parents and teachers are involved in complementary educational tasks. Second, she claims that teachers must understand the family learning environment of the child in order to help that child learn, and parents must understand the learning environment of the school. Third, she indicates that conflict, especially if the culture of the family is different from that of the teacher, is inevitable and necessary. The conflict can be destructive if it is ignored, but it can be productive if it is worked on openly. The different and similar concerns of parents and teachers can be most productively managed if addressed jointly. Fourth, it is difficult and does take time for teachers and parents to learn about each other's "subjective worlds." However, Lightfoot cites several examples where they have done this, with a major impact on teacher–parent relationships and student learning. Her descriptions of these "successes" are very congruent with the findings described early in this chapter: the more the teachers understand and use the home environment, and the more the parents get involved and comfortable in the school and classroom, the better the benefits. Fifth, we must be careful not to define the child's needs solely in the parents' and teachers' terms. Children (all the more as they get older) are part of the triad and have rights and views which must be taken into account. As Willard Waller (1932) warned some fifty years ago, it would be a sad day for childhood if teachers and parents ever succeeded in totally agreeing on what children should learn. (See also Coons & Sugarman, 1978, chs. 3–5, on "the best interest of the child").

Thus, there is a tension among the teacher, parent, and child perspectives which may be greater or less, depending on the circumstances. The issue is not how to make this tension disappear, but to recognize that these phenomenological differences are among the most powerful barriers to *and* resources for change. Compared to other factors the family learning environment, as sociologists have found time and time again, has the strongest effect on children's education.[6] Those programs described earlier which have directly involved parents have latched on to this very powerful force. In Lightfoot's (1978) analysis, the choice is between "boundaries and bridges," and she leaves no doubt that building bridges is the only way to get where we want to go.

Is the situation described by Lightfoot peculiar to inner-city black communities in the United States? Probably not. Sharp and Green conducted a case study of a progressive primary school in Britain. They asked parents about their knowledge of what their school was attempting to do.

Many parents admitted that they did not understand "these modern methods": "I don't really understand them myself but they know what they're doing"; "I can see it's not what I've been used to but I can't make head nor tail of it myself." ... In the absence of a relevant stock of knowledge at hand many of the parents, themselves, seem to recognize that they were at a disadvantage and not necessarily in a good position to play the role of a good parent. (Sharp & Green, 1975, pp. 202–203)

Speaking of parents' being at a disadvantage, Weatherley investigated the implementation of special education legislation in Massachusetts, in which he observed 40 "assessment meetings" involving parents and specialists:

The parents are at a great disadvantage in these meetings. They are outnumbered. They enter a meeting, frequently in a strange room, where they confront a number of people, many for the first time. They are usually outsiders joining an ongoing group; the core evaluation team has generally met together as a group during the previous assessments, and its members work together on a continuous basis ....

A psychologist explains the test results for a seventh grader. The mother and father are present. The father is a manual laborer: "We went over prior tests. Verbal, 109, high average; new learning, a component of the social situation, scale score, 1%; object assembly was perfect—fast, methodical, an incredible gestalt in sight and puzzle completion. Performance was 130, the top 3 percent of the population." (1979, pp. 51–52)

These individual cases raise the general question of how knowledgeable parents and community members are about new policies and programs introduced in their schools.[7] Such knowledge is necessary politically and symbolically for their support of new programs; but more basically, knowledgeable parents and community may be essential *educationally* for getting new programs to work.

---

6 See Marjoribanks (1979) for an excellent summary of this literature and for how family learning environments differ.

7 It should be obvious that if many school people who have to implement changes are unsure about what a particular change is, they are hardly in a position to help parents understand it.

## Logistical barriers

If we take seriously the everyday work situations of teachers (chapter 7), principals (chapter 8), students (chapter 9), and district administrators (chapter 10), we can readily conclude that there are many practical barriers to involving parents. Teachers and administrators receive little or no pre-service training in how to work or cope with parents. Most new program changes do not contain ideas about how to involve parents (unless the program specifically includes a parent involvement component) or how to protect the program from inappropriate interference by small minorities of parents. Students as they get older do not want parents to interfere. And, above all, the daily grind and pressures to survive crowd out good intentions.

A recent statewide study in Maryland of teacher practices regarding "parental involvement at home in instructional matters" provides a good overview of current forms of involvement and associated practical difficulties (Becker, 1981). Some 3700 elementary school teachers and 600 principals responded to the survey. Becker found that virtually all teachers send notices home, regularly interact with parents on parent nights, and so on. However, "only 7% initiate as many as three group meetings or workshops for parents" (p. 7). He also found that teachers who conduct workshops for parents are the ones who most actively emphasize the teaching role of parents at home. At the practical level, Becker discovered that 75% of the teachers believed that parent involvement at home was necessary for achieving educational goals for students, but "many teachers do not know how to initiate and accomplish their programs of parent involvement that would help them most" (p. 8).

Becker asked about the use of 14 specific techniques (e.g., "ask parents to read to their child regularly or listen to the child read aloud"). He found that despite a general endorsement by teachers of parent involvement at home, "very few appear to devote any systematic effort to making sure that parental involvement at home accomplishes particular learning goals in a particular way" (p. 22). Only 9% of the sample "required" parental cooperation; the rest made various "suggestions." Those teachers who were more active users of parent-involvement-at-home techniques were also more likely to involve parents in the classroom as volunteers, aides, or observers. Apparently the other teachers, despite a general endorsement of parent involvement, did not know how to go about it, perceived parents as not interested in becoming involved, or did not take the time to develop a program of participation. Or perhaps many teachers felt that parents could not make a worthwhile contribution to their child's education.

There is no need to go into details of other research studies except to note that an ironic and frustrating picture emerges. On the one hand, most teachers will say they want more contact with parents, but seem to feel that many parents are unavailable or uninterested. On the other hand, parents say that they want to find out more about the curriculum, what their children are supposed to learn, and what they can do at home to help. As most schools go, these interests get expressed (if at all) in negative, episodic ways—"parents interfere" or "teachers blame the parents for not being interested, or for providing a poor home environment" (e.g., Lightfoot, 1978). Yet as the evidence shows, once parents and teachers do interact on some regular basis with a particular program focus, mutual reservations and fears become transformed with positive results.

We cannot lump together all parents and all teachers. There are differences. Some parents do become actively involved; some do not show the slightest interest in their children's school work. Some teachers and some whole schools have developed effective parent–school programs. Others seem determined to keep parents at a distance. However, we can make two generalizations: (1) only a minority of parents and communities have been brought into the picture concerning the purposes and methods (in short, the meaning) of new program changes; (2) many more teachers and many more parents than is currently the case would like more contact about these matters.

Not each and every program change requires parent involvement to become successful. But if we ask the question "Would this change be better implemented, with more positive results, if parents understood it, and if particular activities were designed for parent and student use at home?", we get a sense of the potential power of more explicit school–home involvement in educational reform. On the other hand, school people may respond that they do not want to involve parents in reform, because parents might reject the changes or want to modify them. This raises important political, philosophical, and ethical questions about who has the right to decide on educational reform. The short answer is that it has to be continually negotiated where there are differences of views.

Aside from these issues, the main theme in this chapter is that most educational changes (at least at the elementary school level) would benefit enormously from parents' understanding and participation, and indeed will probably fail to become implemented if parents are ignored or bypassed. If parents are not consulted about a particular change being considered on the grounds that they might oppose it, its proponents have failed to understand that getting a change "adopted" without parents' knowledge only delays problems. If parents continue to be disregarded during attempted implementation, it is only a matter of time before the change is attacked or withers away from lack of substantial impact. Stated another way, if there are differences, it is better to confront and negotiate them during the early stages rather than ignore them in the hope that they will disappear.

# Guidelines for coping

This is not a book on how to fight city hall. Other people have written on citizens' rights and how to use power-based strategies (e.g., Huguenin et al., 1979; Moore et al., forthcoming). Parents also need skills and opportunities for participating at home and/or at the school in implementing educational practices. Guidelines are thus needed for school people about parents as well as for parents about schools. In the guidelines that follow, the limitations of the programs reviewed in this chapter should be noted: most concern elementary schools; most concern impact on basic skills; the parent/teacher/student triad has not been examined in most programs; and the relative roles of mothers and fathers have not been researched.

## Advice to school people

In Part I of the book the process of educational change was presented as consisting of three phases: adoption, implementation, and institutionalization. Advice about parents' roles should be considered according to these phases. It is also necessary to take into account at least two separate levels: the school district and the local school (and classroom). Starting with the district level and moving to the school and classroom level, the following guidelines can be suggested to school people. (See also Lyons et al., 1982: *Involving Parents: A Handbook for Participation in Schools.*)

## District level

1 Concerning the district-wide *adoptions* of new programs or policies, it is not possible (or even an option, if it involves a legislated change) to consult with parents throughout the district. The senior district administrator will have to work with the school board to ensure that the board endorses and has some general understanding of the change, and of the requirements of implementation (see Fullan & Park, 1981). The administrator should have a good understanding of the objectives and needs in the district, so that "needed" reforms are adopted.

2 In considering potential innovations, the district administrator should examine them to see if they have a parent involvement component. Many innovations, as we have seen, do contain materials, activities, and requirements for involving parents. All other things being equal, if there is a choice of programs, select the program which has a well-worked-out parent involvement component.

   If there is no such component, and if the innovation is desired or necessary for other reasons, develop a specific plan as to how parents can be informed and involved at the level of implementation. The precise details would not necessarily be worked out at the district level, but the plans for how schools could work with parents could be designed in consultation with schools.

3 As the innovation moves from adoption through implementation and possible institutionalization, keep the board informed and monitor the reception it is getting at the school level (Fullan & Park, 1981). The better the adoption and implementation processes have been managed, the more clear and more effective will be any decisions about continuing the change.

## School and classroom level

4 It is at the school level that most specific care must be taken. It may be that the school is the unit to decide whether or not to adopt a particular innovation. In this case, parent–school councils, or other ways of testing whether the innovation is right for the community, can be used.

5 Whether or not the school is the decision-making unit, those innovations which have been adopted require an explicit *implementation plan* vis-à-vis parents. At the school level the principal, staff, and parents can decide on the approach. There are a number of school-level activities which could be carried out, including communication with parents about what the change is and how it will be used. In programs which require and provide resources for parent participation (as many do), the selection and training of parents is crucial, as is the development of a clear program focus for exactly how parents should be involved (see Joyce et al., 1978, and Lyons et al., 1982, for additional guidelines).

6 At the classroom level, if the school as a collectivity has worked out an approach, teachers' work with parents can be facilitated. With or without a collective consideration, individual classroom teachers (or small groups) can do more than any other single group. Parent involvement is most productive when the objectives are clear and when parent activities are clearly known (see the six guidelines for effective parent participation in innovation formulated by Bridges, 1976). I do not assume that parent involvement can be easily accomplished. It is complicated by the fact that parents are not a homogeneous lot. Lightfoot (1978), Marjoribanks (1979), and

Bridges (1976), among others, have shown that ethnic and class differences are very significant and difficult to understand especially in those cases where the teacher has a background dissimilar to that of the students and families. (House, 1978, ch. 7, has some suggestions for how teachers can help break down stereotypes and communicate more effectively with parents.)

Involving parents in change is also complicated because the teacher may have to work out the details of implementation as he or she goes along. It may turn out that some form of "mutual adaptation" occurs as teachers with parent involvement or feedback refine or change the innovation in practice.

In introducing a new program to parents, some additional guidelines can be noted. Start small. Hold a meeting with parents. Explain the objectives and methods being used. Establish a few small exercises taking 5 or 10 minutes that parents could do at home with students.[8] Hold a workshop for parents. Link up with one or two other teachers. Use parents to involve or help other parents. Involve parents in the classroom where there is interest. Through interaction, attempt to understand the concerns of parents and the family learning environment. Involve students (the relative involvement of students and parents will vary by grade level). Discuss how performance and progress is to be measured. Do not expect 100% success, but do expect real improvement. In brief, have an explicit, even if small-scale, plan to involve parents. All of this will be facilitated if the school has an approach to and experience with involving parents. Starting small and building incrementally can lead to multiple forms of community involvement which reinforce each other.

Note that the underlying consequence of these sets of activities is the development of *knowledge* on the part of parents, teachers, and students about the purpose of a particular change, and of *skill* in implementing it. It is, in other words, the development of the meaning of change at the level of individuals with some opportunity to achieve shared meanings.

## Advice to parents

*General* advice to parents about what they should know about schools is only marginally helpful. In fact, as outsiders, parents are at a very great disadvantage if the school wants to keep them at a distance, as most do.

The Designs for Change handbook *Child Advocacy and the Schools* (Moore et al., forthcoming) would be a good place to start for parent and citizen groups interested in bringing about improvements in their local schools. The Designs for Change organization attempts to support parent groups through advice, training, and other forms of technical assistance, helping them define their concerns, gather accurate information to document the problems, and carry out a variety of intervention activities designed to get action to make improvements.[9] Some additional guidelines can be suggested:

1  If you have a choice of schools, check out the history and attitude of each school toward parent and community involvement.[10] (More educated parents are likely to check out the school than are less educated parents—see Wimpelberg, 1981.)

---

8 All of this will be easier if the innovation has a parent involvement component with suggestions, materials, training and other activities.
9 The intervention activities range from representing individual families with school-related problems, to training groups of parents, to strategies for getting media coverage, to making public presentations, to negotiating issues with officials, to filing litigation, etc.
10 Coons and Sugarman (1978) make a strong argument for the need for families to control educational choices.

2  Be lucky enough to be in a community where the principal and teachers are doing something to involve parents in instructional matters.
3  Wherever you are, do not assume that teachers do not want you. Teachers have their own beleaguered world. They may be overwhelmed. They may be faced with an innovation adopted by the board or another level of government about which they are unsure, and consequently are reluctant to show their confusion to parents.
4  Become familiar with some of the curriculum your child is using (through workbooks, discussions).
5  Ask the teacher if there is anything you can do at home to help the child. The receptive teacher may be willing to develop a small workshop for parents.
6  If you do not instantly understand the curriculum and other changes being used in the school, you are not alone. It takes time and interaction to develop some understanding.
7  For most educational innovations, parents can learn to do some activities with their child which can be learned in a relatively short time. Moreover, you know things about the family environment and about your child that the teacher doesn't know (and the teacher probably knows things about your child that you don't know). The most powerful combination for learning is the family and school doing complementary things.
8  If you are in a desperate situation of apparent prejudice, lack of caring, and no interest on the part of the school, fight for your rights alone or with other parents. If you are really up against a stone wall, these guidelines will only be minimally helpful. Put another way, read other books on the rights of citizens, power-based strategies, and so on (see Moore et al., forthcoming). Even if the school is uncaring, you can do a number of home-based activities which can be very useful.

Parent involvement is not the only answer. Nor is it free from danger. Some situations of involvement may turn out to have harmful consequences if they result in endless conflict, lowered morale, and the like. As with other educational reforms the implementation of involvement programs should be carefully carried out and monitored as to problems and impact. Moreover, I do not delude myself that the ideas in this and other chapters can be used to accomplish widespread effective reform. Social change does not happen that way, because (1) some educational problems are endemic and may not be solvable (see especially Miles, 1981, on the properties of school systems), and (2) the education system reflects society, and consequently reforms from within may not make much of a difference to the life chances of students once they leave schools (Bowles & Gintis, 1976; Jencks et al., 1972, 1979). The guidelines may seem naive and foolish in some situations in light of societal dominance, daily prejudices, poverty, and simply just surviving physically and psychologically.

Nonetheless, the individual reader has to start somewhere. It may not be noticeable, but there are many, many more effective parent involvement programs in operation than was the case a decade ago. There has been a social movement beyond the rhetoric of general endorsement or rejection of community involvement, toward the development and use of specific programs involving parents in the classroom or at home in instructional activities. These forms of involvement have become purposeful and meaningful at the individual level. And, as we have seen in this chapter, they are making a difference for students, teachers, and parents. We know better what works and why it works. It is not easy to set up effective parent–school activities, but it can be done. Some of the phenomenological barriers have been overcome through interaction. Some of the logistical problems have been addressed through the development of more and better curriculum activities specifically designed to include parents. It is encouraging to note that most of the parent involvement programs are directed at the more educationally disadvantaged parents, where the need is greatest and where the interest may be much greater than most people think (Lightfoot, 1978).

Many parents and teachers are overloaded with their own work-related and personal concerns. They also may feel discomfort in each other's presence due to lack of mutual familiarity and to the absence of a mechanism for solving the problems which do arise. In examining the research presented in this chapter, it is encouraging to observe that parent participation was effective when someone or some group (parents, teachers, district staff, program developers) had the responsibility for organizing and conducting specific activities which brought parents and school people together for a particular purpose. Success did not happen by accident.

In the meantime, the simple conclusion of this chapter is twofold. First, we know very little about what parents think of specific innovations because they are rarely asked; if asked, they might not be able to say much because they do not have enough involvement in educational change activities to obtain sufficient information to know what is going on. Second, much educational reform requires the conjoint efforts of families and schools. Parents and teachers should recognize the critical complementary importance of each other in the educational life of the student. Otherwise, we are placing limitations on the prospects for change which may be impossible to overcome.

# Part III

# Educational Change at the Regional and National Levels

 Chapter 13

# Governments

> ... his obsession with rationalism had isolated him. For four years [he] talked about the big ideas he wanted to talk about. He never once listened to what the public was trying to say to him, about its problems, its fears, its dreams. Above all ... he ignored rationalism's essential flaw. To be systematic is sensible. To be systematic without common sense, without humour, is to treat systems as more important than people.
>
> — Richard Gwynn (on Prime Minister Trudeau), in The Northern Magus (1980), p. 107

Now we get to the biggest culprit of them all—the government. But if we are true to the phenomenological basis of our analysis, we will realize that what government policy-makers and administrators do is perfectly understandable—to themselves. If it is difficult to manage change in one classroom, one school, one school district, imagine the scale of the problems faced by one state or province or country in which numerous agencies and levels and tens or hundreds of thousands of people are involved. It is infinitely more difficult for that government if its personnel do not venture out to attempt to understand the culture and the problems of local school people.

Still, governments seem to be astonishingly obtuse about one implementation fact: the way in which they go about change *within* their own organizations is a fundamental part of the implementation process (what Berman, 1978, calls the macro implementation problem). Stated another way, if governments are poor at launching new programs or at bringing about changes within their own ranks, how can they possibly criticize schools for not changing? I suspect it is this more than anything else that turns teachers, administrators, and others off in dealing with government personnel.

However, to continue our pursuit of the meaning of change, we should attempt to understand the role of governments at least partly from their perspective. They do have a responsibility to protect minorities and to be concerned about the quality and equity of education at the local level. Yet it is incredibly difficult to induce and support or monitor change at a distance. Moreover, the vast majority of government personnel, like the rest of us, are just cogs in the machinery. The daily demands and pressures from superiors and peers in the world of politics are enormous. Programs and politicians are frequently ephemeral. Before one policy has been completely formulated, the next one demands attention. Policy-making is both more compelling and more exciting than policy implementation. There are, overall, many complaints and few satisfactions.

In order to examine the role of governments in educational change, this chapter is divided into four main sections. The first section considers the U.S. federal government; the next section, the role of state departments in the U.S.; the third section, the role of the federal and especially provincial departments of education in Canada; and the final section, a summary of the implications of the chapter in the form of "guidelines for governments." In each of the first three sections, I attempt to provide a brief picture of what governments currently do in relation to educational change, and with what impact.

# The United States federal government

Again reflecting the extremely short history of implementation concerns, the U.S. federal government has only been involved heavily in the business of educational change since the Elementary and Secondary School Act of 1965 and its various Titles.[1] The intention of this Act and other programs soon to be identified is essentially to improve the quality and equality of education in the country. My interest from the point of view of the initiation (adoption) and implementation of change is in two areas: *What* programs and activities have they promoted? What are the main issues, and what is the extent of *impact* of the programs?

## The programs

It will not be possible to identify and report on every federally sponsored educational program, but most of the major ones can be located.[2] The vast majority of federal programs are administered through state departments of education; federal requirements are specified and are supposed to be followed, and compliance is to be evaluated and reported. Total federal monies to local school districts (including all monies administered through state departments) make up on the average only 8 to 9% of district budgets (in 1977/78 it was 8.1% or $6.5 billion—NCES, 1978), but over 40% of state education agency budgets are based on federal funds. At the district level federal money frequently represents

---

1 There was some ad hoc prior involvement, most notably in the 1954 *Brown* v. *Board of Education* segregation decision and its civil rights aftermaths. Some large-scale curriculum development projects were also launched with major federal backing with the passage of the National Defense Education Act in 1958 following Sputnik I, when national concern with deficiencies in the country's scientific capabilities was intensified (see Atkin & House, 1981).

2 Beyond direct education programs there are numerous significant federal activities in other government departments which relate to education indirectly, and which I do not include (e.g., early childhood programs, youth development grants, community development projects, employment programs, etc., etc.). See Williams (1976, 1981) for discussion of implementation issues in a variety of social program areas.

the only substantial source of funds directed explicitly at *program change*. Moreover, some states and some districts get much more depending on eligibility criteria.

The federal role in education is intrinsically complicated from a financial and program point of view, all the more complex because it is currently in flux. (See Institute for Research on Educational Finance and Governance, 1981.) President Reagan announced his intention to disestablish the new cabinet-level Department of Education and reduce it to foundation or bureau-level status. Policy decisions have been made for budget year 1981/82 to reduce and integrate federal expenditure and involvement at the state and local levels. There has already been mounting pressure over the years to consolidate federal funds to states into "block grants" in order to decentralize control. The Reagan philosophy of decentralization of control to states and local authorities and reduction in federal expenditures is resulting in a number of decisions, toward elimination of some programs and consolidation and cutbacks in others. Two major changes are taking place: the move from "categorical" funding to states to "block grant" funding, and reduction in educational expenditures. Generally, categorical grants earmark funds to very specific program objectives, with extensive and detailed application, delivery, and accountability procedures around specific programs for particular populations; block grants allocate money to broad functional areas, with less paperwork and somewhat more general compliance requirements to show that the money was spent for those populations (see Department of Education Weekly, 17 August 1981). Obviously, more flexibility, less hassle, and reduced administrative machinery are the result for both states and federal levels, but so is less specific accountability. While gaining flexibility, states (and education) will receive less money because of overall reduced spending.

On 31 July 1981 the U.S. Congress passed the Education Consolidation and Improvement Act to be effective for school year 1982/83, citing the Act as a long-overdue "dramatic shift in the balance of power" from federal to state levels (Department of Education Weekly, 10 August 1981). Some 33 programs were consolidated, with certain major programs (soon to be discussed) retaining their categorical status.[3] Table 1 (adapted from Department of Education Weekly, 10 August 1981) provides a simplified overview of the new policy.

In the next two subsections I will describe briefly many of the major programs, including some of those to be subsumed in the Title II block grant. Full descriptions of programs will not be possible, but some of the main aspects will be noted.

The programs relating to school change are most easily divided into those under the jurisdiction of the Office of Education (OE)—that is, most of the programs—and those operating out of the National Institute of Education (NIE). OE is responsible for overseeing policy and program development and implementation. NIE is essentially a research, development, and evaluation agency which identifies research priorities and funds individuals and groups in

---

3 Categorical status has two advantages for program proponents: the integrity of program objectives can be retained instead of being swallowed into general grants, and money for the program can be protected (albeit reduced in size in this case).

Table 1    **Education Authorization Levels for**
              **Selected Major Programs,**
              **Funding Year 1982/83**

| Program | Authorization Amount (in millions of dollars) |
|---|---|
| *Elementary and Secondary Education* | |
| Title II (33 programs)* | 589.37 |
| Title I | 3480.00 |
| Bilingual Education | 139.97 |
| Civil Rights Act Title IV | 37.10 |
| Women's Educational Equity | 6.00 |
| Follow Through | 44.30 (to be reduced to 14.8 by 1984 and then to block grant) |
| Impact Aid | 475.00 |
| Refugee Education | 5.00 |
| Indian Education | 81.70 |
| *Special Programs* | |
| Education for the Handicapped | 1039.85 |
| Vocational Education | 735.00 |
| *Research and Development* | |
| National Institute of Education | 55.61 |

*Title II funded by block grant; all others categorical.

the country to carry out the work. Much of NIE's research work is on OE programs, although OE also sponsors evaluation for its own programs.

### Office of Education[4]

Table 2 contains the list and starting dates for selected federal programs of the Office of Education directed at school reform. These nine programs will be described in the following pages. While they represent the major OE school-related projects, the list is not exhaustive.

Title I is by far the largest program in terms of money (over $3 billion annually) and numbers of students (over 5 million) and educational personnel reached (Kirst & Jung, 1980). The purpose of Title I is to provide financial assistance to districts for elementary schools with "concentrations of children from low-income families" (Public Law 89–10 Title I, Sec. 101). It is a categorical program in which monies are earmarked for entitlement to certain categories of students. Funds are administered through state departments to local districts on the basis of program proposals to meet the needs of educationally

---

4 I present only an overview of OE programs. It is beyond the scope of this chapter to analyze the intricacies, overlaps, and complications within and across these programs. While I do raise many of these issues, for precise detail and understanding the reader should consult the official Acts and documented studies. For the best and most comprehensive up-to-date history, description, and analysis which includes virtually all of the programs I discuss here, see Crandall et al.'s report in the DESSI study of dissemination programs within OE. I also include in the Appendix additional specific research references for each program.

Table 2    Major Office of Education Programs
for School Change

| Program | Year of Inception |
| --- | --- |
| Title I | 1965 |
| Title III* (became IVC) | 1965 (1974) |
| Emergency School Aid Act* (ESAA) | 1972 |
| Title VII | 1967 |
| Vocational Education Act | 1968 |
| Right to Read* (became Basic Skills) | 1969 (1978) |
| Bureau of Education Handicapped | 1967 |
| Follow Through* | 1967 |
| JDRP (and NDN) | 1972 (1974) |

*Programs to be incorporated into the block grant (i.e., Title II in table 1).

disadvantaged students in the districts. Specific proposals vary in emphasis, but tend to concentrate on basic skills among elementary school children. There is an elaborate set of criteria, specifications, and requirements for reporting and evaluating programs, including data on progress in upgrading student achievement. As with other programs, noncompliance in the use of funds "theoretically" can lead to withdrawal of assistance (more about compliance later). Almost 90% of the school districts in the U.S. receive at least some Title I funds, with some districts and some schools receiving very substantial amounts. In California, for example, the 33 largest school districts receive more than 80% of the state's Title I funds (Kirst & Jung, 1980, p. 26). These funds provide for the salaries of district project staff and so-called Title I teachers in eligible schools, as well as for a variety of other resources. States receive 2% of the $3 billion to administer the program, which they use to hire staff and to obtain other resources. In effect most staff become permanent, because Title I funds are continuous (with some variation in total amounts) year after year.

Districts and states are not left on their own to develop programs. There are 10 regional Title I "Technical Assistance Centers," which are funded to provide assistance to districts and states in the development, implementation, monitoring, and evaluation of programs. The program implementation packages (PIPS), for example, represent one set of resources (Campeau et al., 1979). Some states have developed considerable resources for assisting local districts. Title I programs are eligible for the National Diffusion Network (see below), which itself becomes a source of Title I programs and technical assistance for interested districts and states. In short, Title I is a major source of federally sponsored educational reform representing close to 40% of the federal funds which end up at the local district level.[5]

5 That is, of the district expenditures of 8.1% or $6.5 billion which derive from federal sources, close to $3 billion comes from Title I (NCES, 1978). The federal government, of course, funds a great many other agencies (e.g., state departments of education), program developments, and dissemination and research activities, not to mention their own staffing and agencies.

Title III, designed initially to support innovative local development, has now been superseded by Title IVC.[6] The program is administered by the states, which use the money in different ways. About 68% of the money is used to fund local "development" projects (usually in relation to program priority areas identified by the state), 23% to support supplementary centers (intermediate units in the state which serve nearby districts), 14% to support adoption of exemplary projects, 12% to dissemination of exemplary projects, and 10% in mini-grants to individual teachers or schools. But states vary greatly in how they administer the program. In some states the funds are distributed in small amounts to nearly all districts; in others the total funds are allocated to "exemplary" proposals among a small number of districts (see McDonnell & McLaughlin, 1980, and the next section in this chapter on the role of the states).

The Emergency School Aid Act (ESAA), passed in 1972, arose out of Title VI, the Civil Rights Act. It is intended to provide "financial assistance to meet the special needs incident to the elimination of minority group segregation and to encourage the voluntary elimination, reduction or prevention of minority group isolation" in schools (cited in Keesling, 1980). It is a non-categorical program in which local districts voluntarily submit proposals (although many proposals arise out of court-ordered desegregation). Some 560 districts (fewer than 5% in the country) received grants in 1979 (ESAA Program Office, cited in Keesling, 1980, p. 46). In Keesling's representative sample the average grant to districts was $460,800 with individual grants to any one district ranging from $23,900 to $9,426,000 (p. 47). The ESAA program also will be incorporated into the block grant for 1982/83.

Title VII—Bilingual Education Act provides financial assistance to local districts to develop programs "to demonstrate effective ways of providing for children of limited English proficiency, instruction designed to enable them, while using their native language, to achieve competence in the English language" (cited in Keesling, 1980, p. 63). The largest number of students who participate are Hispanic, although some seventy languages are included. About the same number of districts participate in Title VII as in ESAA (i.e., about five hundred). The average grants, however, were approximately half the size of ESAA grants, according to Keesling's survey (p. 66).

The Vocational Education Act, 1968, Part D, Exemplary Projects supports the development of projects designed to enhance career readiness and awareness. At present (1981) it has a budget of $735 million, which provides funds for projects being used in districts and schools.

The Right-to-Read program began in 1969 to support the development and use of projects designed to upgrade reading skills of disadvantaged students. In

---

6 A new consolidated Title IV enacted in 1974 consists of two main parts: IVB (formerly Title II and parts of III), which provides funds for school library resources, textbooks, etc., for testing and guidance, and for strengthening instruction in academic subjects; and IVC (formerly parts of Title III and V), related to innovative projects, to strengthening leadership resources at state and local levels, and to projects on dropout prevention and health and nutrition for low-income families. My interest is in Title IVC. For an excellent study of Title IV see McDonnell and McLaughlin (1980). As noted, for 1982/83 it will become incorporated into the block grant, thereby disappearing as a specific federal project (although individual states will no doubt retain it at their own discretion).

1978 it was redefined somewhat more broadly and labeled "basic skills." Its budget for 1980 was $35 million. It too will be consolidated into the block grant.

Follow Through (FT) began in 1967 with the goal of facilitating the development and dissemination/implementation of model programs for making schooling more effective for low-income children from kindergarten through grade 3. While targeted at a portion of the same population (K–3 grades) as Title I, FT is not a "service" program like Title I, but an experimental/development program. The program provides funds for the dissemination of a variety of educational models ranging from behavioral modification approaches to open education—hence the reference to Follow Through as a "planned variation experiment." Models are developed by so-called "model sponsors" (usually in educational laboratories, R&D centers, and universities). Models are evaluated for inclusion in the program, and once included may be selected by local school districts, with the federal government providing the funds for the model sponsor to work with the district in implementing the program. As an experimental program it received a good deal of money in the early stages. At its peak in 1973 it included 22 programs that were being used in 173 districts (Hodges et al., 1980). Rhine (1981) estimates that some $1 billion has been spent by the federal government on FT since its inception in 1967. FT is currently down to 19 active model sponsors. Like other programs, it is also eligible for National Diffusion Network funds (see below). Some 21 FT programs (some models have more than one program, serving different grade levels, etc.) have been "validated" for inclusion in NDN. The NDN affiliation has resulted in the provision of funds to establish 21 FT Resource Centers (one for each validated project). These centers have staff and facilities for responding to requests, disseminating materials and information, and offering demonstrations and other training at the center or on site. FT will be phased into the block grant by 1985, with major cuts over the next three years.

The Bureau of Education Handicapped has funded development, demonstration, and research projects since 1967. The emphasis on programs for the handicapped has intensified considerably since the passage of federal law PL 94–142 in 1975 on the education rights of exceptional children (although many of the individual states had many policies and programs already under way). I mention only the more recent (1977) Market Linkage project of BEH, because it is aimed at the development and implementation of new instructional materials for special education teachers to use with handicapped children and for regular classroom teachers to use within their own classrooms (see Thompson, 1981). BEH subcontracts an intermediary agency (LINC Services Inc.) to facilitate the publication and dissemination of "products" designed to aid schools in addressing the needs of the handicapped. The impact on schools of the marketing strategy is as yet unknown, but Crandall et al. will be reporting shortly their findings in the DESSI research on the effectiveness of the Market Linkage project.

The final federal program effort to be discussed is the National Diffusion Network (NDN) and its screening device, the Joint Dissemination Review Panel (JDRP). A dissemination review panel (DRP) established in 1972 consisted of 11 members of the OE; in 1975 it became the Joint DRP when 11 members from NIE were added. The 22-member panel is appointed on the basis of "their experience in education and their ability to analyze evaluation evidence on the effectiveness of educational products and practices" (Tallmadge, 1977, p. 1). Decisions about the effectiveness of programs are based on the quality of evidence submitted by program developers concerning the nature of materials, the magnitude of effects of the program, and the likelihood that the program can be implemented in new sites (including the commitment and capacity of the developer to assist in implementation).

Once validated by JDRP as "exemplary," the programs become part of NDN—a nationwide system for disseminating, and for assisting local districts in selecting and using, programs that meet their needs. NDN operates through so-called State Facilitators (SF) and Developers/Demonstrators (D/D). OE provides the funds for at least one full-time SF in each state, whose job is to disseminate information, to help people in school districts select desired programs, to arrange for D/Ds (i.e., the developers of the program) to work with the district staff in implementation, and to monitor and collect evaluative information on the use and impact of programs. NDN finances the D/Ds' provision of training, materials, assistance, and monitoring to those who adopt the programs, but it does not pay for any release time for staff in the adopting district.

The programs eligible for submission originally were Title III projects (innovative projects developed by local districts with federal funds from Title III, which has since evolved to Title IVC). Eligibility for inclusion has been increasingly broadened to incorporate projects developed from any federal source (and recently projects developed without the use of federal funds). Thus, all of the programs listed in this section are eligible to have projects approved and funded by NDN. Over the past five years Title I has had more than 50 projects validated which have been funded from its program, Follow Through has some 22 projects, BEH approximately 24, and Title IVC 24 (Neill, 1981). A complete listing of validated programs is compiled annually in a publication titled *Educational Programs That Work* (Far West Lab, 1980). In 1980/81 the total list included 237 projects which were in operation (NDN Report, 1981). Of the 237, 59% or 139 were receiving dissemination funds, while the others were operating locally without these funds. Of the 139 projects, 32% were in the areas of basic skills and 20% in early childhood/parent readiness. The remaining 48% were distributed over ten program areas including special education, bilingual education, in-service education, alternative schools, and so on.

According to the official report, 6126 schools adopted 103 projects in 1978/79; in 1979/80 the figure was close to 10,000 (Neill, 1981).[7] Estimates are that in 1978/79 more than 20,000 teachers and other educators received in-service training and some half-million students were potentially affected (NDN Report, 1981). In 1980/81, it is said, 2.7 million students were involved in NDN-adopted projects (Neill, 1981).

In summary, there are many different federal agencies and sub-agencies involved in school change; most of the programs are directed at low-income, minority, and other disadvantaged groups at the elementary school level; and the programs frequently overlap, with states and local districts piecing together combinations of funds from different programs related to similar populations of students.[8] Given the number of agencies, levels, and year-by-year variations in

---

7 Note that these are "adoption" figures, not implementation.
8 For example, 98% of the districts in which FT projects are operating also receive Title I project funds. The question of overlap and other implications are discussed in the section below, "Issues and impact," after the NIE program is outlined.

fiscal appropriations, figuring out what to ask for, what to do with it once you get it, and how to account for it must be an educator's nightmare. "Meaning, anyone?"

## National Institute of Education

NIE has had a rocky political history since its inception in 1972 (see Sproull et al., 1978). Questions about its mandate, frequent turnover in leadership, reorganizations, continuous doubts about its budget, and many other problems have plagued its short career. After hopes of an initial budget of $150 million, the annual budget never rose to more than half that amount. NIE's political and financial situation is even more shaky today. Its budget for the 1980/81 fiscal year was $75 million. For 1981/82 that has been reduced substantially, to $55 million. NIE has yet another new director since late 1981, with the corresponding ramifications in personnel and program change in its three major divisions: Teaching and Learning, Educational Policy and Organization, and Dissemination and the Improvement of Practice. Continual changes from above in the Department of Education will allow it to uphold its claim to instability as a way of life for the foreseeable future.

Despite these difficulties, NIE has developed a program of research and dissemination in each of the three divisions. To begin with, it inherited a number of projects from the Office of Education, most notably those pertaining to dissemination. The system of regional R&D Laboratories and Centers (17 across the country) was also partially passed on to NIE in the form of mandates to allocate certain proportions of their funds to Lab and Center programs. I will not attempt to summarize all the research activities of NIE. Specific projects and programmatic themes in each of the three divisions have produced significant research knowledge relevant to several of the chapters in this book—instructional practices (especially the time-on-task research), organizational leadership and change, role of the principal, parent involvement, staff development, characteristics of effective change programs, and so on.

However, the area of research most central to change on a large scale concerns the activities of the Dissemination and Improvement of Practice division.[9] Six major NIE dissemination-related projects will be taken up.

ERIC (Educational Resources Information Center): *1965–*

SDGP (State Dissemination Grants Program): *1975–*

RDX (R&D Exchange): *1976–*

RDU (R&D Utilization): *1976–1979*

ES (Experimental Schools): *1972–1979*

DTA (Documentation and Technical Assistance):[10] *1974–1977*

---

9 Dissemination refers to the deliberate spread of new ideas and programs. The intention of most dissemination efforts is to bring new programs to the awareness of potential adopters. Dissemination programs vary in how far they go towards supporting actual implementation. The main goal of some dissemination projects is simply to make available information and to provide access to programs, while other projects explicitly attempt to assist in implementation of programs which are adopted. (For more complete descriptions of NIE dissemination projects see Raizen, 1979, and Thompson, 1981.)

10 The DTA program is the only one not in the Dissemination division; it arose out of the concerns of the "school capacity for problem-solving" subgroup in the Educational Policy and Organization division to provide an alternative to the product-development/dissemination orientation of traditional dissemination approaches.

In the following pages the six programs will be described briefly. As with other programs mentioned in this chapter, the main research studies on each one are listed in the Appendix along with a short statement on the program.

*Educational Resources Information Center*: ERIC is an information-based system in which published and unpublished literature on all aspects of education is actively sought, acquired, indexed, abstracted, and made available in microfiche as well as hard copy. A national office as well as regional clearinghouses with thematic responsibilities continually update the information, which is available through state offices, district resource centers, libraries, universities, and other intermediaries. The system contains some 500,000 entries and continues to grow. Raizen (1979) notes that over 200,000 requests for information are made each week, although use of information is another question. ERIC is used in all OE and NIE dissemination programs and provides the foundation for some of them, such as the State Dissemination Grants Program.

*State Dissemination Grants Program*: The predecessor of SDGP was an experimental program called the Pilot State Dissemination Project (PSDP), which ran from 1970 to 1972 (see Sieber et al.'s 1972 evaluation of the program). The initial program provided federal support for three state education agencies (Oregon, South Carolina, and Utah) to develop and test strategies for bridging the gap between the knowledge needs of local practitioners and the knowledge available on existing research products. The program used a combination of an information base (mainly ERIC) and field or extension agents to work with local personnel to formulate needs and match them to available information. The program was evaluated as relatively successful.

SDGP is a major program in NIE designed to strengthen the capacity of state education departments to provide "comprehensive and generalized" dissemination services to local school districts for the purpose of improving educational practice and equity (see Madey et al., 1979; Royster et al., 1981). "Comprehensive" is defined to include three main components: (1) information resources ("a full range of resources including data, documents, products, and technical expertise"); (2) linkage ("a means of linking the client groups to the resource base"); and (3) leadership/management arrangements "to facilitate provision of services on any problems to all members of the client group." Two types of grants are made: *capacity-building grants*, which average $100,000 each, are potentially renewable for three to five years, to support the development of the state's comprehensive dissemination system; *special-purpose grants*, which average $25,000, are short term and focused on particular problems such as initial planning, training of personnel, and development of certain specified resources.

The Capacity Building Grants began in 1975 with a first cohort of 10 states followed in successive years by cohorts II (14 states), III (six states), IV (four states), and V (10 states). Thus, at the present time 44 states or territories (including Puerto Rico and the U.S. Virgin Islands) have been funded. In short, the 44 states in the program are attempting to build information systems containing research and program knowledge on all aspects of education, and to stimulate access and use of the information throughout the jurisdiction.

*Research and Development Exchange*: There are 17 Regional Laboratories and university-based R&D Centers. Following congressional policy, NIE currently allocates almost one-half of its budget to Lab and Center work. The RDX program is a cooperative effort among several Labs, Centers, and states to exchange information on key topics mostly in the areas of basic skills (math and language arts) and competency-based education. In the RDX program, Labs and Centers (1) synthesize and disseminate information and/or provide training or assistance on topics and products of potential interest to practitioners,[11] and (2) communicate information/product needs in the field to researchers and developers. There are eight regional exchange centers, which are housed in Appalachia Educational Lab (West Virginia), CEMREL Inc. (Missouri), Mid-continent Regional Educational Lab (Missouri), Northwest Regional Educational Lab (Oregon), Research for Better Schools (Pennsylvania), Southwest Educational Development Laboratory (Texas), and Southwest Regional Lab (California). Each center serves from four to 11 states. Four central services support the regional exchanges: the Dissemination Support Service for staff responsible for dissemination (provided by the Northwest Regional Educational Lab); the R&D Interpretation Service, to help transform knowledge resulting from R&D into more usable form (provided by CEMREL); the Resource and Referral service, to build a data bank of people and organizations knowledgeable about R&D in the basic skills and competency areas (at the Center for Vocational Education, Ohio State University); and the System Support Service to facilitate the total R&D exchange by coordinating information so as to inform the R&D community in the country of field-based needs and reactions to existing products and research (at the Far West Lab in San Francisco).

*Research and Development Utilization*: In 1976 NIE established the Research and Development Utilization Program to help schools clarify and solve local problems by drawing on validated R&D knowledge and corresponding technical assistance in the areas of basic skills and career education (see Louis & Rosenblum, 1981; Louis, Rosenblum, et al., 1981). Seven projects were funded, which operated in a total of 20 states and served over 300 schools or districts. The seven projects were the Northwest Reading Consortium, the Georgia Research and Development Utilization Project, the Pennsylvania School Improvement Project, the National Education Association Inservice Education Project, the Florida Linkage System, the Michigan Career Education Dissemination Project, and The Network Consortium Project (Massachusetts). Each project was designed to help school personnel address particular problems through the use of selected programs, as well as to enhance their problem-solving capacity (i.e., their procedures for deciding on and implementing new programs).

*Experimental Schools*: The ES program started in 1970 in the Office of Education, and was transferred to NIE in 1972. Its goal was to provide funds to local school districts who were willing to launch locally planned comprehen-

---

11 For example, one of the regional exchange centers produces a guidebook called *Research within Reach: Reading*, which presents responses by a panel of reading experts to 24 questions most frequently asked about teaching reading. The guidebook contains summary statements on such problems as reading readiness and the difficulties in developing reading skills, and lists references for further reading. Various state, regional, and local reading consultants use the guide to design in-service activities, to increase their own or others' knowledge about reading instruction, and as an aid in identifying or selecting curriculum materials (see Kronkosky et al., 1981).

sive change efforts. "Comprehensive" was defined as including five major components as a minimum: curriculum, community participation, staff development, administration, and organization. Interested districts competed for grants through the development of proposals and revisions. Those that received grants were funded up to five years. A total of 18 school districts (ten rural and eight urban) obtained grants.

*Documentation and Technical Assistance*: In 1973 NIE established a task force called Building Capacity for Renewal and Reform. The ideas of the task force fed into the newly formed NIE group School Capacity for Problem Solving (a subgroup in the current division). The task force had urged NIE "to study and support internal processes of growth and renewal through which local school practitioners identified their problems and found resources, and ideas to meet their needs" (DTA, 1977; Smith & Dyer, 1979). In order to examine and facilitate these "problem-solving" processes NIE awarded grants in 1974 to nine local urban change efforts which were already under way (four in New York City, and one each in Los Angeles, Louisville, San Jose, Minneapolis, and Washington). While the approaches being used at the sites differed, they all concentrated on various collaborative methods involving parents, students, teachers, and administrators.

NIE was interested not just in the nine sites. As a research and dissemination agency it was primarily concerned with documenting the strategies being used and their impact at each site, and finding ways of utilizing this information to help other schools improve their problem-solving capacity. This dual interest in documentation and technical assistance resulted in the DTA project. The DTA contract was awarded in late 1974 to two institutions which had decided to collaborate: the Center for New Schools in Chicago, and the Center for Educational Policy and Management in Eugene, Oregon. The contract was for five years running from the beginning of 1975 to the end of 1979.[12] Their job was to document problem-solving processes and outcomes, develop technical assistance handbooks and resources, and facilitate the transfer of this knowledge to new user sites.

## Issues and impact

Entire books and countless articles can be and have been written on each of the fifteen programs just described. For those interested in detail related to any given program, the Appendix contains a list of the main independent research or evaluation studies conducted on the various projects.

There are several overriding issues which should be considered in the evolving federal role in education. I divide these into three clusters: sources and development of change, macro implementation problems (including expectations, knowledge of the change process, and federal/state/local interrelationships), and impact. These clusters help to explain why federal programs succeed and fail. There are numerous dilemmas faced by federal authorities in the multi-level change process in which they are engaged; recognizing the

---

12 The program was terminated by NIE at the end of three years for a variety of reasons related to slow progress in meeting program objectives (see Miles, 1979; Smith & Dyer, 1979).

nature of these dilemmas is a key requirement for improving the federal role. Let us take a closer look at each of these clusters in order to set the context for considering the role of states.

## Sources and development of change

The federal government expends billions of dollars on elementary and secondary education. We can divide this financial contribution into three main categories:

1 Monies which end up directly in school district budgets (such as Title I). In 1978, as we have seen, this amounted to 8.1% of local budgets, or $6.5 billion.
2 Funds which go directly to state agencies for their own activities (that is, the money is granted to increase the capacity of the state agency). Although this expenditure constitutes on average some 40% of the state educational budgets, it is difficult to cite an overall dollar figure.
3 Money to research, development, and resource centers to support major programs. In 1977, Orlich (1979) reports, the federal government spent $217 million on R&D. This sum does not include the development and technical assistance money that goes directly to particular programs, resource centers, etc. (e.g., Follow Through centers). The total federal expenditure in this third category is also difficult to estimate, since there are so many programs and agencies involved.

Even with the reduction in the education budget under the Reagan administration for 1981/82, it is clear that the federal government is a major source of funds for "new" program initiatives. Moreover, if funds were drastically cut further, the federal government has still contributed billions of dollars over the past fifteen years to the development of new products and programs which are now available for use and being used. In other words, strictly in terms of the *production* of new programs—what I have referred to as the initiation or adoption phase—the federal government has been responsible directly and indirectly for the presence of many new programs and corresponding assistance. These programs, it should be repeated, are intended by and large for disadvantaged groups.[13] In this sense, the federal government is an antidote or counter-force to the "bias by neglect" referred to in chapter 2. We can speculate that without this source of change, only a fraction of the new programs for minority groups over the past fifteen years would have been developed in the face of either inertia or lack of resources at the state and local levels. None of this says that these resources were always used wisely by either federal or other agencies—a topic which is taken up in relation to the other two clusters of variables. But as a source of potentially valuable, needed reform the federal government has played a significant role at the initiation phase.

## Macro implementation

Put most straightforwardly, *how* the federal government goes about educational change starts the implementation process in action. What happens afterwards is to a large extent a continuation of how well or how badly the change process is initiated and followed through. There have been several notable problems in

---

13 This is not to say that states and districts are uninterested in the problems of minority groups, but only that the federal government is one major source of resources and pressures for reform.

what Berman (1978) has called the macro implementation capacity of governments. These problems have to do with inherent difficulties in managing large-scale change; unrealistic expectations by governments; absence of preparation and training of government personnel to manage particular change programs; corresponding inadequate understanding of the nature of the change; non-existent, inconsistent, or otherwise poor communication and relationships with state and local personnel who participate in programs; and overlapping and segmented programs and departments at the federal level. In short, the federal impact on educational change is related to the extent to which the different agencies develop their own capacity to understand and participate in a complex multi-level implementation process.

Some examples. The programs associated with the Elementary and Secondary School Act of 1965 in the early years suffered from unrealistic and vague goals and misspent funds (McLaughlin, 1976). It was assumed that widespread reform could be brought about by good intentions and infusion of new resources. We now know that these expectations were farfetched. The programs themselves were imprecise and underdeveloped. McLaughlin's description of the first several years of Title I provides a good case in point. The regulations were unclear and confusing, and specific programs to address particular goals had not yet been developed. No one in fact knew what to do, although many acted as if they did.

Even if there are realistic goals and good ideas, these often do not get translated in practice *within* government circles, let alone outside. Berman (1978, p. 167) contends that there are at least four main elements to federal-level policies: the general policy (P), the regulations on program which operationalize the policy (G or government program), adoption (A) by a state or local district, and implementation (I) or change in practice. In the move from P to G (i.e., within government) those responsible for G might not understand the program, may even oppose it, and in any case have priorities of their own. Gideonse (1980, p. 68) reminds us that it is "the lower and middle level government officials who actually implement policy." Often they are excluded from the higher-level deliberations on the evaluation and development of policy. And then, as I have discussed previously, programs get further variegated or diluted in the move to adoption and then to implementation.

A related point is that there is little evidence to this day that governments (beyond constant reorganizations) explicitly prepare their own personnel for specific change efforts.[14] As Gideonse (1979, p. 318) notes about the Experimental Schools (ES) project, "While it was assumed that schools would need staff development programs to train the district personnel to carry out the comprehensive programs, no such assumption seems to have occurred to anyone concerning parallel needs of ES/Washington staff." Corwin (1977) explores this problem in the ES project in some detail. He describes how government project officers vascillated between being contract managers and project advis-

14 A tendency that is at least 2000 years old: "We trained hard ... but it seemed every time we were beginning to form up into teams we were reorganized. I was to learn later in life that we tend to meet any situation by reorganizing, and a wonderful method it can be for creating the illusion of progress while producing confusion, inefficiency, and demoralization." —Gaius Petronius, A.D. 66, cited in Gaynor (1977).

ers and technical assisters without any preparation or discussion among themselves as to the nature of their roles.[15] And preparation is indeed needed, because the skills required for facilitating change at a distance, and the dilemmas faced, get more and more complex as one has to deal with more levels of the educational system.

The phenomenology is all wrong for government personnel and local practitioners to recognize and empathize with each others' problems. Government staff have multiple troubles of their own—incessant meetings and paperwork, competition to maintain or increase budgets or stave off reduction or elimination of programs, periodic changes in policy directions as political leaders change, and some impatience to see results for their efforts. In the meantime, districts and schools have their own host of situational problems, with the particular project promoted by a given government department being only one of many concerns. (Cowden and Cohen's 1979 "Divergent Worlds of Practice" contains an illuminating account of the problem.)

The macro implementation problem is related to how government agencies understand and approach regional and local jurisdictions. State and local districts vary in their capacity to implement programs and to deal with countless pressing issues other than specific new programs of interest to particular federal departments. Elmore (1980, pp. 13–14) indicates that there are many reasons other than resistance for states or local districts not to implement new policies: lack of resources or capacity to implement, lack of a sense of urgency or priority, an incompatibility with other commitments, or existing policies which slow or deflect implementation. Whatever the case, it is the quality of the federal/state relationship which is critical to implementation, for a dual reason: nearly all federal initiatives are administered through state agencies, and federal agencies on their own could reach only a tiny fraction of school districts in the country. State agencies can have a significant impact on local program change (see next section).

Finally, the whole business is hard to figure out anyway. As we have seen, there are several major programs attempting to do overlapping things. The separate government agencies and monitoring systems which are in place appear to have little interaction at the federal level. From the local district's perspective it must look bewildering if not a little crazy. Addressing a reading problem could involve any number of possible programs (Title I, IVC, Basic Skills, NDN, Follow Through, RDX, etc.) or combinations of programs. (See Kimbrough & Hill's 1981 study of the problems at the local level of overlapping federal programs.) Legislation requires setting up several parallel parent advisory councils for different programs (see Keesling's 1980 study of Title I, ESAA, Title VII, and Follow Through). Ambivalence about the authority of federal involvement in education fosters further inconsistencies at both the giving (federal) and receiving (states, local districts) ends of the relationship. How best to deal with issues of compliance, decentralization, and consolidation remains

---

15 This phenomenon may be changing in some quarters. Madey et al. (1979, p. 29) report that project monitors on the SDGP at NIE now receive some training. However, technical assistance is downplayed, and contacts between monitors and project directors vary. In the 29 projects Madey studied, about half of the monitors and directors had frequent contact, while the other half had little contact beyond formal requirements.

elusive.[16] Whether we look from the top down or from the bottom up, we get a growing sense that the process of educational change has a lot in common with a labyrinth.

## Impact

It is impossible to assess the full impact of the various programs under discussion. There are too many short-run and cumulative ramifications, both intended and unintended, to detect. Nor, of course, can we know what would have been the impact if different approaches had been used. On the other hand, there are at least two major generalizations that stand out and provide a starting point for further work. The first, as we have learned, is that resources for the development of quality programs combined with resources for ongoing assistance during the first year or two of implementation is effective in bringing about change. The federal government has been a major source of reform in this regard. The second generalization is that effective implementation of federal programs depends on the capacity of states and local districts to manage change within their own jurisdictions—and this capacity varies among states and districts.

Some brief comments on the impact of particular programs are in order. While earlier reviews of Title I (e.g., McLaughlin, 1976) found ambiguous goals, noncompliance, diversion of resources, and limited state scrutiny of local programs, Kirst and Jung (1980) found more implementation of Title I programs. They argue for the necessity of a longitudinal approach in interpreting major ongoing programs. They find, for instance, increasing evidence that funds are reaching targeted children, and that most states have developed "adequate to good" procedures for reviewing local applications for Title I funds. A more detailed implementation study of Title I in eight states found that there has been considerable improvement in the performance of states and local districts in the administration of the program (Goettel et al., 1977). I also indicated earlier that more than fifty Title I programs had been validated for use in NDN as "exemplary" (over 25% of current validated NDN programs come from Title I sources).

Other programs have had impact. The National Diffusion Network continues to have a record of relative success (Emrick & Peterson, 1977; Crandall et al., forthcoming). Several Follow Through models claim (with supporting evidence) significant impact on teachers, parents, and children (Rhine, 1981; Hodges et al., 1980). Title IVC receives very favorable reviews by state and district personnel for providing essential marginal resources to bring about needed changes (McDonnell & McLaughlin, 1980). Independent evaluations of the Research and Development Utilization effort found numerous instances of success (Louis & Rosenblum, 1981). Some states have benefited significantly from "capacity-building" resources from the federal level (see Royster et al., 1981, on the State Dissemination Grants Program). Some specific experiments were on balance admitted failures (except as lessons in what not to

---

16 See Elmore (1980) on compliance vs. capacity, and Turnbull (1980) on consolidation vs. segmentation, for discussions of the pros and cons of these complicated issues. These matters are taken up again in the final section of this chapter, "Guidelines for governments."

do)—the Experimental Schools project and the Documentation and Technical Assistance projects, to name two.

The actual impact of federal efforts is debatable in several respects. Was the result worth the scale of effort? Were the changes real? Do they make any ultimate difference on how well children fare in society? Perhaps the most prominent positive factor resides in a comparison of 1965 to 1981.[17] In 1965 neither the federal government nor anyone else knew much about implementation and had even less to work with in terms of quality programs. In 1981 there appears to be a large number of proven programs available in certain subject areas, a good deal of knowledge about what factors affect implementation and how to address some of them, and a respectable number of success stories. Whether this amount of achievement is adequate is a moot point, but when we compare the situation now to that a few years ago (e.g., 1975) when it seemed that failure of reform was a foregone conclusion, we now know not only that some success can be achieved but also why it is being achieved. In some respects *any* degree of success is remarkable, given what we know about the problems of facilitating or managing large-scale change, and about the corresponding vulnerability of policies as they wend their way through the education system.

We have also learned during this period that the capacity to bring about change varies a great deal among states and districts and is a crucial factor in the equation. The state in many ways is the critical government agency because it has the direct constitutional authority for most aspects of education. The state is also a major step closer to school districts than is the federal government.

# The state education department

The state is the intermediary between the federal government and local districts as well as a force for change in its own right. I consider two aspects of state education departments: a brief descriptive profile of states, and federal/state/local relationships with an emphasis on the orientation of states to educational change in their relationships with the other two agencies.[18]

## Profiles

The U.S. Constitution leaves the authority over public education to the states. The federal government, except for a few areas of jurisdiction, is influential

---

17 The time period in which a research study is conducted is a critical but often unrecognized variable. Research carried out ten years ago may no longer be accurate, although it often is quoted uncritically to support a particular viewpoint (see Kirst & Jung, 1980). Most of the research I use in this book is very recent; when earlier work is cited I have attempted to ensure that it has been replicated or confirmed by later studies.

18 Van Geel (1976, ch. 4) and Wise (1979) are two very useful sources on which I draw for descriptive information. Other research studies on the role of states in federally sponsored programs are also informative and are cited accordingly. Cates et al. (1979) provide capsule profiles on the dissemination status and activities for each state.

mainly because it provides money needed by states and districts. State structures for education consist of a department of education headed by a chief state school officer (the commissioner), who is responsible to a state board of education and to the governor. The commissioner and board members are either elected or appointed, depending on the state.

Leaving aside Hawaii, the District of Columbia, and the territories, which have unique structures (such as single educational agencies with no local districts), there are basically two structural patterns in the remaining 49 states. According to Yin and Gwaltney (1981) 34 states have a three-level structure (the state, intermediate units, local boards), while some 15 have a two-level pattern (the state, local boards). The establishment of intermediate units has been a trend over the past ten years as educational financing and programming have become increasingly more complicated. In a very few cases (e.g., New Jersey) the units are regional offices of the department of education and thus perform a regulatory administrative function. In the majority of cases, however, the intermediate units are service agencies funded by states (using some federal program money) to coordinate and provide supplementary assistance (staff development, evaluation, curriculum development, etc.) to districts which could not otherwise afford the services. There are many different patterns. New York, for example, is organized into 60 Boards of Cooperative Education Services (BOCES), Texas has its Regional Education Service Centers (RESC) and Kentucky its Educational Development Regions (EDR), and so on. Some states have more than one type of intermediate unit. One state studied by McDonnell and McLaughlin (1980, p. 92) had three types: a county-level system of elected officials, state regional education offices to provide assistance, and a third unit to assist districts in adopting validated projects. Eighteen of the 34 states with intermediate agencies have at least two different types of regional units.

States vary in their degree of centralization. In 1976 van Geel classified 20 states as centralized, 23 as decentralized, and six as mixed. Centralized states tend to prescribe minimum competencies; some approve textbooks for state-wide use, take more interest in the content of courses of study, and collect and make public the achievement and other evaluative data. Decentralized states are more inclined to favor local discretion in deciding on the precise nature of school programs. Wise (1979) argues strongly that the trend is toward greater state regulation of narrowly defined competencies. He reports that "minimum competency testing" had been mandated by 33 states by mid-1978, and at least 73 "accountability laws" had been enacted by 1974 (p. 2). Florida's Educational Accountability Act of 1976, New Jersey's Thorough and Efficient (T and E) system mandated by the State Court in 1972, and California's various pieces of legislation promoting school improvement—all provide elaborate requirements (and resources) for improving school performance mostly in basic skills areas. The New Jersey State Court went so far as to require that "if the local government fails, the State government must compel it to act, and if the local government cannot carry the burden, the State must itself meet its continuing obligation" (Wise, 1979, p. 160).

Like most government agencies, states frequently reorganize. In the latest survey of chief state officers, more than half (28) reported that the state agency had been reorganized during the last two years (1979 and 1980). On the average, state education departments have about 600 professionals, and some have as many as 3000 (Madey et al., 1979, p. 23). State agencies have tripled in size in the past fifteen years, to a large extent because of the influx of federal money. Murphy (1974) found that 40% of the operating budget in the nine states he studied came from federal funds. McDonnell and McLaughlin note that from 30% to 80% of state education department budgets come from federal funds. Many of the staff positions in the departments correspond to federal programs (e.g., Title I Project Director). While a sizeable proportion of funds comes from federal programs, the autonomy and program initiative of states, as we will see shortly, vary a great deal. Some states in their use of federal funds act mainly as conduits to local districts; others use federal funds as well as their own to promote particular priorities actively. In addition to federally sponsored programs, most states have developed their own major programs. Baratz et al. (1979) reported that 20 states administer bilingual programs, 16 administer compensatory programs, 34 oversee competency testing programs, and states spend six times as much money as the federal government on education for the handicapped (cited in Murphy, 1980, p. 39).

Another type of state profile more directly related to program change was developed by Hood and Blackwell (1979), who compiled indicators of states' "knowledge production and dissemination capacity." They used five indicators of *knowledge production* (e.g., number of ERIC documents produced in the state) and eight indicators of *dissemination capacity* (e.g., number of ERIC searches, involvement in the R&D Utilization Project). Using all 13 indicators they ranked states into six groups from highest to lowest on most indicators. The states can be dichotomized in a simpler way: those states or territories which are high or moderate on all indicators (21) and those which are low or moderate on all indicators (30). The classification should not be taken too literally, because the study did not measure actual utilization or impact. Nonetheless, the notion of variations in state capacity to facilitate or bring about educational change is an important one, and is central to the next section. (See also Crandall et al.'s forthcoming profiles of the dissemination activities of 10 states; also Royster et al., 1981.)

## Federal/state/local relationships

Murphy (1980) notes several gaps in our knowledge about the state role in education. Little is known about the internal structure and operation of state departments especially at the level of middle and lower management, where there is the most direct contact with school. Very little research has been conducted on the role and effectiveness of intermediate units. (Recent exceptions are Yin & Gwaltney, 1981; Havelock & Huberman, forthcoming; Firestone & Wilson, 1981.) More case studies are needed of *implementation* of federal and state programs including "vertical" studies of different state strategies and state/local relationships, particularly as they influence local practice. Much research on states has apparently excluded a large number of states and has thereby possibly biased generalizations; according to Burlingame and Geske (1979), "In fact, 21 of the 50 states have not yet appeared in any published multiple state case studies—an astonishing 42%" (cited by Murphy, p. 42).

There have been a small number of informative multi-state studies. Five of these can be used to examine the role of states: Goettel et al. (1977) on Title I in eight states; the System Development Corporation study of parent involvement in four programs; the evaluation of the State Capacity Development Grants in 44 states (Royster et al., 1981); the study of the state role in consolidation of Title IV (McDonnell & McLaughlin, 1980); and the Yin and Gwaltney (1981) research of three intermediate units.[19]

## The Title I example

In a broad sense at least three major ingredients at the state level are required for widespread change: the program must be reasonably sound; if it comes from the federal government, it must be congruent with state priorities; and the state must have the capacity to influence/work with local districts. If any one of these ingredients is missing, there will not be much implementation. Goettel et al.'s initial research (1977) and further conceptualization (Orland & Goettel, 1980) based on case studies of the implementation of Title I in eight states support and expand on these points. They cite three state-level variables which influence local implementation of Title I: *knowledge* of the requirements of the program; a *commitment* to implementing it; and *administrative capacity* to facilitate implementation.[20]

In a more simplified version, we could combine knowledge and commitment as one factor, and portray state orientation to educational change in figure 5. Thus, for any given policy or program coming from the federal level, a state could be either more or less knowledgeable about and committed to it, and have either greater or lesser capacity to facilitate or foster its implementation. We would not expect much if any implementation to occur in a Type I situation. Type II situations would be frustrating at all levels: there would be a push for the change, but few mechanisms to assist in productive implementation. A Type III situation arises when the state is not committed to a program but does have a fairly high capacity to get things implemented. In Type IV situations we would expect the most implementation.

Knowledge and commitment, as the figure indicates, do not amount to very much without the capacity to influence the implementation process. To define ideal state capacity for change in detail is a tall order, but the main elements can be identified, because so much is known about what makes for effective implementation. The few state studies tend to confirm what is already known about implementation. In general, state capacity is related to such factors (in combination) as: (1) being clear about expectations and about what the change is; (2) taking an active interest in and finding out what is happening with the program at the local level; (3) providing or making accessible technical assistance in staff development, planning, conducting evaluations and using evaluative data, etc. Goettel et al. (1977) found that local districts frequently lacked the administrative capacity in the area of program development in Title I, and most states provided little help or incentive to districts in such areas as obtaining adequate

19 In addition to these five studies, one component of the DESSI study focuses on federal/state/ local relationships, but the results are not yet available.

20 These three variables parallel the three I suggested. Program quality is similar to knowledge of the program, as is congruence to commitment, and administrative capacity to capacity to influence districts.

**Figure 5**

Knowledge/commitment

|  | | LOW | HIGH |
|---|---|---|---|
| State capacity to implement | LOW | I | II |
|  | HIGH | III | IV |

parent involvement, conducting needs assessment, selecting or developing programs, and evaluation.[21] The ten regional Title I Technical Assistance Centers (TACs) were not well developed at the time of Goettel's research (the federal legislation was passed in 1974, but the centers took some time to develop); however, they represent a good illustration of the capacity-building role of the state. The regional centers were set up to provide free advice and service to the states and local districts on all aspects of Title I. It is quite easy for states to become preoccupied with the evaluation of formal compliance criteria (e.g., targeting and tracking money) without developing program knowledge and capacities necessary for engaging in discussions or work with districts.

The whole question of evaluation represents an important problem area which could easily deserve a separate chapter. Most federal and state programs have elaborate evaluation requirements. The majority of information collected seems to focus on compliance and test-related outcomes, diverts a great deal of energy into form-filling and report-writing, results in reams of paper which often is not read let alone used, and in any case frequently is not related or relatable to program involvement. In Title I, as in other programs, the linkage of evaluation data to instructional improvement is an acknowledged problem (see David, 1981; Fishbein et al., 1980).[22] In 1980, the Office of Education added two new categories to the Title I award program: one on improving the utility of evaluation information, and the other on the management of Title I evaluation (Fishbein et al.). Showing an interest in and facilitating better

---

21 Four of the eight states were what Goettel et al. call "nondirective." They left decisions to the districts and showed little specific interest beyond general compliance concerns. The four directive states were very clear, demanding, and influential about expectations, but in terms of our discussion of capacity they must be viewed in relation to what Goettel calls "orientation to substance." Some directive states dwelt on bureaucratic compliance, while others showed substantive interest in programs and emphasized their technical assistance responsibilities. Orland and Goettel (1980, p. 17) do not specify how many of the four directive states focused on substantive program improvement; but if half of them did, it would mean that two of the eight states combined directiveness and program help.

22 There are some instructive ongoing studies being conducted on the relationship between evaluation and instructional improvement at the district level. See the research of the Center for Educational Evaluation at U.C.L.A. (Lyon et al., 1978; Williams & Bank, 1981), and the work of the Huron Institute (Kennedy, 1981; Neumann, 1981). See also Alkin et al. (1979). In general, these studies find two things: (1) the vast majority of districts do not have procedures for relating evaluation to program development; (2) there are a small number of districts that do (Huron found 18). The districts that do use evaluation effectively by and large model the implementation characteristics described in chapter 5 and chapter 10.

district-level evaluation systems linked to program development is another facet of state capacity for change.

## The parent involvement example

The large-scale study of parent involvement in Title I, ESAA, Title VII, and Follow Through conducted by System Development Corporation corroborates the importance of the role of states in implementation. Effective parent participation at the local level was more likely to occur in states which had developed their own guidelines for parent involvement (e.g., in Title I), actively communicated these expectations and guidelines, provided technical assistance, and monitored projects with some direct contact (see Robbins & Dingler, 1981; Cadena-Munoz & Keesling, 1981; Smith & Nerenberg, 1981; Melaragno et al., 1981).[23]

## The state capacity example

Madey et al.'s (1979) study contains additional information on the role of states. It is based on the 29 states (at the time) who had received grants from the State Capacity Building Program (SCBP) to improve their dissemination capabilities. Some findings of interest: (1) Based on project directors' assessment Madey et al. (p. 24) classify 12 states as taking on the grants for "problem-solving" reasons (to fill an existing need), eight as "opportunistic" (the money was there), and nine as "mixed." (2) Of the 29 project directors, 16 indicated that their state agency was innovative; 10 of the 29 judged the state influence on school improvement in the state to be extensive. (3) Most states developed increasingly comprehensive information resources, coordination of dissemination efforts, and linkage capacity (training of state, intermediate, and local staff on how to link information to needs of people; provision of assistance to local agencies), but there were some notable differences between states. (4) Involvement of middle-level state staff in decision-making regarding dissemination was positively related to the extent to which comprehensive resource and linkage systems were established. (5) States which focused on content-specific dissemination by program (e.g., vocational or special education) were less likely to develop *coordinated* systems than states which were involved in more general dissemination programs such as NDN, RDX, and RDU.[24] (6) About one-half of the NIE monitors interacted frequently with project directors, and this amount of contact was positively related to the degree of development of the state dissemination system. In addition, the provision of technical assistance (by some monitors) was positively related to dissemination development; although project monitors were not officially charged with giving help, some did, and project directors desired more technical assistance from NIE staff. (7) The length of tenure of a project director was very strongly related to dissemination development in the state. (8) Structural placement of the capacity-building project was important — of the 29 projects, seven were placed in a research/evaluation unit, 12 in service divisions, and 10 in administrative units; projects in the

---

23 Recall (chapter 12) that effective parent involvement was achieved in only a minority of districts. State expectations and capacity happens to be the variable under discussion here, but it is only one source of influence; district and school variables are very powerful.

24 That is, the focus on content programs maintained segmentation by program, which inhibited coordination of information and assistance across programs.

service uivisions did better at developing comprehensive linkages than those in the other kinds of unit. Overall, project and state department leadership in promoting development of the system was an important variable in how successful the development was.

The final report of the SCBP evaluation elaborates on the above findings (Royster et al., 1981). The case study profiles of the systems in five states—Illinois, Kansas, Michigan, Rhode Island, and Texas—are very useful for describing the history and development of different systems and for characterizing how particular state systems actually work in practice. More generally, Royster et al. (1981, pp. 4–31) suggest that state systems for linking information between state and other levels (regional and local) can be captured in one of three models: non-coupled (in which the information base and its staff have little formal relationship to linkers working in other state departments or intermediate units); loosely coupled (in which there is general coordination and linkers act as intermediaries between the resource base and local clients); and tightly coupled (in which the resource base and linkers are integrated through managerial structures and line relationships). Aside from the specific conclusions already mentioned (Madey et al.), the actual impact of these different models or the SCBP program as a whole on information *utilization* at the local level is impossible to determine.[25]

## The Title IV example

McDonnell and McLaughlin (1980) describe in considerable detail their research on Title IV programs. The study was comprehensive. It included questionnaires to managers and administrators in all state education departments. Response rates were over 80% for nearly all roles and were 100% for several. Questionnaires were sent to a sample of over 600 local districts involved in IVB projects (60% response) and 453 districts in IVC projects (79% response).[26] Field work was conducted in 24 districts and in the education department office in each of eight states. Their research covered both parts B and C of Title IV. Only the main findings will be discussed.

Title IVB provides grants to states to distribute to districts for the purchase of library, media, and guidance and testing materials (total $154.5 million in 1978). In most states the distribution formula is based on enrollment. Districts have autonomy over how they spend the funds among the eligible services. McDonnell and McLaughlin (1980, p. 8) found that in most states IVB is more of an acquisition service than a focused program, but in their field work they found some states that engage in substantive planning and assistance to districts. States and districts like the IVB program because of its flexibility among the areas covered. In their survey of districts, the researchers asked, "How important have Part B funds been to your district in terms of providing services that you might otherwise have been unable to provide?" Some 66% responded "very important," the highest response category on a five-point scale, and a further 22% answered at the second-highest category.

---

25 In July 1981 ABT Associates received a contract from NIE for a two-to-three-year study of programs in NIE's general dissemination assistance area. The study includes the RDX and State Capacity programs, and should provide information on the actual impact of these multi-year efforts.
26 Questionnaires to Title IV state advisory councils and to non-public school districts and principals were also distributed, but I do not report these findings.

The IVC grants ($184.3 million in 1978) for innovative projects fall into five categories:[27] (1) development of new programs, which is the largest category, taking about two-thirds of the total money; (2) adoption grants, for districts to adopt exemplary projects (e.g., from NDN), which consume a relatively small percentage of total funds; (3) dissemination grants to support the spread of developed projects; (4) grants for supplementary centers awarded to intermediate agencies serving nearby districts; (5) mini-grants to individual schools or teachers for special activities (see McDonnell & McLaughlin, 1980, pp. 18–19).

In considering the significance of the state's role orientation to relationships with districts, McDonnell and McLaughlin suggest that there are three different approaches: states may act primarily as "funding conduits," as "regulatory agencies," or as "providers of technical assistance." Those states which conceive their roles as funding conduits pass on the money to local districts, insisting only on formal compliance (e.g., reports that the money is targeted to the appropriate population). These states do not show a substantive interest in program development, but rather leave it entirely to local districts. The states with this orientation neither know much about local implementation nor have any effect on it. Regulatory-agency states "are more likely to formulate and then carry out policy aims of their own which can be superimposed on an existing federal program. They are also more likely to expect local programs to reflect state priorities" (p. 89). These states are more influential at the local level, but this influence can be a two-edged sword depending on whether state priorities and local priorities are congruent. Some states of the third orientation have established separate technical assistance units either in the state department or in the regional intermediate units referred to earlier. In either case, staff spend a large amount of time in the field. The nature and effectiveness of intermediate units varies. McDonnell and McLaughlin conclude from their eight site visits that these units are more effective if they are an extension of the state agency (although separating assistance from regulation), if they avoid duplication with either other state or local units, and if they do not compete with districts for funds (p. 91). (See also Joyce et al.'s study in California of state/local-district/school interrelationships involving 46 state and federal initiatives with staff development components.)

McDonnell and McLaughlin make a number of recommendations for federal and state agencies to improve their work with each other and with districts, and I will refer to these in the concluding section of this chapter.

### The intermediate agencies example

One of the few comparative studies of regional or intermediate educational agencies in the U.S. has just been carried out by Yin and Gwaltney (1981). They also provide some useful overview information. Of the 50 states, 34 have regional units. The authors note that there are different types of intermediate agencies. Some states have cooperatives with services determined by local districts and funds provided by the districts with some state and federal contribution; others have intermediate agencies which are authorized by state

---

27 The DESSI study, the findings from which have been cited, also includes IVC grants (Crandall et al., forthcoming). In the DESSI study there is some indication that local development of programs through IVC grants results in more "ownership" and a greater degree of implementation than does adoption of NDN programs.

legislation, provide services (but usually with an emphasis on state priorities), and are primarily financed by state and some federal funds. Many states have two (and in a few cases three) different types of agencies.

Yin and Gwaltney (1981) selected three of these agencies for study. They selected "exemplary" units which were intensively involved in providing services to local districts. Of 14 potential sites which they considered, the following were chosen:

1 The Wayne County Intermediate School District (Wayne ISD) in Michigan, linked to the Michigan Department of Education and serving 36 districts.
2 The Northern Colorado Educational Board of Cooperative Services (NCEBOCS) linked with the Colorado Department of Education and serving six districts.
3 The Education Improvement Center—South (EIC–South) linked with the New Jersey Department and serving 144 districts.

The funding pattern varied. In the Wayne ISD, 40% came from federal projects, 37% from a tax levy for special education, 12% from state sources, and small percentages from other projects; local districts contributed only 4% of the total budget of $50 million through service fees. Of its $1 million budget, the NCEBOCS collects only 12% from federal projects; 42% comes from the state and 42% from local districts. In New Jersey, the EIC–South's budget of $3 million derives 65% from federal projects and 35% from state sources; districts pay nothing.

The study examined three types of services: staff development workshops, linker assistance (in-person assistance to individuals related to specific problems), and information retrieval. Intermediate agencies worked with districts to identify needs or respond to needs, helped develop proposals (e.g., to obtain a Title IVC adoption grant), and acted in follow-through capacity to provide assistance during implementation.

The authors offer explanations as to why some arrangements were successful and others less so (p. 63). Five main reasons for success are proposed: (1) the services were user-oriented from the assessment of needs, through assistance, to follow-through; (2) the arrangement enabled intermediate units and local districts to obtain external resources (federal and state); (3) the development of "active, professional networks" between the intermediate agency and the districts as well as across the districts provided opportunities for mutual influence and help; (4) the existence of state legislation mandating and giving direction to collaborative relationships promoted success; and (5) there were mutual benefits (both parties gaining) in the relationship.

The Yin and Gwaltney research is limited in some respects. The cases were selected as exemplary and are therefore probably atypical. The research did not attempt to assess the actual impact of the agencies on local programs and activities. Nonetheless, the study is helpful in presenting some information on the role of intermediate agencies (of which very little is known), in reinforcing ideas about the importance of external assistance under collaborative conditions, and in raising issues about the complex nature and large variations in the size and work of such agencies.[28]

---

28 There has been more attention paid lately to the role of intermediate agencies and to the complexities and impact of "inter-organizational arrangements" in school improvement efforts (see Chin et al., 1981; Havelock & Huberman, 1981; Research for Better Schools, 1981; TDR Associates, 1981; Havelock, 1981).

It is clear that the roles of state departments of education and intermediate agencies are critically important in supporting or inducing school improvement. It is also evident that there is a tremendous range in the configurations of arrangements and conditions across and within states; that we are only beginning to obtain a picture of what some of these variations are; and that we are even more in the dark about what their consequences are for local practice. It seems quite likely that states and intermediate units will receive more attention in the implementation research field over the next decade—a development much needed.

# Canadian federal and provincial governments

Before taking up the main implications of the role of governments in school reform, I turn to a consideration of the Canadian scene.

Educational reform in Canada is less complex to explain than that in the United States, but no more manageable. Three general observations should be made at the outset: (1) the federal role is very limited; (2) there has not been the big push by provincial governments to develop innovative products and projects and provide ongoing support for implementation (although recently there has been more concern); and (3) there is a paucity of research (either individual case studies or comparative provincial studies) on the workings of ministries of education.[29] There has been a great deal of movement during the 1970s by provincial ministries in developing new policies and in attempting to address problems of implementation. And this development appears to be getting more focused. But first some facts about the federal and provincial roles.

## The federal government

The best introduction to the federal role in education is by way of money and policy. The federal government provides some of the former and extremely little of the latter, being explicitly discouraged from doing so by the provinces and by its own reluctance. The British North America Act (1867) states that provinces "may exclusively make laws in education" (Section 93).[30]

There are three ways in which the federal government provides funds for education: direct contributions, indirect contributions, and general grants. Little of the money from any of the three sources directly supports regular elementary and secondary schools, and hardly any of it comes attached to policy directives.[31] If we start with direct costs, the federal government contributes

---

29 Some provinces use the style "Department of Education" and others "Ministry of Education." For simplicity I shall use "ministry" as the general term.

30 However, the federal government is responsible for providing education to Indians and Inuits and to children on armed forces bases; for contributing to minority-group language training; and for vocational and occupational training programs beyond what secondary schools offer.

31 The federal government does provide substantially more funds for postsecondary institutions, but they are outside my concern in this book.

only 2.76% of the $11.7 billion for elementary and secondary schools; the ten provinces and the Yukon and Northwest Territories contribute 67.02%, local taxes 26.38%, and fees and other sources 3.83% (see Brown, 1981, p. 74; figures are for 1978). Even the 2.76% is misleading for the majority of school systems, because most of this ($324 million in 1978) goes to pay for the education of Indians, Inuits, and children in schools on armed forces bases as specified in the constitution. In the second category—indirect contributions— the federal government is involved in two main ways. In 1977/78 $122.2 million was allocated to provinces to supplement minority-language training (French in English-language areas, English in French-language areas) in elementary and secondary schools (Brown, p. 167).[32] A large amount ($790 million in 1977/78) goes to employment training programs, in which the federal government pays 74% of total costs and the provinces the remaining 26% (Brown, p. 160). The third and final category of funds—general grants to provinces—refers to unconditional equalization payments. In 1978/79, seven of the ten provinces received entitlements totalling $2.66 billion to support all government services in those provinces, not confined to education. It is impossible to determine how much of this ends up in education budgets for any given province, but approximately 25% of provincial spending goes to education (including postsecondary— Brown, p. 36).

There are other forms of indirect federal involvement in education through support for research and programs and policies of other federal departments (in science, industry, social welfare, and health). What it all amounts to, even when we include the direct funding, is that the federal government is providing necessary money to support the education system but is not involved in directly influencing educational policy. An external review of Canadian educational policy by the Organization for Economic Cooperation and Development (OECD, 1976) put it this way: "Officially there is *no* federal presence in the area of educational policy ... no federal authority with the word 'Education' in its title" (p. 89; italics in original). But the OECD examiners also note that there is a federal presence in education "as long as nobody calls it educational policy, and as long as there are no overt strings attached to the money coming from Ottawa" (p. 89). The situation is very different from that in the U.S. It is interesting to note that both levels of government—the federal and the provincial— are reluctant to talk about the federal role.[33] One of the results of this avoidance of educational policy discussion, according to the OECD reviewers, is the lack

---

32 Canada is also committed to a policy of multiculturalism at the federal level, but there is not much direct support for schools in developing specific multicultural programs. Most medium-sized and large cities in the country, and some rural areas, have substantial percentages of a variety of ethnic groups. Policies and programs for these groups have been established in varying degrees by local boards of education.

33 There has been some discussion in various conferences and professional associations about the desirability of greater cooperative exchanges and joint endeavors across the provinces, and possibly of establishing a federal office of education in cooperation with the provinces, but the latter is very unlikely. The two most relevant national groups currently are the Council of Ministers of Education (which operates more as a semi-private, diplomatic discussion forum for the ministers of education) and the Canadian Education Association (which promotes professional policy debate and study among government and school system officials across the country but has no official status). Another source of debate and information is a recent national conference (see Ivany & Manley-Casimir, 1981).

of a national policy or set of goals for education. So it is at the provincial level where we must look for policy, program, and implementation action.

## The provincial governments

There are fewer than 1000 school districts in Canada. Among the ten provinces, Quebec has the largest number of districts (255) and Prince Edward Island the smallest (2); the rest range between 33 and 188. The numbers include Catholic school districts, which are under the constitution part of the public system.[34] On average, school districts in Canada are larger in size (geographically and in numbers of students) than those in the United States. Educational policy is the responsibility of each provincial ministry of education with certain responsibilities defined for local boards of education. Nearly every province (British Columbia being an exception) has regional offices, which, unlike most intermediate units in the U.S., are formally an arm of the provincial ministry.

Despite provincial autonomy, the goals, educational trends, and problems of implementation in all provinces are similar in many respects. Program and curriculum policy come in the form of official curriculum guidelines for each subject area produced by the provincial ministry. These guidelines are usually developed by provincial committees or task forces with membership drawn from among teachers, administrators, university professors, and ministry personnel. The guidelines are developed, disseminated, reviewed, and revised on a cyclical basis every several years. In addition to the main curricula, ministries develop other education policies governing all aspects of education—special education legislation, programs mandating or supporting parent advisory councils, work education programs, and so on.

Because of the decentralized nature of the Canadian education system, and because of the lack of careful comparative information, we have to be cautious in attempting to generalize. There are some clear impressions, however, backed up by a small number of research studies and policy decisions being taken in the different provinces. I summarize these issues in four categories. The first three correspond to the phases of curriculum decision-making and use referred to above: namely, (1) curriculum or policy *development*, (2) *implementation*, and (3) *evaluation* or review and revision. In the fourth and concluding section I discuss current orientations and directions being taken by provincial ministries.[35]

### Development

Up until the early 1960s curriculum guidelines in most provinces were highly content-specific. Since that time they have gone through a period of general statements or suggestions (approximately 1965 to 1975) to the current trend of increasing specificity of goals, activities, and expected outcomes. In the period of general guidelines (1965–75) there were enormous problems. The guidelines

34 In some provinces funding is provided only to certain grade levels. In Ontario, for example, Catholic schools are funded only to the end of grade 10.
35 The discussion relating to the first three categories attempts to characterize the past fifteen years and as such comes across more negatively than some of the current trends warrant. The fourth category redresses this imbalance by indicating what is now being done to confront some of the issues.

were deliberately left general on the assumption that local boards and teachers would develop the details. The main problem faced by districts and teachers was that it was not at all clear what the proposed policies really meant in practice.[36] Nearly every province in the past few years has taken to defining the curriculum more carefully.[37] There are still two major dilemmas. First, even with further definition, the latest curriculum guidelines and documents are not in "implementable" form. Goal statements are more clear, content to be covered is set down more specifically, reference to expected learning outcomes is tighter. But, the *means* of implementation (e.g., teaching strategies and activities) are not well developed or integrated. Resource or support documents are frequently produced, but serve as a range of suggestions only. This lack of direction is not a bad thing, as it allows decisions to be made at other levels (e.g., the district and the classroom). But the initial dilemma remains that it is still not clear in many guides what it is that is being proposed, particularly in relation to implementation (see especially Robinson, 1982).

The second set of problems at the development stage arises because the process is beset with political and ideological difficulties—many of them quite innocent, but just as consequential. The task forces or committees which develop the guidelines are formally representative of different groups. The fact that there is selectivity on committees is only a small part of the problem. Unrealistic time-lines (politically driven and in many ways inevitable), value conflicts within the committees and certainly outside them, and insufficient resources, skills, or time to develop details and a reluctance to do so—they all add up to an inauspicious start for many guidelines. Fowler (1979) comments on his experience in working with committees in Saskatchewan:

Chief decision-makers pressure committees to produce a "final" product at the earliest possible date. Sometimes these work schedules produce undue stress on the working committee. With the introduction of such stress, decisions unfortunately often become based on unsubstantiated evidence and complex problems become oversimplified or glossed over in the rush to produce an end product. (p. 7)

Governments can't win. If they encourage widespread debate during the development phase, as most do, the policy gets delayed and the discussions bog down in abstract goals (not on what practice changes are at stake). By the time the new guideline hits the streets it may be discredited for many and insufficiently developed for others.

There are positive features to this process depending on one's viewpoint. It allows for pluralistic debate at the development phase and great latitude at the implementation phase (since the policies usually are not highly specified). Moreover, in most provinces guideline revision is just reaching its second or third major cycle, so that there is some *cumulative* development occurring in terms of greater clarity of and agreement on goals, and better materials and resources for implementation (see, for example, the second major assessment

---

36 Quebec may be an exception, as the OECD (1976) review noted, in that it had a comparatively clear set of goals.

37 Guidelines typically include a list of objectives, topics and content to be covered, and ideas and resource suggestions for teaching activities and evaluation. Most guidelines are by subject area and cover several grade levels according to the particular province's organization of the grade-level divisions. Thus, they do not constitute courses of study.

of reading in British Columbia, Tuinman & Kendall, 1980). Major debates still remain in social studies, special education, and multicultural programs, as well as generally in the degree of emphasis on core subjects, basic skills, and testing.[38]

## Implementation

Regardless of what happens at the development phase, a lot of things can be done or undone when a guideline is introduced for use. There are no studies available which describe the details of what ministry personnel do in introducing and providing for or facilitating implementation. A picture of some of the main issues can be derived from research on how school people perceive the role of ministries of education, and from some inferences based on (1) what is known on the surface about the role of the ministry and (2) what implementation theory and research tell us. (See Fullan & Park, 1981, for a discussion of implementation problems vis-à-vis curriculum guidelines in Ontario.)

The problems of implementation are essentially the same as those examined in chapter 5. At this point, I am more interested in the particular role of the ministries of education. Two aspects that stand out relate to *guideline/materials development* itself, and *how the ministry goes about implementation*.

The first matter that should be recognized is that the curriculum guidelines are not (and are not intended to be) the actual curriculum materials to be used. Depending on the subject area and the province, they can go some distance in providing sources of ideas and activities but they are not the intact curriculum for use. And many teachers do not use them. For example, in the recent provincewide assessment of reading in British Columbia, Tuinman and Kendall (1980, pp. 140, 152) found that two-thirds of the elementary school teachers and one-half of the secondary school teachers had not consulted the Curriculum Guide in the previous six months; only 17% and 26% of elementary and secondary school teachers respectively reported that the guide had a "significant impact" on their teaching. In other curriculum areas in B.C. similar results are found: in social studies, for instance, almost 50% of the teachers responded at the low end of a helpfulness scale in rating the guide on "helpful teaching suggestions" (Aoki et al., 1977, pp. 62–66).[39]

For most teachers the "curriculum in use" is derived from one or more of the following sources: textbooks from commercial publishers, materials developed by their local districts, materials borrowed or adapted from other districts which have developed curriculum, or piecemeal planning and use of resources by individual teachers. There are several problems with this approach. Textbooks by themselves, although they are approved by the ministry, are incomplete matches to the curriculum guideline; districts that produce curriculum do

---

38 In social studies, for example, several issues are identified in the provincewide review conducted in British Columbia (Aoki et al., 1977). In the area of core requirements and basic skills a good example of the issues is reflected in the Alberta Department of Education policy discussion paper on Alberta Education and Diploma Requirements and various reactions to it (see Van Manen & Stewart, 1978). Another general debate on education in Ontario is contained in the final report of the Commission on Declining Enrolment (Jackson, 1979) and the Ministry of Education's response to the report (Ontario Ministry of Education, 1980).

39 There are no comparable data available from other provinces, but implementation research in several other provinces suggests that the results would not be radically different.

not have the resources to develop the best, validated products; and there is often limited knowledge across districts about what has been developed in other locations, little money for obtaining the materials, and less for engaging in in-service education to use them. Put more generally, provincial governments have not put much money into the development of validated exemplary curriculum materials or innovative projects.[40] Minor amounts have been provided in some provinces for learning materials development, and the Canada Studies Foundation (largely supported by federal funds) has attempted to address the absence of Canadian materials in social studies (Anderson & Benoit, 1980). But these add up to only a pittance. Nor am I suggesting that there should have been large amounts of money directed to curriculum materials. Development without a system of access to information and people (e.g., in-service assistance) would have been a waste of resources. The problem remains, however, that Canadian-based curriculum materials are not widely available,[41] and ways of aligning appropriate materials of high quality from whatever source with curriculum guidelines have not yet been well worked out.

The second aspect of the role of provincial ministries concerns how they go about introducing and following through on new and revised guidelines. They may do this either directly (using their own staff) or indirectly (by providing resources for implementation). In the direct role, most ministries of education provide orientation sessions throughout the province about the nature of the particular curriculum. This approach presents at least two problematic issues: geographical distances and the number of districts to reach may allow for only brief orientation sessions to district *representatives*;[42] and the ministry person conducting the sessions may not be thoroughly knowledgeable about the guideline and how to implement it, since it was probably developed by another group or another department.

Even if the orientation goes well, the real implementation difficulties lie beyond the introduction. In some cases, ministries have funded regional orientation workshops conducted by teachers, consultants, and others who had participated in developing the new guideline—that is, by those who were most knowledgeable about it. These pre-implementation workshops, no matter how stimulating, are at best limited to producing awareness, ideas, and interest in *attempting* implementation. As we have seen so often, it is *during* the initial attempts at implementation that assistance is most needed and is frequently unavailable.[43] The primary assumption about follow-up is that implementation is the responsibility of school districts, schools, and individual teachers. But whether they accept this responsibility depends on their priorities and processes as described in the relevant chapters in Part II. The ministries' role in follow-up

---

40 The exception may be Quebec, where the necessary French-language curriculum materials are otherwise unavailable.

41 There is serious concern that the Canadian curriculum is too influenced by textbooks and other materials developed in the United States, which are adapted or borrowed or otherwise find their way into the school (see Anderson & Benoit, 1980).

42 Thus, the individual teacher may receive *no* orientation; over 45% of the secondary school teachers in the Reading Assessment Survey said that they received no formal orientation to the Guide (Tuinman & Kendall, 1980, p. 152).

43 Downey et al.'s (1975) large-scale study of the social studies curriculum in Alberta found that pre-implementation workshops were not followed by much implementation in the classroom.

has varied over time and across provinces—from providing technical assistance, to clarifying and monitoring implementation, to conducting reviews for further policy revision. Not the least of the difficulties is vascillation and ambiguity as to whether ministry personnel are there to assist or to monitor implementation; and more fundamentally, there may be disagreement among ministry personnel about what should be emphasized in a curriculum guideline. Assistance is problematic for reasons already stated: numbers of people to reach, lack of knowledge about the change and/or the change process, and overlap or ambiguity—either in the minds of ministry personnel or in the views of school people—about the assistance vs. regulation roles.

Research studies asking teachers how helpful they find external groups confirm the relatively limited impact of ministry personnel. A representative sample of teachers in the British Columbia Social Studies Assessment rated the ministry of education lowest of eight external sources: on a helpfulness scale of 1 to 5 the mean rating for ministry personnel was 1.56 (Aoki et al., 1977, p. 55). Similar findings are reported in other surveys (Leithwood & MacDonald, 1981; Kormos, 1979). The limited impact of ministry personnel on local implementation is not surprising. Their numbers and resources are small in the face of the overwhelming number of schools and personnel within their jurisdiction. And it is a thankless task to bear responsibility for policies and programs which by virtue of the inherent difficulties in the implementation process never go smoothly.

Regulation or monitoring is just as difficult as providing assistance, since for many guidelines it is not at all clear exactly what implementation would look like, and since it is not easy to obtain valid implementation information concerning what is really happening in the classroom. In short, ministry personnel have their own problems of meaning about educational change.

### Evaluation/review

A third major responsibility of ministries of education is to assess the use and impact of public policy in education. There has been the familiar "accountability" trend in defining core subjects and testing student achievement, but it reaches nowhere the degree of specificity or compulsion that the "competency-based" movement has in the United States (see Wise, 1980). There are no compulsory provincial examinations. Nonetheless, most ministries have geared up for more evaluative data gathering. The most systematic and thorough by far is the British Columbia Learning Assessment Program (LAP). Mussio and Greer (1980, p. 29) state that the main objectives are to:

1. Monitor student achievement over time.
2. Assist curriculum developers at the provincial and local levels in the process of improving curriculum and developing suitable resource materials.
3. Provide information which can be used in determining the allocation of resources at provincial and district levels.
4. Provide direction for change in teacher education and professional development.
5. Provide direction for educational research.
6. Inform the public of some of the strengths and weaknesses of the public school system.

Provincewide data are gathered on student attitude and achievement and on attitudes and perceptions of parents, teachers, administrators, and other district staff on a wide variety of matters relating to the curriculum and its use. The assessments are carried out by independent teams, usually headed by a university faculty of education professor and including teachers, administrators, and ministry members. The general results are made public to all concerned; student achievement data by district are fed back to the districts for information and possible use (other data from the surveys are not separated and fed back by district). The assessments began in 1976 and operate on a cyclical schedule. The reading assessment is the first second-round evaluation to be completed, producing comparative, longitudinal information (Tuinman & Kendall, 1980); other assessments are in various stages of production according to the schedule.

The other provinces conduct regular reviews of curriculum and are moving in the direction of collecting more detailed, systematic information. Ontario is in the process of developing the Ontario Assessment Instrument Pool (OAIP), which is designed to provide an inventory of testing instruments to assess the achievement of objectives in the curriculum guidelines in each subject area (Ontario Ministry of Education, 1979). Program reviews are conducted in the various curriculum areas by ministry personnel, although most of the reviews are not seen as very effective by school people (see Fullan & Park, 1981). Cooperative reviews may also be carried out by agreement between a school system and the ministry and seem to be more successful. Whatever the case, all of the ministries of education in Canada are engaged in developing procedures for reviewing curriculum needs and quality, and are considering the question of how best to assess student learning.

The collection of evaluation data presents additional difficulties. The field of educational evaluation has burgeoned over the past decade, and in the same period has come the recognition that it is a very complicated business.[44] There are three major interrelated problem areas that seem to plague provincial curriculum assessments (and any program evaluation): *what information to collect*, *how to gather it*, and above all *how to use it*. I can only highlight some of the main issues. In simple terms the question of what information to collect can be divided into two categories: data on student achievement or what we might call *implementation outcomes*, and information on *implementation practice and difficulties* (e.g., teacher use in the classroom, quality of materials, forms of help available). The "what" question, then, concerns the range of information which is targeted for collection. Information on learning outcomes without other implementation data is very difficult to interpret and use; on the other hand, implementation data are very difficult to collect, particularly so because it is not always clear what implementation would look like in practice.

The question of how to gather information raises another set of issues. I leave aside the more technical methodological matters and mention what might be called "relationship" questions. These include questions of who does the review, of validity, and of ethics. The ministry may take greater or less control over the review, conducting the review itself or, as in the case of B.C., contracting it to a third party. Validity refers to whether the information obtained is an accurate reflection of what is actually happening (e.g., in terms of practices and

---

44 On the relationship between evaluation and implementation see Leithwood and Montgomery (1980) and Fullan (1980). I will not attempt to cite references from the mammoth and rapidly growing evaluation literature, but one very useful source is House (1980).

outcomes). Ethics refers to several delicate issues concerning how the information is to be used fairly and justly (see House, 1980).

The third key question—how to use the information—ties together the three sets of questions. What information is collected obviously shapes what can be potentially used. Information on learning outcomes, for example, without information on implementation practices/difficulties can create pressure for reform but not very constructive pressure, because it only indicates what the problem is, not how to address it. Additional information would be needed to confront the latter. How the data are collected affects the validity (for example, people don't usually provide accurate responses if they think the information might be used against them). If the information is not valid or is too general, it is poor for use.

Finally, even if reasonably accurate data have been obtained, the real problem lies in figuring out how the information can be used. Frankly, this gets us back to the *beginning* of the implementation process. Having information about what should be changed only puts us in a position of knowing (or thinking we know) *what* should be changed, not *how* to go about changing it—that is, how to set up an effective implementation process.[45] While finding ourselves back at GO sounds discouraging, evaluations can and do have an impact. Evaluators frequently make a distinction between summative and formative evaluation. The summative impact of provincial assessments is more visible, because the information can be used to revise policy, i.e., the curriculum guidelines, or materials. Note that this use of data does not directly affect *practice*—it alters policy and development, which may or may not lead to subsequent implementation (depending on the presence or absence of other factors). Formative impact occurs when the evaluative data are used to improve practice. Linking evaluative data to instructional improvement, as we saw earlier, requires a sophisticated system of relationships and activities. A large part of the problem relates to the lack of attention to the "black box" of implementation. Testing data provide information on the achievement of desired educational objectives. Implementation involves questions of which *instructional activities* would best address objectives. Unfortunately, much of the conflict and debate in education focuses on objectives and outcomes without attending to the critical intervening activities (i.e., instruction and learning activities) which link them together.[46]

The process of linking objectives, implementation activities, and evaluative data on achievement outcomes must operate at the district and school levels, as it has in some cases (see chapter 10, and Bank & Williams, 1981). Government agencies are limited in how much they can influence this level of utilization of evaluative information. Certainly they cannot command improvement to happen, any more than they can legislate any change into practice. They can, however, develop resources (materials, access to people) which provide support to districts (even put on pressure) to strengthen evaluation utilization procedures within the district.

---

45 Stated another way, the evaluation system should be integrated as part and parcel of any implementation plan (see Bank, 1981; Williams & Bank, 1981; Fullan, 1982; Alkin et al., 1979).
46 In chapter 3 and throughout the book I have suggested that implementation involves changes in the use of new materials, in new teaching behaviors, and in beliefs. Attention must be devoted to these kinds of changes as means to accomplishing particular educational objectives, if learning outcomes are to improve.

## Ministries' orientations to change

The ministries' role in development, implementation, and evaluation sum-marizes their major involvement in educational change, but more must be said about what the current trends seem to be. Three aspects that come to mind pertain to personnel, organization, and resources. The personnel question quite simply asks whether government agencies prepare their own members for roles as policy implementers. We have seen that preparation involves at least two components—knowledge of the policy or change, and knowledge of how to go about implementing the policy. How ministries approach these internal staff development needs is indicative of the extent to which they prepare for imple-mentation (as distinct from policy promulgation). We do not get the impression that governments in fact have attended to their own staff development needs regarding clarity, knowledge, and skills for engaging in major change efforts. If we insist that the school district's and the individual school's capacity for pro-cessing change is crucial, then government departments, inasmuch as they are in comparable learning situations, must also have the capacity for introducing and following up on new programs. Once again, professional development is not just for teachers and administrators.

Personnel development can be facilitated or constrained by the second aspect—organization. The internal communication and rapport across depart-ments within the ministry is at issue. If development, implementation, and evaluation are in separate departments which do not communicate and develop ongoing working relationships, we can predict that these matters will not be interrelated at the local-district level. Matters that cannot be resolved at the macro level should not be expected to coalesce at the micro level.

Resources, the third issue, concern the relative allocation of budget to each of the three main functions. Disproportionate allocation to any one or two areas would portend problems. Financial analyses are not available, but it would seem on the surface that ministries of education in the past have allocated vastly more to formulation of policy and to reviews than to supporting imple-mentation. This pattern may be partly related to the lack of explicit awareness of implementation issues (i.e., both what implementation is and what causes it) which have only been articulated in the past few years. If so, we can see how ministries will respond in the future to the press of implementation problems now that they have come to the fore.

In every province there are major policy initiatives—task forces to review the curriculum, new policies and services for special education and minority groups, emphasis on continuing education, and so on. The question of central interest in this section is whether ministries of education are approaching the issue of *implementation* differently. There are some indicators showing that they are. Most ministries have established implementation departments or units over the past few years. Several are taking concrete action. As an illustration, a new unit in British Columbia's Ministry of Education, entitled Program Implementation Services, began in 1978. It has developed a series of regional sessions and follow-through contacts focusing on new and revised curriculum guidelines. The work is heavily interactive, with staff spending most of their time in the field. A curriculum resource center was established in 1980 in the division to collect and disseminate locally developed and other curricular materials and guides related to all subject areas. Emphasis has been placed on implementation by providing in-service workshops on planning and implementation both for its own staff and for representatives from the 75 districts in the province. The unit is small, having only about five full-time members, but it draws heavily on staff from local districts as resources for summer institutes and regional workshops.

A second more specific example: In Alberta, to assist teachers in implementing the new social studies curriculum, the province has allocated $2 million in 1981/82; 125 experienced teachers (there are 138 school districts in the province) will have conducted workshops and provided follow-up assistance during the first months of attempted implementation from September 1981 to January 1982. The teachers were to be still employed by their boards, but with their salaries paid by the province.[47] In two other government reports the requirements for in-service education to support implementation are costed out with corresponding recommendations to provide resources for the introduction and follow-through on all new curricula (Alberta Department of Education, 1980; Fennell, 1980).

In Ontario, serious attention to implementation is reflected in the approach to new special education legislation (called Bill 82) passed in December 1980. Implementation is to be gradually phased in over five years (1980–85), with the province contributing to local boards by 1985 annual additional resources of $75 million. An elaborate implementation strategy has been formulated using regional teams, pilot boards during the first year, the orchestration of curriculum and other program resources, and in-service education through regional university faculties of education.

It is too early to tell whether these endeavors and those in other provinces will be successful, as most are just being launched. None will be sufficient to resolve all the problems of implementation, but it appears that provincial governments are taking a more explicit interest in changes at the level of practice.

# Guidelines for governments

Governments get lots of advice, and I will not attempt to add another long list of the ills of governments and what they should do differently. It is easy to treat governments as distant villains in the educational change process. While it is the case that government agencies and personnel should do some things differently if they wish to maximize their influence, our theory of meaning and change should generate considerable sympathy for their lot. The multi-level implementation process is, in a word, capricious. Government staff cannot abdicate their responsibility to oversee changes called for through legislative policy-making. Local educational personnel do not see the constant pressures on government staff to get a high-priority program delivered, to balance countless competing demands from above and below, when the total amount of time and resources is not nearly equal (and getting less equal) to the requirements of getting the job done. There is no reason to believe that civil servants are any less virtuous than the rest of us in wanting to see school improvements made.

---

47 The characteristics of effective in-service or assistance programs are taken up in chapter 14. How much impact the new approach in Alberta will have will depend on whether the assistance program possesses or develops many of these characteristics. It is also obvious that the number of teachers and the time-line may not be enough. But it is a step in the right direction.

Within this context of the difficulties of bringing about large-scale change, I will suggest a small number of major guidelines to highlight some of the things governments will have to do and emphasize, if they expect their policies and programs to stand a better chance of becoming implemented in practice.[48] In the most general sense, of course, the advice is to understand the principles and processes of what makes for effective change (as, for example, described in this book) as a basis for generating particular approaches and follow-through support for implementation. Beyond this I will suggest five broad, mutually reinforcing guidelines relating to (1) compliance vs. capacity; (2) relationships and expectations among government levels and between government agencies and local districts; (3) resources for program development and in-service and technical assistance among government levels; (4) the question of how governments prepare their own staff for introducing, facilitating, and monitoring change; and (5) the need for an explicit implementation plan, and government commitment and interest in *implementation results*.

## 1. Understanding the difference between compliance and capacity

The most insightful and simply stated version of this guideline is contained in Elmore's (1980) 39-page booklet. He writes: "There is a critical difference between the ability or willingness of implementors to comply with rules and their capacity to successfully deliver a service. Implementation depends more on capacity than it does on compliance" (p. 37). Governments are legally responsible for ensuring compliance with policies, but there are limits to what can be accomplished through regulation. If governments confine themselves to a regulatory role, two things happen which actually interfere with implementation.

First, because the levels and parts of educational systems are "loosely coupled," and because program change is not simple to assess, it requires tremendous energy to find out what is happening; the more preoccupied governments become with surveillance in such a situation, the more energy must be spent at all levels on administrative paperwork, reporting, and other compliance-type information.[49]

The second and related reason why preoccupation with compliance hinders implementation is that it diverts energies and attention away from developing local capacity to make improvements. Elmore (1980, p. 12) suggests that policy-makers should tend more to discovering the state of local capacity for program delivery and to figuring out ways of supporting, guiding, and prodding its further development. As we have seen, some government agencies are primarily concerned with their regulatory and bureaucratic role, while others

---

48 For those interested in more extended discussions of the role of governments in educational and other social program implementation there are several recent good sources in the U.S. See Bardach (1977); Berman and McLaughlin (1978); Chabotar, Louis, and Rosenblum (1980); Cowden and Cohen (1979); Crandall et al. (forthcoming); Elmore (1979–80); Gideonse (1979, 1980); Kirst (1979); Levin (1981); McDonnell and McLaughlin (1980, ch. 5); Turnbull (1980); Williams (1980).

49 Turnbull (1980) refers to testimony before Congress that federal regulations in education account for 40% of all paperwork in the local school districts; Hill (1980) found that 25% of the administrative paperwork of school principals related to federal requirements.

take a more direct interest in the substance of the program and whether it is actually working.[50] Stated another way, if a program is not working in certain settings, governments should know whether the reasons have more to do with competing priorities, lack of resources, skills, and leadership (i.e., capacity issues) or with diversion of funds, outright resistance, etc. (i.e., compliance). If capacity is the problem, increased surveillance will not help and may hinder actual implementation.[51] There is no simple solution, because governments must be concerned with both compliance and capacity; it will be necessary to decide on the balance of attention and resources to be devoted to each of these two aspects.

Focusing on capacity, as Elmore indicates, is more challenging, difficult, and interesting than only gathering compliance information. The implication of guideline 1 is that U.S. federal government program grantors should pay attention to how the capacity of state education agencies can be supported and further developed. (The move to block grants may facilitate this stance, since less federal resources are required for regulatory information-gathering.[52]) State agencies in turn should determine how they could relate to intermediate and local agencies. In Canada provincial ministries of education would consider how they can work with local districts more effectively in this regard.

*Guideline 1, then, advises governments to concentrate on helping to improve the capacity of other agencies to implement changes.*

## 2. Relationships and expectations

It may seem as if de-emphasizing compliance is tantamount to allowing receiving agencies to do as they please. Paradoxically, concentrating on capacity requires more interaction and yields greater knowledge of what local agencies are attempting to do. We have seen several problems in the federal/state/local and provincial/local relationships. Ambitious and unique goals, unclear expectations, and episodic or nonexistent contact characterize government/local relationships in many program change efforts.

*Guideline 2 stresses the importance of governments' being clear about what the policy is and spending time interacting with local agencies about the meaning, expec-*

---

50 To illustrate the importance of this distinction, information on how many children participated in a program, how many teachers were involved in in-service sessions, etc. tells nothing about whether the program is working to bring about the intended changes. I said earlier in this chapter that evaluation information frequently does not have an impact; it requires a sophisticated evaluation system for program improvement to be effected, and this system is related more to capacity-building than to control through compliance.

51 Cowden and Cohen (1979, p. 91) observe that for the odd major program governments can pour in tremendous resources (money, power, and knowledge) and have an impact, but it is not feasible to do this very often, because the resources required to enforce the change in this manner are prohibitive (not to mention the value question of whether governments should make changes this way).

52 The implication of consolidation (block grants) vs. categorical programs is controversial because of the various pros and cons (see Levin, 1981; Turnbull, 1980). Block grants allow states more leeway in deciding on priorities, which in some cases may result in less money being directed at groups now targeted by federal policy, but may result in more implementation for those priorities which are selected (because they are the priorities selected by the state). In any case, the major categorical programs still exist (e.g., Title I); and furthermore, a capacity-development orientation can be taken regardless of whether the basis of funding is block or categorical.

*tations, and needs in relation to local implementation.* There are some cases of outright rejection of change when local districts simply do not value or actively dislike certain policies; but in most of the research studies cited in this chapter, local districts (or state agencies vis-à-vis federal departments) desired *more* clarification and *more* assistance in implementing adopted programs, which government personnel were often reluctant to provide (perhaps because they did not really understand how the policy could be implemented). At the outset, Elmore (1980, p. 29) recommends, the smart policy-maker will say, "Before we go too far with this idea, can you tell me what it will look like in practice?" Once a policy is on its way, it is necessary for government personnel to devote time to interacting with implementers and to demonstrating that program change in practice is a priority. The benefits are in both directions. First, since the problem of meaning is inevitable when people first contend with a new policy, there must be plenty of opportunities to ask for clarification and assistance. When federal or state agencies clarify expectations and respond to requests for assistance, it increases the likelihood of implementation.[53] Second, through this interaction government personnel find out about the realities and needs of implementation. But it is a more challenging role, because it requires going beyond the superficial piety of espousing new social policies into the reality of the implementation quagmire.

## 3. Resources for program development and technical assistance

Governments do seem to have had an impact on change in practice in some program areas in recent years, and they have done this by providing resources for two essential aspects of implementation. They have funded the development and validation of quality products or programs, and they have allocated corresponding resources to support in-service assistance during implementation. But it is only in the past few years and only in some program areas that these twin requirements have been met. Most school systems and individuals within them are caught up in the demands of coping with everyday problems. When new policies are introduced, there is little resource slack available for program development and/or learning on one's own.

*Guideline 3, therefore, recommends that for any new policy, governments should see to it that they or someone else is addressing and looking at the program development and in-service assistance needs.*

## 4. The preparation of government staff

The previous three guidelines assume that the government has its own house in order. If this is not the case, we can hardly expect government staff to extend clarity and support to others. Gideonse (1980, p. 67) comments on the problem: "What is needed is a consciousness on the part of top management on down that the daily life of the organization is at least as important as the delib-

---

53 We saw this in several studies: for example, in Title I (Orland & Goettel, 1980); in parent advisory councils (Keesling, 1980; Melaragno et al., 1981); in Title IV (McDonnell & McLaughlin, 1980); and so on.

erations on high policy, for it is in the daily life that that policy is implemented. If the atmosphere is sour, so will be the implementation." Middle- and lower-level government staff are the ones who are more directly responsible for implementation, and, says Gideonse (p. 68), "they are often quite unknowledgeable about the background rationale that shaped the thinking of key decisions." The problem can be especially acute when there are regional as well as central offices (as is the case in most provinces in Canada and most states in the U.S.). Williams (1980, p. 112) stresses the importance of knowledge and competence among field (regional) staff for implementation.

*Whether central or regional staff are being considered, guideline 4 suggests that government agency leaders should take special steps to ensure that their own staff, especially those who have the most direct contact with the field, have the opportunity to develop knowledge and competence regarding the policy and program, as well as in how to facilitate implementation* (again, competence in the *content of the change* and in the *change process* respectively). This is not just a matter of having periodic workshops or other training opportunities for staff; it really must be accomplished in the daily decision-making, communication, planning, and implementation activities engaged in by government staff. (See also Berman's 1978 description of macro implementation.)

## 5. The need for an explicit implementation plan

*Guideline 5 is implicit in the previous guidelines: namely, the underlying assumption is that an explicit implementation plan is needed to guide the process of bringing about change in practice.* One of the foundations for such a plan, as Williams (1980, p. 101) observes, is that top leaders must really *want* better implementation to the point of continually asking staff and local personnel about implementation, committing resources to support implementation, and being realistic but insistent about progress. "At basic issue," says Williams, "is whether the agency can alter its orientation and style of decision making to develop the resources and the organizational structure needed for *implementing* the implementation perspective" (italics in original).

A few writers have offered more specific guidelines as to how "implementation analysis" and planning may be carried out. Elmore (1980, p. 3) talks about the importance of "reasoning through implementation problems *before* policy decisions are firmly made" (his italics). He outlines a set of guiding questions for doing "backward mapping": "instead of beginning at the top of the system with a new policy and reasoning through a series of actions required to implement it, begin at the bottom of the system, with the most concrete set of actions, and reason backward to the policy" (Elmore, 1980, p. 29). Bardach (1977, pp. 264–66) recommends a series of guidelines for writing "an implementation scenario" and stresses the importance of having a "fixer": someone at the top who takes an active interest in probing and fixing implementation problems.

As implementation gets under way, the critical supporting elements are those identified in the previous guidelines: balancing the relative emphasis on compliance and capacity; setting up information-gathering procedures which are most likely to influence local action; fostering interaction between local personnel and government staff and others external to the local district; promoting program development and technical assistance resources; and enhancing the capabilities of in-house staff to work effectively among themselves and with local and regional agencies.

A final word of caution. Leaving aside the question of whose values and goals should be pursued, there are serious practical limitations to how much governments can directly determine what happens in practice. We might think of two kinds of roles for governments in social change, both of which would be carried out depending on the policy area: one role could be labeled *social experimentation* or development, and the other *legislative implementation*.

Bearing in mind a combination of factors (the impossibility of forcing widespread change in practice, the uncertainty about what programs are most needed and soundly developed, and the lack of resources at the local level to plan for needed changes), some authors suggest that one major role (among others) for governments is to support the development and dissemination of promising programs (see Cowden & Cohen, 1979, p. 98; McDonnell & McLaughlin, 1980, pp. 102–107). The chief source of change is not pressure but the promotion of bright ideas and programs and the stimulation of exchanges and assistance in relation to using them. This works as a form of social experimentation and voluntarism, somewhat similar to the way the Follow Through and NDN programs operate.

Legislative implementation concerns the putting into practice of high-priority social policies such as education for the handicapped or improving the learning of basic skills. Here the interest and role on the part of government in insisting on implementation are much stronger, although the earlier guidelines still apply: that is, it is not possible to enforce program improvement by legislation and surveillance alone.

The length of this chapter gives some indication of just how entangled and dilemma-ridden the role of governments in implementation really is. Federal/state/regional/local relationships in the U.S. and federal/provincial/regional/local relationships in Canada represent intimidating challenges for those who wish to comprehend—let alone influence—school improvement. Opportunity for input into shaping reforms is needed at all levels. Inequality of education is not likely to be addressed adequately at the local level either because of discrimination (intended or not) or because of lack of resources for developing and learning to use needed program changes. Similarly, acceptable solutions are not likely to be designed at the policy level, because variations in local situations and priorities require variations in solutions, and/or because local institutions vary in their commitment and capacity to implement new policies.[54] In either case governments have a legitimate and essential role in educational reform because *problems of equity and program quality are unlikely to be resolved at the local level*.

Nor are we talking about the achievement of perfect solutions. The more realistic goal is to achieve better implementation in a greater number of situations. What with the rapidity of change and expansion and the lack of knowledge about implementation over the past fifteen years, government leaders can

---

54 See Wise (1979, ch. 6) for one useful discussion of equity and program improvement.

be forgiven for devoting resources to policy and program *development* in education, and for not understanding how socially complex and difficult the *implementation process* is. They are in a better position now to redress this imbalance and to test in the next decade whether significant educational change is indeed possible.

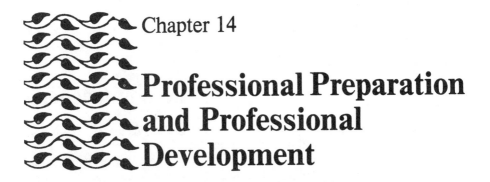

Chapter 14

# Professional Preparation and Professional Development

*The fact is that our primary value concerns our need to help ourselves change and learn, for us to feel that we are growing in our understanding of where we have been, where we are, and what we are about, and that we are enjoying what we are doing . . . . To help others to change without this being preceded* and *accompanied by an exquisite awareness of the process in ourselves is "delivering a product or service" which truly has little or no significance for our personal or intellectual growth.*

— *Sarason (1972), p. 122 (his emphasis)*

Educational change involves *learning* how to do something new. It is for this reason that if any single factor is crucial to change, it is professional development.[1] As obvious as that is, it is extremely difficult to establish effective professional development programs either at the pre- or in-service stages. I consider first, and comparatively briefly, the pre-service question. What training do teachers receive which makes it more likely or less likely that they will be prepared to cope with change? In the second section I pursue the question of the continuous professional development of teachers, for it is the role of in-service education which is most central to school change. In-service education is central for two reasons. First, under the best of circumstances, pre-service education can only scratch the surface of the realities of educational change for the simple reason that these realities can only be fully grasped once people are on the job. The second reason why in-service education is more significant is that relatively fewer new teachers are being hired: so that for any given change effort the vast majority of participants are those with some experience.[2] Thus, the chances for change depend on educators in the existing work force and their opportunities for development.

In a later section of this chapter the preparation and professional development of non-teaching personnel—administrators/consultants—will be examined to see how these would-be change agents learn or don't learn to manage,

---

1 I use the terms "in-service education," "staff development," and "professional development" interchangeably.

2 New teachers still represent a very important group, because their overall numbers spread across the whole system can be substantial and because their attitudes, skills, and experiences in the first years of teaching obviously can influence them for the rest of their careers.

lead, and support change efforts. In the final section I summarize the main implications in the form of a set of guidelines for effective professional development.

# The preparation of teachers

The time-frame I use for considering the preparation of teachers covers the pre-service teacher education program and the first year or two of teaching (often called the induction years).[3] The first year of teaching provides the first critical moment for examining the issues surrounding preparation.

In considering teacher education, I will not attempt to do justice to all the specialized and alternative programs which may be found among the 1300 teacher education institutions in the U.S. and the 50 faculties of education in Canada. Instead, I take up three themes most directly related to the question of change: the theory/practice dilemma (including the practicum), preparation within the formal program for engaging in educational change, and the experiences of the beginning teacher.

The question of balance and integration of theory and practice has plagued teacher educators and student teachers for decades. The learning theories in psychology, the socialization and social interaction theories in sociology, the philosophies of education, and the application of theory-based teaching techniques across the subject areas have remained sources of promise, frustration, and confusion. Most student teachers will say that they get too much theory, that it is irrelevant and a waste of time. Many professors of education, especially those in the social science disciplines, will argue that students get too little theory, that they are uninterested in developing a solid grounding in theories of education and teaching. Most seem to agree, however, that the *integration* of theory and practice is a desirable if elusive goal. For example, in a Canada-wide survey of faculty and students in 11 English-speaking faculties of education (25% of the total number in Canada) we asked a sample of 1400 students and 500 faculty members for their assessment of how much importance was actually attached to certain goals in their institutions, and how much importance they thought should be attached to them. One of these goals was "to prepare teachers who can integrate theory and practice." Students and faculty had essentially the same views: while about 30% of each group thought that their institution actually attached a strong emphasis to this goal (calculated by those who responded "great" or "very great" on a five-point scale), about 90% thought that this goal should receive a strong emphasis (Fullan, Wideen, et al., forthcoming). This discrepancy between the real and the ideal was one of the largest among the nine goal areas we asked about.

As the teaching market has become tighter, the trend in teacher education has been to attempt to make the preparation period more practically useful. Internships, collaborative relationships between universities and local school

---

3 The Instructional Improvement and Implementation group at NIE are conducting a major research program on teacher staff development covering all phases of development divided into three parts: pre-service, induction (first three years of teaching), and in-service. My thanks to Joe Vaughan of NIE for sending me various reports from several of the projects (see Vaughan et al., 1980).

systems, and the gradual extension of the practice teaching component characterize this trend. It has been greeted with some satisfaction on the part of student teachers, school people, and some faculty of education professors (along
with unease on the part of other professors). The more recent debate on the
value of lengthening the practice teaching component has also sharpened the
dilemma. First, there is the problem of overall amount of time. For each hour
the field-based component is increased, there is a corresponding decrease in
academic training. Many educators observe that the total amount of time available to prepare teachers is insufficient, and that teachers get less preparation for
their work than any other professionals (see Denemark, 1979). Whether this
problem can be practically resolved at the pre-service stage is an open question,
but its existence reinforces the view that support at the induction phase and
continued in-service education are essential.

Second, there is the question of whether increasing the field component will
result in better-prepared and more thoughtful teachers. Tabachnick et al.
(1979–80) in the United States report on an intensive study of 12 student
teachers in a four-semester program which had one semester devoted to practical work in the classroom and seminar discussions about it. They note:

Student teaching typically involved a véry limited range of classroom activities. When
student teachers were observed, they were most often engaged in the rather routine
and mechanical teaching of precise and short-term skills, in testing and grading children, or in "management procedures." (p. 14)

They also observed that student teachers frequently worked with prepackaged
curriculum materials: "Typically, the students tended to follow the lessons contained in these materials somewhat rigidly rather than using them as guides"
(p. 15). The student teachers' work was determined by several factors: "the
structure of the school day; the pre-determination of curriculum and content
and materials; an emphasis on order, control and busyness" (p. 14). The
finding is similar to what Clifton (1979) reports in his Canadian study—that
practice teaching is very much a question of "survival in a marginal situation."
Tabachnick et al. conclude: "There is no justification in our results for the naive
notion that practical experience *must* be useful in introducing students to a wide
range of teaching abilities" (p. 27; their italics). They recall Dewey's admoni-
tion: "It is a mistake to assume that any experience is intrinsically desirable,
apart from its ability to evoke a certain quality of response in individuals."

Teaching, as we have seen earlier (chapter 7), suffers from the lack of opportunity that teachers have as individuals and particularly in interaction with other
teachers to reflect, to observe, to discuss, to plan. Field-based student teaching,
if Tabachnick, Clifton, and others are correct, can have even more of an
unreflective quality if the students' energies are devoted to adjusting and to
attempting to follow other people's orders. There is nothing wrong with this in
itself. Student teachers must learn how to cope with the demands of the classroom. Nor is the problem of lack of reflection in field-based programs inevitable. Smith (1980) formulates a "design for a school of pedagogy" which is
heavily field-based but also attempts to relate field experiences to the types of
knowledge and pedagogical theories necessary for effective teaching. However,
it is only a "design," not an implemented program. By most empirical counts,
the actual field experience of student teachers tends toward learning how to

adjust to the existing system (see also Fenstermacher, 1979), not preparation for change—the theme to which I now turn.[4]

To implement educational changes, teachers have to be able to assess the potential need for and quality of the changes, have certain basic skills in a range of teaching methods, planning, diagnosing, and evaluation, and be able to modify instructional activities continually in an attempt to meet the needs of individual students. More broadly, they must have abilities which are barely (if at all) touched by the formal teacher education program: interacting with and learning from peers, using and relating to subject consultants, relating to the principal, talking to and working with parents. In short, not only are there difficulties in learning how to use new methods (such as applying theory to practice), but also there is almost a total neglect of the phenomenon of how changes are and can be introduced and implemented. In our national survey in Canada we asked student teachers and faculty to what extent the program did and should "prepare teachers who have the perceptions and skills to implement changes in the schools." There was agreement in the two groups: only 15% in each group indicated that this goal was receiving "great" or "very great" emphasis, while 73% of the faculty and 64% of the students thought that it should.[5] Goals that were viewed as actually receiving the highest emphasis involved preparing teachers "who were knowledgeable in subject areas" and "who can adapt to and work within existing school systems."

Let us take one final indicator of teacher preparation: what happens to the beginning teacher. There is a word which sums up the experiences of most first-year teachers—nerve-racking. Until the past few years not much attention has been paid to the plight of the beginning teacher, who in most cases has to step in on Day One and attempt to do the same work as the twenty-year veteran (and maybe more if the first-year teacher is given some of the worst classes). Ryan and his colleagues (1980) provide one of the more readable accounts of the ups and downs of the beginning teacher in their brief profiles of the personal and professional lives of 12 teachers during their first year on the job. The National Institute of Education sponsored a detailed study of induction programs for beginning teachers carried out by Educational Testing Services (in four volumes, listed under McDonald & Elias, 1980). The title of the first volume indicates the nature of the story: *The Problems of Beginning Teachers: A Crisis in Training*. In the study the authors examine several programs across the U.S. and review the research literature on the beginning teacher. They report

---

4 The issue of internships, the extended practicum, and the like is much more complicated than I have been able to address. Some studies find that the practicum is the most valued part of the program (again, not necessarily that which produces change); others, that student self-concept and motivation to become a teacher actually can decrease during extended practice teaching (e.g., Covert & Clifton, 1980). For a review of some exemplary programs based on internships, support during induction, and collaboration between the university, local districts, and sometimes state agencies, see Elias et al. (1980, vol. II) and Howey and Bents (1979). Ratsoy et al. report on the evaluation of the extended practicum in Alberta. While some programs attempt to give students more practical experience and even focus on innovative practices and skill development, the main point of the above discussion is that there is a tendency in both the status and experience of student teaching toward *routine*, and that this should be examined critically in any program. In any case, more research is needed on evaluating field components of pre-service programs (Vaughan et al., 1980). See Gitlin (1982) for program integrating theory/practice.

5 The 15% was the lowest percentage among nine different goals we asked about, although another goal was rated equally low: "to prepare teachers who have the ability to analyze critically the existing school system."

that the experiences of the first-year teacher have not been studied to much extent, and that the research which has been conducted indicates that it is a traumatic period in which the teacher receives little help. They describe what they call some "facts" of their investigation:

1. Almost all teachers experience the transition period into teaching as the most difficult aspect of their teaching life and career. There apparently are some teachers who move into teaching smoothly and efficiently, but the majority report the period is one of great difficulty and even trauma.
2. The major kinds of problems and difficulties that teachers experience are readily identifiable. Most of them relate to the management and conduct of instruction. These problems are so critical that it is easy to overlook the equally obvious fact that the range of problems includes difficulties with evaluating pupils, being evaluated by the administration, working with parents, developing a consistent teaching style, finding out how the school functions, knowing the rules that must be followed, and a variety of other problems.
3. The least studied aspect of this transition period is the fear, anxiety, and feelings of isolation and loneliness which appear to characterize it. There is sufficient information in existing reports to indicate that these feelings are not uncommon; however, individual conversations with teachers are far more revealing than the current literature.
4. Almost all teachers report that they went through this transition period "on their own." They had little or no help available, and found help only through their own initiative. This help usually took the form of seeking out some other teacher in whom they could confide....
5. There is probably a strong relationship between how the teacher passes through the transition period and how likely they are to progress professionally to higher levels of competence and endeavor. (McDonald, 1980, vol. I, pp. 42–43)

McDonald and Elias (Elias et al., 1980, vol. II) also identified 24 exemplary programs which were attempting to help the new teacher through the first year or years of teaching. They carried out case studies of four of these programs and provided brief profiles of the others. All of the exemplary programs were characterized by considerable inter-agency cooperation (e.g., a consortium of school districts, co-planning and cooperation between universities and school systems). People seemed mostly satisfied with the results of the programs. Two qualifiers should be noted: the programs in question were selected as exemplary, had innovative designs, etc.—that is, they were atypical; and there is still an absence of data on the relationship between these programs and innovative behavior of their graduates.

Nonetheless, there is a growing interest in the needs of the beginning teacher and the relationship between pre-service and in-service needs of new teachers. One of the more influential documents in this regard was the James Report (1972) in the United Kingdom. In this government report on teacher education, it was recommended that probationary teachers have a reduced teaching load (75% load) and additional release time to attend induction workshops within their schools or at regional teacher centers; that professional tutors be appointed within each school to provide training and support for probationers; and that external centers be developed in teacher education institutions and teacher centers to conduct workshop activities for tutors and probationers. Bolam et al. (1979) conducted an independent evaluation of the first pilot scheme of the program involving two large districts. They found not only that the program had a major effect on the new teachers, but that other staff members benefited, as did inter-agency cooperation between the teacher education institution and/or teacher centers and the local authority. Questions of how best to train tutors, how to extend the benefits to the rest of the staff, and especially how to establish the program nationally in all local authorities (given both financial and technical difficulties) as was the intention of the recommendation, remain as serious problems. But some progress is being made, partially sustained by the success of the pilot efforts.

In the meantime, in the U.S., programs such as those identified by McDonald and Elias (1980) and others continue to be developed.[6] The vast majority of new teachers, however, do not have access to such programs. As Ryan (1979) observes with all seriousness, the main goal of the first-year teacher is often simply (actually not so simply) to become a second-year teacher.

An underlying implication of much of this research is that student teachers and new teachers have certain developmental needs. The work of Frances Fuller (1969) and those who have built on her research formalizes this idea. Essentially, this work shows that new teachers tend initially to be preoccupied with self and management concerns (e.g., feeling adequate, being accepted, maintaining class control) and more gradually come to focus on task and impact concerns (e.g., instructional materials, teaching approaches, student learning).[7]

Let us return to the overall question of the initial preparation of teachers in order to draw several conclusions. The first and foremost idea I would suggest is that no matter how well prepared the student teacher is, there are fundamental social and developmental needs once he or she begins in that first job. Second, there is a natural conservative tendency on the part of the student teacher and beginning teacher, the school in which he or she works, and the teacher education institution: the pressure is on to get, adjust to, and keep a job. Third, we can speculate that what happens to the new teacher in his or her first exposure to the classroom—as a student and in the first one to three years of teaching— will have lasting effects on attitudes and behavior on the job. Fourth, some pre-service programs and some induction-year programs have been established to support and facilitate the development of new teachers.

Initial teacher education, no matter how wonderful the program is, is severely limited in what it can do to prepare teachers to implement changes. The amount of curriculum to be covered in terms of available time, the practical necessity of preparing students who can get jobs, the situation of the beginning teacher who enters as a junior member of an ongoing organization with established patterns of work, and above all the fact that learning how to implement educational changes requires skills and experiences which must be to a significant extent learned on the job—all inhibit the likelihood that the first-year teacher will be an influential change agent.[8]

---

6 See also Howey and Bents (1979) and Zeichner (1979). Zeichner compares induction programs in the U.S. and the U.K. He identifies 11 programs in the U.S. and reports generally favorable results.

7 For one application of this research see Adams et al. (1980); Loucks and Hall (1979) have further developed and applied the concept of developmental concerns or stages of concern to how teachers react to innovations (see the next section below).

8 The first-year teacher, of course, can bring fresh ideas and/or can be more open to learning new things on the job, but these are only *potentials*. The conditions for in-service education for new and continuing teachers, throughout their careers, represent the most critical variables in relation to whether these potentials get further developed.

# The professional development of teachers

How often do you hear statements to the effect that the continuous professional development of teachers is the key to school improvement? Like so many other single-factor solutions to multifaceted phenomena, the *general* endorsement of in-service education means nothing without an accompanying understanding of *the characteristics of effective as compared to ineffective in-service education efforts.* Nothing has promised so much and has been so frustratingly wasteful as the thousands of workshops and conferences which led to no significant change in practice when the teachers returned to their classrooms. Neither teacher participants nor workshop leaders are satisfied with the results of their efforts.

In a review of in-service education two years ago, I summarized the reasons for failure in seven points:

1 One-shot workshops are widespread but are ineffective.
2 Topics are frequently selected by people other than those for whom the in-service is intended.
3 Follow-up support for ideas and practices introduced in in-service programs occurs in only a very small minority of cases.
4 Follow-up evaluation occurs infrequently.
5 In-service programs rarely address the individual needs and concerns (see Hall & Loucks, 1978).
6 The majority of programs involve teachers from many different schools and/or school districts, but there is no recognition of the differential impact of positive and negative factors within the systems to which they must return.
7 There is a profound lack of any conceptual basis in the planning and implementing of in-service programs that would ensure their effectiveness. (Fullan, 1979, p. 3)

Ironically, despite education being our bread and butter, our approaches to in-service education of our own members have been based on weak conceptions of how learning occurs.[9]

In building an understanding of what constitutes effective professional development, and why most approaches fail, I will start with two basic questions. What is educational change? What makes it succeed? From these two questions I will proceed to describe five case examples of effective in-service programs in order to illustrate why and how they succeeded. I will then (somewhat obviously) return to the issue of why the majority of professional development efforts do not work. Finally, I will conclude with the overview question of what professional development opportunities are available to teachers.

## What is change and what makes it succeed?

Now to the first-order question: What is educational change? Or, more pointedly, what is teacher change? Professional development, when it occurs,

---

9 For other reviews of in-service education see Howey and Joyce (1978), Lawrence (1974), McLaughlin and Marsh (1978), Rubin (1978). Flanders (1980) reports other relevant views on the dissatisfaction of teachers with professional development experiences.

implies, of course, that there has been or will be some *development*, some *change*. So I start with the question of what is meant by development or change. In chapter 3 I discussed the meaning of change around the notion of what it entails for the individual. I suggested that it involves at least two broad components, pertaining to what one *thinks* (new beliefs, philosophy, theories, knowledge, attitudes, etc.) and what one *does* (use of new materials, new skills, new behavior, etc.). At this abstract level—some illustrations will come shortly— when teachers engage in a professional development activity, they are partaking in something which raises and/or advocates the possibility of changes in beliefs and behavior with all that this might involve regarding new theories, knowledge, and skills in attempting to improve practice.[10]

And the second basic question: What makes change succeed? In chapter 5 the analysis of the implementation process provided some answers to this question. Four sets of characteristics were discussed: those relating to the innovation itself, to the school district, to the school, and to factors external to the local school system. The general relationship of these factors to professional development is fairly clear. For change to succeed, we found, (1) the innovation has to represent a real need; it has to be reasonably clear or at least become clear over time; and (2) the school district, (3) the schools, and (4) the external system have to support the implementation process in various ways. Professional development is central to each of these four sets of characteristics—that is, it is central to the entire process of change. Specifically, we found (1) that professional development must focus on a need; (2) that the emphasis on in-service education on the part of the school district in relation to principals and teachers is essential; and (3) that teachers must have the opportunity to interact with each other, share ideas, and help one another, and must have some external assistance from the principal, district consultant, or others outside the school. If we define professional development as learning new things thought to be desirable, we can see that the implementation process is precisely the same. The extent to which the relatively formal (e.g., workshops) and informal (e.g., sharing ideas and help) professional development activities succeed is the extent to which change succeeds.

## Case examples of successful professional development

We can now consider several specific examples of successful professional development endeavors in order to see what their characteristics are. Five particular and diverse illustrations will be used: (1) Stallings's (1980) description of the in-service approach used to teach basic reading skills at the secondary level; (2) Pratt et al.'s (1980) and Melle et al.'s (1981) study of the in-service program in Jefferson County school district to improve the teaching of science at the elementary school level; (3) Huberman's (1981) case study of the ECRI reading program adopted in Masepa school district (one of the case studies of the DESSI program—Crandall et al., forthcoming); (4) Elliott's (1976–77, 1979, 1980) action research in the United Kingdom based on how teachers learn;

---

10 This applies both to situations in which teachers decide on the direction of the change and to those cases where someone else makes the initial decision (e.g., the principal or superintendent).

and (5) the work of Bruce Joyce and his associates in California (Joyce & Showers, 1980, 1981; Joyce, 1978; McKibbin & Joyce, 1980).

## A secondary school reading program

Stallings carried out a four-phase study in several districts in California focusing on the teaching of secondary school teachers to improve reading skills of students. In phase I the researchers observed in 46 classrooms to examine the relationship between what teachers did to address reading problems and what students achieved. The result of this phase was the identification of specific instructional approaches which seemed to work.[11] In phase II, they used the findings from phase I to work with 51 teachers—half were trained, and the other half (the control group) received training only at the end of the experimental period. In phase III teachers were trained to conduct workshops (16 days training time) and subsequently conducted the basic series of workshops for other teachers in the district. In phase IV, selected teachers were trained to act as leaders of training programs in their own districts.

When the most successful activities in phase I were identified, in the second phase a group of 26 teachers were trained in the use of these activities (a control group of 25 teachers received no training). The teachers who were trained attended seven workshops, held one week apart. Each workshop was 2½ hours in duration, a total of 17½ hours of training. Using pretest and posttest data the authors found that the teachers who were trained did use the instructional activities and did achieve greater gains in student reading ability over the year. Of the 31 criterion variables (measuring the implementation of specific instructional activities) the trained teachers changed over the school year on 25, while the control teachers changed on only three. Phase III was interesting because it allowed comparison of the effectiveness of workshops led by teachers with workshops led by the project leaders. In following up the impact on classroom practice, the authors found that teacher-led groups performed equally as well as the group led by the project leaders. (Both groups implemented 17 of the 26 criterion activities used as indicators.)

Taking the project as a whole, various evidence is presented which shows changes in classroom practice and gains in student achievement. Stallings concludes that the project "left the districts with a cadre of teacher trainers to carry on the process of teaching secondary teachers effective instructional methods ...." Based on the evidence the project was validated by the Joint Dissemination Review Panel and is now in the National Diffusion Network (see chapter 13).

## A school district in-service program

We have already seen something of Jefferson County in chapter 10. The Pratt et al. (1980) paper focuses on the relationship of staff development to implementation of a new science curriculum. The district linked up with the Concerns Based Adoption Model team at the University of Texas (Loucks & Hall, 1979).

---

11 The researchers found, for example, that students made more gains in classrooms where the teachers spent more time instructing, discussing homework, providing corrective and supportive feedback, having students read aloud in small groups, etc. They then designed workshops for phase II which were based on these findings.

They collaborated in designing an approach to in-service which included the following elements: (1) 23 teachers were selected and trained as in-service leaders; (2) the district altered the original intention so that, instead of conducting a three-day in-service workshop for all teachers at the beginning of the school year, it spread the in-service activities over the year, working with one-third of the schools at a time; (3) the individualized developmental nature of the in-service was stressed: care was taken to provide teachers with some one-to-one contact between in-service sessions; workshops were designed around small-group activities matched to needs and interests of teachers (with the "stages of concern" model[12] used to do the matching); (4) at later phases of the work (when its critical importance was discovered) principals were trained to provide support for implementation. The extent of change in classroom practice was measured and found to be progressively more evident (see Melle & Pratt, 1981, and the description of Jefferson County in chapter 10). One of the interesting aspects of their program is the systematic attention to all teachers new to the district. New teachers to a program, whether they are first-year teachers, those from other districts, or even those within the district who change teaching assignments from school to school or grade level to grade level, receive in-service training.[13]

## An NDN program

Huberman (1981) conducted a case study of one school district's use of the JDRP-validated ECRI program. He found widespread implementation in the classrooms of Masepa school district (pseudonym). Two of the explanatory factors singled out were related to professional development: "the quality and amount of technical assistance" and "sustained central office and building level support" (Huberman, 1981, p. iii). The district arranged for certain principals and teachers (who would serve as in-service leaders) to receive training at the developer's "exemplary center for reading instruction."[14] All teacher users received training and follow-up assistance from the principal (trained as an ECRI leader) and/or other resource staff who were trained in the use of the model, including a part-time "helping teacher" at the school level. Huberman comments:

It was also decided that ongoing assistance should be provided, hence the idea of a "helping teacher" who would give workshops, demonstrate the ECRI techniques,

---

12 Hall and Loucks (1978), building on Fuller's (1969) work with pre-service teachers, have developed a "stages of concern" model in relation to the in-service needs of those who are implementing change. Hall and Loucks found in their various studies that when teachers are first involved in considering a change, they have informational and personal concerns about the implications of the change for them, and later (if the first stages are dealt with adequately) come to have more concerns about how to implement it and about its impact on learning. Hall and Loucks contend that in-service activities must be designed and timed to address these different needs.
13 The in-service program for all teachers new to the district was one of the four exemplary cases in McDonald and Elias's (1980) study of induction programs referred to in the previous section. Adam's County also has a systematic and thorough emphasis on staff development for all employees (Fullan et al., 1978).
14 The training of teachers as trainers of other teachers—often referred to as the "turnkey approach"—can be very powerful, as it lessens dependence on external consultants (i.e., it builds the internal capacity) and allows teachers to be helped by other teachers, who frequently are seen as the most valued (not to say only) sources of help.

provide supplies and materials, chair a monthly in-service meeting between users, provide on-demand consultancy. (p. 68)

The developmental nature of learning something new was also recognized by a policy of easing teachers into ECRI rather than expecting comprehensive implementation all at once. Huberman (p. 43) found that the first users saw the program as complex, unclear, or confusing and difficult to use. The lack of requisite skills, absence of good materials, and feelings of being poorly prepared to use the program were cited as early problems. Says Huberman, "Teachers, trainers and administrators all talk of a 'difficult', 'overwhelming', sometimes 'humiliating' experience during the first 6 months and, for some, during the initial two years" (p. 81). He notes that almost every respondent attributed the survival of ECRI in the precarious first year to two factors and their associated activities: (1) the helping teacher and (2) the presence of a strong administrative support at the school and central-office level (1981, p. 70). Activities mentioned as valuable included frequent in-service meetings "during which teachers exchange tips, war stories, encouragements, complaints and formulated requests to the helping teacher" (1981, pp. 70–71).[15] Most participants "refer spontaneously to neighboring districts where the program has sputtered or died, they claim, because there was no helping teacher and only token administrative commitment" (1981, p. 70). Huberman reports that it was not until the end of the first year of use that there was some "settling down" of the anxiety, and two to three years before people felt comfortable with the program.

This gradual clarity and development in the minds and behavior of those using something new captures the essence of *meaning* in the process of educational change. All new programs of any complexity, no matter how well developed and described in advance, appear psychologically overwhelming when people first experience them, even when the people have voluntarily chosen the program.[16] As Huberman describes it, the initial six months is a period of high anxiety and confusion. After some settling down, there still remains a very significant period of relating the separate specific behaviors to the underlying rationale of the new program. Huberman captures the behavioral and conceptual (beliefs, theory, etc.) dimensions of implementation which were stressed above in response to the question "What is change?" After six months use,

there is cognitive mastering over the individual pieces of ECRI, but little sense of the integration of the separate parts or, more globally, of why certain skills or exercises are related to specific outcomes. Concern for understanding the structure and rationale of the program grows as behavioral mastery over its parts is achieved. (p. 91)

---

15 Note the combination of frequent *informal* exchanges and *formal* requests which resulted in in-service sessions. Effective professional development depends on both ongoing exchanges among users and regular training sessions.

16 There are some very difficult philosophical questions about the purpose and value of any given change, in terms of *who* decides on the direction of change. Whether the particular change in fact is needed, and is of high quality, are open questions as I have stated before (chapter 2). What I am saying here is that even well-developed innovations, and even if voluntarily selected by users, will be reacted to with initial anxiety about how to implement them and about whether they are worthwhile (i.e., better than what exists at present).

The fundamental importance of meaning to successful educational change could not be more succinctly stated.

The sources for professional development can be multiple and varied, as the ECRI case study shows. In one of the schools examined, in which there were nine users of the program, Huberman (1981, p. 101) found that several sources of assistance were used: the NDN State Facilitator, ECRI trainers, district-office curriculum coordinator, trainers and teachers in neighboring schools, and the helping teacher who was located in the school. Within the school there was "frequent and unthreatening" assistance from other teachers, a resource which ECRI strengthened as more teachers used a relatively common program. The principal was able to help substantively as well as administratively after having been trained at the ECRI developer's home site.

The more concrete forms of assistance are too detailed to report here. In the DESSI study, the researchers make a useful distinction between *event-specific assistance* (e.g., in-service workshops, meetings) and *ongoing assistance* (e.g., one-to-one assistance, exchanges of ideas).[17] The pattern of assistance over time is also noteworthy. Huberman (1981, p. 105ff.) reports that the pre-implementation training of both trainers and trainees was weak, but ongoing assistance became stronger during implementation. At the beginning, the central district office provided impetus and support—arranging for the training of teachers who would act as trainers of other teachers, selecting and arranging for the training of helping teachers, and obtaining state staff development funds to support the various in-service training sessions and to purchase needed materials. During initial implementation the central office role diminishes as the school principal and helping teacher become more active and as teachers begin to help each other more.

One final set of observations on the amount of professional development training and the financial sources of support for it: Of the formal training aspects, trainers received intensive one-week (helping teacher) or three-week (turnkey trainers) sessions at the developer's home site. These were seen as the most useful. Teacher users received four to five days of pre-implementation training, and one to two days of formal in-service during implementation. This amount of time was seen as inadequate by the users. The crucial forms of in-service for users were the ongoing assistance (monthly meetings, helping teacher, exchanges among teachers) and the help and interest on the part of administrators. More opportunity to observe other classrooms in which teachers were using ECRI was the most commonly cited type of "assistance not received" but desired. As to financial sources of support, the NDN system provided the support for the developer's work, and state staff-development funds were used to provide release time for teachers. Monthly meetings and other forms of informal support occurred during the school day or after hours. Note that it is very difficult to calculate how much professional development activity was going on, for much of it was informal. The formal time (five to seven days for users over the year), as we also saw in the Stallings case study, is not large; that is, small amounts of ongoing in-service can have major payoffs, if they are combined with other factors necessary to support the implementa-

---

17 This distinction is similar to one made above between relatively formal professional development activities and relatively informal exchanges. Both are important.

tion process.[18] Moreover, not all innovations are as demanding as the ECRI program, Innovations vary as to how much help is needed.

## Action research with teachers

The fourth case example is based on the work of Elliott and his colleagues in the United Kingdom, who conducted several years of classroom research with teachers in order to identify how they best learn on the job. In their earlier research, they worked with 40 teachers in 12 schools on a project in which the focus was on problems of implementing inquiry/discovery approaches to learning (Elliott, 1976–77). In the course of the project they identified 43 "practical hypotheses" connected with the issue of developing teachers' abilities to monitor their own work. This study is particularly reinforcing of the importance of teacher–teacher interaction, which, as we have seen (chapter 7), normally— unless someone does something about it—does not occur. To illustrate, I cite only the last six of the 43 hypotheses:

38 The more access teachers have to other teachers' classroom problems, the more open they are to student feedback.
39 The more access teachers have to other teachers' classroom problems, the more open they are to observer feedback.
40 The more access teachers have to other teachers' classroom problems, the more open they are to feedback from other teachers.
41 The more access teachers have to other teachers' classroom problems, the more able they are at self-monitoring in their classroom practice.
42 The more access teachers have to other teachers' classroom problems, the more they experience a tension between their accountability as educators for process-values and their accountability to society for knowledge outcomes.
43 The more access teachers have to other teachers' classroom problems, the more they are able to bring about fundamental changes in their practice. (Elliott, 1976–77, pp. 20–21)

The project team and teachers used a variety of methods to collect systematically classroom patterns and facilitate teacher reflection on them. Methods included listening to or viewing recordings of their teaching behavior, having a dialogue with participant observers (project members, other teachers) about salient patterns, discussing teaching styles with students, and attempting and monitoring changes over time.

In later work, Elliott carried out further analyses directly related to professional development. He examined, for example, his experience in leading in-service courses in curriculum studies to find out "how teachers learn" (Elliott, 1979). His observations are most revealing on the relationship between meaning and professional development in bringing about change. Based on his attempts, Elliott concludes that "genuine theoretical statements about practice cannot be understood a priori. One does not first understand a theoretical principle about education and then apply it in an analysis of practice" (Elliott, 1979, p. 2). He goes on to suggest that "theoretical knowledge contributes to the learning of a

---

18 The role of technical assistance in the DESSI study as a whole (Huberman's was one case study within the larger set of case studies and surveys) confirms the existence and importance of this finding (see Crandall et al., forthcoming). The RDU project also found that the amount and variety of assistance during attempted implementation were important to achieving significant and successful change (Louis & Rosenblum, 1981).

skill only after a certain level of practical knowledge has first been acquired" (p. 7). Further, "teachers learned new techniques on the basis of their perceived instrumentality, congruence with existing practice, and cost in time and effort, rather than on the basis of a knowledge of underlying theoretical principles" (p. 28). We are not considering solutions at this stage, but we can see that the seemingly "rational" tendency of university consultants and other developers to dwell on the underlying theoretical rationale of a new program in pre-implementation introductory sessions is ill-timed. Elliott, like Huberman, found that some experience with practical application is necessary before the theory can begin to make sense (and subsequently generate more fundamental applications). Stated another way, internalization of the theoretical principles of new change attempts is central to fundamental implementation, but it must arise from the interaction of practical application and theory-based analyses and reflection. The sequence is important—the movement from practice first to theory second, and the enlargement of understanding which comes from moving back and forth between practice and theory as changes are attempted.

Elliott's work, along with other similar projects (see Tikunoff & Ward, 1979), indicates that collaborative research between an outsider and teachers on practical and theoretical aspects of instruction can constitute a fundamental staff development experience.

### Joyce's research

The final case example, represented by the work of Joyce and his associates, corroborates many of the principles embedded in the previous four cases. Joyce and Showers (1980, 1981) closely reviewed the relevant literature in order to derive some "lessons from research" for improving in-service education. They concluded that the following five components of in-service education programs were essential for fundamental change: theory, demonstration, practice, feedback, and application with coaching (see especially Joyce & Showers). They show why staff development is less effective when some of the components are missing. For example, theory (or the presentation of the underlying philosophy and rationale of a change) by itself may stimulate interest or awareness, but contains no practical guidelines for use. Or demonstrating or modeling a new teaching approach, as many studies have found, is very effective because it shows concretely what the application would look like in practice; however, by itself it may lead to imitation, but not necessarily to serious or lasting use. Or leaving out theory in order to stress practical application leads to superficial change. However, application in the regular classroom setting, combined with a system of coaching, feedback, and discussion of underlying principles involving peers and consultants, is effective. Moreover, it is precisely the kind of system we have referred to as essential *during* the implementation process. Joyce and Showers leave us with the powerful idea that professional development programs designed to bring about fundamental change should incorporate all five components in some combination over time.

An analysis of the role of staff development in the large-scale Rand Change Agent study (FPSEC) reinforces Joyce and Showers's conclusions. McLaughlin and Marsh (1978, p. 76) found that staff training activities which were well done and skill-specific, with clear demonstrations, were effective, but *"only in the short run"* (their italics). The authors explain:

Skill specific training activities only have a transient effect, because, by themselves, *they do not support staff learning and teacher change*. Skill specific training enabled teachers to implement new project methods and materials .... But this implementation was often mechanistic and did not constitute teacher assimilation of the new techniques and procedures. (p. 77; their italics)

Conceptual clarity, as I have suggested earlier, cannot be achieved at the outset through specific goal statements, lectures, and packaged materials; it must be accomplished during implementation as people try things and discuss them. And it is important for understanding and consolidating the change in practice. Joyce (1979, p. 30) notes that he has seen approaches where the theory has been dropped because it was impractical, and instead demonstration, practice, and feedback were stressed. That the subsequent performance was weak, says Joyce, "was kind of nice to know" because "we do have to know what we are doing." And as Flanders (1980, p. A–12) notes, teachers are not necessarily uninterested in theory. He reports that at certain stages of their careers, many teachers show "a growing, intensifying interest in theory in education and philosophies of knowledge."

In their later work Joyce and Showers (1981) have become more systematic in attempting to integrate staff development components and changes in practice. They make a distinction between "fine tuning" of teaching skills (acquiring new skills to enhance existing ones) and mastering new teaching models or programs (the latter obviously representing more complex and fundamental change). Even within the "fine tuning" skill-acquisition domain, Joyce and Showers raise serious questions about whether these skills get "transferred" into the teachers' repertoire for other applications or whether they remain rooted in their original, literal application. The latter type of application can be effective for accomplishing certain specific goals (such as sharpening a teacher's question-asking ability in a new social studies curriculum), but the potential for transfer (e.g., knowing when and under what conditions to use question-asking) may be missed. Joyce and Showers (1981), using their five components of training cited earlier, are developing some working hypotheses in which they suggest ways of maximizing transfer. In any case, Joyce and Showers are working on what is probably the most fundamental problem in in-service education— the transfer of knowledge and training from workshops to classroom situations.

In some other more specific studies, Joyce and his associates have contributed more detailed knowledge of staff development in schools. McKibbin and Joyce (1980) studied the professional development lives of 21 teachers in one school over a four-year period. The school (in California) has a very well funded and staffed in-service program with release time, staff trainers, and so on.[19] Teachers had numerous (almost unlimited) opportunities to request in-service activities. The study examined how much variation there was among teachers in using these opportunities, and what accounted for the differences. All teachers were rated on the basis of participation, training requests, and use of training. The range was from 13 to 88 on the point system used. The teacher who rated 13 participated only in training that was mandatory, while the teacher who rated 88 took advantage of a variety of opportunities. McKibbin and Joyce

---

19 In a later subsection on "opportunities for professional development," I expand on the question of availability of in-service for teachers.

also introduced the interesting notion of variations in individual psychological orientations to one's work, and used Maslow's hierarchy to characterize teachers' levels of need. Teachers were rated according to whether they were primarily interested in individual development and growth (roughly Maslow's self-actualization characterization) or were mainly concerned with maintenance of basic needs (economic security, having a job, showing little interest in growth). The authors theorize that establishing rich, multi-option staff development programs without considering individual orientations to take advantage of them may lead to a serious mismatch and waste of resources.

In a large-scale study of the federally sponsored Urban/Rural School Development Program, Joyce (1978) evaluated the impact of the project in 25 communities. The program was designed to involve community members and school staff from poor communities in equal decision-making; they were to plan and implement staff development activities within each school to improve the quality of education in the school. Joyce found that the school–community councils took time to get started, but once they got under way they led to active and successful school-focused activities. The sequence consisted of establishing the council, conducting a staff-development needs survey within the school, translating needs into diverse programs, implementing the programs at the school level, evaluating them, and recycling with new needs identified. The details of the findings should be examined in the original report. There were some variations in success, but the project as a whole was successful in accomplishing community involvement and satisfaction, teacher satisfaction, staff development formats and activities addressing focused, school-based needs, and reported positive impact on student learning. Joyce (p. 8) comments: "It appears that onsite-hands-on-inservice experiences which are made part of the teacher's job can function effectively. Teachers in the Urban/Rural program received most of their training during school hours and in or near their schools .... They reported greater satisfaction with these activities than did the comparison populations in California, Michigan, and Georgia."

These five case examples of relatively successful professional development programs are consistent in showing the combination of components which are necessary to bring about change in practice. These and other ideas will be used in the final section of the chapter, in which I summarize a small number of basic guidelines for staff development. It is but a short step to reconsider why the majority of professional development programs seem to fail.

## Why most professional development programs fail

The majority of in-service education experiences fail to meet the needs of teachers, and particularly needs connected with new programs, because they do not incorporate characteristics similar to those in the five successful case examples just described. Most experiences that teachers have with in-service tend to be of the one-shot type, or a university or district course, with little focus or follow-up support to use the ideas. Three of the most typical forms of in-service activities illustrate this point—the university course, the district professional development day or workshop, and pre-implementation training in connection with newly adopted programs or policies.

The university extension course is a common form of in-service education for teachers seeking upgrading, master's degrees, recertification, and so on. There is the usual criticism that many of the courses are too theoretical, impractical, and downright useless, for they are given by professors who have been long away from the classroom (if they were ever in it). But even in the smaller number of cases where the course is stimulating and contains interesting ideas, it is usually difficult to use the ideas. If the individual attempts to put them into practice, when problems are encountered there is no convenient source of help or sharing. It is very hard to be a lone innovator.

School-district planning of professional development programs represents another instance of frequently missed opportunities. There are great variations in how much emphasis districts place on staff development (see the next section), but there is less variation in the formats used. The one-shot, large-scale conference or workshop using external speakers is a typical format. We do not need to guess why it does not work.[20] Some districts establish on-site courses in cooperation with local universities which count for master's or certification credit. These at least provide some incentive for engaging in in-service, but they are usually not integrated with approaches described in the previous section.

Another interesting aspect is that the nature of school-district in-service programs does not seem to change very much when teachers plan their own programs. Joyce (1979, p. 31) comments: "When teachers plan their own in-service, it just amazes me how quickly they plan the same workshops, the same approaches, and so forth that they have complained about." Teacher representatives on school professional development committees find themselves planning activities which they probably know in their hearts will not work. If they spend the bulk of their time conducting needs surveys, identifying topics, and scurrying around finding guest speakers—in short, getting the professional development calendar filled—they will feel in the final analysis that their efforts have not been appreciated by other teachers. There are of course good workshops and programs sponsored and run by teacher groups. The point is not so much that teachers are just as poor as the rest of us at planning in-service, but more a commentary on how the existing system of professional development constrains or structures what is done. Representatives on committees have only so much time and authority, and the professional development system is often segmented from the program planning and implementation system.[21]

The third example of problematic professional development occurs when there is an attempt to provide some training in relation to a new program which has been adopted. In this case the relationship between staff development and

---

20 I am not implying that there should never be conferences or university courses. They can be very worthwhile, stimulating awareness and contributing to the general knowledge base. They usually are not very effective at helping translate that knowledge into changes in practice.

21 This is an important point in two senses. First, poor planning of in-service cannot be blamed on people being obtuse. The fact is that it is extremely difficult to launch an effective program because it is virtually impossible to control all the factors necessary to establish an ongoing program and make it work. The second and related point is that those responsible for program and other policy development and those responsible for staff development are frequently two (or more) different groups working on their own agendas, with little mutual coordination or even knowledge of each other's activities and needs.

program use is potentially more direct than in the other two illustrations. Downey's (1975) study of the introduction of a social studies curriculum in Alberta provides one example among many of what typically happens. Pre-implementation workshops were provided for all teachers who were to use the new curriculum. Let us assume (a big assumption) that the workshops contained many of Joyce's components—demonstration, theory, practice, etc. As a result of the workshops teachers were expected to go forth and implement. They didn't, and it is easy to see why in retrospect. Many teachers probably did not attempt implementation because they had other priorities, or because they saw the new curriculum as representing another in a long string of arbitrary changes. Other teachers may have seriously attempted to use the new curriculum, and they would have found that it was then, during the first attempts, that they had the most specific questions, doubts, and confusions about how to make it work, and *it was precisely then that they had no one to ask*. In-service opportunities during initial implementation are absolutely crucial.

To conclude, let us take the simple notion of incentives. Why should a teacher engage in professional development activities of the kind illustrated here? Presumably, a teacher would be attracted to the idea that professional development would expand knowledge and skills, contribute to growth, and enhance student learning. But what are the costs? Will professional development make the job easier or harder? The rhetoric of innovation underestimates, if it does not totally ignore, the real costs of attempting something new. Consider a few of them. Especially at the beginning, innovation is hard work. It takes extra time and energy, even when release time is provided. It can add significantly to the normal workload. As for increased competence on the job— another incentive—it is more likely that our competence actually *decreases* during first attempts at trying something new (recall Huberman's 1981 case study).[22] Our tendency is to return to familiar ways of doing things, or to practice the new ways privately so as to not expose our inadequacies to peers and supervisors. It is exactly the opposite that is needed—exchanges among peers and others about the *natural* problems of learning new skills. It takes an enlightened, supportive, and ongoing approach to staff development of the types described in the previous section to counteract the tendency to avoid confronting problems of implementation. All of this is compounded by the possibility that the particular change may not necessarily be well developed or be the most appropriate one for the situation.

In short, professional development, one of the most promising and powerful routes to growth on the job, to combating boredom and alienation, to school improvement, and to satisfaction, has gotten a bad name. Despite poor experiences (and possibly because of a few good experiences) people still seem to have faith in its potential, probably because it makes such obvious, intuitive good sense. But why the majority of attempts have been less than successful should be equally obvious: effective staff development programs, like effective educational change efforts, are not accomplished by good intentions alone.

---

22 Joyce, in his lectures, uses the analogy of learning a new tennis grip under the instruction of a professional. In first trying the new grip, we feel awkward and *less* able to hit the ball properly.

# Opportunities for
# professional development

When we start adding up the number and variety of professional development opportunities for teachers, what we find is rather staggering in magnitude. It is also out of control to the point that we do not know how much staff development goes on, nor do we know how best to coordinate and take advantage of the opportunities. The result is that staff development resources are frequently squandered. To help identify the promise and problem of the professional development "system" I consider four aspects: (1) staff development resources attached to policies and programs, (2) staff development at the local district level, (3) teacher centers, and (4) the work of university teacher education institutions and teacher federations.

## Staff development resources attached to
## specific policies/programs

The first illustration is in the area of staff development resources attached to policies and programs that are new. We have already seen a number of specific examples of this type of program in chapter 13. But what does this area look like in toto? Joyce, Bush, and some colleagues examined the question for the California State Department of Education in considering the matter of how the various staff development activities in the state could be evaluated (California State Department of Education, 1979). They found a bewildering array of programs and an uncoordinated and to a certain extent undecipherable system for using the allotted resources. They categorized the programs into three areas: agency-building efforts (e.g., programs to create teacher centers and resource centers), programmatic efforts (e.g., targeted curriculum efforts), and programs with a proportion of their funds allocated to staff development (e.g., in special education, bilingual education, vocational education). In total, they found more than forty specific federal or state-sponsored programs related to staff development. While most of the initiatives were administered through school districts, a few programs went directly to schools. There was a general lack of coordination; rather, a number of piecemeal activities were going on with little interrelationship. An undetermined amount of the resources theoretically intended for staff development was not actually spent on such activities; instead it went to purchase materials or to pay salaries. The researchers drew a number of conclusions which basically focus on the absence of organization and missed opportunities:

Many teachers are presently engaged in almost no formal staff development activities. Because there is no staff development organization, as such, in-service activities are generally planned on an ad hoc basis. Teachers are rarely visited by administrators, consultants, or other teachers who work near them and could help them in their teaching. (California State Department of Education, 1979, p. 7)

Multiple programs and agencies were essentially isolated from each other, with duplicative administrative structures side by side at the district level having little formal or informal linkage (see Gordon, 1980). The researchers are currently conducting a comprehensive follow-up evaluation of 46 federal and state initiatives involving staff development components. (See Joyce et al., 1981, for a first preliminary report, in which they characterize staff development as "an awkward adolescent.")

A comparatively simpler version of the problem is emerging in Ontario in reference to the new special education legislation (Bill 82). The provincial ministry of education will be providing an additional $75 million to support implementation. One of several major categories in which the money is to be spent is staff development (with the other categories including new staff, curriculum, etc.). School boards are required to submit annual plans as to how they will be addressing the various needs. The critical question will be whether school boards will be able to develop effective staff development activities (e.g., of the types described in the previous section) for special education teachers and especially for regular classroom teachers who will be affected by Bill 82. There are also a number of questions about how external agencies will be used (e.g., regional faculties of education that offer special education courses). The point of all this is that, while there is an array of staff development resources *potentially* available, they will not make much contribution if they are not identified and coordinated to provide some focused, ongoing support.

## School-district staff development activities

The second illustration comes from the school-district level, which is perhaps the most critical sorting and coordinating point because most programs pass through or are incorporated into the district administrative structure. In chapter 10 we looked at the basic picture at the district level, which included, of course, the need for staff development activities. We can now isolate the staff development component and ask how districts approach it. Not much is known about the extent of actual activities and costs, but there has been one careful and revealing in-depth study which demonstrates what a morass school-district professional development is, analyzes and provides specific information on the configuration of staff development, and formulates a set of guidelines for analyzing programs and costs (see Moore & Hyde, 1978, 1979, 1981). Moore and Hyde set out to "make sense of staff development" in three urban school districts, which were selected on the basis of apparent levels of staff development activity (high, medium, and low). In all three districts they found that the actual costs of staff development were *fifty* times more than district staffs estimated. One reason for the discrepancy related to the hidden costs of personnel time for staff development; another reason was that the responsibility for staff development was dispersed among a large number of people and departments, so that much of the work was not commonly known:

Frequently staff leaders were unaware of the activities of their colleagues, even when these activities placed demands of time and energy on the same teachers. In general, offices designated to coordinate staff development played a minor role in this swirl of activity. (Moore & Hyde, 1981, p. 4)

There were also marked differences among the three districts in the proportion and type of monetary incentives used. The total budgets of the three districts were $163.6 million for Seaside district, $122.4 million for Riverview district, and $123.9 million for Union district (the three names are pseudonyms). The amount (and proportion) of the budget spent on staff development was $9.3 million (5.7%), $4.6 million (3.8%), and $4.0 million (3.3%) respectively (1981, p. 33)[23]—not small amounts by any reckoning.

There is a wealth of detail in the report, and it is worth describing some of the specific findings. In two of the three districts (Seaside and Union) five major types of activities were found: (1) conducting seminars and workshops, usually in local schools; (2) providing individual assistance to teachers; (3) administering and coordinating staff development; (4) conducting district-wide conferences; and (5) training resource teachers to carry out staff development (p. 39).[24] Staff development activities were conducted in each of several departments or divisions. For example, in Seaside six departments/divisions were all involved substantially in professional development work: career education department, in-service department, compensatory education department, curriculum department, student services division, and personnel division. Riverview district had substantial federal funds because of higher proportions of minority and poor students. They had nearly two dozen different federal programs each containing specific staff development components (30 staff members altogether), as well as a curriculum department, a special education department, a vocational education department, a magnet schools division (to facilitate racial desegregation), a personnel division, and a teacher corps project.

A more specific breakdown of the source of funds is interesting. The vast majority of the monies supporting staff development came from district general funds in Seaside (92%) and Union (85%), while in Riverview only 56% came from general funds and the remainder was largely from federal grants. When these percentages are linked to the earlier information on percentage of revenue spent on staff development, Seaside, with hardly any external funds, spent proportionately about one-third more than did Riverview, which had substantial external funds (5.7% vs. 3.8%); Union spent about the same as Riverview.

Moore and Hyde (1981, p. 76) also calculated the total amount of time in three categories, coming up with the following figures for the average number of hours per teacher spent in staff development during the school year:

|  | Seaside | Riverview | Union |
|---|---|---|---|
| Salaried time* | 101.71 | 33.45 | 45.67 |
| Release time | 5.92 | 7.04 | 3.52 |
| Stipend time | .83 | 23.25 | 1.07 |
| Totals | 108.46 | 63.74 | 50.26 |

*Salaried time was defined as time created by shortened school days, or after-hours time—i.e., neither release time nor stipends were involved.

23 Staff development was defined as "any school district activity that is intended partly or primarily to prepare paid staff members for improved performance in present or possible future roles in the school district" (Moore & Hyde, 1981, p. 9).

24 The third district—Riverview—concentrated on three of the activities: administering staff development, conducting district-wide conferences, and providing individual services. They did not offer school-based workshops or train resource teachers to lead staff development, as did the other two districts.

Three points can be made about these figures. First, considerable time is spent on staff development (even in the district with the least amount it is 50 hours).[25] Second, Seaside teachers participate in much more staff development than do teachers in the other two districts. Third, Riverview relies on teacher stipends much more than the other two districts (especially Seaside), which build the time into the regular jobs of the teachers.[26] As the authors note, the salaried worktime spent in staff development can be increased within certain limits (e.g., shortened days, after-school workshops) without adding any additional "cost," because the staff are on fixed salaries.[27]

Another aspect of the analysis which is instructive relates to the pattern of expenditures on staff development in the three districts (1981, p. 94). Seaside allocated almost 75% of its staff development funds (recall the total was $9.3 million) to teachers (salaried worktime, salary increases, etc.); Riverview allocated only 55% to teachers, and Union 67%. At Riverview, 37% of the funds went to central-office staff development positions (compared to 19% and 27% for Seaside and Union). Riverview also spent much more on external consultants ($212,000 or 4.6%) compared to Seaside ($158,000 or 1.7%) and Union ($48,000 or 1.2%). In other words, Riverview had a larger group of central-office personnel doing staff development; it was they who decided on the topics and conducted district-wide activities. In Seaside, district staff both initiated their own activities and supported activities initiated at the school level, whereas in Riverview there was "virtually no school-based staff development" (1981, p. 79).

There are several conclusions to draw from Moore and Hyde's fascinating excursion into the finances and patterns of school-district staff development.[28] First, if teachers are dissatisfied with the quality of current staff development experiences—and most of them seem to be—Moore and Hyde (1981, p. 108) say, "One must logically ask why the substantial resources presently devoted to staff development are not being translated into adequate experiences for teachers." Second, and in partial answer to the question just posed, the study shows that there is limited coordination and communication among the leaders of staff development at the district level. It seems as if professional development activities have simply evolved piecemeal without any conscious policy or effort to examine what works and doesn't work and how to improve programs and prac-

---

25 Moore and Hyde calculate that from $1000 to $1700 per teacher is invested by the districts in staff development. Since this and the figures on number of hours are "averages," some teachers do considerably more, while others may do virtually nothing. There are also great variations across schools within the same district. For example, in Seaside the percentage of salaried time spent on staff development ranged from 2.4 to 18.3 in the lowest- and highest-activity schools respectively. A familiar explanation was found: in higher-activity schools the principal was making extensive use of every opportunity for staff development (Moore & Hyde, 1981, p. 60).

26 Berman and McLaughlin found that extra pay for staff for professional development was slightly negatively correlated with extent of implementation.

27 Teachers in Seaside still receive extra money indirectly through salary increases, which are tied to taking workshops, courses, etc. in order to move to higher salary schedules (more about this shortly).

28 Moore and Hyde (1979) also studied the politics of staff development in three school districts (one was Seaside and the other two were different districts from those in the study reviewed here). They used an interview approach and found many issues similar to the ones raised in their later report. Teacher dissatisfaction with staff development, the role of teacher unions, and the lack of district commitment and leadership in staff development were some of the main issues which loomed large.

tices. The unwieldy evolution of practices is especially noticeable in the variety of federal and state categorical programs which come into the district with each having its own domain. (See Joyce et al.'s 1981 study of this issue in California.) But it is also evident across the basic program divisions in the district. Third, Moore and Hyde did not study the actual impact of staff development on change in practice. If we take their two studies together, however, there are enough indicators to suggest that most staff development activities do not lead to change. In most districts, teachers participate in workshops largely designed and led by central-office staff or external consultants; there is little evidence of follow-through support for implementation; and participation seems to be based on meeting formal requirements (mandated participation, extra pay, recertification requirements, etc.). Financial incentives can induce attendance, but not the willingness to try new practices in the classroom. Only one (Seaside) of the five districts in the two reports appears to have a strong program, with relatively high participation and school-based involvement. Fourth, the commitment to staff development on the part of leadership at the district and school level is critical, but is missing in most cases as measured by what leaders *do*.[29] Moore and Hyde summarize some of the positive features of leadership when it is exercised:

The amount of time that can be gleaned from the regular workday by committed teachers and administrators is clearly demonstrated in our study. Through early dismissal policies, the creative use of teacher preparation periods and staff meetings, and concerted efforts to build a spirit of collaboration among the members of a particular school staff, greatly heightened participation has been achieved in individual schools without dramatic cost increases. If the staff development aspect of central office administrative roles is emphasized and these administrators are trained to support school-based staff development, and if in addition school building administrators are trained to make maximum use of non-instructional salaried worktime, it appears that the resources for staff development can be increased substantially. (1981, p. 116)

Fifth, there is a vicious circle at work. If most current professional development activities are not seen as worthwhile by teachers, there is little incentive to participate or, having participated, to apply the ideas in practice. If participation is low, or if improvement in practice is not seen as an outcome, policy-makers, the public, and senior administrators are more likely to reduce resources for professional development; diminished resources in turn diminish enthusiasm and incentive to become involved. Resources are needed for staff development and can serve to support considerable participation in educational experiences for professional staff at the school level, as the Seaside case study demonstrates. Professional development and improvement in practice are closely intertwined. It should be patently clear why the latter cannot be accomplished without the former.

Devising and implementing a quality professional development system at the district and school levels is obviously a complex undertaking, as Moore and

---

29 For other examples of districts committed to staff development, see the brief descriptions of Jefferson County and Kamloops in chapter 10. Adam's County School District 12 also provides a prime example of a superintendent and central staff who stress staff development and have established a wide array of opportunities which combine an emphasis on individual development *and* district needs (Fullan et al., 1978).

Hyde's intricate analysis indicates. By examining the various case studies of success in the previous section, and considering the issues raised by Moore and Hyde, we know much more about what to do and not to do, what elements to exclude and include. The basis for optimism may reside in the fact that there has not yet been a serious attempt to harness staff development resources for professional growth and improvement in practice. In-service education and staff development practices have evolved somewhat randomly and thoughtlessly from a social system point of view.[30] The fact that some districts and some schools have figured out how to establish and support profitable staff development experiences, under these confusing circumstances, is a credit to them. Their knowledge can provide one useful resource for others who want to move in the same direction. The more general message is that any serious change effort must contain an effective professional development component.

In addition to staff development opportunities tied to particular programs, and local district practices, a third type concerns the establishment and activities of teacher centers—to which I now turn.

### Teacher centers

There is no typical teachers' center (Devaney, 1977). Some centers serve a whole district, and some several districts. Some are funded by foundations or federally; others are funded from a variety of sources including school district budgets. Some have staff with specialized expertise; the staff of others offer more general resource capabilities. Teachers' centers tend to be small (perhaps two or three staff, although some are much larger) and housed in available school buildings. They conduct or arrange for workshops on identified topics of need, as well as providing one-to-one assistance, a place to meet other teachers, and a place to discuss and obtain curriculum materials. Participation in workshops, other center activities, or informal visits is usually voluntary. Advisory boards of teachers, administrators, and sometimes the public are responsible for making general policy and program decisions. Teachers' centers are primarily meant to be run by and for teachers, although administrators and other groups or agencies supplying the funding also participate in various ways in guiding and evaluating their work.

The straightforward introduction to teacher centers is to say that they can be very effective *if* they offer professional development activities with the characteristics described earlier. Devaney (1977) claims that good teacher centers have the advantage of providing the "warmth, concreteness, time, and thought" which teachers usually do not get in typical staff development programs. (See also other articles in Devaney, 1977.) They can also have the advantages of being close to the local school, offering opportunity for informal and formal exchanges among peers, and in general forming a relatively stable, ongoing resource base of both people and materials. Like any other innovation, they can also fail. Put another way, the quality of implementation—how the center is decided upon, is introduced, is set up, goes about its work, and is monitored—is important.

---

30 That is, it is not necessarily that each individual responsible for planning in-service has been thoughtless, but that the *combination* resulting from countless ad hoc uncoordinated decisions and activities has been ineffective and wasteful. For some suggestions as to how to conceptualize, improve, and evaluate staff development programs, see Schlecty (1981).

The variety of formats and governance arrangements makes it difficult to generalize. However, recent evaluation by Mertens and Yarger (1981) of 37 of the 89 federally funded teacher centers in the United States provides some useful data on the nature and extent of activities. The centers are governed by policy boards (average membership 21), with teachers having a majority position on the boards (65%), followed by administrators (20%), representatives from higher education groups (7.5%), and parents/paraprofessionals (7.5%). Mertens and Yarger found that the policy boards were active and influential in making policy and administrative decisions governing the work of the centers. They examined four types of work engaged in by the centers: material resources and equipment, consultative services, facilitative services, and monetary resources. Material resources, which nearly all centers offered, was the most frequently used type of resource: 58.1% of the services offered by the centers related to material resources (without direct consultative service). The second most frequent use of service (25.3%) related to one-to-one consultation between center staff and individual teachers. This one-to-one assistance mostly involved help in materials development or adaptation. The third category (11.4%) concerned facilitative assistance—that is, center staff, unable to provide direct assistance themselves, helped teachers locate the appropriate resources elsewhere. Monetary aid is available more sparingly (5.2% of all services), but can be helpful in freeing some teachers through the payment of substitute teachers, payment for conferences, and so on.

Mertens and Yarger (1981, p. 14) suggest that teacher centers may be most clearly distinguished from other approaches to in-service education by the priority that is placed on addressing the needs of individual teachers. They indicate that the turnaround time is short, and that an individual teacher can get assistance tailored to his or her needs even though other teachers may not have the same need at the same time. They calculated that there were over 55,000 instances of individuals' utilization of the four types of services during the school year studied without any extrinsic benefits (no salary stipends; course credit available in 8% of the activities). Participation was almost always on the teacher's own time (free periods, lunch, after school). The themes of collegiality and responsiveness permeated the data on services and resources.

While individual services dominated, there were a considerable number of group activities. At the informal level, teachers who go to the center will frequently find and interact with other teachers as well as center staff. At the more formal level, Mertens and Yarger identified 1658 group activities (bringing groups of teachers together for professional development activities on a given topic), in which 43,185 teachers participated. The activities were usually targeted on instructional matters, basic skills, or materials development in specific curriculum areas. The one-shot workshop (which, as we have seen, is questionable in its impact on practice) was the predominant activity—about 70% of the 1658 group activities. Another 22% involved multiple activities spanning one month or less, and only 8% spanned a period of five weeks or more.

More than half the group activities (57%) were led by teachers (practicing classroom teachers, or center staff whose primary affiliation was that of teacher). The most frequent instructional approach (70%) consisted of verbal presentations and group discussion. Demonstrations were used frequently (38%). Scheduling of activities was important. Many teachers did not like to leave their classes for in-service. More popular was time during the school day, if it could be found. The proximity of the location of the group activity was a major attraction. Most of the activities were evaluated via questionnaires to participants, who rated the experiences positively.

Mertens and Yarger's study raises just as many questions as it answers. What was the impact of the individual and group activities on what teachers did in the classroom? Did it improve student performance? Who were the participants, what were their characteristics, and what proportion of potential users in the region did they represent? How did the work of the center relate to the work of the local district? Was it a substitute, a reinforcement, a counter-force? Are teacher centers better than other approaches to professional development? These questions cannot be answered from the Mertens and Yarger research, but their study raises two general issues. The first is that some of the findings corroborate what we know about effective professional development—focus on individual needs, help from other teachers, materials and consultative services on both a one-to-one and a group basis targeted on specific curricular and instructional practices. The second issue is more fundamental and philosophical, because it raises the dilemma of individual vs. collective approaches to professional development. I will take up this tension at the end of the chapter, but we should note a familiar problem: should more homogeneous, collective, programmatic approaches to educational change be taken, or more heterogeneous, individualized, varied approaches? It is the difference between fidelity and variation in change. Teacher centers promote individual teacher development; school-based and school-district-based staff development frequently stresses more programmatic concerns involving all teachers in a certain direction of change. The differences are not always incompatible, but there is a tension between them.

## Teacher education institutions and teacher associations

The fourth and final element in the ecology of in-service education involves the vast array of individual courses, workshops, and other professional development activities engaged in by colleges of education and teacher associations and unions. There are so many formats and options that only a few general issues can be raised. First, in total, these offerings do represent a rich array of options open to *individuals*. Second, their relationship to change in practice is not at all clear. As one-shot workshops and short courses, they can make teachers aware of new ideas and can touch on skill development; but most such activities do not have the follow-through or application component necessary to support the actual use of new ideas. (For a potential exception, see AFT, 1982.)

Third (and somewhat related), in many cases in-service workshops and courses are tied to the school district's or the state or province's system of certification, recertification, degree credit, and upgrading for salary purposes. As such, they provide an obvious incentive for participation, but it is very easy for participation to be no more than simple compliance to meet formal requirements rather than an effort to effect program improvement.

Fourth, there is the dilemma of how in-service activities of teacher education institutions and teacher associations relate to school-district program directions. Some differences are useful, for they provide additional options for individuals; the danger is that completely independent systems may result in duplication, confusion of choices, absence of coordination, and inability to implement the ideas if school district and school personnel are not actively supporting their application. All other things being equal, professional development needs are best served when there is some congruence and collaboration between the teachers' colleges and associations on the one hand, and the school-district and school programs on the other.[31] This is a matter of the former's not just taking into account the goals of local districts but also recognizing that it is local factors which largely determine (facilitate or constrain) change in practice.

Fifth, the two agencies (colleges and associations) both have special problems and potentials of their own. Teachers' colleges have generally endorsed the notion that an increase in in-service activities is necessary because of declining pre-service enrolments. But colleges and universities are not set up to contribute to the kind of professional development that requires a *continuing* relationship between individual faculty members and local-district and school staffs. Teacher associations have struggled with their involvement in professional development, with results ranging from collective agreement clauses which prohibit after-hours participation to strong endorsements of the concept of professional development as a career-long responsibility of individuals and of the associations.[32] Both teacher education institutions and teacher associations are still at the relatively early stages of defining a stance and, more important, of engaging in intensive professional development programs and activities. But what they are doing is worth watching, because it represents some important external resources for teachers.

# The preparation and professional development of administrators and consultants

The bulk of this chapter has concentrated on the preparation and professional development of teachers because of their large number and their importance for change at the level of practice. Equally important in a strategic sense is the preparation and the in-service education opportunities designed for those who lead and facilitate the change process.

We can start with a generalization about the formal training received by administrators and consultants prior to entering their positions: with a few exceptions they do *not* receive much preparation for their roles as change leaders or facilitators.[33] Let us consider the kind of preparation received by administrators and consultants respectively.

---

31 Many school districts do have an arrangement with regional universities, but it takes special efforts for collaboration to go beyond a credit system for completing requirements to a developmental instructional improvement approach (see TDR Associates, 1981; Havelock & Huberman, 1981; Havelock, 1981).

32 See Leiter and Cooper (1978) for a discussion of why teacher unionists are not enthusiastic about typical forms of in-service education, and AFT (1982) for an alternative.

33 For a discussion of the relevant change leadership roles see the chapters on the principal (chapter 8), the district administrator (chapter 10), and the consultant (chapter 11).

## Administrators

To become a principal or district administrator, candidates are typically required to take (or have taken) a combination of advanced degrees or courses, usually in educational administration, and short courses designed by the appropriate authority (the state or province). The advanced courses frequently deal with the theory of educational administration, and the short courses with particular laws, policies, regulations, and general expectations for the role. Most people take all of this training part-time in summers and in the evenings.

Miklos and Nixon (1979) give a brief overview of the formal preparatory programs for educational administrators from reports on five countries (Australia, Britain, Canada, New Zealand, and the United States). They note that most preparatory programs are based in colleges or faculties of education, are taken part-time, and lead to degrees or certificates. Topics such as administrative theory, leadership, and decision-making appear in nearly all programs. In some programs there is an emphasis on technical skills through internships or practica, but in most programs the participants perceive that conceptual issues receive the greater emphasis. In some institutions and states, Miklos and Nixon report, there is a trend toward specifying competencies and skill training. With regard to instructional methods, they comment that the greatest reliance is on lectures and discussion.

Most people who write about the preparation programs for administrators seem to agree that by and large they constitute a rather unexciting and unproductive experience (see, for example, Bridges, 1977; March, 1973; Saario, 1979). Moreover, they neglect essential skills. March (1973) talks about the need for administrators to have at least the abilities to analyze and manage five elements: expertise, coalitions, ambiguity, time, and information. Deal and Nutt (1980) recommend a number of conceptual political skills required, but frequently absent, in administrators. Those administrators who do possess the necessary abilities are likely to report that on-the-job experience contributed the most to their development. A sure-fire indicator of the problem of preparation is the frequent reference in the research literature to lack of leadership as a major explanation of failed change efforts.

Another indicator of the problem is the demand for and development of in-service programs focusing on the administrator as a change leader. Leithwood and Montgomery (1981) in Ontario, for example, are developing and testing such a program for principals. Most state and provincial associations of administrators advocate and in some cases have developed professional development programs for principals and district administrators (e.g., Olivero, 1979). Some school districts, as we have seen, are placing a major emphasis on such programs.

It is too early to say anything about the overall effectiveness of these trends. In many ways, professional development activities for administrators are less well developed than those for teachers.[34] It does not take much imagination,

---

34 Professional development emphasis is inversely related to status hierarchies: more stress is placed on the in-service education of elementary than secondary teachers, of teachers than principals, of principals than district administrators, of school-district personnel than of government personnel or university professors. As they move up, incumbents seem to think that they have less need to learn—a very questionable assumption when it comes to how to manage change.

however, to realize that many of the same *principles* of professional development will apply to administrators. There is no reason to believe that workshops or courses—even good ones—will lead to much improvement in the job. They need to be integrated with other aspects of effective professional development. If demonstration, theory, practice, feedback, and application are necessary for teachers, if follow-through after workshops is necessary, if professional development activities are more beneficial when they are linked to specific program changes, if interaction among peers is essential, if both peers and others are needed to provide formal and informal assistance and support—then professional development programs for administrators should include these components. The content of the skills may differ, but not *how* they are learned.

## Consultants

District, regional, and state curriculum and program consultants, project directors, and the variety of people concerned with providing technical assistance, linkage, and training are directly involved in attempting to bring about change. While the depth of skills in different areas may vary depending on the job, I have suggested that consultants need some degree of knowledge and skills in both the *content* of changes being considered and in the *process* of change.[35] The latter, in reference to this chapter, is none other than the consultant's ability to establish effective professional development activities with his or her clientele. The formal preparation of consultants for their roles as change agents is, to understate the case, not well developed. Most do not receive any special training other than the pre-service and in-service courses available to teachers and administrators. At best (or worst, depending on whether you favor the program in question) consultants can develop considerable expertise in the substance of the curriculum or program area in which they work. However, capacity to plan, conduct, and follow through on professional development activities and other aspects of the change process is much more rare.

As with other areas, there have been some recent responses to the professional development needs of program consultants. I mention only two. Over a period of years The Network Inc. has developed a *Linking Agent's Tool Kit* (The Network, 1979, parts One, Two, and Three). The Northwest Regional Educational Laboratory has also developed a series of training packages, *Preparing Educational Training Consultants* (NWREL, 1976). A careful search might locate a few other examples of training materials and activities for specified personnel (e.g., in bilingual education, Title I, special education, vocational education), but good training materials and opportunities are scarce. In particular, district consultants—a potentially powerful source of ongoing support for change—receive little pre- or in-service training in how to establish and facilitate an effective professional development and implementation process.

The professional development of district and other consultants seems all the more important when we realize that the skills they require are varied, somewhat abstract, and difficult to learn; yet when these skills are mastered, consult-

---

35 See chapter 11. There are a number of more special skills, which would have to be identified for any particular role (see Crandall, 1977, and Lippitt & Lippitt, 1978, for a discussion of the range of skills which might be involved).

ants can be very effective in helping to bring about positive changes in practice (Crandall et al., forthcoming; Louis & Rosenblum, 1981).

# Guidelines for effective professional development

There are already a number of guidelines available on different aspects of professional development. Harris (1980) provides an extensive textbook on designing, conducting, and evaluating in-service education programs. Wood and Thompson (1980), Orlich (1980), and Dawson (1978) all list specific guidelines and components necessary for effective in-service for teachers. Moore and Hyde (1979) contribute a handbook for analyzing, costing, and planning staff development at the district level. Each of the five case examples of successful professional development described earlier contains important ideas about what should constitute programs. Materials for the in-service training of principals are now developed or being developed (Rosenblum et al., 1980; Leithwood & Montgomery, 1981). There are training designs and materials for linkage agents (The Network, 1979; NWREL, 1976). And conceptual and practical suggestions have been made for increasing professional education through the development of more explicit "theories-in-use" and a more critical examination of "espoused theories" (Argyris & Schon, 1974, ch. 10), and through guidelines for "learning to work in groups" more effectively (Miles, 1981).

In formulating some guidelines for effective professional development two cautions should be borne in mind. First, at a specific level, guidelines will differ depending on particular role responsibilities. A project director interested in implementing a certain program will have somewhat different interests from a staff developer responsible for coordinating all the professional development activities in the district, or a principal interested in general in fostering professional growth among staff. Second, there are several different types of staff development, all of which might be useful. For example, some approaches stress district-wide priorities, others school-based goals, and still others individual choice of direction in which to go. Indeed, we might ask the general question of whether establishing a rich array of professional development options to be selected by teachers as *individuals* is more effective than attempting to coordinate the activities into more programmatic efforts involving *groups* of teachers in a school or school district all working to implement the same innovation. The following general guidelines do not attempt to resolve this question, but they do draw together from this chapter some of the factors common to effective programs.

1 Professional development should focus on job- or program-related tasks faced by teachers.
2 Professional development programs should include the general components found by Joyce and Showers (1981) to be necessary for change in practice: theory, demonstration, practice, feedback, and application with coaching.
3 Follow-through is crucial. A series of several sessions, with intervals between in which people have the chance to try things (with some access to help or to other

resources), is much more powerful than even the most stimulating one-shot workshop.

4  A variety of formal and informal elements should be coordinated: training workshops and sharing workshops, teacher–teacher interaction, one-to-one assistance, meetings. Note that both teachers and others (principals, consultants, etc.) are significant resources at both the informal sharing or one-to-one level and the formal level of workshops or courses.

5  It is essential to recognize the relationship between professional development and implementation of change. It is in this recognition that the *continuous* nature of professional development can be understood, and that the link between professional development and change in practice (and all the things that interfere with that link) can be most readily identified and addressed.

As long as there is the need for improvement through making changes in education, there will be the need for professional development. To say it another way, professional development is a career-long proposition. It should be very clear that we are talking about a fundamental change in the professional life of teachers and others. People in the education profession, if the lessons of this chapter are to be learned, will have more contact with each other; there will be more support and more vulnerability as what people do becomes the subject of observation and discussion. Staff development coordinators and leaders, whether they be consultants, teachers, principals, or faculty of education personnel, will be involved in designing better workshops and better ways to support follow-through application of ideas. *The absence of follow-up after workshops is without doubt the greatest single problem in contemporary professional development.* Note also that it is neither realistic nor desirable to expect the small number of staff development leaders to provide all the follow-up for the large number of participants. The cases of success we examined consisted of systems of *peer-based interaction* and feedback among teachers combined with external assistance (see especially Joyce & Showers, 1981). Large numbers of people will be affected only when the system of support and interaction becomes established as a regular, normal part of the ongoing work of schools. In short, there is a serious change at stake.

Establishing better professional development programs is not only a means to change but also an innovation in itself, because it involves attempting to implement new approaches to initial preparation and continuing education of teachers, administrators, and other specialists. If we are interested in a theory of "changing"—in identifying those factors most possible to alter, and most instrumental in bringing about change at the level of practice—professional development would be at the very top of the list. Increasing the resources for and emphasis on staff development, establishing more effective programs, and integrating continual professional development into the regular work of school personnel are goals to which all educational agencies should be committed; for sustained improvements in schools will not occur without changes in the quality of learning experiences on the part of those who run the schools.

# Chapter 15

# The Future of Educational Change

> More is learned from a single success than from multiple failures. A single success proves it can be done—what is, is possible.
>
> — R.K. Merton

Where are we in the history of educational change? Surprisingly, given all the technological brouhaha of modernity, we are near the beginning, if we use serious attempts at *change in practice*—at implementation—as the criterion of progress. Being at the early stages of a complex undertaking, we have an obligation to be neither insultingly optimistic nor boringly pessimistic. We have seen many failures, but also some successes even under adverse circumstances. What is more, we understand better why things turn out as they do. Our knowledge is catching up to our information. Both are getting better.

I will not attempt to predict the future of educational change, except to suggest nine themes or dilemmas central to this future, and to note where we currently stand in relation to each theme. The themes concern (1) cognitive and social-development goals of education, (2) fidelity and variation in change, (3) privatism and professional development, (4) specific and generic capacity for change, (5) time and change, (6) leadership and change, (7) grandeur and incrementalism, (8) meaning and change, and (9) school and society, or what we should be satisfied with from the educational system.

## Cognitive vs. social-development goals

There are contradictions within and between what I refer to as the cognitive/academic goals and the personal/social-development goals of education. Cognitive/academic goals concern the acquisition of knowledge and the intellectual tools to obtain and interpret information. They include basic academic skills (reading, math) and higher-order thinking skills (problem-solving abilities). The goals of personal and social development involve individual traits. Such goals relate to the values and abilities that allow people to work and live in groups: work skills and life skills, independence, creativity, empathy, initiative, interpersonal skills, and the like.

Theme 1 concerns the issue of where do we (and should we) put our energies in educational change, and with what chances of success. Fundamentally, it is a question of balance among cognitive and social goals. Currently, the main attention and content of reform is largely imbalanced in favor of the more basic of the cognitive goals, to the relative neglect of higher-order cognitive goals, and to a very strong passivity when it comes to personal/social-development goals.[1] Put in other words, the resources for and emphasis on much innovative reform (and, more revealingly, the small number of successes we have noticed) are in the area of *basic cognitive skills and knowledge at the elementary school level*. To learn how to bring about success at this level is indeed a significant accomplishment. No one would deny that much more remains to be done, and should be done. But we must also raise the question of bias by neglect: in what ways are new educational policies *failing even to attempt* changes in practice in the area of cognitive skills at the secondary school level, and in the personal and social skills areas? There are a few programs which focus on personal and social development, but it takes no special insight to observe that the internal and external pressure on schools is squarely in the cognitive domain.[2]

We cannot leave this theme without acknowledging what consequences, wittingly or not, schools now have on personal and social development. Bowles and Gintis (1976, p. 40) suggest that schools reward conformity, subordination to authority, discipline, intellectually as opposed to socially and emotionally oriented behavior, and hard work independent from intrinsic task motivation. The authoritarian, undemocratic structure of the school replicates the hierarchical order of the work place. Not only does the school overtly neglect personal- and social-development goals, it covertly shapes development in certain directions. Whether or not the educational system is intentionally insidious, and it probably is not, the fact remains that Bowles and Gintis's identification of the *consequences* of the school system on personal and social development may be largely correct. (See also Dale, 1981, and Sarason, 1971, ch. 11, for discussion of how the constitution of the classroom is established.)

The future agenda for educational change should have a place for testing the "implementability" of basic personal- and social-development goals. They do not have to be abstract goals of democracy. As Sarason and Doris (1979, p. 402) observe, school and classroom living contains all of the problems and opportunities of group living. The personal- and social-development goals which might be involved are not foreign to existing espoused policies of school boards and government agencies. Not only do the large-scale reforms in racial integration and special education include specific references to them; so do the regular curricula (e.g., in social studies, language communication, career and life skills). We cannot expect the school to be much more democratic than

---

1 It may seem at first glance that educational policy is very much concerned with social reform (racial integration, mainstreaming for special education, additional entitlements to poor areas). These are of course "social" reforms, but the programs usually focus on cognitive achievement compared to social development. To suggest that social equality (attitudes and skills conducive to mutuality in living) should receive at least as much explicit attention, however, is not to deny the importance of equality in cognitive achievement.
2 The relationship between cognitive and social development is too complicated to analyze here. Obviously, highly developed cognitive skills are necessary for social development, but they also may work against it, depending on one's values and on one's relational skills.

society. We certainly cannot expect the school to *produce* democracy. But on a much smaller scale, it does seem fair to raise the question of what changes in practice (in the curriculum, in instructional activities and behavior, in beliefs and assumptions about how students are treated) would be necessary to achieve some of the personal- and social-development goals already on the books. Attention to the secondary school and to the school/work interface seems especially critical in order to examine what personal and social skills are most neglected and most needed. If we intend to address these goals seriously, it would be wise to use our recently acquired knowledge of implementation.[3] Theme 1 does not imply that a grand social reform should be contemplated, but rather that the balance of cognitive and social goals of educational change should be examined with a view to taking at least some small steps to ensure that some of the changes related to the non-cognitive goals stand a chance of being implemented.

# Fidelity vs. variation

Theme 2—fidelity or variation in change—is equally important because it concerns matters of centralization and decentralization, homogeneity and heterogeneity, authority and discretion. The fidelity–variation dilemma runs through this entire book. It is, however, a book on *planned* (as distinct from naturally occurring) change, and any time we attempt to engineer social change, however oriented to allow for individual choice, the tendency is toward limiting variation and maximizing consistent or faithful implementation. Variation can be of two types: the what and the how. In the case of variation at the "what" level, individuals or groups are allowed to choose different innovations or priorities; with variation at the "how" level, they are permitted, even encouraged, to work out different means of implementing the same innovation. (And, of course, when different means are used, the innovation—even its goals—does not necessarily remain the same.) Dilemmas represent choices between desirable but mutually exclusive possibilities. The problem is that we can never be sure if the best choice is being made, or if we are sure, we can also be sure that someone else is equally sure that the wrong choice is being made.

I have taken the stance that every individual and group should reflect critically on the variation question. If the direction of the change is seen as desirable, and if the means of implementation are proven and clear, there is nothing wrong with consistent, homogeneous implementation (see Berman, 1980). But these conditions are not always or even usually the case, and we don't know whether they are until there is some experimentation with priorities and with different means. I have attempted to mitigate the dilemmas by suggesting that variations be respected, and that interaction and dialogue operate in a checks-

---

3 It would also be wise to reexamine Dewey (1916) for potential ideas for the curriculum. Instead of vaguely reading Dewey as a philosopher of education whose time has passed or never was, it might be worth asking if his ideas did not work because they were unworkable or because implementation was never carefully attempted. The issue is not whether wholesale implementation of Dewey's ideas is desirable or possible, but whether some of them are timely today.

and-balances fashion. I have also advocated that there be more sustained inter-action around the goals and means of reform among small groups of users. Such interaction, while it can generate more ideas in the aggregate, definitely limits *individual* freedom. The individual principal or teacher, for example, would not be left alone to do (or not do) what he or she wanted; there would be some pressure on individuals to do "something," even if there was some choice as to precisely what.

There are other countless subdilemmas. Should the final choice reside at the individual level, the school level, the district, the region, the state or province? What if the individual at whatever level is not doing his or her job? The position taken in this book is that optimum implementation consists in maximizing interaction, planning change in a way such that groups of people must interact and make choices, and such that individuals influence and are influenced by the group. Each of the chapters in Part II calls for particular involvement on the part of those who have the most at stake in sorting out the nature of change according to individual and collective choices about the ends and means of education. The issue of how much variation should occur is left open.[4] In any case, the bias of planned change is that *collectivities* (whatever the size and level) are involved in some deliberate attempt to change practice. The process can lead to more or less variability, but the individual is no longer the isolated decision-maker.

# Privatism vs. professional development

Theme 3, privatism and professional development, directly attacks the desultory isolationism of the educational system.[5] Educational systems are "loosely coupled": teachers rarely directly observe other teachers; the principal has limited contact about instructional practices with the teacher; one school has little to do with another; the district administration is not close to local schools; and the regional or state office has even less contact (Weick, 1976). Yet we have seen that change in practice—whether it be of the programmatic or variation persuasion—*requires* interaction. When a new direction is attempted, there will be uncertainty, anxiety, lack of clarity, a faltering of resolve, a tendency for regular events to preempt the attention needed to figure out how to make it work—all natural, inevitable aspects of the process. People need specific ideas, sounding boards, and social support during this critical early period, or else the

---

4 Stated another way, the principles of change described in the various chapters can be used to encourage either uniform or variable changes in practice. For example, peer interaction, active involvement on the part of the principal, staff development during implementation, etc. can be more or less programmatic, or more or less permissive, in selecting particular changes and ways of implementing them.

5 This statement should be qualified, for looseness of the education system is not always a bad thing (see Weick, 1976). Looseness allows different innovations to appear in different parts of the system; it also protects people from bad central decisions and simple conformity (see also Wilson, 1966).

initial momentum never gets established. If we are to accomplish change in practice, we have to, in Bruce Joyce's coruscating phrase, "crack the wall of privatism" in education. Privatism and professional development are closely (and inversely) linked. In opening up contact, there are dangers of misjudgment, improper evaluation, imposition of ideas, and impatience with those who don't seem to be "with it." We are not used to receiving and giving help, or to minimizing the judgmental nature of feedback. Breaking down privatism means having some *continuous* exchanges about particular changes in instructional practices and their relationship to outcomes—between two teachers, between two or more teachers and the principal, the consultant, and so on.[6] Privatism inhibits the spread of ideas. Individuals, local schools and school boards, teacher associations, governments, and other agencies should find ways of promoting the generative resources of small-group and one-to-one interaction during attempts at change.

# Specific vs. generic capacity for change

Theme 4 reminds us that implementing a particular specific change is not the primary goal. We should always keep an eye on the cumulative record. Each failure lessens the motivation and confidence for the next effort. Even a single success, if it has exacted heavy personal costs in time and energy, may be at the expense of future changes. *The goal is to get good at change.* It is to learn to decide when *not* to attempt a change, as well as to select a smaller number of changes and do them well. It is to find ways of avoiding hopeless and wasted efforts, and to become more proficient at discovering untapped resources in the system. It is to focus on the *consequences* of specific changes—to not lose sight of the fact that innovation is only a means of accomplishing something desired.

Understanding the inevitable sources of problems in the implementation process involves a way of thinking about people and the situations they are in. It may require a paradigm shift towards "the implementation perspective." The assumptions we make in attempting to bring about change in ourselves or others have powerful ramifications throughout the change process. Increasing our basic capacity for implementing change in practice involves altering these assumptions in the direction of consistency with the principles embedded in earlier chapters. We do need a new way of thinking about educational change which places a lot of emphasis on what happens *during* the first year or more (depending on the scope and complexity of change) of attempted implementation. Moving toward the more generic capacity for balancing maintenance and change, for knowing what changes are needed and how they should be introduced, is to place change on a coequal footing with stability.

---

6 It should be clear that privatism does not just apply to teachers. Principals rarely indicate to teachers or to other principals what assumptions they make in dealing with difficult problems, how they go about addressing problems, what works and doesn't work. The same could be said of other roles in the educational system.

# Time and change

Theme 5 is closely related to how change can be built into the regular job. The single most frequently cited barrier to implementation is lack of time. Sarason (1972, ch. 5) refers to "the myth of unlimited resources," and time is one of them. There probably never will be adequate time—it costs too much and there is so much to do. So we should face the fact that we are talking about obtaining small amounts of time on some regular basis. Part of the responsibility lies with decision-makers to provide time for learning to work with new programs through their policies (such as shortened work days). Another part resides with principals, teachers, and the community, who must figure out—as some of them do—more imaginative ways of creating time through scheduling, use of aides, or whatever.[7] The gravity of the goal should be recognized. Until some time for change becomes a regular part of the job (*not* evenings and weekends), we should not expect substantial changes in practice to occur. We know that change involves psychological and organizational processes of some complexity, which do not progress by accident. The note of optimism, as we have seen in some of the case studies of success, is that small amounts of regular time (such as a half-day a month with some one-to-one interaction in between), if used wisely, can produce real benefits. In the meantime, we should only spend so much energy (and time) in lamenting the lack of time available for the personal and social changes which might interest us, or which others expect us to undertake. We are all short on time. It is a question of priorities and of know-how in establishing productive change processes under less than optimal conditions.

# Leadership and change

Theme 6—leadership and change—brings to the fore the quality of those who will direct and manage change. I cannot tell whether leadership for change is getting better or worse. I do know that abstract theories of leadership which call for vision, management of conflict, proactive orientations, and the like do not inspire practical confidence, not because they are in error but because they seem to be full of words which have no concrete referents. We have also seen that the great expansion in leadership positions in the 1960s and early 1970s did not occur (nor could it have been expected to occur) with selection criteria geared to qualities necessary for leading change in practice. In-service programs addressing some of these qualities are only now beginning to become available. One of the potentially more productive longer-term levers for educational change resides in the criteria and mechanisms for the appointment of upcoming leaders over the next fifteen years as new positions become available through retirements. Another depends on continuous professional development programs for leaders being established in more and more school systems (see the

---

7 Recall the differences between Seaside district and the other two districts in how much time per teacher was devoted to professional development over the course of a year (chapter 14).

chapters on the principal and the district administrator, and chapter 14 on professional development). Every chapter in this book, every factor affecting change, implicates the leader in establishing the kind of organizational climate and conditions which make it possible to contend with the inevitable problems of implementation.

# Grandeur vs. incrementalism

Theme 7 raises a dilemma about the scope and magnitude of change. Should we put resources into large-scale reform (the alternative of grandeur) or into smaller, step-by-step efforts (the alternative of incrementalism)?[8] In a literal sense this is a false question, or at least put in the wrong way. The more precise question is about large- and small-scale change. The number of large-scale efforts depends on the priorities and resources in society. If a problem is important enough, it will elicit major and widespread attention. In either case, large or small, the issue in theme 7 is one of *strategy*. If the grandeur alternative means grand visions and expectations without any grounding in the reality of how to get there, it clearly has no warrant in the history of implementation. Watzlawick et al. (1974, p. 159) comment on the problem in their treatise on change:

> It is our contention that ... change can be implemented effectively by focusing on minimal, concrete goals, going slowly, and proceeding step by step, rather than strongly promoting vast and vague targets with whose desirability nobody would take issue, but whose attainability is another matter altogether.

Both large-scale and small-scale change should be attempted depending on the importance of the problems and the resources available for addressing them. *In either case, implementation will be incremental.*[9] Those interested in large-scale change should pay attention to implementation detail, to how they are going to move from one phase to another and make revisions along the way. Vagueness and grandiosity is the problem, not large-scaleness per se. Abstraction and vague or nonexistent plans are the bane of implementation. Concreteness is common to success in both large- and small-scale change.

A second tendency detrimental to change of any scale concerns single-factor (or at best linear) thinking about change. We must remember that there are a set of interacting factors which impinge on attempts at change, even though we find it psychologically more reassuring to deal with one factor at a time. What is required is *multivariate* thinking—attention to *all* of the factors that interact with each other in the change process: the nature of the change; the role of school systems, of principals, of the community, of teachers; communication and climate; integrating professional development with program improvement; and so on. In short, concreteness and multivariate realities are tensions which must be continually addressed. There are many different ways to fail; there are also alternative ways to succeed. While I have outlined some basic principles

---

8 See Smith and Keith's (1971) discussion of these alternatives.
9 We might imagine a revolutionary change in which the basic institutions and people in key positions are replaced. Nevertheless, they must still *begin* the implementation process of establishing a new order.

and guidelines, those who are knowledgeable about particular situations will be in the best position to derive, test, and modify specific strategies.

# Meaning and change

Theme 8 is indeed the meta-theme of the book, which might be rephrased as "Meaning—The Key to School Improvement." Every change has two components: an implicit or explicit *theory of education* (what the change is) and an implicit or explicit *theory of change* (the process being followed to implement it). Individuals must find meaning in both aspects: What does the change mean for what I do? What does the process of introduction and follow-through look like from my perspective? All the problems of change can be compressed into these two aspects.

When we try to look at change directly from the point of view of each and every individual affected by it, and aggregate these individual views, the task of educational change becomes a bit unsettling. When we are dealing with reactions and perceptions of diverse people in diverse settings, faulty communication is guaranteed. People are a nuisance. But the theory of meaning says that individual concerns come with the territory; addressing these concerns *is* educational change.

I have stressed the need for meaning in earlier chapters, and it is worth stressing one time more. At various points, we have discussed incentives and disincentives for putting forth the extra effort to bring about change in practice. The psychological process of change is not smooth, even if everything is done right (which it usually is not) to foster and support it. Clarity, concreteness, practicality, the connection between change in practice and outcomes, and the underlying logic of change are not all apparent at the outset. We have difficulty understanding an innovation without trying it. And trying it raises anxiety and doubts as well as excitement and promise. We need help in moving beyond these problems. In brief, the key to school improvement is to recognize that *individual meaning is the central issue*, and to do things that will enhance this meaning. Several aspects of change become integrally related in this definition. We cannot have successful change if individuals responsible for making it happen do not come to experience the sense of excitement, the mastery of new skills, and clarity about what the change is and why it is working.[10] When people do experience excitement, mastery, and clarity in attempting something new, we are witnessing professional development at its best. It is the development of this personal efficacy and collective confidence in bringing about school change that is so sorely needed.

Let me be clear that I am referring to the need for increased meaning and efficacy for everyone who has a role to play—not just the teacher, but the principal, the consultant, the student, the government official. The theory of meaning suggests that it is necessary and humane to try to understand what change and the change process looks like at every level in the educational system.

---

10 The alternative, of course, is to come to the conclusion that the change is not working and will not work and therefore should be rejected.

One last point on this theme: meaning, the quality of life in the organization, and service are intimately related. If teachers, principals, and others do not experience intellectual and professional growth on the job, how can they make school learning stimulating and productive for children (Sarason, 1972, p. 124)? The quality of the working conditions of the adults in schools deserves serious attention in its own right. It is folly to justify a change only on the abstract (frequently unproven) grounds that it is "for the good of the kids." If it is to succeed, it must also have some good in it for the teacher.

Selected educational changes which take individual meaning and development seriously not only stand a better chance of being implemented; they offer some hope for combating the stagnation, burnout, boredom, and cynicism of professional educators which in the long run will lead to the desiccation of all promising change.

# School and society

The final theme takes us back to the role of education in society. What can we expect from the educational system? Educational change is no substitute for social and political reform. More accurately, educational change is shaped considerably by whatever stability or change exists in the sociopolitical system.[11] Therefore, the expectations must be modest. However, we ought to be able to expect that specific modifications in practice would get implemented more effectively than they currently do, and that students would obtain at least more short-term benefits from innovations introduced than they now do. If educational institutions cannot be held accountable for longer-term effects on society, they should at least be responsible for first-order conditions. Jencks et al. (1972, p. 256) put it this way:

Some schools are dull, depressing, even terrifying places, while others are lively, comfortable and reassuring. If we think of school life as an end in itself rather than a means to some other end, such differences are enormously important. Eliminating these differences would not do much to make adults more equal, but it would do a great deal to make the quality of children's (and teachers') lives more equal. Since children are in school for a fifth of their lives, this would be a significant accomplishment.

It is appropriate that implementation and the meaning of change in education are so closely related to processes of learning and socialization. Principles of learning (for children and adults) represent important resources for principles of change. Unless it has the shoemaker's syndrome (where the shoemaker's children go shoeless), the educational system should turn its own knowledge about learning inward on its own problems of change. It is truly ironic that the usual ways of introducing and supporting change violate so many of the principles of learning so dearly held and advocated in other learning situations by

---

11 Incidentally, it is interesting that implementation theory may have been initiated and is certainly most developed in the field of education (with some important developments occurring in the political science field). Other social program areas and corresponding government agencies would do well to borrow from education, and to develop their own implementation theories (as some are: see Williams, 1981).

the very people responsible for guiding (or allowing themselves to be carried along by) the process.

One of the impressive features of viewing change from the perspective of meaning lies in the realization that there are problems and responsibilities at *every* level in the educational system. We should recognize our own responsibilities, and at the same time attempt to understand the conditions faced by those in other roles as a precondition for engaging them in change. We should approach educational change with the renewed respect which comes from the realization that it demands multi-level responsibilities.

It is too early in the history of change in practice to tell where the new knowledge of implementation will take us. The application of new knowledge frequently creates new unanticipated problems. The more we know, the more we need to know. It is hard work to accomplish change in practice. We have seen that it can be done, and we have ideas about what makes it succeed and fail. The fact that the specific reasons for success and failure make so much common sense should be encouraging. We may not be able to introduce needed educational changes at will, nor be successful with all those which are introduced, and we have no reason to be more optimistic about change in education than in other societal institutions. But we can no longer hide behind the excuse that worthwhile change in practice through deliberate means is impossible.

# Appendix

Each of fifteen selected major innovative programs and research studies in the United States is briefly defined below, and the main references in the Bibliography dealing with each are noted.

1. Dissemination Efforts Supporting School Improvement (DESSI)
2. Emergency School Aid Act (ESAA)
3. Educational Resources Information Center (ERIC)
4. Experimental Schools (ES)
5. Federal Programs Supporting Educational Change (FPSEC)
6. Follow Through (FT)
7. National Diffusion Network (and JDRP)
8. Pilot State Dissemination Program (PSDP)
9. Research and Development Exchange (RDX)
10. Research and Development Utilization (RDU)
11. State Dissemination Grants Program (SDGP)
12. Teacher Corps Program
13. Title I, Elementary and Secondary Education Act (ESEA)
14. Title IV
15. Title VII

*Dissemination Efforts Supporting School Improvement (DESSI)*: A comprehensive three-year study of a broad range of federal and state dissemination programs. Conducted by The Network Inc., Andover, Mass., and assisted by several other institutions, the study examined local implementation in four program areas: National Diffusion Network (including Title I and Follow Through); Market Linkage in Special Education; State Administration of Disseminating through Title IVC adoption grants; and local development through Title IVC adoption grants. Implementation associated with these four program areas was investigated in a sample of 146 schools in 10 states through questionnaires and interviews, and more intensively in detailed case studies of 12 schools. In addition to the local focus the study also examined the role of external agents and assistance in relation to the four mentioned programs, federal dissemination activities (a survey related to 46 programs, and detailed profiles of 14 of these programs), and state-level dissemination activities in the 10 states in the sample. (For references to the DESSI work see Crandall et al.'s forthcoming master report; Cox & Havelock, 1982; Loucks & Cox, 1982; Huberman, 1981; & Miles, 1981.)

*Emergency School Aid Act (ESAA)* is a federal program passed in 1977. It is intended to provide "financial assistance to meet the special needs incident to the elimination of minority group segregation to encourage the voluntary elimination, reduction or prevention of minority group isolation in schools." (See Keesling, 1980; Robbins & Dingler, 1981; Wellisch et al., 1978.)

*Educational Resources Information Center (ERIC)* is an information-based system in which published and unpublished literature on all aspects of education is actively sought, indexed, abstracted, and made available in microfiche and hard copy. A national office, as well as regional clearinghouses with thematic responsibilities, continually updates the information, which is available through state offices, district resource centers, libraries, universities, R&D labs and centers, and other intermediaries. ERIC is used in all major dissemination programs (See Raizen, 1979.)

*Experimental Schools (ES)* program started in 1970 in the Office of Education, and was transferred to NIE in 1972. Its goal was to provide funds to local school districts that were willing to launch locally planned comprehensive change efforts. "Comprehensive" was defined as including five major components as a minimum: curriculum, community participation, staff development, administration, and organization. Interested districts competed for grants through the development of proposals and revisions. Those that received grants were funded up to five years. A total of 18 school districts (ten rural and eight urban) obtained grants. (See Corwin, 1977; Cowden & Cohen, 1979; Herriott & Gross, 1979; Rosenblum & Louis, 1979.)

*Federal Programs Supporting Educational Change* (FPSEC, also known as the Rand Change Agent Study). A multi-year (1973–77) research study funded by the Office of Education to the Rand Corporation. Four major federally sponsored change-oriented programs were examined: Title III, providing funds for locally developed innovations (later became Title IVC—see Title IV below); Title VII—Bilingual Education, Vocational Education, Part D—on enhancing career awareness and readiness; and the Right-to-Read program, which provided funds for demonstration projects on reading, especially for disadvantaged students (later became the Basic Skills program).

The study consisted of two phases. In Phase I (1973–75) the four programs were examined in a national survey sample of 293 sites in 18 states, and in 29 case studies selected from among the survey sites. In Phase II (1975–77) the two largest programs (Title III and Title VII) were investigated to find out what happens to local projects when federal funding stops; a sample of 100 Title III projects were surveyed, along with field work and follow-up on the Title VII projects in phase I. The study is reported in eight volumes (vols. I–V from phase I, and VI–VIII from phase II), mostly authored by Berman and

McLaughlin. (See Berman & McLaughlin, 1975, 1977, 1978, 1979; for secondary analysis see Emrick & Peterson, 1978; Datta, 1981.)

*Follow Through (FT)* began in 1967 with the goal of facilitating the development and dissemination/implementation of model programs for making schooling more effective for low-income children from kindergarten through grade 3. While targeted at a portion of the same population (K–3 grades) as Title I, FT is not a "service" program like Title I, but an experimental/development program. The program provides funds for the dissemination of a variety of educational models ranging from behavioral modification approaches to open education. Models are developed by so-called "model sponsors" in educational laboratories, R&D centers, and local districts. Models are evaluated for inclusion in the program, and once included may be selected by local school districts, with the federal government providing the funds for the model sponsor to work with the district in implementing the program. As an experimental program it received a good deal of money in the early stages. There are also a number of FT Resource Centers based on the particular models, in which staff and facilities are available for responding to requests, disseminating materials, and offering demonstrations and other training at the center or on site for local schools or districts interested in adopting and implementing the model selected. Major reductions in federal funds for FT are planned over the next three years. (See Bereiter & Kurland, 1981–82; Emrick & Peterson, 1980; Hodges et al., 1980; Keesling, 1980; Rhine, 1981; Smith & Nerenberg, 1981; Stebbins et al., 1977; Crandall et al., forthcoming.)

*National Diffusion Network (and JDRP)*: NDN is a nationwide system of dissemination to assist local districts in selecting and using innovative programs. A Joint Dissemination Review Panel from the Office of Education and the National Institute of Education screens programs using criteria of quality and effectiveness. Once validated by JDRP the programs are included in NDN, which operates through a system of state and regional facilitators, who help school districts select programs of interest and arrange for the Developers/Demonstrators (D/Ds) of the projects to provide training to local district staff. NDN finances the work of the D/Ds.

The programs eligible for submission normally involve projects developed from other federal programs (and recently from any sources). Thus, Title I has more than 50 projects validated, Follow Through some 22, Title IVC approximately 24. A complete listing of validated programs is compiled annually in a publication titled *Education Programs That Work* (Far West Laboratory). The programs cover such areas as basic skills, early childhood, special education, bilingual education, in-service education, and alternative schools. In 1980–81 the total list included 237 projects. (See Neill, 1976, 1981; Far West Laboratory 1980; Lebby, 1981; Tallmage, 1977; Emrick & Peterson, 1977; Crandall et al., forthcoming.)

*Pilot State Dissemination Program* (PSDP) was a two-year program which provided federal support for three state education agencies to develop and test strategies for bridging the gap between the knowledge needs of local practitioners and the knowledge available on existing research findings and/or programs. The program used a combination of an information base (mainly ERIC) and field or extension agents to work with local practitioners to formulate needs and match them to available information. (See Emrick & Peterson, 1978; Sieber et al., 1977.) The PSDP experiment led to the State Dissemination Grants Program (see below).

*Research and Development Exchange (RDX)*: The RDX program is a cooperative effort among several Labs, Centers, and states to exchange information on key topics mostly in the areas of basic skills (math and language arts) and competency-based education. In the RDX program, Labs and Centers (1) synthesize and disseminate information and/or provide training or assistance on topics and products of potential interest to practitioners, and (2) communicate information/product needs in the field to researchers and developers. There are eight regional exchange centers, which are housed in Appalachia Educational Lab (West Virginia), CEMREL Inc. (Missouri), Mid-continent Regional Educational Lab (Missouri), Northeast Regional Exchange (Massachusetts), Northwest Regional Educational Lab (Oregon), Research for Better Schools (Pennsylvania), Southwest Educational Development Laboratory (Texas), and Southwest Regional Lab (California). Each center serves from four to 11 states. Four central services support the regional exchanges: the Dissemination Support Service for staff responsible for dissemination (provided by the Northwest Regional Educational Lab); the R&D Interpretation Service, to help transform knowledge resulting from R&D into more usable form (provided by CEMREL); the Resource and Referral service, to build a data bank of people and organizations knowledgeable about R&D in the basic skills and competency areas (at the Center for Vocational Education, Ohio State University); and the System Support Service to facilitate the total R&D exchange by coordinating information so as to inform the R&D community in the country of field-based needs and reactions to existing products and research (at the Far West Lab in San Francisco). (See Kronkosky, 1981; Raizen, 1979.)

*Research and Development Utilization (RDU)*: In 1976 NIE established the Research and Development Utilization Program to help schools clarify and solve local problems by drawing on validated R&D knowledge and corresponding technical assistance in the areas of basic skills and career education. Seven projects were funded, which operated in a total of 20 states and served over 300 schools or districts. The seven projects were the Northwest Reading Consortium, the Georgia Research and Development Utilization Project, the Pennsylvania School Improvement Project, the National Education Association Inservice Education Project, the Florida Linkage System, the Michigan Career Education Dissemination Project, and The Network Consortium Project (Massachusetts). Each project was designed to help school personnel address particular problems through the use of selected programs, as well as to enhance their problem-solving capacity (i.e., their procedures for deciding on and implementing new programs). (See Louis, Rosenblum, & Molitor, 1981; Louis & Rosenblum, 1981; Louis, Rosenblum, et al., 1981; Louis, Kell, Chabotar, & Sieber, 1981; Louis, Kell, et al., 1981; Molitor, 1981; Spencer & Louis, 1980.)

*State Dissemination Grants Program* (SDGP): SDGP is a major program of the National Institute of Education designed to strengthen the capacity of state education departments to provide "comprehensive and generalized" dissemination services to local school districts and intermediate agencies. Comprehensive is defined to include information resources, linkage (linking clients to information), and leadership/management arrangements. Capacity-building grants are awarded to states on a three-to-five-year renewable basis. The grants began in 1975 with a first cohort of 10 states. At the present time 44 states and territories have been funded. (See Madey et al., 1979; Royster et al., 1981.)

*Teacher Corps Program*: Teacher Corps is a federally funded program to provide support for collaborative university/school-district projects to improve and/or develop pre-service and in-service projects for teachers and teacher aides in geographical areas having a concentration of low-income families in order to strengthen educational programs and services. (See Corwin, 1973; Reinhard et al., 1980; Rosenblum & Jastrzab, 1980.) Stanford Research Institute (SRI), Menlo Park, California is currently conducting a major evaluation of the program.

*Title I, Elementary and Secondary Education Act* (ESEA): Title I is a federal program with the purpose of providing financial assistance to districts for elementary schools with "concentrations of children from low-income families." It is by far the largest federal program, with an annual budget of over $3 billion and serving some 5 million children. It is a categorical program in which monies are earmarked for entitlement to meet the needs of disadvantaged students. Funds are administered through state departments to local districts on the basis of program proposals. Almost 90% of the school districts in the United States receive at least some Title I funds, with some districts and some individual schools receiving substantial amounts for staff and program assistance. There are 10 regional Title I "Technical Assistance Centers," which are funded to provide assistance to districts and states in the development, implementation, monitoring, and evaluation of programs. (See David, 1981; Fishbein et al., 1980; Goettel et al., 1977; Keesling, 1980; Kirst & Jung, 1980; McLaughlin, 1976; Melaragno et al., 1981; Orland & Goettel, 1980; Crandall et al., forthcoming.)

*Title IV* consists of two parts. Title IVB provides grants to states to distribute to districts for the purchase of library, media, and guidance support materials. Title IVC for innovative projects (formerly Title III) is of more direct interest for our purposes. The IVC grants fall into five categories. The largest category involves grants to local districts for the *development* of new programs. A second category is for *adoption*, for districts to adopt exemplary projects (e.g., from NDN). Other smaller-scale grants are available for dissemination, individual school projects, and the like. (See McDonnell & McLaughlin, 1980; Crandall et al., forthcoming; Berman & McLaughlin, 1977, 1978).

*Title VII*—Bilingual Education Act provides financial assistance to local districts to develop programs "to demonstrate effective ways of providing for children of limited English proficiency, instruction designed to enable them, while using their native language, to achieve competence in the English language.'' The largest number of students who participate are Hispanic, although some 70 languages are included. (See FPSEC; Cadena-Munoz, 1981; Keesling, 1980.)

# Bibliography

Adams, R., Hutchinson, S., & Mattray, C. A developmental study of teacher concerns across time. Paper presented at American Educational Research Association annual meeting, 1980.

Alberta Department of Education. *Inservice education for implementation of new and revised programs.* Edmonton: Department of Education, Tri-partite Committee on In-service Education, 1980.

Alkin, M., Daillak, R., & White, P. *Using evaluations.* Berkeley, Calif.: Sage, 1979.

American Federation of Teachers. *AFT educational research and dissemination program.* Washington: AFT, 1982.

Anderson, R., & Benoit, R. *Reflections concerning the Canada Studies Foundation.* Toronto: Canada Studies Foundation, 1978.

Aoki, T., et al. *British Columbia social studies assessment*, Vols. 1–3. Victoria: British Columbia Ministry of Education, 1977.

Apling, R., & Kennedy, M. *Providing assistance to improve the utility of information from tests and evaluations.* Cambridge, Mass.: Huron Institute, 1981.

Apple, M. Analyzing determinations: Understanding and evaluating the production of social outcomes in schools. *Curriculum Inquiry*, 1980, *10*(1), 55–76.

Argyris, C., & Schon, D. *Theory in practice: Increasing professional effectiveness.* San Francisco: Jossey-Bass, 1977.

Armour, D., et al. *Analysis of the school-preferred reading program in selected Los Angeles minority schools.* Santa Monica, Calif.: Rand Corporation, 1976.

Atkin, J., & House, E. The federal role in curriculum development, 1950–1980. *Educational Evaluation and Policy Analysis*, 1981, *3*(5), 5–36.

Bailey, A. A re-examination of the events at Cambire school. Unpublished paper, University of Sussex, England, 1975.

Bailey, G. Management and change. In M. Milstein (Ed.), *Schools, conflict, and change.* New York: Teachers College Press, 1980.

Baldridge, J. Organizational change and the consultant's role: Rules for effective action. In J. Baldridge & T. Deal (Eds.), *Managing change in educational organizations.* Berkeley, Calif.: McCutchan, 1975.

Baltzell, C. Selection of elementary and secondary school principals: Preliminary findings. Paper presented at American Educational Research Association annual meeting, 1981.

Bank, A. School district management strategies to link testing with instructional change. Evaluation Network Meetings, October 1981.

Bank, A., Snidman, N., & Pitts, M. Evaluation, dissemination and educational improvement: How do they interact? Paper presented at American Educational Research Association annual meeting, 1979.

Bardach, E. *The implementation game: What happens after a bill becomes a law.* Cambridge, Mass.: MIT Press, 1977.

Barth, R. Home based reinforcement of school behavior: A review and analysis. *Review of Educational Research*, 1979, *49*(3), 436–58.

Bass, G. *A study of alternatives in American education*, Vol. I, *District policies and the implementation of change*. Santa Monica, Calif.: Rand Corporation, 1978.

Bass, G., & Berman, P. *Federal aid to rural schools: Current patterns and unmet needs*. Santa Monica, Calif.: Rand Corporation, 1979.

Bass, G., & Berman, P. Analysis of federal aid to rural schools, part II: *Special needs of rural districts*. Santa Monica, Calif.: Rand Corporation, 1981.

Bassin, M., & Gross, T. Organization development: A viable method for change for urban secondary schools. Paper delivered to American Educational Research Association annual meeting, 1978.

Becker, H. Teacher practices of parent involvement at home—a state wide survey. Paper presented at American Educational Research Association annual meeting, 1981.

Behn, W., et al. School is bad: Work is worse. In M. Carnoy & H. Levin (Eds.), *The limits of educational reform*. New York: McKay, 1976.

Bennett, N., et al. *Teaching styles and pupil progress*. Cambridge, Mass.: Harvard University Press, 1976.

Bennett, N., et al. *Focus in teaching: Readings in the observation and conceptualization of teaching*. London: Longman, 1979.

Bennis, W. *Changing organizations*. Toronto: McGraw-Hill, 1966.

Bentzen, M. *Changing organizations: The magic feather principle*. New York: McGraw-Hill, 1974.

Bereiter, C., & Kurland, M. A constructive look at Follow Through results. *Interchange*, 1981, *12*(1), 1–21.

Berger, P., & Luckmann, T. *The social construction of reality*. New York: Anchor Books, 1967.

Berman, P. The study of macro- and micro-implementation. *Public Policy*, 1978, *26*(2), 157–84.

Berman, P. Thinking about programmed and adaptive implementation: Matching strategies to situations. In H. Ingram & D. Mann (Eds.), *Why policies succeed or fail*. Beverly Hills, Calif.: Sage, 1980.

Berman, P. Toward an implementation paradigm. In R. Lehming & M. Kane (Eds.), *Improving schools*. Beverly Hills, Calif.: Sage, 1981.

Berman, P., & McLaughlin, M. Implementation of educational innovation. *Educational Forum*, 1976, *40*(3), 345–70.

Berman, P., & McLaughlin, M. *Federal programs supporting educational change*, Vol. VII, *Factors affecting implementation and continuation*. Santa Monica, Calif.: Rand Corporation, 1977.

Berman, P., & McLaughlin, M. *Federal programs supporting educational change*, Vol. VIII, *Implementing and sustaining innovations*. Santa Monica, Calif.: Rand Corporation, 1978.

Berman, P., & McLaughlin, M. *An exploratory study of school district adaptations*. Santa Monica, Calif.: Rand Corporation, 1979.

Berman, P., et al. *Federal programs supporting educational change*, Vol. IV, *The findings in review*. Santa Monica, Calif.: Rand Corporation, 1975.

Bickel, W., & Bickel, D. A study of a district teacher organization's impact on educational policy. Paper presented at American Educational Research Association annual meeting, 1979.

Blake, R., & Mouton, J. *Consultation*. Reading, Mass.: Addison-Wesley, 1976.

Blumberg, A., & Greenfield, W. *The effective principal*. Boston: Allyn & Bacon, 1980.

Bolam, R., Baker, K., & McMahon, A. *The T.I.P.S. project national evaluation report*. Bristol, England: University of Bristol, School of Education, 1979.

Bowles, D. School–community relations, community support, and student achievement: A summary of findings. Madison: University of Wisconsin, R&D Center for Individualized Schooling, 1980.

Bowles, S., & Gintis, H. *Schooling in capitalist America*. New York: Basic Books, 1976.

Boyd, W. The changing politics of curriculum policy making for American schools. *Review of Educational Research*, 1978, *48*(4), 577–628.

Bridge, G. Parent participation in school innovations. *Teachers College Record*, 1976, *77*(3), 366–84.

Brookover, W. Effective secondary schools. Philadelphia: Research for Better Schools, 1981.

Brown, L. Problems in implementing statutory requirements for Title I ESEA Parent Advisory Councils. Paper presented at American Educational Research Association annual meeting, 1980.

Brown, W. *Education finance in Canada*. Ottawa: Canadian Teachers' Federation, 1981.

Bussis, A., Chittenden, E., & Amarel, M. *Beyond surface curriculum*. Boulder, Colo.: Westview Press, 1976.

Butler, M., & Paisley, W. *Factors determining roles and functions of educational linking agents*. San Francisco: Far West Laboratory, 1978.

Byrne, D., Hines, S., & McCleary, L. *The senior high school principalship, The national survey*, Vol. I. Reston, Va.: National Association of Secondary School Principals, 1978.

Cadena-Munoz, R., & Keesling, J. *Parents and federal education programs*, Vol. IV, *Parental involvement in Title VII projects*. Santa Monica, Calif.: System Development Corporation, 1981.

California State Department of Education. *Recommendations for the evaluation of staff development in California: A preparatory study*. Sacramento, 1979.

Calliste, A. Educational and occupational expectations of high school students: The effects of socioeconomic background. Unpublished doctoral dissertation, University of Toronto, 1980.

Campbell, R. The world of the school superintendent. *New York University Education Quarterly*, 1977, *9*(1), 14–20.

Campeau, P., Binkley, J., Treadway, P., Appleby, J., & Bessey, B. *Final report: Evaluation of Project Information Package dissemination and implementation*. Palo Alto, Calif.: American Institute for Research, 1979.

Canadian Education Association. *Results of a Gallup poll of public opinion in Canada about public involvement in educational decisions*. Toronto: CEA, 1979.

Carew, J., & Lightfoot, S. *Beyond bias: Perspectives on classrooms*. Cambridge, Mass.: Harvard University Press, 1979.

Carlson, R. *School superintendents: Careers and performance*. Columbus, Ohio: Charles Merrill, 1972.

Carnie, C. Assisting school districts to use evaluation results effectively: Techniques that work. Paper presented at American Educational Research Association annual meeting, 1982.

Cates, C., Malkas, M., Sulkis, B., & Hood, P. (Eds.). *The state of the states: Report of discussions at the 1978 Dissemination Forum*. San Francisco: Far West Laboratory, 1978.

Center for Equal Education. Effects of parents on schooling. *Research Review of Equal Education*, 1977, *6*, 30–40.

Chabotar, K., Louis, K., & Rosenblum, S. *RDU study and its policy context: Perspectives of educational policy makers*. Cambridge, Mass.: ABT Associates, 1980.

Charters, W., & Pellegrin, R. Barriers to the innovation process: Four case studies of differentiated staffing. *Educational Administration Quarterly*, 1973, *9*(1), 3–14.

Cherniss, C. *Staff burnout: Job stress in the human services*. Beverly Hills, Calif.: Sage, 1980.

Chin, R., et al. Utilization models for types of knowledge. Paper presented at American Educational Research Association annual meeting, 1981.

Clark, C., & Yinger, R. Research on teacher thinking. *Curriculum Inquiry*, 1977, *7*(4), 279–304.

Clark, C., & Yinger, R. The hidden world of teaching. Paper presented at American Educational Research Association annual meeting, 1980.

Clark, D., Lotto, L., & McCarthy, M. Factors associated with success in urban elementary schools. *Phi Delta Kappan*, March 1980, pp. 467–70.

Clifton, R. Practice teaching: Survival in a marginal situation. *Canadian Journal of Education*, 1979, *4*(3), 60–74.

Cohen, E. Open-space schools: The opportunity to become ambitious. *Sociology of Education*, 1973, *46*(2), 143–61.

Cohen, E. Sociology looks at team teaching. In R. Corwin (Ed.), *Research in Sociology of Education and Socialization*, Vol. 2. Greenwich, Conn.: JAI Press, 1981.

Cohen, M. Effective schools: What the research says. *Today's Education*, April–May 1981, pp. 46G–50G.

Coleman, J., et al. *Equality of educational opportunity*. Washington: U.S. Government Printing Office, 1966.

Connell, R., et al. Class and gender dynamics in a ruling-class school. *Interchange*, 1981, *12*(2/3), 102–17.

Connelly, F., & Elbaz, F. Conceptual bases for curriculum thought: A teacher's perspective. In A. Foshay (Ed.), *1980 Yearbook, Association for Supervision and Curriculum Development*. Alexandria, Va., 1980.

Coons, J., & Sugarman, S. *Education by choice: The case for family control*. Berkeley: University of California Press, 1978.

Corbett, D. School contingencies in the continuation of planned educational change. Philadelphia: Research for Better Schools, 1982.

Corcoran, T. Ordinary knowledge as a constraint on the use of research: The case of the comprehensive basic skills review. Paper presented at American Educational Research Association annual meeting, 1982.

Corwin, R. *Reform and organizational survival—The teacher corps as an instrument of educational change*. New York: Wiley, 1973.

Corwin, R. *Patterns of federal-local relationships in education: A case study of the rural experimental schools program*. Cambridge, Mass.: ABT Associates, 1977.

Covert, J., & Clifton, R. An examination of the effects of extending the practicum on the professional dispositions of student teachers. Unpublished paper, Memorial University of Newfoundland, 1980.

Cowden, P., & Cohen, D. *Divergent worlds of practice*. Cambridge, Mass.: Huron Institute, 1979.

Cox, P., & Havelock, R. External facilitators and their role in the improvement of practice. Paper presented at American Educational Research Association annual meeting, 1982.

Crandall, D. Training and supporting linking agents. In N. Nash & J. Culbertson (Eds.), *Linking processes in educational improvement*. Columbus, Ohio: University Council for Educational Administration, 1977.

Crandall, D. Emulation and replication. *Teacher Education and Special Education*, 1981, *4*(2), 13–22.

Crandall, D., et al. Master report series of the study of dissemination efforts supporting school improvement. Andover, Mass.: The Network, forthcoming.

Crowson, R., & Porter-Gehrie, C. The school principalship: An organizational stability role. Paper presented at American Educational Research Association annual meeting, 1980.

Cusick, P. *Inside high school*. Toronto: Holt, Rinehart & Winston, 1973.

Cussons, R., & Hedges, H. Volunteers in Halton schools. Unpublished report, Ontario Institute for Studies in Education, 1978.

Daft, R., & Becker, S. *The innovative organization: Innovation adoption in school organizations*. New York: Elsevier North-Holland, 1978.

Dale, R. From expectations to outcomes in education systems. *Interchange*, 1981, *12*(2/3), 65–85.

Dalin, P. *Limits to educational change*. London: Macmillan, 1978.

Dalin, P., & Rust, V. Can schools learn? Unpublished manuscript, International Movements toward Educational Change, Oslo.

D'Amico, J. *The effective schools movement: Studies, issues and approaches*. Philadelphia: Research for Better Schools, 1980.

Datta, L. Changing times: The study of federal programs supporting educational change and the case for local problem solving. *Teachers College Record*, 1981, *82*(1), 111–16.

David, J. Local uses of Title I evaluations. *Educational Evaluation and Policy Analysis*, 1981, *3*(1), 27–40.

Davies, D., et al. *Federal and state impact on citizen participation in the schools*. Boston: Institute for Responsive Education, 1978.

Dawson, A. Criteria for the creation of in-service education programs. *Canadian Journal of Education*, 1978, *3*(1), 49–60.

Dawson, J. *Teacher participation in educational innovation: Some insights into its nature*. Philadelphia: Research for Better Schools, 1981.

Deal, T., & Nutt, S. *Promoting, guiding—and surviving—change in small school districts*. Cambridge, Mass.: ABT Associates, 1979.

Denemark, G. The case for extended programs of initial teacher preparation. Paper presented to the Forum of Education Organization Leaders, Arlington, Va., 1979.

Denham, C., & Lieberman, A. *Time to learn: A review of the beginning teacher evaluation study*. Washington: National Institute of Education, 1980.

Devaney, K. (Ed.). *Essays on teachers' centers*. San Francisco: Far West Laboratory, 1977.

Dimond, E. (Ed.). *Issues of sex bias and sex fairness in career interest measurement*. Washington: National Institute of Education, 1975.

Dow, I., & Whitehead, R. *New perspectives in curriculum implementation*. Report prepared for Ontario Public School Men Teachers' Federation, 1981.

Downey, L., and associates. *The social studies in Alberta—1975*. Edmonton, Alta.: L. Downey Research Associates, 1975.

Doyle, W., & Ponder, G. The practicality ethic in teacher decision making. *Interchange*, 1977–78, *8*(3), 1–12.

Drew, C. (Ed.). *Case studies in program improvement*. Andover, Mass.: The Network, 1979.

*DTA project: Overview 1977*. Chicago: Center for New Schools, Documentation and Technical Assistance in Urban Schools, 1977.

Duignan, P. The pressures of the superintendency: Too many deadlines, not enough time. *The Executive Educator*, November 1979, pp. 34–35.

Eastabrook, G., & Fullan, M. *School and community: Principals and community schools in Ontario*. Toronto: Ontario Ministry of Education, 1978.

Edmonds, R. Effective schools for the urban poor. *Educational Leadership*, 1979, *36*, 15–27.

Edmonds, R. Programs of school improvement: A 1982 overview. Paper prepared for Conference on Implications of Research on Teaching for Practice, National Institute of Education, 1982.

Eggleston, J. *The sociology of the school curriculum*. London: Routledge & Kegan Paul, 1977.

Elliott, J. Developing hypotheses about classrooms from teachers' practical constructs: An account of the work of the Ford teaching project. *Interchange*, 1976–77, *7*(2), 2–22.

Elliott, J. How do teachers learn? Unpublished paper, Cambridge Institute of Education, 1979.

Elliott, J. The implications of classroom research for the professional development of teachers. *World Year Book in Education*, 1980.

Elmore, R. Organizational models of social program implementation. *Public Policy*, 1978, *26*(2), 185–228.

Elmore, R. Backward mapping: Implementation, research and policy decisions. *Political Science Quarterly*, 1979–80, *94*, 601–16.

Elmore, R. *Complexity and control: What legislators and administrators can do about implementing public policy*. Washington: National Institute of Education, 1980.

Emrick, J., & Peterson, S. *Evaluation of the National Diffusion Network*. Menlo Park, Calif.: Stanford Research Institute, 1977.

Emrick, J., & Peterson, S. *A synthesis of findings across five recent studies in educational dissemination and change*. San Francisco: Far West Laboratory, 1978.

Emrick, J., & Peterson, S. *San Diego implementation study: Case study report and first-year measurement development*. Los Altos, Calif.: Emrick & Associates, 1980.

Epstein, J. A longitudinal study of school and family efforts on student development. In S. Mednick & M. Harway (Eds.), *Longitudinal research in the U.S.* Boston: Nijhoff, 1982.

Estes, G. Assisting school districts to improve evaluation use: Issues and approaches. Paper presented at American Educational Research Association annual meeting, 1982.

Etzioni, A. *Studies in social change*. New York: Holt, Rinehart & Winston, 1966.

Evans, C. *The micro millenium*. New York: Washington Square Press, 1979.

Fantini, M. Community participation: Alternative patterns and their consequence on educational achievement. Paper presented at American Educational Research Association annual meeting, 1980.

Far West Laboratory for Educational Research and Development. *Educational programs that work*. San Francisco: Far West Laboratory, 1980.

Farrar, E., DeSanctis, J., & Cohen, D. *Views from below: Implementation research in education*. Cambridge, Mass.: Huron Institute, 1979.

Fennell, B. *Teacher in-service training costs*. Edmonton: Alberta Department of Education, 1980.

Fenstermacher, G. What needs to be known about what teachers need to know? Paper presented to Exploring Issues in Teacher Education conference, R&D Center, Austin, Tex., 1979.

Firestone, W., & Herriott, R. Images of the organization and the promotion of change. In R. Corwin (Ed.), *Research in sociology of education and socialization*, Vol. 2. Greenwich, Conn.: JAI Press, 1981.

Firestone, W., & Wilson, B. *Political and technical linkage: The contribution of regional educational agencies*. Philadelphia: Research for Better Schools, 1981.

Fishbein, R., Anderson, J., & English, J. Increasing the relevance of Title I evaluation data to school practice. Paper presented at American Educational Research Association annual meeting, 1980.

Fisher, C., et al. Teaching behaviors, academic learning time, and student achievement: An overview. In C. Denham & A. Lieberman (Eds.), *Time to learn*. Washington: National Institute of Education, 1978.

Flanders, G. *Summary report: Professional Development Study*. Vancouver: British Columbia Teachers' Federation, 1980.

Fullan, M. Overview of the innovative process and the user. *Interchange*, 1972, *3*(2/3), 1–47.

Fullan, M. *School-focused in-service education in Canada*. Report prepared for Centre for Educational Research and Innovation, OECD, Paris, 1979.

Fullan, M. The relationship between evaluation and implementation. In A. Lewy & D. Nevo (Eds.), *Evaluation roles in education*. London: Gordon Breach, 1980.

Fullan, M. Research on the implementation of educational change. In R. Corwin (Ed.), *Research in Sociology of Education and Socialization*, Vol. 2. Greenwich, Conn.: JAI Press, 1981.(a)

Fullan, M. School district and school personnel in knowledge utilization. In R. Lehming & M. Kane (Eds.), *Improving schools*. Beverly Hills, Calif.: Sage, 1981.(b)

Fullan, M. The use of external resources for school improvement by local education agencies. Prepared for Far West Laboratory, San Francisco, 1982.

Fullan, M., & Eastabrook, G. The effects of Ontario teachers' strikes on the attitudes and perceptions of grade 12 and 13 students. In D. Brison (Ed.), *Three studies of the effects of teachers' strikes*. Toronto: Ontario Ministry of Education, 1979.

Fullan, M., Eastabrook, G., & Biss, J. Action research in the school involving students and teachers in classroom change. In R. Carlton, L. Colley, & N. MacKinnon (Eds.), *Education, change and society*. Toronto: Gage, 1977.

Fullan, M., & Leithwood, K. Guidelines for planning and evaluating program implementation. Prepared for British Columbia Ministry of Education, 1980.

Fullan, M., Miles, M., & Taylor, G. *Organizational development in schools: The state of the art*, Vol. IV, *Case studies*. Washington: Report to National Institute of Education, 1978.

Fullan, M., Miles, M., & Taylor, G. Organization development in schools: The state of the art. *Review of Educational Research*, 1980, *50*(1), 121–84.

Fullan, M., & Park, P. *Curriculum implementation: A resource booklet*. Toronto: Ontario Ministry of Education, 1981.

Fullan, M., & Pomfret, A. Research on curriculum and instruction implementation. *Review of Educational Research*, 1977, *47*(1), 335–97.

Fullan, M., Wideen, M., Hopkins, D., & Eastabrook, G. *The management of change in teacher education*, Vol. II, *A comparative analysis of faculty and student perceptions*. Final report to Social Sciences and Humanities Research Council (in progress).

Fuller, F. Concerns of teachers: A developmental conceptualization. *American Educational Research Journal*, 1969, *6*(2), 207–26.

Gaines, E. School superintendents describe the job: Short and sour. *Education Daily* (Washington, D.C.), 23 May 1978, p. 5.

Galanter, W. Elementary school staff support system effects on program implementation and job satisfaction. Unpublished doctoral dissertation, Fordham University, 1978.

Galton, M., & Simon, B. *Progress and performance in the primary classroom*. London: Routledge & Kegan Paul, 1980.

Galton, M., Simon, B., & Croll, P. *Inside the primary classroom*. London: Routledge & Kegan Paul, 1980.

Gaskell, J. Sex inequalities for education for work: The case of business education. *Canadian Journal of Education*, 1981, *6*(2), 54–72.

Gaynor, A. A study of change in educational organizations. In L. Cunningham et al. (Eds.), *Educational administration*. Berkeley, Calif.: McCutchan, 1977.

Gersten, G., Carnine, D., Zuref, L., & Cronin, D. Measuring implementation of educational innovations in a broad context. Paper presented at American Educational Research Association annual meeting, 1981.

Giacquinta, J. The process of organizational change in schools. In F. Kerlinger (Ed.), *Review of research in education*. Itasca, Ill.: Peacock, 1973.

Giacquinta, J., & Kazlow, C. The growth and decline of public school innovations: An analysis of the open classroom. Paper presented at American Educational Research Association annual meeting, 1979.

Gideonse, H. Designing federal policies and programs to facilitate local change efforts. In R. Herriott & N. Gross (Eds.), *The dynamics of planned change*. Berkeley, Calif.: McCutchan, 1979.

Gideonse, H. Improving the federal administration of education programs. *Educational Evaluation and Policy Analysis*, 1980, *2*(1), 61–70.

Giroux, H. Hegemony, resistance, and the paradox of educational reform. *Interchange*, 1981, *12*(2/3), 3–26.

Gitlin, A. Reflection and action in teacher education programs. Paper presented at American Educational Research Association annual meeting, 1982.

Goettel, R., et al. *A study of the administration of ESEA, Title I in eight states*. Syracuse: Syracuse Research Corporation, 1977.

Gold, B., & Miles, M. *Whose school is it anyway? Parent teacher conflict over an innovative school*. New York: Praeger, 1981.

Goldhammer, K. Role of the American school superintendent. In L. Cunningham et al. (Eds.), *Educational administration*. Berkeley, Calif.: McCutchan, 1977.

Goodlad, J. *The dynamics of educational change*. Toronto: McGraw-Hill, 1975.

Goodlad, J. Can our schools get better? *Phi Delta Kappan*, January 1979, pp. 342–47.

Goodlad, J., Klein, M., and associates. *Behind the classroom door*. Worthington, Ohio: Charles A. Jones, 1970.

Gordon, D. An approach to the evaluation of state initiatives in staff development. Paper presented at American Educational Research Association annual meeting, 1980.

Gordon, I. Rebuilding home–school relations. *Planning and implementing parent/community involvement into the instructional delivery system*. Proceedings from a parent/community involvement conference sponsored by the Mid-West Teacher Corps, 1978.

Gorton, R., & McIntyre, K. *The senior high school principalship: The effective principal*, Vol. 2. Reston, Va.: National Association of Secondary School Principals, 1978.

Greenfield, W. Empirical research on principals: The state of the art. Paper presented at American Educational Research Association annual meeting, 1982.

Grieve, T. The role of a curriculum director at the school district level. Unpublished paper, Kamloops School District, Kamloops, B.C., 1980.

Gross, N. Basic issues in the management of educational change efforts. In R. Herriott & N. Gross (Eds.), *The dynamics of planned educational change*. Berkeley, Calif.: McCutchan, 1979.

Gross, N., Giacquinta, J., & Bernstein, M. *Implementing organizational innovations: A sociological analysis of planned educational change*. New York: Basic Books, 1971.

Grubb, W., & Lazerson, M. Rally round the workplace: Continuities and fallacies in career education. *Harvard Educational Review*, 1975, *45*(4), 451–74.

Hall, G., Hord, S., & Griffin, T. Implementation at the school building level: The development and analysis of nine mini-case studies. Paper presented at American Educational Research Association annual meeting, 1980.

Hall, G., & Loucks, S. A developmental model for determining whether the treatment is actually implemented. *American Educational Research Journal*, 1977, *14*(3), 263–76.

Hall, G., & Loucks, S. The concept of innovation configurations: An approach to addressing program adaptation. Paper presented at American Educational Research Association annual meeting, 1981.

Hall, G., Rutherford, W., & Griffin, T. Three change facilitator styles: Some indicators and a proposed framework. Paper presented at American Educational Research Association annual meeting, 1982.

Halsey, A., et al. *Origins and destinations: Family class and education in modern Britain*. Oxford: Clarendon Press, 1980.

Handbook of Canadian consumer markets, 1979. Toronto: Conference Board of Canada, 1979.

Hargrove, E. *The missing link: The study of implementation of social policy*. Washington: Urban Institute, 1975.

Harris, B. *Improving staff performance through in-service education*. Boston: Allyn & Bacon, 1980.

Harris, R. (Ed.). *Reflections on the experience of educational linking agents*. Andover, Mass.: The Network, 1979.

Hauser-Cram, P., & O'Leary, K. Parents and schools: A partnership model. Paper presented at American Educational Research Association annual meeting, 1981.

Havelock, R. *Planning for innovations*. Ann Arbor: Institute for Social Research, University of Michigan, 1969.

Havelock, R. *The change agent's guide to innovation in education*. Englewood Cliffs, N.J.: Educational Technology Publications, 1973.

Havelock, R. *School-university collaboration supporting school improvement*, Vols. I–IV. Washington: Knowledge Transfer Institute, American University, 1981.

Havelock, R., & Havelock, M. *Educational innovation in the United States*, Vol. I, *The national survey*. Ann Arbor: Institute for Social Research, University of Michigan, 1973.

Hergert, L. Beyond decision making: Helping schools during implementation. In R. Harris (Ed.), *Reflections on the experience of educational linking agents*. Andover, Mass.: The Network, 1979.

Herriott, R. The federal context: Planning, funding and monitoring. In R. Herriott & N. Gross (Eds.), *The dynamics of planned educational change*. Berkeley, Calif.: McCutchan, 1979.

Herriott, R., & Gross, N. (Eds.). *The dynamics of planned educational change: An analysis of the rural experimental schools program*. Berkeley, Calif.: McCutchan, 1979.

Hill, P., Wuchitech, J., & Williams, R. *The effects of federal education programs on school principals*. Santa Monica, Calif.: Rand Corporation, 1980.

Hodges, W., et al. *Follow Through: Forces for change in the primary schools*. Ypsilanti, Mich.: High Scope Press, 1980.

Holborn, P., et al. *The management of educational change in teacher education*, Vol. IV, *A research agenda*. Final report to Social Sciences and Humanities Research Council (in progress).

Holcomb, J. Superintendents should push programs—not paperwork. *American School Board Journal*, 1979, 66, 34.

Holliday, F. *Building on cultural strengths: The experience of the Chicago region in building capacity in educational problem solving in local urban schools*. Chicago: Center for New Schools, 1977.

Holmes, M. An examination of two technical assistance styles within one project. Chicago: Center for New Schools, DTA Project, 1977.

Hood, P., & Blackwell, L. *Indicators of educational knowledge production, dissemination, and utilization: An exploratory data analysis*. San Francisco: Far West Laboratory, 1979.

Hood, P., & Blackwell, L. The role of teachers and other school practitioners in decision making and innovation. San Francisco: Far West Laboratory, 1980.

Hood, P., & Cates, C. *Alternative approaches to analyzing dissemination linkage roles and functions*. San Francisco: Far West Laboratory, 1978.

Horst, D., et al. *An evaluation of project information packages (PIPs) as used for the diffusion of bilingual projects*. Mountain View, Calif.: RMC Research Corporation, 1980.

Hottois, J., & Milner, N. *The sex education controversy*. Lexington, Mass.: D.C. Heath, 1975.

House, E. *The politics of educational innovation*. Berkeley, Calif.: McCutchan, 1974.

House, E. *Evaluating with validity*. Berkeley, Calif.: Sage, 1980.

House, E., & Lapan, S. *Survival in the classroom*. Boston: Allyn & Bacon, 1978.

Howes, N., & Quinn, R. Implementing change: From research to a prescriptive framework. *Group and Organizational Studies* 1978, *3*(1), 71–83.

Howey, K., & Bents, R. *Toward meeting the needs of the beginning teachers*. Midwest Teacher Corps Project and University of Minnesota/St. Paul Schools Teacher Corps Project, 1979.

Howey, K., & Joyce, B. A data base for future directions in in-service education. *Theory into Practice*, 1978, *27*(3), 206–11.

Howey, K., Yarger, S., & Joyce, B. *Improving teacher education*. Washington: Association of Teacher Educators, 1978.

Huberman, M. Microanalysis of innovation implementation at the school level. Unpublished paper, University of Geneva, 1978.

Huberman, M. Finding and using recipes for busy kitchens: A situational analysis of knowledge use in schools. Prepared for the Program on Research and Educational Practice, National Institute of Canada, 1980.

Huberman, M. *Exemplary center for reading instruction (ECRI) Masepa, North Plains: A case study*. Andover, Mass.: The Network, 1981.

Huguenin, K., Zerchykov, R., & Davies, D. *Narrowing the gap between intent and practice*. Boston: Institute for Responsive Education, 1979.

Huling, L., Hall, G., & Hord, S. Effects of principal interventions on teachers during the change process. Paper presented at American Educational Research Association annual meeting, 1982.

Hull, C., & Rudduck, J. Introducing innovation to pupils. Norwich, England: Centre for Applied Research in Education, University of East Anglia, 1980.

Hyde, A. *Capacities for solving problems: Problems and problem solving methods of school principals*. Chicago: Center for New Schools, 1977.

Institute for Research on Educational Finance and Governance. Federal categorical aid: Emerging patterns of support. Published by the Institute, Stanford University, 1981.

Ivany, J., & Manley-Casimir, M. *Federal–provincial relations: Education Canada*. Toronto: OISE Press, 1981.

Jackson, P. *Life in classrooms*. New York: Holt, Rinehart & Winston, 1968.

Jackson, P. The uncertainties of teaching. Paper presented at American Educational Research Association annual meeting, 1980.

Jackson, R. *Implications of declining enrolment for the schools of Ontario: A statement of effects and solutions*. Final report of the Commission on Declining Enrolments. Toronto: Ontario Ministry of Education, 1978.

Jencks, C., et al. *Inequality: A reassessment of the effects of family and schooling in America*. New York: Basic Books, 1972.

Jencks, C., et al. *Who gets ahead*. New York: Basic Books, 1979.

Joyce, B. In-service education: New perspectives on an old term. In M. Wideen, D. Hopkins, & I. Pye (Eds.), *In-service: A means of progress in tough times*. Vancouver: Simon Fraser University, 1979.

Joyce, B. Organizational homeostasis and innovation: Tightening the loose couplings. Unpublished paper, Booksend Laboratories, Palo Alto, Calif., 1982.

Joyce, B. (Ed.). *Involvement: A study of shared governance of teacher education*. Syracuse, N.Y.: National Dissemination Center, Syracuse University, 1978.

Joyce, B. (Ed.). From thought to action: How teachers think in the classroom. Special issue of *Educational Research Quarterly*, 1978–79, *3*(4).

Joyce, B., Bush, R., & McKibbin, M. Information and opinion from the California staff development study: The compact report. Sacramento: California State Department of Education, 1981.

Joyce, B., & Showers, B. Improving inservice training: The messages of research. *Educational Leadership*, 1980, *37*(5), 379–85.

Joyce, B., & Showers, B. The coaching of teaching: Ensuring transfer from training. Unpublished paper, Booksend Laboratories, Palo Alto, Calif., 1981.

Karweit, N. Time in school. In R. Corwin (Ed.), *Research in sociology of education and socialization*, Vol. 2. Greenwich, Conn.: JAI Press, 1981.

Katz, D., & Kahn, R. *The social psychology of organizations*. 2nd ed. New York: Wiley, 1978.

Katz, E., Lewin, M., & Hamilton, H. Traditions of research on the diffusion of innovation. *American Sociological Review*, 1963, *28*(2), 237–52.

Keesling, J. *Parents and federal education programs: Some preliminary findings from the study of parental involvement*. Santa Monica, Calif.: System Development Corporation, 1980.

Keidel, G. *A profile of public school superintendents of the State of Michigan*. Lansing: Michigan Association of School Administrators, 1977.

Kennedy, M. How evaluators can help policy makers. Cambridge, Mass.: Huron Institute, 1981.

Kennedy, M., Apling, R., & Neumann, W. *The role of evaluation and test information in public schools*. Cambridge, Mass.: Huron Institute, 1980.

Kimbrough, J., & Hill, P. *The aggregate effects of federal education programs*. Santa Monica, Calif.: Rand Corporation, 1981.

Kirst, M. Strengthening federal–local relationships supporting educational change. In R. Herriott & N. Gross (Eds.), *The dynamics of planned educational change*. Berkeley, Calif.: McCutchan, 1979.

Kirst, M., & Jung, R. The utility of a longitudinal approach in assessing implementation: A thirteen year view of Title I, ESEA. *Educational Evaluation and Policy Analysis*, 1980, *2*(5), 17–34.

Kormos, J. Educator and publisher perceptions of quality curriculum and instructional materials during declining enrolments. Unpublished report, Ontario Institute for Studies in Education, 1978.

Kormos, J., & Enns, R. *Professional development through curriculum development*. Toronto: Ontario Teachers' Federation, 1979.

Kratzmann, A., Byrne, T., & Worth, W. *A system in conflict: A report to the Minister of Labour by the fact finding commission*. Edmonton: Alberta Department of Labour, 1981.

Krawchenko, K., et al. Curriculum in Alberta: A study of perceptions. Unpublished paper, Department of Education, University of Alberta, 1979.

Kronkosky, P. A case study of three states' dissemination of *Research within research: A research guided response to concerns of reading educators*. Austin, Tex.: Southwest Educational Development Laboratory, 1981.

Lambright, W., et al. *Educational innovations as a process of coalition building: A study of organizational decision-making*. Washington: Report to National Institute of Education, 1980.

Lawrence, G. Patterns of effective in-service education. Tallahassee: Florida Department of Education, 1974.

Lebby, A. State and federal validation and dissemination systems. *Teacher Education and Special Education*, 1981, *4*(2), 33–38.

Lehming, R., & Kane, M. (Eds.). *Improving schools*. Beverly Hills, Calif.: Sage, 1981.

Leiter, M., & Cooper, M. How teacher unionists view in-service education. *Teachers College Record*, 1978, *80*(1) 107–25.

Leithwood, K. The dimensions of curriculum innovation. *Journal of Curriculum Studies*, 1981, *13*(1), 25–36.

Leithwood, K., & MacDonald, R. Decisions given by teachers for their curriculum choices. *Canadian Journal of Education*, 1981, *6*(2), 103–16.

Leithwood, K., & Montgomery, D. Evaluation in program implementation. *Evaluation Review*, 1980, *4*(2), 193–214.

Leithwood, K., & Montgomery, D. The role of the elementary school principal in program improvement: A review. *Review of Educational Research*, forthcoming.

Leithwood, K., et al. An empirical investigation of teachers' curriculum decision making processes and strategies used by curriculum managers to influence such decision making. Unpublished report, Ontario Institute for Studies in Education, 1978.

Levin, H. Educational reform: Its meaning. In M. Carnoy & H. Levin (Eds.), *The limits of educational reform*. New York: McKay, 1976.

Levin, H. Categorical grants in education: Rethinking the federal role. Publication of the Institute for Research on Educational Finance and Governance, Stanford University, Spring 1981.

Lezotte, L., et al. *School learning climate and student achievement*. East Lansing: Michigan State University, Center for Urban Affairs, 1980.

Lieberman, A., & Miller, L. Teachers, their world and their work: Implications for school improvement. Unpublished manuscript, 1982.

Lightfoot, S. *Worlds apart: Relationships between families and schools*. New York: Basic Books, 1978.

Lightfoot, S. Exploring family–school relationships: A prelude to curriculum designs and strategies. Paper presented at American Educational Research Association annual meeting, 1980.

Lighthall, F. Multiple realities and organizational nonsolutions: An essay on anatomy of educational innovation. *School Review*, February 1973, pp. 255–87.

Lindblom, C. The science of muddling through. *Public Administration Review*, 1959, *19*, 155–69.

Lindblom, C., & Cohen, D. *Usable knowledge*. New Haven, Conn.: Yale University Press, 1979.

Lippitt, G., & Lippitt, R. *The consulting process in action*. La Jolla, Calif.: University Associates, 1978.

Lippitt, R. Consultation: Traps and potentialities. In R. Herriott & N. Gross (Eds.), *The dynamics of planned educational change*. Berkeley, Calif.: McCutchan, 1979.

Little, J. The power of organizational setting: School norms and staff development. Paper adapted from final report to National Institute of Education, *School success and staff development: The role of staff development in urban desegregated schools*, 1981.

Lortie, D. *Schoolteacher: A sociological study*. Chicago: University of Chicago Press, 1975.

Loucks, S. Conceptualizing and measuring program implementation: A variable use for planned change and evaluation. Paper presented at American Educational Research Association annual meeting, 1978.

Loucks, S. & Cox, P. School district personnel: A crucial role in school improvement efforts. Paper presented at American Educational Research Association annual meeting, 1982.

Loucks, S., & Hall, G. Implementing innovations in schools: A concerns-based approach. Paper presented at American Educational Research Association annual meeting, 1979.

Loucks, S., & Melle, M. Implementation of a district-wide curriculum: The effects of a three year study. Paper presented at American Educational Research Association annual meeting, 1980.

Louis, K. Meet the project: A study of the R&D utilization program. Cambridge, Mass.: ABT Associates, 1980.

Louis, K. External agents and knowledge utilization: Dimensions for analysis and action. In R. Lehming & M. Kane (Eds.), *Improving schools*. Beverly Hills, Calif.: Sage, 1981.

Louis, K., Kell, D., Chabotar, K., & Sieber, S. *Perspectives on school improvement: A casebook for curriculum change.* Final report to National Institute of Education. Cambridge, Mass.: ABT Associates, 1981.

Louis, K., Kell, D., et al. *The human factor in dissemination: Field agent roles in their organizational context.* Cambridge, Mass.: ABT Associates, 1981.

Louis, K., & Rosenblum, S. *Linking R&D with schools: A program and its implications for dissemination.* Washington: National Institute of Education, 1981.

Louis, K., Rosenblum, S., & Molitor, J. *Strategies for knowledge use and school improvement.* Final report to National Institute of Education. Cambridge, Mass.: ABT Associates, 1981.

Louis, K., Rosenblum, S., Spencer, G., Stookey, J., & Yin, R. *Designing and managing interorganizational networks.* Final report to National Institute of Education. Cambridge, Mass.: ABT Associates, 1981.

Louis, K., & Sieber, S. *Bureaucracy and the dispersed organization.* Norwood, N.J.: Ablex, 1979.

Lucas, B., Lusthaus, C., & Gibbs, H. Parent advisory committees in Quebec: An experiment in mandated parental participation. *Interchange*, 1978–79, *10*(1), 26–39.

Lyon, C., Doscher, L., McGrahanan, P., & Williams, R. *Evaluation and school districts.* Los Angeles: Center for the Study of Evaluation, U.C.L.A., 1978.

Lyons, P., et al. *Involving parents: A handbook for participation in schools.* Santa Monica, Calif.: System Development Corporation, 1982.

Madaus, G., Airasian, P., & Kellaghan, T. *School effectiveness.* New York: McGraw-Hill, 1980.

Madey, D. A study of the relationships among educational linker roles and selected linker functions. Unpublished doctoral dissertation, Duke University, 1979.

Madey, D., Royster, E., Decad, J., Baker, R., & Strang, E. *Building capacity for improvement of educational practice: An evaluation of NIE's state dissemination grants program.* Durham, N.C.: NTS Research Corporation, 1979.

Majone, G., & Wildavsky, A. Implementation as evolution. In H. Freeman (Ed.), *Policy studies annual review*, Vol. II. Beverly Hills, Calif.: Sage, 1978.

Mann, D. Education policy analysis and the rent-a-troika business. Paper presented at American Educational Research Association annual meeting, 1981.

March, J. Model bias in social action. *Review of Educational Research*, 1972, *42*(4), 413–29.

March, J. Analytical skills and the university training of educational administrators. Paper presented at National Conference of Professors in Educational Administration, 1973.

Marjoribanks, K. *Families and their learning environments: An empirical assessment.* London: Routledge & Kegan Paul, 1979.

Marris, P. *Loss and change.* New York: Anchor Press/Doubleday, 1975.

Martin, J., & Zichefoose, M. The school superintendent in West Virginia. Unpublished report, West Virginia University, 1979.

Martin, W., & Willower, D. The managerial behavior of high school principals. *Educational Administration Quarterly*, 1981, *17*(1), 69–90.

McDonald, J., & Elias, P. *Study of induction programs for beginning teachers*, Vols. I–IV. Final report to National Institute of Education. Princeton, N.J.: Educational Testing Service, 1980.

McDonnell, L., & McLaughlin, M. *Program consolidation and the state role in ESEA Title IV.* Santa Monica, Calif.: Rand Corporation, 1980.

McKibbin, M., & Joyce, B. An analysis of staff development and its effects on classroom practice. Paper presented at American Educational Research Association annual meeting, 1980.

McKinney, W., & Westbury, I. Stability and change: The public schools of Gary, Indiana, 1940–1970. In W. Reid & D. Walker (Eds.), *Case studies in curriculum change*. London: Routledge & Kegan Paul, 1975.

McLaughlin, M. Implementation of ESEA Title I: A problem of compliance. *Teachers College Record*, 1976, *77*(3), 397–415.

McLaughlin, M., & Marsh, D. Staff development and school change. *Teachers College Record*, 1978, *80*(1), 69–94.

McLean, L. The chastening of educational research. Unpublished paper, Ontario Institute for Studies in Education, 1979.

McNair, K., & Joyce, B. Thought and action, frozen section: The South Bay study. In B. Joyce (Ed.), *Educational Research Quarterly*, special issue, 1978–79, *3*(4), 16–25.

Melaragno, R., Lyons, M., & Sparks, M. *Parents and federal education programs*, Vol. VI, *Parental involvement in Title I projects*. Santa Monica, Calif.: System Development Corporation, 1981.

Melle, M., & Pratt, H. Documenting program adaption in a district-wide implementation effort: The three year evolution from evaluation to an instructional improvement plan. Paper presented at American Educational Research Association annual meeting, 1981.

Merten, S., & Yarger, S. A comprehensive study of program estimates, staff services, resources, and policy board operations in 37 federally funded teacher centers. Paper presented at American Educational Research Association annual meeting, 1981.

Miklos, E., & Nixon, M. Comparative perspectives on preparation programs for educational administrators. Paper presented at Canadian Society for the Study of Education annual meeting, 1979.

Miles, M. Linkage on a new key: The DTA experience. New York: Center for Policy Research, 1979.

Miles, M. School innovation from the ground up: Some dilemmas. *New York University Education Quarterly*, 1980, *11*(2), 2–9.

Miles, M. *Experience-based career education in Perry-Parkdale schools mid-west: A case study*. Andover, Mass.: The Network, 1980.

Miles, M. *Learning to work in groups*. 2nd ed. New York: Teachers College Press, 1981.

Miles, M. Mapping the common properties of schools. In R. Lehming & M. Kane (Eds.), *Improving schools*. Beverly Hills, Calif.: Sage, 1981.

Miles, M., Fullan, M., & Taylor, G. *Organizational development in schools: The state of the art*, Vol. III, *OD consultants/OD programs in school districts*. New York: Center for Policy Research, 1978.

Miles, M., et al. *Project on social architecture in education: Final report*. New York: Center for Policy Research, 1978.

Molitor, J. Linking R&D with local schools: A federal program and its outcomes. Paper presented at American Educational Research Association annual meeting, 1981.

Moore, D., & Hyde, A. *Rethinking staff development: A handbook for analyzing your program and its costs*. Chicago: Designs for Change, 1978.

Moore, D., & Hyde, A. *The politics of staff development in three school districts*. Report to the Ford Foundation. Chicago: Designs for Change, 1979.

Moore, D., & Hyde, A. *Making sense of staff development programs and their costs in three urban school districts*. Final report to National Institute of Education. Chicago: Designs for Change, 1981.

Moore, D., Hyde, A., Blair, K., & Weitzman, S. *Student classification and the right to read*. Chicago: Designs for Change, 1981.

Moore, D., Weitzman, S., Steinberg, L., & Manar, U. *Child advocacy and the schools*. Chicago: Designs for Change, forthcoming.

Murphy, J. *State education agencies and discretionary funds*. Lexington, Mass.: D.C. Heath, 1974.

Murphy, J. The state role in education: Past research and future directions. *Education Evaluation and Policy Analysis*, 1980, *2*(4), 39–52.

Mussio, J., & Greer, N. The British Columbia assessment program: An overview. *Canadian Journal of Education*, 1980, *5*(4), 22–40.

Nash, C., & Ireland, D. In-service education: Cornerstone of curriculum development or stumbling block? Paper presented at Canadian Society for the Study of Education annual meeting, 1979.

National Center for Education Statistics. *Statistics of public, elementary and secondary day schools 1977–78 school year*. Washington: NCES, 1978.

National Diffusion Network. *NDN reporter*. San Francisco: Far West Laboratory, 1981.

National Education Association. *Nationwide teacher opinion poll 1979*. Washington: NEA.

Neill, S. The National Diffusion Network: A success story ending. *Phi Delta Kappan*, May 1976, pp. 598–601.

Neill, S. The National Diffusion Network. *Phi Delta Kappan*, June 1981, pp. 726–28.

Nelson, M., & Sieber, S. Innovations in urban secondary schools. *School Review*, 1976, *84*, 213–31.

Network, The. *Linking agent's tool kit*. Part One: An Overview; Part Two: Background Readings; Part Three: Stages of Intervention. Andover, Mass.: The Network, 1979.

Neumann, W. Evaluators and principals: The aim is self-reliance. Cambridge, Mass.: Huron Institute, 1981.

New York State. *The superintendent of schools: His role, background and salary*. New York: Office of Education Performance Review, 1974.

Nisbet, R. *Social change and history*. New York: Oxford University Press, 1969.

Nisbet, R. *History of the idea of progress*. New York: Basic Books, 1980.

Northwest Regional Educational Laboratory. *Preparing educational training consultants*. Portland, Oreg.: NWREL, 1976.

Olivero, J. The changing role of the school principal—and what to do about it. Unpublished paper, Association of California School Administrators, 1979.

Olson, J. Teacher constructs and curriculum change. *Journal of Curriculum Studies*, 1980, *12*(1), 1–11.

Ontario Ministry of Education. *Issues and directions: The response to the final report of the Commission on Declining School Enrolments in Ontario*. Toronto: Ontario Ministry of Education, 1980.

Ontario Ministry of Education. The Ontario Assessment Instrument Pool: A curriculum-based aid to evaluation. *Review and Evaluation Bulletins*, 1979, *1*(1).

Organization for Economic Cooperation and Development. *Review of national policies for education: Canada*. Paris: OECD, 1976.

Orland, M., & Goettel, R. Toward a conceptual framework for understanding the intergovernmental implementation of federal aid programs in education. Paper presented at American Educational Research Association annual meeting, 1980.

Orlich, D. Federal educational policy: The paradox of innovation and centralization. *Educational Researcher*, 1979, *8*(7), 4–9.

Orlich, D., Ruff, T., & Hansen, H. Stalking curriculum: Or where do elementary principals learn about new programs. *Educational Leadership*, 1976, *33*(8), 614–21.

Paddock, S. The myth of parent involvement through advisor councils. Paper presented at American Educational Research Association annual meeting, 1979.

Partlow, H., Turner, J., & Cummins, A. *The supervisory officer in Ontario*. Toronto: Ontario Ministry of Education, 1980.

Peterson, K. Making sense of principals' work. Paper presented at American Educational Research Association annual meeting, 1981.

Pharis, W., & Zakariya, S. *The elementary school principalship in 1978: A research study*. Arlington, Va.: National Association of Elementary School Principals, 1979.

Pincus, J. Incentives for innovation in public schools. *Review of Educational Research*, 1974, *44*, 113–44.

Pratt, H., Melle, M., Metsdorf, J., & Loucks, S. The design and utilization of a concerns-based staff development program for implementing a revised science curriculum. Paper presented at American Educational Research Association annual meeting, 1980.

Pratt, H., Winters, S., & George, A. The effects of a concerns-based implementation plan on the achievement of elementary science students. Paper presented at American Educational Research Association annual meeting, 1980.

Pressman, J., & Wildavsky, A. *Implementation*. Berkeley: University of California Press, 1973.

Raizen, S. Dissemination programs at the National Institute of Education, 1974 to 1979. *Knowledge: Creation, diffusion, utilization*, 1979, *1*, 259–92.

Ratsoy, E. *Evaluation of the education practicum program, 1977–78*. Edmonton: Faculty of Education, University of Alberta, 1978.

Rayder, N. *Summary of external evaluations: Bringing unity into language development*. Vancouver School Board, 1979.

Regan, E., & Winter, C. Tasks performed by consultants to influence the curriculum decisions of teachers. In K. Leithwood (Ed.), *Studies in curriculum decision making*. Toronto: OISE Press, 1982.

Reinhard, D., et al. Great expectations: The principal's role and in-service needs in supporting change projects. Paper presented at American Educational Research Association annual meeting, 1980.

Research for Better Schools. *Annual report on study of regional education service agencies: Fiscal year, 1981*. Philadelphia: RBS, 1981.

Rhine, R. (Ed.). *Making schools more effective: New directions from Follow Through*. New York: Academic Press, 1981.

Robbins, A., & Dingler, D. *Parents and federal education programs*, Vol. III, *Parental involvement in ESAA projects*. Santa Monica, Calif.: System Development Corporation, 1981.

Roberts, D. Theory, curriculum development and the unique events of practice. In H. Munby, G. Orpwood, & T. Russell (Eds.), *Seeing curriculum in a new light*. Toronto: OISE Press, 1980.

Robinson, F. Superordinate curriculum guidelines as guides to local curriculum decision-making. In K. Leithwood (Ed.), *Studies in curriculum decision-making*. Toronto: OISE Press, 1982.

Rosenblum, S., & Jastrzab, J. *The role of the principal in change: The Teacher Corps example*. Cambridge, Mass.: ABT Associates, 1980.

Rosenblum, S., & Louis, K. *Stability and change: Innovation in an educational context*. Cambridge, Mass.: ABT Associates, 1979.

Rothman, J., Erlich, J., & Teresa, J. *Promoting innovation and change in organizations and communities*. New York: Wiley, 1976.

Royster, E., Madey, D., Decad, J., & Baker, R. *Building capacity for improvement of educational practice: An evaluation of NIE's state dissemination grants program*. Durham, N.C.: NTS Research Corporation, 1981.

Rubin, L. *The in-service education of teachers*. Boston: Allyn & Bacon, 1978.

Runkel, P., Schmuck, R., Arends, J., & Francisco, R. *Transforming the school's capacity for problem solving*. Eugene: Center for Educational Policy and Management, University of Oregon, 1978.

Rutherford, W., & Hall, G. Describing the concerns principals have about facilitating change. Paper presented at American Educational Research Association annual meeting, 1982.

Rutter, M., Maugham, B., Mortimer, P., Ouston, J., & Smith, A. *Fifteen thousand hours: Secondary schools and their effects on children*. Cambridge, Mass.: Harvard University Press, 1979.

Ryan, K. The stages of teaching and staff development. Paper presented at American Educational Research Association annual meeting, 1979.

Ryan, K., et al. *Biting the apple: Accounts of first year teachers*. New York: Longman, 1980.

Saario, T. Leadership and the change process: Preparing educational administrators. In R. Herriott & N. Gross (Eds.), *The dynamics of planned educational change*. Berkeley, Calif.: McCutchan, 1979.

Sarason, S. *The culture of the school and the problem of change*. Boston: Allyn & Bacon, 1971; 2nd ed., 1982.

Sarason, S. *The creation of settings and the future societies*. San Francisco: Jossey-Bass, 1972.

Sarason, S. The nature of problem-solving in social action. *American Psychologist*, April 1978, pp. 370–80.

Sarason, S., & Doris, J. *Educational handicap, public policy, and social history*. New York: Free Press, 1979.

Schlecty, P. *A social theory based framework for evaluating staff development*. Final report to National Institute of Education, 1981.

Schmuck, R., Murray, D., Smith, M., & Runkel, P. *Consultation for innovative schools: OD for multiunit structure*. Eugene: Center for Educational Policy and Management, University of Oregon, 1975.

Schmuck, R., Runkel, P., Arends, J., & Arends, R. *The second handbook of organizational development in schools*. Palo Alto, Calif.: Mayfield, 1977.

Schon, D. *Beyond the stable state*. New York: Norton, 1971.

Schulz, D. *Teachers adapt to innovation*. Final report to National Institute of Education, 1979.

Schutz, A. *On phenomenology and social relations*. Chicago: University of Chicago Press, 1970.

Sharp, R., & Green, A. *Education and social control: A study in progressive primary education*. London: Routledge & Kegan Paul, 1975.

Sieber, S. Research on knowledge utilization: The pilot state dissemination program. *Bulletin of the School of Education*, Indiana University, Fall 1974.

Sieber, S. The solution as the problem. Paper delivered to Society for the Study of Social Problems annual meeting, 1978; revised 1979.

Sieber, S. Knowledge utilization in public education: Incentives and disincentives. In R. Lehming & M. Kane (Eds.), *Improving schools*. Beverly Hills, Calif.: Sage, 1981.

Sieber, S., Louis, K., & Metzger, L. *The use of educational knowledge*, Vols. 1 and 2. New York: Columbia University, Bureau of Applied Research, 1972.

Silberman, C. *Crisis in the classroom*. New York: Vintage Books, 1970.

Simms, G. The implementation of curriculum innovation. Unpublished doctoral dissertation, University of Alberta, 1978.

Sirotnik, K. What you see is what you get: A summary of observations in over 1,000 elementary and secondary classrooms. Paper presented at American Educational Research Association annual meeting, 1982.

Smith, A., & Nerenberg, S. *Parents and federal education programs*, Vol. V, *Parental involvement in Follow Through programs*. Santa Monica, Calif.: System Development Corporation, 1981.

Smith, B., et al. *A design for a school of pedagogy*. Washington: Department of Education, 1980.

Smith, L., & Dwyer, D. Federal policy in action: A case study of an urban education project. St. Louis: Graduate Institute of Education, Washington University, 1979.

Smith, L., & Geoffrey, W. *The complexities of an urban classroom.* New York: Holt, Rinehart & Winston, 1968.

Smith, L., & Keith, P. *Anatomy of educational innovation: An organizational analysis of an elementary school.* New York: Wiley, 1971.

Spencer, G., & Louis, K. *Training and support of educational linking agents.* Cambridge, Mass.: ABT Associates, 1980.

Sproull, L., et al. *Organizing an anarchy.* Chicago: University of Chicago Press, 1978.

Stallings, J. Follow Through: A model for in-service teacher training. *Curriculum Inquiry*, 1979, *9*(2), 163–81.

Stallings, J. The process of teaching basic reading skills in secondary schools. Menlo Park, Calif.: SRI International, 1980.

Statistics Canada. *Elementary–secondary school enrolment 1980–81.* Ottawa, 1981.

Stearns, M., Greene, D., & David, J. *Local implementation of PL94–142: First year report of a longitudinal study.* Menlo Park, Calif.: SRI International, 1980.

Stebbins, L., et al. *Education as experimentation: A planned variation model*, Vol. IV A, *An evaluation of Follow Through.* Cambridge, Mass.: ABT Associates, 1977.

Tabachnick, R., Popkewitz, T., & Zeichner, K. Teacher education and the professional perspectives of student teachers. *Interchange*, 1979, *10*(4), 12–29.

Tallmadge, K. *Ideabook.* Washington: U.S. Government Printing Office, 1977.

Taylor, B. *The "inside" outsiders: A study of three consortium linking agents.* Andover, Mass.: The Network, 1979.

TDR Associates, Inc. *Case studies of three urban university–school colaboratives mandated for the improvement of educational practice.* Report to National Institute of Education. Newton, Mass.: TDR Associates, 1981.

Thomas, M. *A study of alternatives in American education*, Vol. II, *The role of the principal.* Santa Monica, Calif.: Rand Corporation, 1978.

Thompson, C. Dissemination at the National Institute of Education: Contending ideas about research, practice, and the federal role. Paper presented at American Educational Research Association annual meeting, 1981.

Tikunoff, W., & Ward, B. Interactive research on teaching: An overview of the strategy. San Francisco: Far West Laboratory, 1979.

Toffler, A. *Future shock.* New York: Bantam Books, 1970.

Toffler, A. *The third wave.* New York, Bantam Books, 1980.

Toronto Board of Education. *We are all immigrants to this place.* Toronto, 1976.

Truch, S. *Teacher burnout and what to do about it.* Navato, Calif.: Academic Therapy Pub., 1980.

Tucker, H., & Zeigler, H. *Professionals versus the public: Attitudes, communication, and response in school districts.* New York: Longman, 1980.

Tuinman, J., & Kendall, J. *The British Columbia reading assessment: General report.* Victoria: British Columbia Ministry of Education, 1980.

Turnbull, B. Program consolidation at the federal level: An answer to problems in federal aid? Paper presented at American Educational Research Association annual meeting, 1980.

Van der Berg, R., et al. *Large scale strategies for supporting complex innovations in participating schools.* 's Hertogenbosch, Netherlands: Katholiek Pedagogisch Centrum, 1981.

Van Geel, T. *Authority to control the school program.* Lexington, Mass.: D.C. Heath, 1976.

Van Manen, M., & Stewart, L. (Eds.). *Curriculum policy making in Alberta education.* Edmonton: University of Alberta, 1978.

Vaughan, J., et al. *Staff development research area plans.* Washington: National Institute of Education, 1980.

Venezky, R., & Winfield, L. Schools that succeed beyond expectations in teaching reading. University of Delaware Studies on Education, 1979.

Volp, F., & Heifetz, L. School superintendents in New York State: Role perceptions and issues orientations. Paper presented at American Educational Research Association annual meeting, 1980.

Waller, W. *The sociology of teaching*. New York: Wiley, 1932.

Waring, M. *Social pressures and curriculum innovation*. London: Methuen, 1979.

Watzlawick, P., Weakland, J., & Fisch, R. *Change*. New York: W. W. Norton, 1974.

Weatherley, R. *Reforming special education: Policy implementation from state level to street level*. Cambridge, Mass.: MIT Press, 1979.

Weatherley, R., & Lipsky, M. Street-level bureaucrats and institutional innovation: Implementing special-education reform. *Harvard Educational Review*, 1977, *47*(2), 171–97.

Weick, K. Educational organizations as loosely coupled systems. *Administrative Science Quarterly*, 1976, *21*, 1–19.

Weick, K. Loosely coupled systems: Relaxed meanings and thick interpretations. Paper presented at American Educational Research Association annual meeting, 1980.

Weiss, C. Knowledge creep and decision accretion. *Knowledge: Creation, diffusion, utilization*, 1980, *1*(3), 381–404.

Welch, W. Twenty years of science curriculum development: A look back. In D. Berliner (Ed.), *Review of Research in Education, 7*. Washington: American Educational Research Association, 1979.

Weldy, G. *Principals: What they do and who they are*. Reston, Va.: National Association of Secondary School Principals, 1979.

Wellisch, W., MacQueen, A., Carriere, R., & Duck, G. School management and organization in successful schools. *Sociology of Education*, 1978, *51*, 211–26.

Werner, W. Implementation: The role of belief. Unpublished paper, Centre for Curriculum Studies, University of British Columbia, 1980.

Whiteside, T. *The sociology of educational innovation*. London: Methuen, 1978.

Williams, R., & Bank, A. Linking testing and evaluation activities with instruction: Can school districts make it happen? Paper presented at American Educational Research Association annual meeting, 1981.

Williams, W. *The implementation perspective*. Berkeley: University of California Press, 1980.

Williams, W. (Ed.). *Studying implementation: Methodological and administrative issues*. Chatham Publishers, 1981.

Williams, W., & Elmore, R. (Eds.). *Social program implementation*. New York: Academic Press, 1976.

Willis, P. *Learning to labour*. Westmead, England: Saxon House, 1977.

Wilson, J. Innovation in organization: Notes toward a theory. In J. Thompson (Ed.), *Approaches to organizational design*. Pittsburgh: University of Pittsburgh Press, 1966.

Wimpelberg, R. Parent choice in public education: The preferences and behaviors of parents related to their children's schooling. Paper presented at American Educational Research Association annual meeting, 1981.

Wise, A. Why educational policies often fail: The hyperrationalization hypothesis. *Curriculum Studies*, 1977, *9*(1) 43–57.

Wise, A. *Legislated learning*. Berkeley: University of California Press, 1979.

Wolcott, H. *The man in the principal's office*. New York: Holt, Rinehart & Winston, 1973.

Wolcott, H. *Teachers vs. technocrats*. Eugene: Center for Educational Policy and Management, University of Oregon, 1977.

Wood, F., & Thompson, S. Guidelines for better staff development. *Educational Leadership*, 1979, *36*, 374–78.

Wynne, E. *Looking at schools*. Lexington, Mass.: D.C. Heath, 1980.

Yin, R., & Gwaltney, M. *Organizations collaborating to improve educational practice.* Cambridge, Mass.: ABT Associates, 1981.

Yin, R., Herald, K., & Vogel, M. *Tinkering with the system.* Lexington, Mass.: D.C. Heath, 1977.

Yin, R., Quick, S., Bateman, P., & Marks, E. *Changing urban bureaucracies: How new practices become routinized.* Santa Monica, Calif.: Rand Corporation, 1978.

Zaltman, G., Duncan, R., & Holbek, J. *Innovations and organizations.* Toronto: Wiley, 1973.

Zaltman, G., Florio, D., & Sikorski, L. *Dynamic educational change.* New York: Macmillan, 1977.

Zeichner, K. Teacher induction practices in the United States and Great Britain. Paper presented at American Educational Research Association annual meeting, 1979.

# Index